Hugo Grotius's *Remonstrantie* of 1615

Hugo Grotius is one of the six jurists whose statues stand outside the Supreme Court of the Netherlands in The Hague.

SCULPTURE BY JOHAN POLET, PHOTO BY RENÉ & PETER VAN DER KROGT, HTTP://STANDBEELDEN.VANDERKROGT.NET

Hugo Grotius's *Remonstrantie* of 1615

Facsimile, Transliteration, Modern Translations and Analysis

By

David Kromhout
Adri K. Offenberg

BRILL

LEIDEN | BOSTON

Cover illustration: *Portret van Hugo de Groot (1583–1645), Michiel Jansz. van Mierevelt (atelier van), 1631*, https://www.rijksmuseum.nl/nl/collectie/SK-A-581

Library of Congress Cataloging-in-Publication Data

Names: Grotius, Hugo, 1583–1645, author. | Kromhout, David, 1976- writer of added commentary. | Offenberg, A. K., contributor. | Blankman, Marijke, contributor. | Heertum, Cis van, 1958- translator.
Title: Hugo Grotius's remonstrantie of 1615 : facsimile, transliteration, modern translations and analysis / by David Kromhout, Adri Offenberg.
Other titles: Remonstrantie nopende de ordre dije in de landen van Hollandt ende Westvrieslandt dijent gestelt op de Joden. English. | Remonstrantie on the regulations to be instituted in Holland and West Friesland regarding the Jews
Description: Leiden ; Boston : Brill, 2019. | Includes bibliographical references.
Identifiers: LCCN 2019005678 (print) | LCCN 2019006792 (ebook) | ISBN 9789004397446 (ebook) | ISBN 9789004396074 (hardback : alk. paper)
Subjects: LCSH: Jews–Legal status, laws, etc.–Netherlands–17th century.
Classification: LCC KKM2467.M56 (ebook) | LCC KKM2467.M56 G764 2019 (print) | DDC 342.49208/73–dc23
LC record available at https://lccn.loc.gov/2019005678

Typeface for the Latin, Greek, and Cyrillic scripts: "Brill". See and download: brill.com/brill-typeface.

ISBN 978-90-04-39607-4 (hardback)
ISBN 978-90-04-39744-6 (e-book)

This book is printed on acid-free paper and produced in a sustainable manner.

Contents

Foreword

In 2015 it was four hundred years ago that the eminent jurist Hugo Grotius, then pensionary of Rotterdam, wrote his *Remonstrantie* at the request of the States of Holland and West Friesland. To mark the occasion, chairman Jaap Sajet of the *Morasha* foundation took the initiative in 2014 for a scholarly study that placed the *Remonstrantie* in its historical and social context, including a new complete edition of the *Remonstrantie* with explanatory notes, a facsimile of the original, a retranslation into modern Dutch and an English translation. As fellow board members of *Morasha* at the time we could not imagine the vast scope of this project. Sajet's vision surpassed our imagination.

The *Remonstrantie* marks the beginning of the debate on the Jewish presence in the Dutch Republic, by one of the greatest contemporary jurists. Grotius discusses the issue of the rights of Jews in connection with the political and religious situation in the Dutch Republic. It is the principal purpose of the *Morasha* foundation to promote publications on aspects of Dutch-Jewish history which have so far been insufficiently explored. As such, this edition is highly appropriate to the objectives of *Morasha*.

In 1615 Hugo Grotius gave his view on how to deal with the influx of Sephardi Jews at the request of the States of Holland and West Friesland. In this *Remonstrantie nopende de ordre dije in de landen van Hollandt ende Westvrieslandt dijent gestelt op de Joden* (A *Remonstrantie* on the Regulations to be Instituted in Holland and West Friesland Regarding the Jews), Grotius first raised the question whether Jews ought to be admitted in the first place. After having answered in the affirmative, he considered the terms and conditions to be applied to their admission. That the *Remonstrantie* was eventually shelved is no reflection on its contents. If anything, it had to do with the political situation in the Dutch Republic at the time.

Dr Jaap Meijer previously published an edition of the *Remonstrantie* in 1949, though without a retranslation or an English translation, so that it was not accessible internationally. It was time to engage with the *Remonstrantie* once more.

Publishing the work of a scholar as exceptional and eminent as Hugo Grotius requires much of everyone in the project. The researcher has to be well acquainted with the period and the issues Hugo Grotius was faced with in 1616. We are very fortunate that Dr David Kromhout expressed a great interest in the project and was available and willing to do the research. Not only did he write the article on the backgrounds to Grotius' advisory report, he also had to identify and translate the numerous Latin references and notes in the *Remonstrantie*. We appreciate the advice provided to Dr Kromhout by Prof. Marc de Wilde and Prof. Henk Nellen. Dr Adri Offenberg brought his great expertise as a book specialist at the *Bibliotheca Rosenthaliana* to bear on the transcription of the seventeenth-century manuscript.

As a historical text can be challenging to read even when presented in a contemporary font, a retranslation into modern Dutch in the edition was included. This was a formidable task, and we are delighted with the result provided by Marijke Blankman MA. She has come up with a contemporary retranslation that nevertheless remained as close as possible to the source text. Dr Cis van Heertum translated this retranslation into English, using the Authorized Version of 1611 for the biblical quotes so that these, too, are consonant with the period of the *Remonstrantie* itself. Will Kelly carefully read the final version of David Kromhout's English text. We are honoured by the introduction by Piet Hein Donner LLM, who as former Justice Minister and Vice-President of the Council of State operated at the interface of politics and science, as Grotius before him.

A scientific council was established to supervise the project and ensure a high academic standard, consisting of Prof. Irene Zwiep, Prof. Emile Schrijver, Dr Adri Offenberg and Steph Scholten MA, who was succeeded by Rachel Boertjens MA after he left for Scotland. We are very grateful to them all for their dedication, their valuable contributions and their commitment in seeing this book through to completion. We also thank Rachel Cilia Werdmölder MA for her expert assistance in the final editing process of the book.

Dr Ruud Koster coordinated all aspects of this complex project from beginning to end with great enthusiasm and determination, from grant applications to contacts with the publisher.

In addition to a great deal of work and effort, it was necessary to find sponsors to make sure this edition would see the light of day. We thank our sponsors and donors for having responded generously to our request for support, and so having provided the financial means to realise this edition.

Our deep gratitude goes to Jaap Sajet, chairman of *Morasha* until his death in 2015, who was so committed to the history of the Jews in the Netherlands. He was the inspiring force behind this publication, and it is sad that Jaap has not been able to see his vision reach fruition.

This book is dedicated to his memory.

Marianka van Lunteren-Spanjaard
President of *Morasha*
October 2018

Prologue

Hugo Grotius's *Remonstrantie*

The book you have in your hands is one of Hugo Grotius's lesser-known works, translated into modern Dutch, entitled: *Remonstrantie betreffende de regelgeving die in Holland en West-Friesland moet worden opgesteld ten aanzien van de Joden* (Remonstrance regarding regulations that should be drawn up in Holland and West Friesland regarding the Jews). Grotius was commissioned to write the text by the States of Holland, in his capacity as pensionary of Rotterdam. This request was prompted by unrest surrounding the settlement of Jews in towns in Holland after it transpired that a resident of Hoorn had converted to Judaism. Because Amsterdam and Rotterdam were, at that time, the only Holland towns with a Jewish community, their pensionaries were asked by the States to draw up a concept of regulations governing the settlement and residence of Jews.[1]

Today, the *Remonstrantie* is primarily of interest as a historical document, an illustration of the problems confronting the young Dutch Republic as a beacon of toleration and prosperity in a world where both were in short supply. As such, it sheds lights on the thinking and political relationships of early 17th-century Holland, at the beginning of the Golden Age. But it also holds up a mirror to our own time, in which to examine recurring issues like migration, identity and coexistence in diversity.

Background

Around 1592/1593 groups of Sephardic Jews began settling in the towns of Holland. This was a new phenomenon for the time, though Jewish communities had existed in a number of towns in the Low Countries during the Middle Ages. As far back as the late 13th century, for example, there was a Jodenstraat (Street of the Jews) in Maastricht, and by the 14th century there is evidence of Jewish communities elsewhere. But after the devastation of the Black Death in the mid-14th century, Jews were persecuted in many places for being the supposed cause of the epidemic. By the 15th century the communities had seemingly vanished completely; there is, at any rate, no further mention of them in the historical record.

Following the *Reconquista* in Spain, Ferdinand and Isabella (the 'Catholic Monarchs') increasingly turned against the country's Jews, who had lived there for hundreds of years under the protection of Moorish rulers. In 1492 the Jews of Spain were presented with a stark choice: convert to Christianity or leave the country; in 1497 a similar ultimatum was issued in Portugal. Some of the Jews who chose exile ended up in Antwerp or in towns in the Rhineland. There, the pattern was repeated: in 1549 Charles V, the grandson of the Catholic Monarchs, ordered Jews who had sought refuge in Antwerp to leave the city. This did not trigger Jewish migration to Holland, since Charles was the ruler of that province as well. Indeed many Jews simply remained in Antwerp; even then, the city fathers knew a thing or two about 'toleration'. But once Antwerp fell into Spanish hands and the Dutch Republic seemed to be gaining the upper hand in its war with Spain, Jews who had initially fled elsewhere (especially Hamburg and Cologne), began to seek safety in Holland, attracted by the spirit of toleration in the Dutch Republic and the opportunities created by its economic boom. For example, in the 1590s a group of Sephardic Jews settled in Amsterdam, while a group of German Jews made their home in the area around Groningen.[2] In the entry for 1598 in his *Jaerboeken en Historiën* (Annals and Histories) Grotius mentions the

1 Hans Blom, et al., *Geschiedenis van de Joden in Nederland* (Amsterdam: Uitgeverij Balans, 2017), p. 85.

2 Jonathan I. Israel, *The Dutch Republic* (Oxford: Oxford University Press, 1995), p. 376.

arrival of Portuguese Jews, citing fear of the Inquisition and the hope of setting up a profitable business in Amsterdam as the twin motives for their decision. To translate this into contemporary language: they were a mixture of asylum seekers and economic migrants.

Although we now talk about Jewish immigrants, contemporary sources describe them as 'new Christians'; in any event they were not always open about their religion. According to Swetschinski[3] it was not until 1602 that the first public expression of Judaism is found, in the form of a statement by a man accused of trafficking in stolen goods who gave his religion as Jewish. In the years that followed, other Sephardic Jews started coming 'out of the closet' and began looking into the possibility of opening their own synagogue. During that same period Lutherans and Mennonites were also pushing the bounds of toleration in the Republic, while a number of towns had substantial Roman Catholic minorities. It was chiefly the town authorities that were competent to decide on such matters. It therefore made sense for Jews to approach the towns with the most tolerant attitude. In his study of the Republic, Jonathan Israel notes how a group of Jewish families who had come to Amsterdam from Venice and Thessaloniki sought permission from the town council of Haarlem to establish a synagogue there.[4] When that request was denied because of opposition from local Calvinist consistories (church boards), they tried their luck in Rotterdam in 1610. There they were initially granted permission, but when that permission was revoked a few years later they returned to Amsterdam, where the Jewish community had managed to organise itself without explicit permission from the authorities.[5]

The consistories' opposition to the establishment of synagogues in the towns and cities was not rooted in antipathy towards the Jewish religion. The Republic had no tradition of being either for or against Jews,[6] and Calvinism was not by definition hostile to them. Their standpoint should be seen in the context of the 'confessionalisation'[7] of the population, the struggle over the position of Calvinism within society and its political influence on government policy. The Dutch Revolt was accompanied by a revolutionary reform of the Roman Catholic Church and the introduction of a new (Reformed) ecclesiastical order.[8] In that sense the new Church was now established as an institution, but Calvinists were still in the minority. Around the transition from the 16th to the 17th century, the Calvinists' aim was to expand their position in society, in the face of competition from Lutherans and Roman Catholics. Although the States of Holland had recognised freedom of religion (and the freedom to practise one's religion) at Dordrecht in 1572—to win over the public for the revolt against Spain and not to alienate anyone—the prevailing opinion among patricians and municipal authorities was that toleration of the public practice of other religions jeopardised social unity. Although the town councils were often accused of 'free thinking' by orthodox Calvinists, they too viewed toleration with great suspicion, not unlike those who look askance at multiculturalism today.

Why Did Grotius Write the *Remonstrantie*?

The background to the *Remonstrantie* can be found in Blom's *History of the Jews in the Netherlands*.[9] The sheriff of Hoorn had arrested a certain Hans Joostensz, who had converted to Judaism and together with his wife had begun making kosher cheese for Jews in Amsterdam. The conversion of Jews to Christianity was not a problem, but

3 D.M. Swetschinski in Blom et al., *Geschiedenis van de Joden in Nederland*, p. 85.

4 Ibid., pp. 376–377. See also p. 74 et seq.

5 A.T. van Deursen, *De last van veel geluk* (Amsterdam: Uitgeverij Bert Bakker, 2004), p. 183 et seq.

6 D.M. Swetschinski, ibid. pp. 80–84.

7 See J.I. Israel, op. cit., p. 361 et seq. See also H.A. Enno van Gelder, *Vrijheid en onvrijheid in de Republiek* (Haarlem: H.D. Tjeenk Willink & Zn, 1947).

8 H.A. Enno van Gelder, *Revolutionnaire Reformatie* (Amsterdam: Van Kampen & Zn, 1943).

9 Blom op. cit., pp. 78/79 and 85.

the same could not be said for the reverse. In this particular case the States of Holland and West Friesland decided to banish the couple from the province, but by then, the case had already touched off a debate about policy on the settlement and treatment of Jews. Against this backdrop the pensionaries of Amsterdam and Rotterdam—Adriaan Pauw and Hugo Grotius—were commissioned to draw up a set of regulations to which Jews 'should adhere in order to prevent any scandal, nuisance or sanctions'. According to Swetschinski these two cities were chosen because they were the only ones with a Jewish community, though Van Eysinga suggests that Rotterdam was regarded as more liberal minded and Amsterdam as more Calvinist, so that the States may have hoped that a combination of the two would yield a 'golden mean'.[10]

Hugo Grotius was appointed pensionary of Rotterdam in 1613. In practice this simply meant that he was the paid adviser to the municipal government, but holding a permanent appointment gave the pensionary a strong position vis-à-vis the town magistracy, which changed every year. With the help of his staff, which he was expected to pay out of his own pocket, the pensionary was the de facto head of the municipal civil service. At the time of his appointment Grotius was not yet 30 and already advocate general of the States of Holland. There had been talk of a possible appointment to the High Court of Holland and Zeeland, but in the end Grotius preferred a more political career.[11]

At the time of his appointment the Dutch Republic was embroiled in a heated politico-religious debate surrounding the disagreement between Arminius and Gomarus about predestination. In 1611 the States had adopted a resolution ordering the Remonstrants (the followers of Arminius) and the Counter-Remonstrants (those of Gomarus) to accept each other's views, and as advocate general Grotius was involved in the implementation of that resolution. Grotius was also involved on a personal level. As a member of the Reformed congregation in Leiden he had supported calling Arminius as its minister; moreover he was a friend of Johannes Wtenbogaert, the future leader of the Arminians, and had lived in his house during his time in Leiden. It is important to note that this theological dispute had a political dimension as well, concerning the relationship between church and state. Arminians, who were well represented in municipal government, championed a role for the state in matters like Church governance and the appointment of ministers, partly as a counterbalance to the intolerance of orthodox viewpoints. Gomarists, who were more strongly represented in consistories, sought greater influence over government policy and thus a more popular (i.e. democratic) influence on the oligarchic municipal authorities.

Obviously, the dispute between Remonstrants and Counter-Remonstrants had nothing to do with the issues that gave rise to the request to draw up a set of regulations governing the Jews in Holland and West Friesland. But the request was premised on the notion that the States had the power to adopt such regulations. The Amsterdam municipal authority was evidently of a different opinion. In 1616 it adopted ex proprio motu an ordinance that prohibited Jews from slandering the Christian faith, converting Christians to Judaism and having relations with Christian women, even if they were prostitutes.[12] It is not clear if the Amsterdam authorities then regarded the matter as closed. According to Van Eysinga, Adriaan Pauw also submitted a proposal for a set of regulations, which was discussed by the States in 1619, together with the request (*Remonstrantie*) of Rotterdam. In so far as the *Remonstrantie* assumed that the States were competent to regulate religious matters, it bears on the question at the heart of the debate and a related issue that arose two years later, namely

10 W.J.M. van Eysinga, *Mededelingen der Koninklijke Nederlandse Akademie van Wetenschappen*, Literature division, new series, vol. 13, no. 1 (1950), included in *Sparsa Collecta* (Leiden: A.W. Sijthoff, 1958), p. 423 et seq.

11 H. Nellen, *Hugo de Groot: Een leven in strijd om de vrede*, (Amsterdam: Balans, 2007), p. 144 et seq.

12 Blom op. cit., p. 79.

whether a synod could be convened by the States General, or only by the individual provinces, which was the standpoint of the States of Holland.

Peculiar or Shrewd?

The *Remonstrantie* consists of three parts: a general explanation, the articles themselves and explanatory notes to the individual articles. It is beyond the scope of this foreword to examine each of these parts in full, but the general explanation merits further attention. Seen through modern eyes, it will appear offensive, anti-Semitic and discriminatory. But it is informed by a rationale that led to regulations that were relatively liberal for the time. It remains unclear if the general explanation accurately reflects Grotius's own views or whether it should instead be seen as a piece of advocacy, intended to persuade potential opponents with their own arguments. If the latter, it is an ingenious piece of rhetoric.

First, Grotius explains the need for these regulations by noting that Jews were starting to settle in the towns of Holland on a large scale, a state of affairs which was permitted by the municipal authorities with a view to the economic benefits these new residents would generate. Accordingly, he proceeds to examine the issue from the perspective of the common interest. To do so, it is first necessary to address two preliminary questions: should Jews be admitted to the country in the first place, and if so, should they be permitted to practise their religion? A third question is: what can be done to ensure that such practice does not undermine the Christian faith or disrupt public order?

Grotius begins by stating that there are two good arguments for not admitting Jews to the country. Admitting people of another religion weakens social unity. What is more, Jews hate Christians and could therefore pose a danger to public order and security. We hear echoes of these same arguments in the immigration debate of our own time: migrants are a danger to social cohesion and security. Grotius does not attempt to minimise the dangers to security; indeed he emphasises them by repeating alarmist stories about Jews that were then in circulation. Truly, he concedes, these are all good reasons not to let the Jews into the country, but on the other hand, he points out, Paul wrote that the entire Jewish people would eventually convert. And if that is the case, then surely they should be admitted—otherwise how can they embrace the true faith? Apart from this religious argument, there is also an obligation to extend hospitality on the basis of a shared humanity. On this point Grotius invokes a natural principle which he would develop into 'natural law' in later works, including *De iure Belli ac Pacis*. He also contends that even if Jews do hate Christians, they should not be treated in the same way, if only to ensure that Christians give no cause for such hatred (Grotius suggests that Jews actually have reason to hate). Furthermore, on the risks to security and the possibility that the faith of 'weaker' Christians might be undermined, he maintains that laws and official oversight should be sufficient.

If the conclusion is that Jews can and should be allowed into the country, the question arises of whether they should be permitted to practise their faith. Grotius identifies two possible objections to this: first, the Biblical prohibition on idolatry, and second, the paradox that Jews will then be permitted something that is denied to Catholics. But, he argues, if Jews are not permitted to practise, they must be forced to convert to Christianity or, failing that, society will have to accept a group of people with no religion at all. The first option would be improper, and the second wrong, since pure godlessness is even worse than Judaism. Besides, he claims, Judaism is not idolatry; Jews worship the same God, albeit with an admixture of superstition. In response to the second objection Grotius points out that Catholics do the same: allow Jews to observe their religion but deny that privilege to members of other Christian denominations. Moreover, Grotius notes, given their obedience to the Pope, the enemy of the Dutch Republic, Catholics are actually much more dangerous than Jews.

In this way Grotius uses the force of logic to convince his readers that Jews should be allowed into the country and permitted to practise their religion. In addition to invoking hospitality and the Christian duty to love one's neighbour, his argument rests on two pillars: 1) a conviction that Jews would eventually convert of their own accord and that Holland was as good a place as any for them to do so, and 2) a belief that observing the wrong religion was better that having no religion at all, given that forced conversion was out of the question. The Biblical dimension of Grotius's logic is difficult for modern-day readers to follow. But it also demonstrates that without a shared frame of reference, debates on fundamental questions never move beyond the stating of opposing viewpoints without ever bridging the differences between them. In any case, it must be acknowledged that Grotius himself ultimately offers no answer to the two main objections he raises: that allowing people to practise their faith freely undermines social unity and that by extending this right to Jews, they would be allowed something denied to Roman Catholics. And these were considerations that carried a great deal of weight with more liberal-minded patricians and municipal authorities. When the States eventually got round to debating the *Remonstrantie*, they could not resolve these contradictions either, and by resolution of 13 December 1619 they left the matter of the residency of Jews to the wisdom of the municipal authorities.[13] By then, however, in a swift reversal of fortunes, Johan van Oldenbarnevelt had been beheaded, and Grotius was serving a life sentence in Loevestein Castle.

The Article-by-Article Explanatory Notes

Assuming that Jews should be allowed into the country and permitted to practise their faith, there was still the matter of what rules should govern them. The *Remonstrantie* is based on the principle that Jews should be treated the same as Christians, so that they may experience Christian love. The only exception to this policy is in cases where it could harm 'the welfare of the Christian religion or of the state'.[14] It is striking how Grotius situates the imperative of 'equal treatment' as an extension of the Christian commandment to love one's neighbour. Earlier in the text he distinguishes between the 'deeper love' between Christians and the 'neighbourly love' we owe our fellow man, after the example of the good Samaritan. The latter form of love is also the source of the hospitality which he previously cited as a reason for allowing Jews into the country and of the duty to accord them equal treatment. In this way we can trace the evolution of his thinking about natural law.

When Grotius writes about equal treatment, he is referring to Jews as a group and not as individuals. The political and social concept of a society of equal citizens with inalienable rights still lay in the distant future. Hobbes's *Leviathan*, the first work in which the state is derived from the individual, would not appear for nearly half a century after the *Remonstrantie*. At the start of the 17th century the conception of society was still very much rooted in the medieval notion of an assemblage of different groups and 'estates'. Relations between these groups were regulated by public law, while the position of individuals was primarily determined by the group to which they belonged and their legal status within that group, in line with its own rules and customs.

These are the concepts that determine the form and content of the regulations proposed in part II of the *Remonstrantie*. They form the background for the compartmentalisation of society that is taken for granted: between Christian and Jew, between urban and rural. They are also the basis for two absolute prohibitions: Jews must not be allowed to live outside the towns (4) and marriage between Jews and Christians is forbidden, on

13 Van Eysinga, as quoted in *Sparsa Collecta* p. 426.

14 In the modernised language of the text, Grotius's original word *politie* ('police' in modern Dutch) has been replaced by *staat* ('state'). However, something along the lines of 'government and public order' is presumably closer to what the author had in mind.

penalty of death (27).[15] It should be noted that Jews are defined in terms of their religion. Only two provisions concern Jews on the basis of religion and origin: the obligation to register with the authorities within eight days of arriving in a town (1) and the ban on holding public office (40). But because Jews are defined by their religion, the profession of faith is an essential part of public oversight and must be made in the presence of the municipal authorities (2). Opinions or statements incompatible with this profession of faith are subject to corporal or even capital punishment (13). This is also the reason that a Jew who has been excommunicated for 'bad conduct or wicked opinions' has the right to appeal the decision to the local authorities (20), since excommunication has direct consequences for his legal status.

Along with the profession of faith, Jews are required to swear an oath of loyalty to the Republic (3); being of a different faith made one's patriotism suspect. Therein lies a difference in the treatment of Jews and Christians. Another distinction can be observed in the relationship between the religions. Blasphemous remarks or profanation of the Christian faith in speech (14) or in writing (16) are prohibited; according to the explanatory note accompanying article 16, this proscription also extends to the possession, use or printing of the Talmud. Jews are permitted to interact freely with Christians, provided they do not attempt to convert them (25). Conversely, ministers are allowed to visit gatherings of Jews, after notifying the authorities, and offer them instruction; those present are not allowed to leave (21). A Christian who converts to Judaism will be banished (33), but a Jew who converts to Christianity should be allowed to do so freely (34–37). A final key difference is the restriction on the number of Jewish families allowed to settle in a given town—200 (300 in Amsterdam) (4), so as to prevent them from becoming too numerous.

Modern readers of the *Remonstrantie* are struck by the numerous provisions *allowing* Jews to do one thing or another. The implicit principle here is that everything which is not explicitly allowed is forbidden. This constitutes a fundamental difference from modern law, which is premised on the principle that everything which is not explicitly forbidden is allowed. The article-by-article explanatory notes are also striking. Roman law and the writers of classical antiquity serve as authoritative sources for Grotius, given that he had no direct example on which to model his work. The towns had no regulations on the matter, and when he turned his gaze elsewhere he could find only repressive examples. Catholic countries and Rome were often held up as examples of what not to do, although Grotius is selective on that front. The fact that Jews were allowed to reside in Catholic countries and Rome is cited as proof that, with a few legal provisions in place, the presence of Jews need not be a problem. But on the matter of whether Jews should be forced to pay a special tax in order to practise their religion freely, Grotius denounces a similar tax in Rome as tyranny and greed and compares it to the practices of the ancient emperors (article 6).

What Happened Next

The *Remonstrantie* was never implemented, so we can only speculate as to whether it would have worked in practice. The States of Holland referred the question of regulation back to the municipal authorities with the sole restriction that Jews should not be forced to wear any distinguishing sign. In practice, though, few towns got around to taking regulatory measures. In 1632 Amsterdam tightened up its own rules by prohibiting Jews from

15 Van Eysinga (op. cit. 429) points out how this prohibition differs from the foundational principle articulated in *De Iure Belli ac Pacis* that marriage with foreigners is in principle permitted. Leaving aside the fact that the *Remonstrantie* is mainly concerned with the issue of 'two faiths in one bed', to quote a Dutch proverb, it should be acknowledged that the *Remonstrantie* is a political text. With these two prohibitions Grotius presumably aims to alleviate unease in both the countryside (about the possible settlement of Jews) and in the towns (about mixed marriages).

engaging in occupations governed by guilds. But starting in 1672 the status of Jews in the towns was gradually liberalised, partially in recognition of the staunch support they had given to the Republic during that 'year of disasters', in contrast to the Roman Catholics, who, in various towns, had welcomed Louis XIV with open arms. Yet it was not until 1796 that Jews attained full equality in law with other citizens.

The *Remonstrantie* was not a central work in Grotius's career as a jurist. Even his biographer gives it no more than scant attention.[16] It was a product of his day-to-day duties as pensionary. Nevertheless, the *Remonstrantie* is one of his few works which deals with the lives of ordinary citizens. Working from a number of basic assumptions he arrived at a set of regulations that were exceptional for their time, but as it turned out, the work was merely an academic exercise. The problems it addressed were not a major concern in contemporary political life. Jewish communities flourished in a number of towns and cities, especially Amsterdam, even in the absence of official regulations governing their lives. In the early 17th century, moreover, the debate about the place of Jewish communities was almost entirely eclipsed by the political debate surrounding the convening of a national synod, the dispute between Remonstrants and Counter-Remonstrants and the debate about continuing the war against Spain.

A Beacon at Sea

This brings me to my final question. Is the *Remonstrantie* more than a historical document, a phase in the development of Dutch society and a step in the evolution of Hugo Grotius's thinking?

The *Remonstrantie* is based on a different conception of society than ours: a *Ständestaat*, a society of groups, collectives or 'estates', in which the status, liberty and duties of individuals depended on their position within their own group and the position of that group in relation to others. This society was assailed on all sides by religious disputes, which served to undermine intra-group solidarity. Hence the concerns about religious diversity and irreligion which permeated society and indeed underpinned the *Remonstrantie* itself. It sounds odd to modern ears, and we are more likely to see it as an illustration of the dangers of the intermingling of church and state. But is building social cohesion on the basis of a shared Dutch identity so different from pursuing the same end with religion as the binding factor? Is the fear of foreigners who do not respect our values or of Muslims who threaten our Judaeo-Christian culture so very different from the fear of religious diversity in the 17th century? And do we not continue to think in terms of groups when we talk about Moroccans, Turks, Muslims and ethnic minorities?

From within the social framework discussed above, the *Remonstrantie* attempted to find a rational solution to an age-old question: how can we, as members of different communities, live and work together in a single society? Over the centuries many solutions have been attempted: territorial separation, whether by street, neighbourhood, city or country (*cuius regio, eius religio*); cultural, religious or ethnic compartmentalisation, or apartheid. In Western Europe over the past half century we have tried to resolve the issue by eliminating it entirely, stressing instead individualism and equality. Against this backdrop, cohesive religious, cultural or ethnic communities are increasingly viewed with suspicion. With respect to the differences that remain, both toleration and tolerance are invoked as solutions. But as a rule, tolerance only extends to those differences that do not matter to us. Religious, cultural or ethical customs or views that strike us as objectionable or wrong must be altered swiftly by legislation to conform to majority opinion. But tolerance is only genuine if we are willing to put up with behaviours, opinions or customs that we regard

16 Nellen op. cit. mentions the *Remonstrantie* in the index of people and works, and once in the footnotes. The main body of the text only refers to it obliquely, in a subordinate clause on p. 99.

as incorrect, wrong or objectionable. The *Remonstrantie* is Hugo Grotius's attempt to find an enduring answer to that conundrum. To do so, he ingeniously employed the convictions and arguments of his opponents.

Before consigning the *Remonstrantie* to history, therefore, we should ask ourselves whether the questions Grotius sought to answer are truly no longer relevant and whether the answers we have come up with are so much better. Because if not, it might be useful to draw attention to the *Remonstrantie* from time to time, as the present publication does. Not because it offers a more appealing solution, but because we need to realise that with all the debate about identity politics, all the indignation about what deviates from the norm or is culturally different, and all the arguments that religion has no place in public life, sooner or later we revert to the thinking that forms the foundation of the *Remonstrantie* and the questions that text attempts to address. In that sense the *Remonstrantie* is a warning to us to learn from the experience of the past, or in the words of the Dutch proverb, it is a stranded ship that serves as a beacon to other vessels at sea.

Piet Hein Donner

Illustrations

Notes on Contributors

Marijke J. Blankman
(*1948) studied Dutch Language and Literature (cum laude 1988), University of Amsterdam, with a specialization in Historical Literature. She contributed to several books on Early Modern Dutch literature and served as picture editor for similar publications. From 2006 till her retirement in 2013 she worked as co-ordinator of Internal Communications at the Van Gogh Museum in Amsterdam.

Jan Pieter Hendrik (Piet Hein) Donner
(*1948) began his career as a civil servant in the Ministry of Economic Affairs and then in the Ministry of Justice. He was a member and chairman of the Scientific Council for Government Policy and joined the Council of State in 1998. From 2002 to 2011 he was, with a year's interruption during which he was a member of the House of Representatives, successively Minister of Justice, of Social Affairs and Employment, and of Home Affairs. In 2012 he returned to the Council of State as vice president until he reached the upper age limit in 2018. He fulfils various other functions including the chairmanship of the Interchurch Council in Government Affairs and membership of the scientific board of the T.M.C. Asser Institute.

Cis van Heertum
(*1958) read English literature at Nijmegen under Professor T.A. Birrell and had the wistful pleasure of being the last of his PhD students (doctorate degree 1989). She worked as a curator in The British Library in 1990–1991, then joined the staff of the Bibliotheca Philosophica Hermetica in Amsterdam. Her main responsibilities in this library are curatorial and editorial. Since 2011 she has also worked as a translator and editor, specializing in book history and art history.

David Kromhout
(*1976) studied Hebrew and Jewish Studies with minors in Greek, Latin and Arabic at the University of Amsterdam. His research interest is the intellectual world of the long seventeenth century, with emphasis on the dynamics of intercultural and inter-confessional exchange. He wrote a dissertation on the Synod of Dort (1618) as a foucauldian event and its repercussions on the literary discourse of the Leiden humanists. Presently, he is a teacher of Classics at the Stedelijk Lyceum in Zutphen.

Adri K. Offenberg
(*1939) studied Dutch Philology, Bibliology, and Hebrew and Danish language at the University of Amsterdam. He joined the staff of the Bibliotheca Rosenthaliana, University of Amsterdam, in 1965 and was curator from 1974 to his retirement in 2004. He was editor-in-chief of *Studia Rosenthaliana* from 1987 to 2004 and of the *volume Bibliotheca Rosenthaliana. Treasures of Jewish Booklore* (Amsterdam, Amsterdam University Press 1994). He works mainly in the field of Jewish bibliography with emphasis on Hebrew incunabulistics and Jewish printers and authors in Amsterdam. He authored several books and articles in various scholarly journals, among which many on early modern Sephardic Amsterdam.

Notes on This Edition

Adri K. Offenberg and David Kromhout

The manuscript of Hugo Grotius' (Hugo de Groot's) *Remonstrantie* of 1615 is kept by the library of the Portuguese-Israelite Community of Amsterdam Ets Haim-Livraria D. Montezinos under shelfmark EH 48 A 02. It was acquired by David Henriques de Castro (1826–1898), a Jewish collector from Amsterdam, in 1867.[1] He bought the manuscript along with a few other items relating to the history of the Jews in the Netherlands at Nijhoff's famous Grotius auction in The Hague on 15 November 1864.[2]

These manuscripts auctioned by Nijhoff have a remarkable provenance. They were still in the possession of Hugo Grotius' direct descendants, afterwards called Cornets de Groot, as late as 1864. The last descendant, Hugo Cornets de Groot, His Majesty's tax collector in Cuijk, left them to his landlord Baptiste Ragouins out of gratitude. The latter then sold them for 700 guilders to tobacco dealer G. Snelleman in Rotterdam, who had the larger part auctioned by Nijhoff 'for the fun of it'. The manuscripts raised over 1,247 guilders.[3]

1 Cohen, *Onder de hamer*. Henriques de Castro published articles on the history of the Portuguese-Israelite Community in Amsterdam; a commemorative text to mark the second centenary of the Portuguese Synagogue (1875) and a monumental edition, *Keur van grafstenen* (1883), on Beth Haim in Ouderkerk aan de Amstel, the Portuguese-Jewish cemetery that was restored at his expense.

2 *Catalogue de manuscrits autographes du célèbre Hugo Grotius et de documents importants qui ont servi à la composition de ses ouvrages dont la vente aura lieu le 15 nov. 1864 sous la dir. de Martinus Nijhoff*. Nijhoff also published a second edition of this catalogue, with notes by W.J.M. van Eysinga and L.J. Noordhoff, in The Hague in 1952. The manuscript of the *Remonstrantie* is described under No. 73 in the catalogue with the additional remark "MS. important du 16e siècle. Avec quelques notes marginales de la main de Grotius." (Important 16th-century MS. With a number of marginal notes in Grotius' hand).

3 Kleffens, "Over zes brieven uit het bezit van Hugo de Groot."

David Henriques de Castro commissioned a modern transcription of the text, which had been written in a graceful though not easily legible gothic script. This he had bound with the original manuscript. He died on 10 October 1898, after which his extensive collection of art objects and his library were auctioned the next year.[4] The manuscript of the *Remonstrantie* can be found in the catalogue under No. 509, with the additional remarks "avec copie moderne" (with a modern transcription) and: "La belle écriture faite sans doute par le secrétaire de Grotius qui lui même a fait des annotations autographes en marge" (The fine handwriting is undoubtedly that of Grotius' secretary, while Grotius himself added the marginal annotations in his own hand).

This item was bought for sixty guilders by the bibliophile and owner of one of the most comprehensive collections in the field of Dutch Jewry, David Montezinos (1828–1916), librarian of Ets Haim from 1866 to 1916.[5] In 1889 he donated his entire collection of over 20,000 printed works, manuscripts and prints to the library, which has been held under the name Livraria D. Montezinos since.

The manuscript, written on good quality chancery paper in folio (31.1×20.8 cm) contains 34 leaves (68 pages), preceded by two blank leaves. The leaf after the 25th leaf is not numbered, so that leaves 26 to 33 are actually leaves 27 to 34. The manuscript has 1,406 lines of text. It was bound together with the late nineteenth-century transcription of the text in a half vellum binding with marbled sides and three ties. The two texts have now been separated.

4 *Catalogue de vente de la succession de feu D. Henriques de Castro Mz.*

5 Silva Rosa, "David Montezinos, de stichter van de 'Livria D. Montezinos.'"

FIGURE 1
Portrait of David Henriques de Castro by his brother Gabriel Haim Henriques de Castro, painted between 1865 and 1875

The text is written in a graceful Old Dutch round cursive Gothic script; the Latin quotes are in a clear Italian cursive. The manuscript was not written in Grotius' own hand, but was probably made by his secretary or a professional scribe. The remark in both auction catalogues according to which the marginal notes were made by Grotius is incorrect, they are by the same hand as the text itself (with the possible exception of the marginal note on f. 8r, though this cannot be established with any certainty).[6] A slip of paper with a comment by "Mr Frederiks" was unprofessionally pasted over half of the title above the text on f. 1r.[7] This probably happened after the nineteenth-century transcription had been added to the manuscript. According to the comment the manuscript was in the hand of Hugo Grotius, which is not the case.

Gothic script occasionally features variants of the letters a and e. The use of capitals is not always very consistent. The capitals J and H are sometimes used in the middle of a sentence.[8] The capitals are more florid in the part containing the regulations, which is amply laid out. The number of abbreviations is limited and solved by italicizing the letter or letters so as to avoid abbreviation marks in the transcription. Whether the corrections and underscores are part of the original editing of the text or were made by a later hand could not always be established with certainty. The marginal notes in

6 Comment by Prof. Henk Nellen (5-10-2016).

7 This is probably J.G. Frederiks (1828–1896), who published articles on seventeenth-century Dutch history in the periodical *Oud Holland*, on Johannes Uytenbogaert (1873) and on Petrus Scriverius (1894), two individuals in Grotius' direct environment. He also co-authored a two-volume biographical lexicon, *Biographisch woordenboek der Noord- en Zuidnederlandsche letterkunde* (1875–1878; [2] 1888–1891), which contains an entry on Henriques de Castro on pp. 150–151.

8 The difference between the small letter 'j' and the capital 'J' can be clearly distinguished in line 720.

FIGURE 2 David Montezinos and his assistant Jacob da Silva Rosa at Ets Haim/Livraria Montezinos around 1910

the manuscript are to be found in the left margin; in the transcription they were included in the right margin.

The strictly diplomatic transcription is based on the "reading eye" principle introduced by W.G. Hellinga, meaning we offer the text the way it looked after the manuscript had been finished. This makes any form of textual criticism unwanted.[9] As a result, there is no question of any regularisation of the text: *iaer* for instance is not written as *jaer*; *ouer* does not become *over*; *vuijt* is not written as *uuijt* and *jn* does not become *in*. If in the text words like *jaar, jong* or *jeugd* begin with an i, therefore, the i is not automatically replaced by a j. Conversely, when *in* begins with a j, that letter j is not replaced by an i, etcetera.

The translation into modern Dutch aims to make the text readable for contemporary readers, but to maintain the style and reasoning of Grotius. The name of the text *Remonstrantie* is maintained in Dutch when referring to Grotius's text, when referring to the general term, it is translated as "Remonstrance".

The text was published by Dr Jaap Meijer in 1949 with a very extensive historical introduction and appendices.[10] It is obvious from a number of minor errors and inaccuracies in the transcription of the text of the *Remonstrantie* that Meijer—without acknowledging it—based himself on the admittedly excellent nineteenth-century transcription of the original manuscript.[11] He left the Latin

9 Hellinga, *Van den vos Reynaerde. Diplomatisch uitgegeven naar de bronnen vóór het jaar 1500. I Teksten*, v–vii.

10 Groot, *Remonstrantie.*

11 Some examples: in line 72 Meijer offers the word *versos* in the passage from Juvenal, which is meaningless

FIGURE 3
Jaap Meijer was a Dutch Jewish writer, historian, and poet who studied and wrote about the *Remonstrantie*. He is seen here in his home library in Heemstede in 1980.

quotes untranslated, though not without including (occasionally perfunctory) references to sources in the footnotes. In 1955 Meijer published an English summary of his edition in *Jewish Social Studies. A quarterly journal devoted to contemporary and historical aspects of Jewish life*, Vol. 17 (April 1955), pp. 91–104.

The text of Grotius' commentary on his own regulation is really an independent text which reveals much of Grotius' thought and method. The main purpose of this commentary would appear to be to substantiate the rules in the actual regulation. This would seem to be obvious, though it should be borne in mind that these learned quotes provided the document with extra authority and *gravitas*. It may even have been the principal aim of the text. Van Ittersum for instance writes about the use of references like these in Grotius' *De Jure Praedae*: 'The aim would have been to increase the number of authorities in the treatise's margins, rather than to elucidate an existing argument. When it suited Grotius, even texts from which he had once derived real intellectual sustenance could quickly be turned into "authorities", littering a manuscript's margins and, paradoxically, obscuring the argument.'[12]

Grotius mainly, though not exclusively, refers to legal sources to underpin his arguments. These are primarily relevant texts drawn from Roman and canonical law, but there are also references to the so-called Consiliators or Commentators such as Baldus de Ubaldis, Julius Clarus and other jurists. In the manuscript these references are distinguished by a different script; in our transcription they are presented in italics. These references have been moved to the footnotes and replaced by mod-

in the context, whereas the original manuscript clearly has *verpos* (the circumcised); the 19th-century transcription has the same. In line 562 the word *getal* is missing, as in the transcription. In line 926 *hemluijden* is missing, as in the transcription. In line 951 Meijer has *quod super devoto*, where the original has *quod super his de voto*. In line 1165 *t'eentmael*, again as in the transcription. In line 1250 the manuscript reads *gereguleert*, Meijer has *geregneert*, as does the transcription. Similarly line 1264/65 has *leste tijden*, Meijer has *eerste tijden* as does the nineteenth-century transcription, a significant difference in meaning. That he uncritically based himself on the nineteenth-century transcription without consulting the original is obvious from line 1309, where he has *horibus*, whereas the manuscript has *honoribus* in a clear Italian italic.

12 Ittersum, "The Working Methods of Hugo Grotius," 190.

ern source references in the modern retranslation and in the English translation. Occasionally a reference is an integral part of an argument, in such cases a suitable solution was always sought and found. The Latin has been translated by the editors unless otherwise stated. When a reference was clearly incorrect or untraceable, we decided not to include it. Meijer in his edition relied on Feenstra, Duyvendak and De Smidt to research the references (see p. 122, n. 8), though there are still many mistakes. It is incidentally uncertain in quite a few cases whether Grotius actually found the sources he quoted from himself, as he very often gleaned them from other sources: 'Always a man in a hurry, Grotius never lost the habit of incorporating second-hand quotations and references into his writings.'[13]

13 Ittersum, 176.

CHAPTER 1

Introduction and Analysis of the *Remonstrantie*

David Kromhout

1 The Historical Context of the *Remonstrantie*

Grotius's *Remonstrantie nopende de ordre dije in de landen van Hollandt ende Westvrieslandt dijent gestelt op de Joden* suffered a peculiar fate: initially, it was a policy document that was written to solve a particular and actual situation. As happens often, the consciously assembled document was neglected and was consigned to a personal archive without having exerted any political influence that we know of.[1] However, the disregarded policy document had a remarkable afterlife, and there may be few other documents that, after having been completely neglected in their own days, suddenly receive quite some attention from modern historians.[2] The reason that it does receive this much attention is probably the fact that it represents one of the great cultural intersections of the Dutch 17th century. On the one hand, the document is ascribed to Hugo de Groot, or Grotius in his Latinized form, 'the miracle from Holland', who in his own right is studied intensively as a jurist, a statesman, a humanist, a biblical scholar, and as a poet.[3] Although it might seem evident to study the *Remonstrantie* for its legal and political implications, it is Grotius's humanist world view that underlies the text and cannot be neglected. On the other hand, the *Remonstrantie* addresses the settlement of Jews in the cities of Holland and West Frisia—an occurrence that would have a profound influence not only on the Dutch economy and overseas networks, but also on the perception of Holland and the Dutch Republic as an open and tolerant society. Holland was already a cultural staple market and the establishment of Menasseh ben Israel's printing press would make Amsterdam one of the most important centres of Jewish book printing in the world.

Since the text has been written by one of the greatest representatives of Dutch 17th-century culture and concerns regulating the settlement of Jews, it is often read as proof of Grotius's opinions on Jews and Judaism and as either an example of tolerance in the 17th century or evidence of its absence. For, as we shall see, both interpretations are indeed possible. This approach is not unproblematic, however. Grotius writes about Jews and Judaism only on a few occasions and in all these cases the texts are embedded in a specific historical context. It should be remembered that Grotius wrote many of his letters and texts as a politician

1 A resolution of the States of Holland and West Frisia, dated 13 December 1619, speaks of concepts of a regulation, written by the Pensionaries Pauw and Grotius. It remains a matter of debate whether our *Remonstrantie* is the same text. The text of the resolution can be found in Groot, *Remonstrantie*, 101.

2 Among them: Wilde, "Offering Hospitality"; Eyffinger, "'How Wondrously Moses Goes Along with The House of Orange!': Hugo Grotius' 'De Republica Emendanda' in the Context of the Dutch Revolt"; Peterse, "Hugo Grotius und sein Gutachten über die rechtliche Stellung der Juden in Holland (1615)"; Swetschinski, *Reluctant Cosmopolitans*; Bodian, *Hebrews of the Portuguese Nation*; Swetschinski, "Tussen middeleeuwen en Gouden Eeuw, 1516–1621"; Rabbie, "Hugo Grotius and Judaism"; Vlessing, "על ראשית יהודי פורטוגאל באמסטרדאם"; Rosenne, "Hugo Grotius: An Israeli Appreciation"; Michman, "Historiography of the Jews in The Netherlands"; Groot, *Remonstrantie*; Zwarts, *Eerste rabbijnen*.

3 There is no complete certainty that the text of the *Remonstrantie* is only from Grotius's hand, although much in the style of the text would suggest that this is the case. For the purposes of the discussion here it has been assumed that Grotius either wrote the complete text by himself or else incorporated texts written by Pauw into the first and second parts of the *Remonstrantie*. See p. 52.

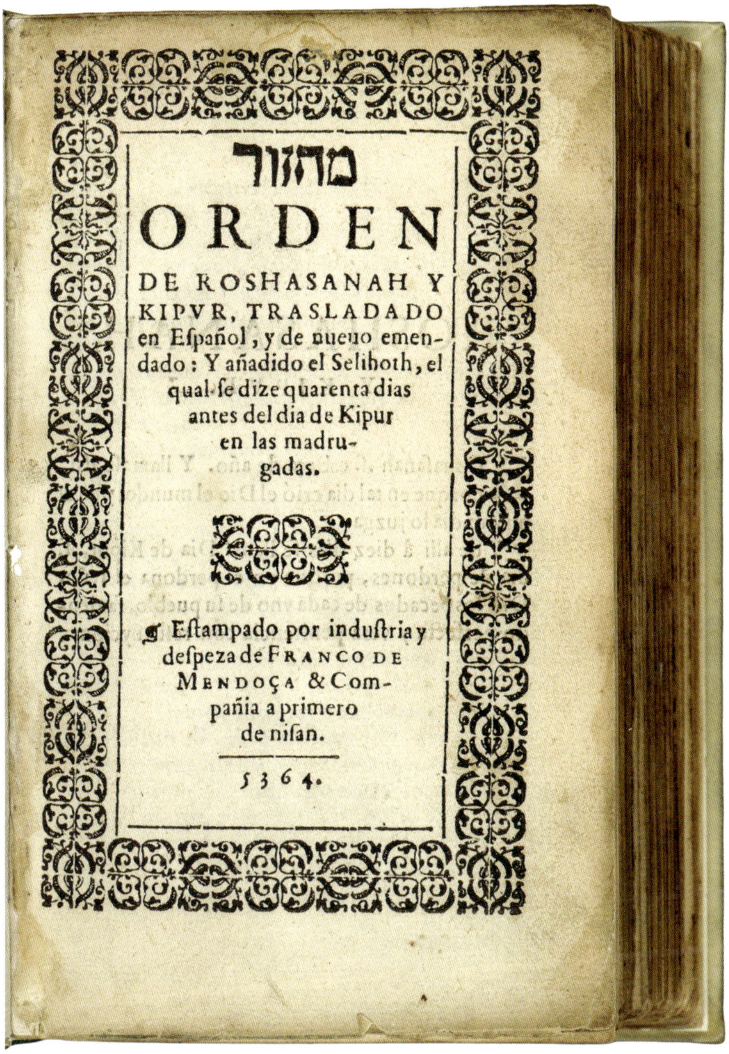

מחזור
ORDEN
DE ROSHASANAH Y KIPVR, TRASLADADO en Eſpañol, y de nueuo emendado: Y añadido el Selihoth, el qual ſe dize quarenta dias antes del dia de Kipur en las madrugadas.

Eſtampado por induſtria y deſpeza de FRANCO DE MENDOÇA & Compañia a primero de niſan.

5364.

FIGURE 4
Title page of a Sephardi Machzor printed in 1604 where both Hebrew and Spanish were used

in unstable times. It is therefore impossible to read his texts as if they are unpolluted expressions of Grotius's inner convictions. Grotius acted as one of the main protagonists on the political scene of the 1610s, a complex role that would consume all his energy and would lead to his imprisonment and exile. More than reflections of a secluded scholar, the *Remonstrantie* offers an insight into the complex negotiations between Calvinists, humanists, pragmatists, mercantilists and others.

The Portuguese merchants were not the first Jews to arrive in the Northern Netherlands. During the later Middle Ages, Jews had lived in various places in the Northern Netherlands, particularly in the eastern provinces of present-day Overijssel, Gelderland (Gelre) and Limburg. These Jews, however, arrived under very different circumstances and were different Jews themselves. The Jewish diaspora is traditionally divided in two parts, namely 'Ashkenaz' and 'Sepharad'. Ashkenaz is the Jewish designation for Northern and Eastern Europe, and Sepharad, simply meaning 'Spain' or the Iberian Peninsula, is the designation for the Jewish culture of the Mediterranean world, including the Near and Middle East. This division may seem artificial and does no justice to the many local differences between Jewish communities; yet it is a division that is still felt today.

Jews of Ashkenaz, or Ashkenazim, shared some basic cultural features, such as their day-to-day use of Yiddish as their language, a special way of pronouncing Hebrew, a calligraphy that resembles Gothic Latin script, and the centrality of the Talmud in the religious curriculum. Sephardim used a different pronunciation of Hebrew, especially concerning the guttural sounds, and their calligraphy resembled Arabic script, using a pointed reed pen, and they spoke either Ladino (Judeo-Spanish) or Judeo-Arabic in their daily lives. There was a relatively strong focus on the study of the Bible and the mystics.

The Ashkenazim who had lived in the parts of the Low Countries that would go on to become part of the Dutch Republic in the provinces of Gelre and Overijssel came from the larger communities in the Rhineland, especially Cologne. They were completely dependent on the ruling nobility, who usually both needed them for loans and allowed them to settle for a longer or shorter time to engage almost exclusively in moneylending. When in the course of the 15th and 16th centuries the economic opportunities decreased and anti-Judaic sentiment increased, Jews almost completely disappeared from these provinces.

The Jews for whom the *Remonstrantie* was intended had seen their own long range of restrictions and repressions before they were finally able to settle under more favourable conditions in Amsterdam. The Iberian Peninsula had had a large Jewish population since time immemorial; it is generally assumed that Jewish merchants already had communities there in Roman times. Under Visigoth rule (fifth to eighth centuries), the situation worsened gradually from complete freedom under the first kings to expulsions and forced baptism. Already under the Visigoths, suspicion of crypto-Judaism existed and measures were devised to isolate and persecute insincere converts. It is no surprise, then, that in 711 the Iberian Jews hailed the Ummayad Muslim conquerors as liberators, which they were for them. For the Iberian Jews, Muslim rule signified an era of unknown freedom, possibilities and cultural exchange. However, the dynasties of the Almoravids and the Almohads brought an end to this Golden Age from the 11th century onward, with restrictive measures, forced conversions and expulsion. Jews of Al-Andalus fled to the Christian North or Islamic countries in the Mediterranean with a more moderate rule.

The Christian kingdoms gladly received the refugee Jews and for a while Jews enjoyed a certain freedom and privileges. They could occupy positions in armies and at the Court, own property, etc. However, as the story repeats itself, the 14th century sees a growing tendency towards repression with the year 1391 as its apex, when it is alleged that 100,000 or 200,000 Jews were forcibly baptized in a pogrom that swept across Spain. Apparently, this pogrom became the instigator of a series of events that led to the diaspora of Spanish and Portuguese Jews.[4] For although the Jewish communities were severely damaged and diminished, they managed to regroup and recover to the extent that they could. Many communities disappeared, but others survived. This created a situation which had existed earlier under the Visigoths, namely of a large group of converted Jews living next to unconverted Jews. Whether converts had become sincere Christians or not, they still associated with former friends and family, which created a possible ground for relapse.[5] The converted Jews, or *conversos* were able to fully participate in Spanish society and some of them were very successful. They managed to marry into wealthy, noble families and some even served at the King's court. It is probably this combination of success and contact between Jews and *conversos* that gave rise to a new form of stigma: a division was made in the public discourse between Old and New Christians. Whereas Old Christians came from undisputed Roman Catholic families and were regarded as completely trustworthy as to their religious motives, New Christians were suspected of secretly adhering to the faith of their ancestors.[6]

4 Bodian, *Hebrews of the Portuguese Nation*, 6.

5 Bodian, 7–8.

6 Bodian, 8–9.

FIGURE 5
Queen Isabella I of Castile who, along with her husband Ferdinand II of Aragon, was the instigator of the Spanish Inquisition in 1480

This sentiment received impetus with the marriage of Ferdinand II of Aragon (1452–1516) and Isabella I of Castile (1451–1501). This royal pair had enormous religious ambition, which meant that they first of all wanted to reconquer the parts of Spain under Muslim rule, but also wanted to prevent any convert from relapsing into Judaism. As the rumour continued that *conversos* were secretly practising Jewish rituals and deflecting from Catholicism under the influence of their contact with unbaptized Jews, Isabella received papal permission in 1478 to establish a Spanish Inquisition, which was effected in 1480.[7] Contrary to the Roman Catholic Inquisition, which responded to Church authority, the Spanish Inquisition, much to papal dismay, fell solely and directly under royal authority. The Inquisition was set to work and confirmed the circulating rumours. As Ferdinand and Isabella saw it as their prime responsibility to prevent converted Jews from relapsing, and as the Inquisition confirmed their suspicion that converts remained in close contact with Jews and Jewish tradition and were still practising Jewish rituals, they decided to banish all Jews who resisted conversion from their lands in 1492.

This measure created a mass emigration of Jews from Spain in every direction. Portugal was the nearest refuge and many Jews fled from Spain to Portugal, where King John II allowed the Jewish immigrants. Many others, however, fled from the Iberian Peninsula to existing Jewish communities in the Mediterranean. Italy, the Balkans, Turkey and North Africa were favourable destinations, where large communities of Iberian refugees soon

7 Kamen, *Inquisition and Society in Spain in the Sixteenth and Seventeenth Centuries*, 29–43; Nicholas, *The Transformation of Europe, 1300–1600*, 171–172.

grew. The fact that these Jews were expelled did not, however, mean that all ties with their converted relatives were severed. On the contrary, the expulsion from Spain and the establishment of Iberian Jewish communities all over the Mediterranean created an enormous, closely connected network of expelled Jews who had resisted conversion and who stayed in some way in contact with their converted relatives.

Those who had fled to Portugal were soon to find out that their relief was only temporary; under pressure from the most Catholic King and Queen, the same measures against Jews were enacted in Portugal. All Jews were forcibly converted in 1497. Officially, those who refused baptism were allowed to leave the country; however, they had to leave their children and possessions behind. Actually, many Iberian Jews managed to escape with their belongings and children. This meant in theory that from 1497 onwards no Jews were left on the Iberian Peninsula. Again, many fled, mostly to the Mediterranean lands where Spanish Jews had already settled.[8] However, there were also many Jews who decided to stay and let themselves be baptized. These were Jews who had resisted baptism several times already, which meant that they were less disposed to embrace Christianity wholeheartedly. It is assumed that this group in particular was most inclined to live outwardly as Christians, but continued to practise Judaism secretly at home.[9] The Portuguese King Manuel I had promised not to look too closely into the personal beliefs of the newly, forcibly converted. For a while, these New Christians were left alone, until in 1537 the Portuguese Inquisition was established.

The situation for *conversos* in Portugal became increasingly more difficult to bear, and many returned to Spain after the Iberian Unification of Philips II, where pressure was temporarily lighter. The unification with Spain offered the *conversos* considerably more options to escape from the Inquisition.[10] These returning New Christians formed a complex group who became known as *Portuguese*, although many or probably most of them were (descendants of) emigrant Spanish Jews who returned as New Christians. Apparently, they were perceived as a peculiar, distinct group, part of whom were influential merchants and bankers, who lent money to the King, and by now, partly or largely due to the anti-Judaic measures of both kingdoms, had an enormous commercial and social network. To this group belonged the Portuguese merchants, or the Jews from the Portuguese Nation who came to Amsterdam in the years around 1600.

1.1 *Legendary Beginnings*

The earliest beginning of Portuguese Jewish presence in Amsterdam and in the Dutch Republic has been clouded in myths. We have no real, solid evidence of the first phase of this new settlement. We do know that future members of the Sephardic community frequented Amsterdam from as early as 1595, as notarial records have been found from this year onward.[11] However, concerning the establishment of the Jewish community, all we know stems from two obviously embellished sources, both of them written more than 50 years after the actual events and neither of them by eyewitnesses. The best-known of these is the *Triumpho del govierno popular* (1683), by the poet and historian Daniel Miguel de Barrios (c. 1625–1701).[12] A secondary source, of which the original has been lost, but found some interest in the 18th and 19th centuries, is the *Memória para los siglos*

8 Swetschinski, *Reluctant Cosmopolitans*, 58; Israel, *European Jewry in the Age of Mercantilism, 1550–1750*, chap. I.

9 Israel, *European Jewry in the Age of Mercantilism, 1550–1750*, 24–25.

10 Swetschinski, *Reluctant Cosmopolitans*, 60–61.

11 Koen and Pieterse, "Notarial Records in Amsterdam Relating to the Portuguese Jews in That Town up to 1639".

12 Barrios, *Triumpho del Govierno Popular*, 5. On Daniel de Barrios, see Pieterse, "Daniel Levi de Barrios als geschiedschrijver van de Portugees-Israelietische gemeente te Amsterdam in zijn 'Triumpho del govierno popular'". [Barrios p. 5 (403 / GoogleBooks: 333)]

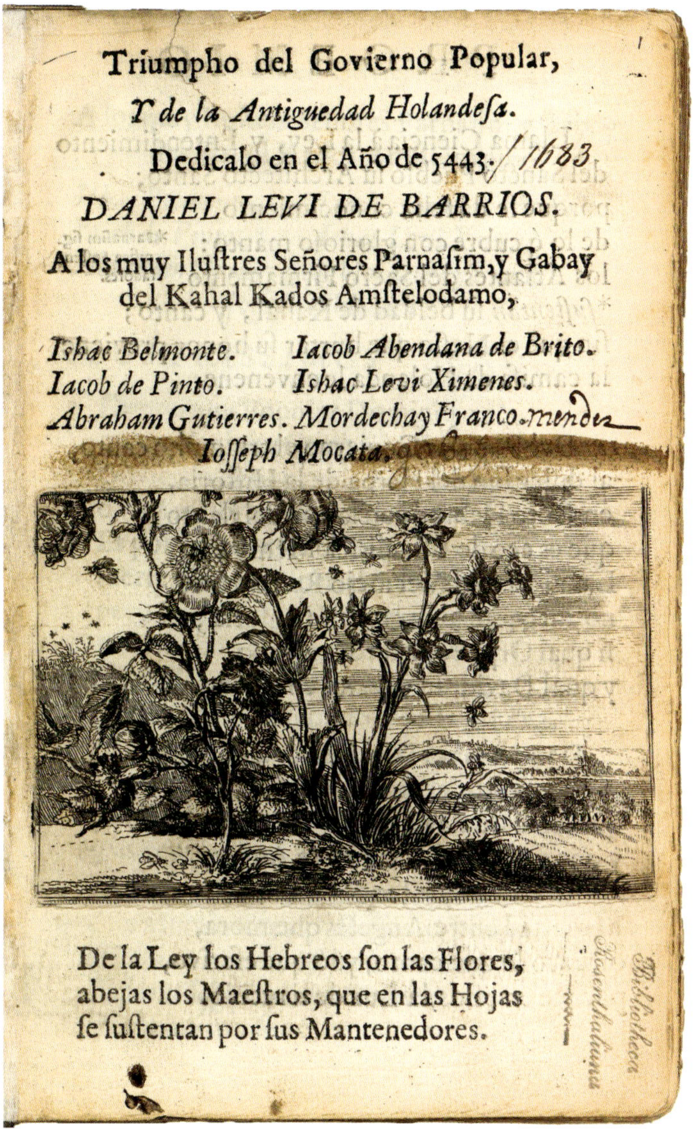
Triumpho del Govierno Popular,
Y de la Antiguedad Holandeſa.
Dedicalo en el Año de 5443.
DANIEL LEVI DE BARRIOS.
A los muy Iluſtres Señores Parnaſim, y Gabay
del Kahal Kados Amſtelodamo,
Iſhac Belmonte. Iacob Abendana de Brito.
Iacob de Pinto. Iſhac Levi Ximenes.
Abraham Gutierres. Mordechay Franco.
Ioſſeph Mocata.

De la Ley los Hebreos ſon las Flores,
abejas los Maeſtros, que en las Hojas
ſe ſuſtentan por ſus Mantenedores.

FIGURE 6
Title page of *Triumpho del govierno popular*, one of the main sources of the foundation myth of the Portuguese Jewish community in Amsterdam

futuros, written by Uri Halevi the Younger (1627–1715), grandson of the supposed first rabbi of the Sephardim in Amsterdam. Both accounts share some basic features, but differ considerably in the details nonetheless.[13]

The first foundational myth, told by Daniel de Barrios, tells of the beautiful Maria Nuñez, who set sail from Lisbon in 1593, together with her brother and her uncle. According to De Barrios, they wanted to flee to Holland from the horrors of the Inquisition. During their voyage, the ship was captured by the English navy and as the English and the Portuguese were at war, the ship was brought up to England. There, Maria in particular made a great impression on both the Queen and her entourage. Even a duke fell for her beauty and wanted to marry her, and the Queen, stricken by her beauty, modesty and manners, proposed that she would be shown to the people of London in her own royal carriage. However, Mary refused both the duke and the royal hon-

13 Both accounts can be found in translation in Salomon, "Myth or Anti-Myth".

ours offered to her by the Queen and instead said that she wanted to proceed on her journey towards Amsterdam in order to live a Jewish life. And so it happened.

The second myth, told by Uri Halevi the Younger, speaks about 10 men and four boys, all New Christians, who reached the city of Emden in 1603 or 1604 [5364]. The story does not inform us whether they were fleeing from the Inquisition or were simply Portuguese merchants who happened to be in Emden, which was not uncommon. Two of these men find out that there are Jews living in Emden and that they can practise their religion there more or less freely. They find out where a rabbi lives in Emden, named Uri Halevi, and they pay him a visit. The grandson informs us that Halevi himself was unable to speak Spanish, so his son Aaron is brought in to interpret their words. The merchants tell Halevi that they are a group of 14 Iberian Jews who desperately want to be circumcised. Halevi explains to them that this is impossible in the Lutheran city of Emden, but that if they go to Amsterdam, he will follow them as soon as he can and they will be circumcised there. They agree on where and how to meet and everything goes to plan. Aaron serves as *hazzan*, or cantor, and Uri Halevi as *haham*, or rabbi, who introduces these men into the principles and traditions of a Jewish life.

The third myth is told by both authors and is probably the best known. By now, the young community has started meeting regularly in the house of a certain Jacob Tirado. According to Daniel de Barrios, the members of this community had locked themselves in on Yom Kippur (Day of Atonement), when the bailiff and his men appeared and demanded to be let in. When they entered the room, they began to search for signs of Roman Catholic worship. It turned out that a neighbour had complained about the Portuguese merchants and accused them of secretly celebrating the Holy Mass. When the bailiff learned that these men were no Catholics but Jews, he apologized and asked to include them in their prayers. In other versions, Uri Halevi was taken away to jail and brought before the magistrates.[14] In the version of Uri Halevi the Younger, no mention about Yom Kippur is made. Again, Uri Halevi and his son are taken prisoner, and when they are brought before the magistrates, they convince them by pointing out the great economic value of these merchants to the city of Amsterdam. When consequently the Portuguese were brought before the magistrates and questioned as well, they confirmed Halevi's words and the magistrates allowed them to stay and practise their religion freely.[15]

These myths are very interesting and have been assessed in very different ways. Zwarts, for example, seems to regard them as reliable and goes to great lengths to sift information from the legendary stories and make them correlate with notarial archival findings.[16] He upholds the basic

14 In Uri Halevi's *Memória* and in Barrios' poem *Dialogo harmonico, Triumpho del Govierno Popular*, 134–137.

15 Salomon, "Myth or Anti-Myth", 281–282.

16 'De mededeelingen omtrent de eerste Rabbijnen en Synagogen van Amsterdam, waarover wij tot dusverre beschikten, waren geen primaire, doch secundaire bronnen, eerste vele jaren later opgeteekend. Zoowel Seeligman als Mr. Prins hebben deze verhalen reeds naar het rijk der legenden verwezen, doch tevens de historische kern van het verhaal van Maria Nunez vastgesteld. Het geldt ook voor deze verhalen, […] hoe nl de legende enkele episoden voor het nageslacht bewaarde, deze echter met elkander willekeurig in verbinding brengt en de hiaten alsdan met rijke phantasie omspint. Buiten deze Maria Nunez-legende, bestaat er nog het bekende Emdensche verhaal en, daarmede later samengeweven, dat van Jacob Tyrado, Don Samuel Palache en Jacob Belmonte, die alle drie als stichters der eerste Amsterdamsche Synagoge gelden. Terwijl reeds de historische kern der Nunez-legende op *verschillende* vestigingen wees, heb ik getracht die der overige uit de primaire bronnen vast te stellen.' ['The accounts of the first rabbis and synagogues of Amsterdam, which we hitherto possess, were no primary, but secondary sources, written down many years later. Both Seeligman and Prins have judged them not trustworthy, yet established the historical kernel of the Maria Nunez story. It can be said of these stories as well, […] how legends preserve a few episodes for posterity, and yet arbitrarily interconnect them and fills in the blanks with unfettered imagination. Apart from the Maria Nunez

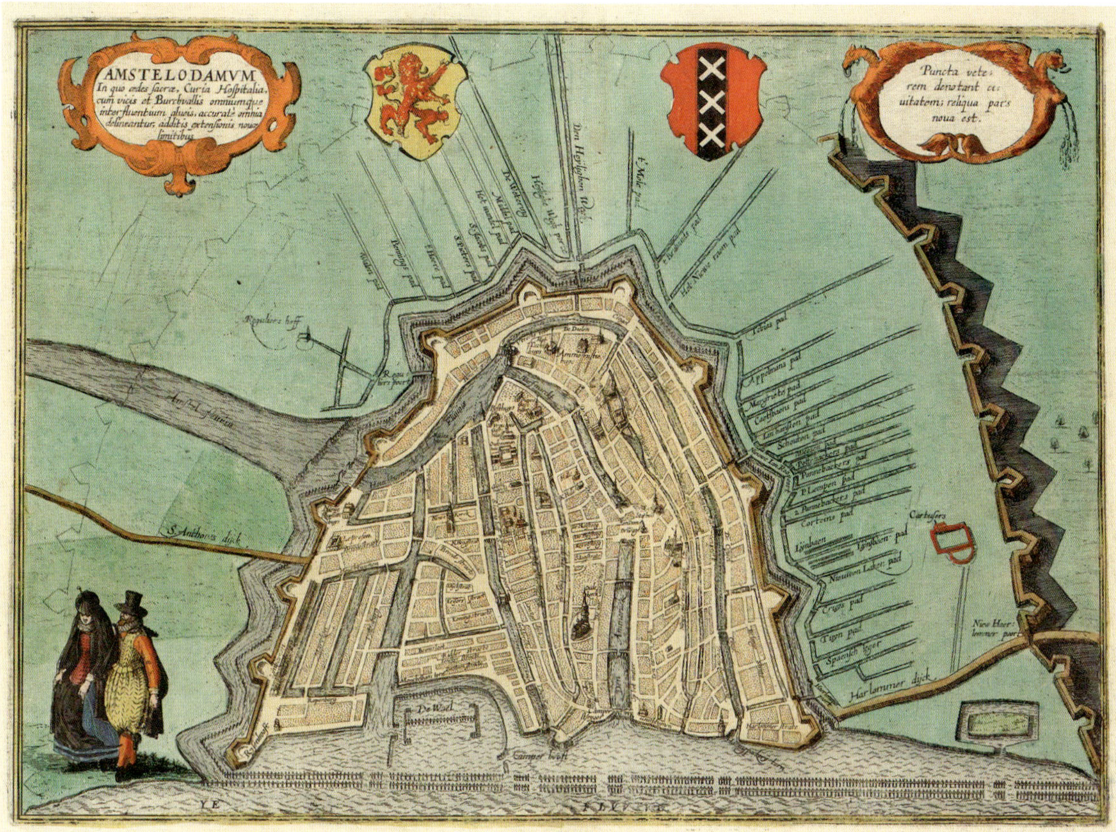

FIGURE 7 Map of Amsterdam dating to ca. 1612, depicting the city as it was around the time of the publication of the *Remonstrantie*

storyline of Maria Nuñez fleeing from Portugal to embrace Judaism, and the contact between Portuguese merchants and Uri Halevi in Emden, which resulted in the founding of a Jewish community in Jacob Tirado's house. The group of 14 Portuguese visiting Emden is identified in this version as a group being led by Jacob Tirado. Vlessing on the other hand is very critical of this attitude and dismisses the legends as historically unreliable and blames historians who use them to create an impression of the first beginnings of the Sephardic community in Amsterdam.[17]

It is interesting to see that both Zwarts and Vlessing make extensive use of the archives of the Portuguese community in Amsterdam. However, where Zwarts used them to fill in the blanks of the legends told above, Vlessing prefers to stick with the archival testimonies only. There are good reasons to handle the legendary material with caution. One reason, of course, is the fact that both accounts have been written relatively late and were possibly meant to embellish one's own history instead of providing a factual representation. But another reason is that the archival findings pose some serious questions, especially about the role

legend, there is the famous Emden story and, related to it, the stories about Jacob Tyrado, Don Samuel Palache and Jacob Belmonte, who are reckoned founders of the first Amsterdam synagogue. Whereas the historical kernel of the Maria Nunez legend hinted already at several phases in the foundation, I have tried to corroborate those of the others from primary sources.'] Zwarts, *Eerste rabbijnen*, 4.

17 Vlessing, "על ראשית יהודי פורטוגאל באמסטרדאם," 81–82.

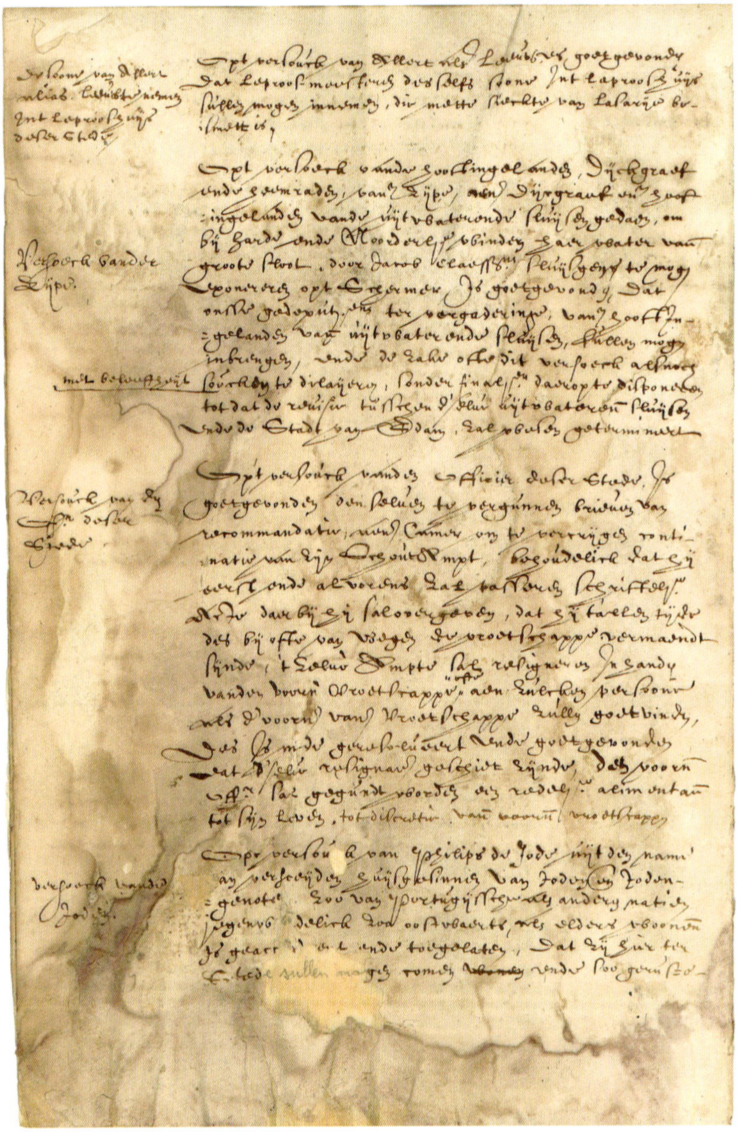

FIGURE 8
This document, written on 10 May 1604, gave permission for Jews to settle in the city of Alkmaar. The last paragraph on this page, captioned 'Request from the Jews', mentions Philips the Jew in the first line.

of Uri Halevi. He does appear in official records, though not as the leader of a Portuguese community but rather as a butcher who was arrested on suspicion of selling stolen goods. In the records of his interrogations it is mentioned that he came from Emden, was a rabbi and a teacher there, and now lived as a Jew and butcher in Amsterdam. No mention is made of Portuguese merchants appearing on his behalf and convincing the burgomasters of the benefits of allowing wealthy merchants into their city. Instead, Halevi stayed in jail for three weeks before he was released without any condemnation.[18] And more awkward is the case of Maria Nuñez, who according to the legend had rejected all signs of honour in order to live a Jewish life freely, but seems to have returned to Seville by 1612—that is if she followed her husband, of whom it is certain that he did return. It has been suggested that she served as a model there for Cervantes's *La Española inglesa*, the story of a beautiful Spanish girl who was kidnapped by the English,

18 Zwarts, *Eerste rabbijnen*, 108–110; Vlessing, "על ראשית יהודי פורטוגאל באמסטרדאם," 82.

raised secretly as a Catholic, rejects the advances of an English count and in the end, comes to Seville where she can openly live a Catholic life![19]

Although the exact beginnings of the Portuguese Jewish communities remain clouded in mist, it is clear that somewhere in the first years of the 17th century a group of Portuguese New Christians decided to try to establish for themselves a Jewish community and that Uri Halevi and his son Aaron were helpful in this process. The legendary Jacob Tirado is assumed to have been a leading personality among these pioneers, and has been identified as being the same person as Guimes Lopes da Costa (c. 1540–1620).[20] According to the legend, the first Portuguese community was named *Beth Jacob* after him, as he was the initiator and the small community assembled in his house. It is clear that this community was established without official approval from the municipal authorities.

The first approval for the foundation of a Jewish community was not granted by the city of Amsterdam, but by the city of Alkmaar. On 10 May 1604 the city informed Philips the Jew (de Joode) that a community of Jews was welcome to settle within the city of Alkmaar, both Portuguese and others, and freely exercise their religion as long as they respected the city regulations.[21] As the City Council of Amsterdam was unhelpful in finding a suitable burial site and building of a synagogue in later years, Zwarts assumed that Uri Halevi negotiated first a burial site in 1602 and later, in 1604, this first official approval with the city of Alkmaar as leverage against the city of Amsterdam. He assumed that the settlement of these Portuguese merchants was of considerable importance to the city and that the migration of this community to another city could be seen as a considerable economic loss for Amsterdam. According to Zwarts, it remains questionable whether the Portuguese merchants ever seriously intended to move from Amsterdam to Alkmaar. Meijer followed Zwarts in his argumentation to a certain extent, but was more outspoken in his conclusions: in any place where orthodox Calvinists ruled, there were hardly any chances for a Jewish community to be established or to grow. Philips the Jew's request to settle in Alkmaar should be interpreted as a desperate action from the orthodox part of the Portuguese community that seriously intended to migrate from Amsterdam to Alkmaar in order to be able to establish a Jewish community under more favourable conditions.[22]

Vlessing however is very critical about this line of reasoning and with some cause. Her first point is that nowhere in the resolution of the City Council of Alkmaar is any mention made either of Amsterdam or of the specific Amsterdam Sephardic community. The resolution speaks of the liberty for Jews to settle in Alkmaar, either from the Portuguese nation or from any other.[23] This means that any group of Jews from anywhere was the-

19 Cohen, "Memoria Para Os Siglos Futuros: Myth and Memory on the Beginnings of the Amsterdam Sephardi Community", 70–71; Israel, "Manuel López Pereira", 115.

20 Pieterse, "Daniel Levi de Barrios als geschiedschrijver van de Portugees-Israelietische gemeente te Amsterdam in zijn 'Triumpho del govierno popular' ", 51.

21 The text can be found in Groot, *Remonstrantie*, 38.

22 'Overal waar de Calvinisten aan het bewind waren werden de Joden buitengewoon veel moeilijkheden in de weg gelegd en kwam het in genen dele, zelfs niet tot een officieuse erkenning van hun status. [...] Het eerst dachten aan verhuizing uiteraard de orthodoxe elementen onder leiding van Uri Halevi. In Amsterdam niet tot een zekere godsdienstvrijheid te kunnen geraken was voor hen aanleiding deze stad te verlaten en de steven naar Alkmaar te wenden.' ['Anywhere the Calvinists ruled, Jews were confronted with considerable resistance and here were even unable to receive an official recognition of their status. [...] Naturally, the more orthodox elements under the direction of Uri Halevi were the first to consider moving. Being unable to acquire the desired degree of religious freedom was for them sufficient reason to leave this city and steer towards Alkmaar.'] Groot, 37–38.

23 'Opt versouck van Philips de Jode uyt den name van verscheyden huysgesinnen van joden ende jodengenoten, zoo van Portugijssche als andere natien, jegenwoordelick zoo oostwaerts als elders wonende, is geaccordeert ende toegelaten, dat zij hier ter Stede mogen comen, [...].' ['At the behest of Philips the Jew on behalf of several families of Jews and proselytes, both from Portuguese and other nations, living both eastwards

oretically invited. Her second critique is that the Philips the Jew named in this resolution is reckoned to be the same as Philips Joosten from Amsterdam. Zwarts has clearly proven that Philips Joosten was Uri Halevi's secular alias and of course Philips the Jew could very well be the same person as Philips Joosten. However, there is no definite proof that he is.[24]

Zwarts suggests that the Portuguese merchants never seriously intended to move to Alkmaar, but sent Uri Halevi to negotiate these favourable conditions in order to put some pressure on the City Council of Amsterdam. According to Zwarts, the Alkmaar charter gave Jacob Tirado the right leverage to obtain from the City Council a monopoly for the silk production in Holland for a period of five years. The city was very keen to keep the Jewish merchants in Amsterdam. However, as the orthodox Calvinists kept a close eye on the granting of liberty by the city to the various religious denominations, the burgomasters were as yet unable to allow Jewish public worship.[25] They could however guarantee them that they could continue practising their religion unhindered in the privacy of their homes. It should be kept in mind that, although there is proof that the silk monopoly was granted to the Portuguese, the connection made between the Alkmaar charter and this monopoly is all speculation. If Philips the Jew is actually Uri Halevi, then it might be true, but even then any solid evidence for the relation between these events is still lacking.[26]

The following year, spring 1605, a group of the Portuguese went to Haarlem with the intention of establishing a Jewish community there. It is not clear why this group went to Haarlem; Zwarts supposes that these initiators were unsatisfied with the secretive nature of the Amsterdam Jewish community and were less connected to Jacob Tirado and his associates, whereas Huussen is convinced that the group desired freedom of religious practice.[27] In any case, the City Council of Haarlem received the merchants benevolently. They were readily given permission to settle and live with their families as Jews—in their private homes. The Jewish merchants objected politely by pointing out to the City Council that there were many places in Germany and Italy where Jews had comparable rights and more. If the city really intended to attract wealthy Jewish merchants, they needed

and elsewhere, it has been approved and accepted that they may come to this city, (…).'] Zwarts, *Eerste rabbijnen*, 43.

24 "לא ידוע אם הכוונה לקבוצת יהודים מאמסטרדאם, כפי שנרשם כמעט בכל ספרי ההיסטוריה, שכן אפשר גם להסיק שהקבוצה היתה ממקום אחר. בתעודה נאמר, שהבקשה לקבל זכות לחופש פולחן דתי באה מקבוצה של יהודים פורטוגאלים ויהודים מאומות אחרות שהתגוררו במזרח ובמקומות אחרים. אמסטרדאם אינה מוזכרת כלל. אפשר להציע השערה, שהקבוצה רצתה לעבור מאמסטרדאם לאלקמאר, אולם אין הוכחה לכך. גם אין כל עדות לזהותו של מנהיג הקבוצה. היהודי פיליפס שהגיש את העצומה לשלטונות העיר אלקמאר אינו בהכרח פיליפס יוסטן, שנחקר באמסטרדאם בשנת 1603. השם פיליפ הינו תרגום הולאנדי לאורי וגם לשמות: פייבל, פייפס, פאיס ופייבלמן. איזיק פרינס היה הראשון ששיער, כי היהודי פיליפ הוא אולי פיליפס יוסטן, אך הוא נהג בזהירות רבה ואילו היסטוריונים אחרים הפכו את השערתו לודאות, בלי עדות משלימה."

['It is unknown whether it had been intended for Jews from Amsterdam, as is printed in almost all history books, as it is equally possible to assume that the community came from somewhere else. The document states that the request for freedom of religious exercise came from a group of Portuguese Jews and Jews from other countries who lived in the East and in other places. There is no mention of Amsterdam. The assumption can be made that the group wanted to move from Amsterdam to Alkmaar, but there is no evidence of that. Neither is there any proof of the identity of the leader of the group. Philips the Jew, who brought the petition before the City Council of Alkmaar, is not necessarily the same person as Philips Joosten, who had been investigated in Amsterdam in 1603. Philip is the Dutch translation of Uri, and also of the names: Faybl, Fayfs, Fays and Fayblman. Izak Prins was the first to suggest that Philip the Jew is perhaps Philips Joosten; he, however, acted with prudence, whereas other historians have taken from his suggestion a degree of certainty without offering sufficient proof.'] Vlessing, "על ראשית יהודי פורטוגאל באמסטרדאם," 83.

25 Bodian, *Hebrews of the Portuguese Nation*, 56–61.

26 Zwarts, *Eerste rabbijnen*, 42–44 and 107.

27 Zwarts, 45; Huussen Jr, "De toelating van Sefardische joden in Haarlem in 1605", 49.

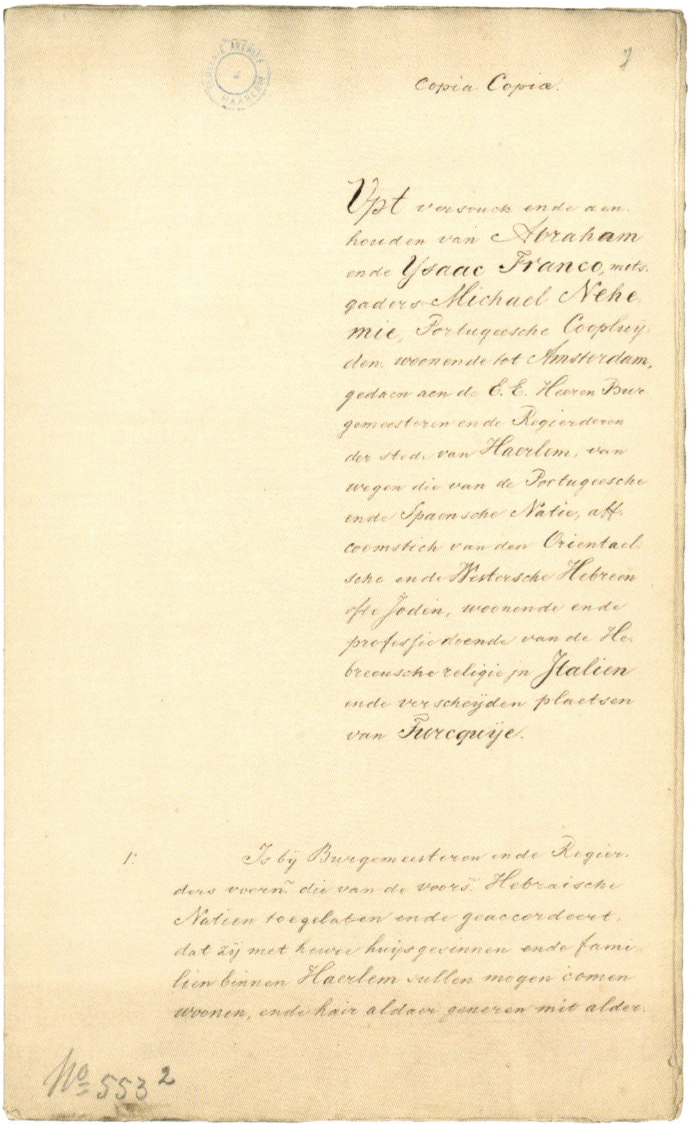
Copia Copia.

Vpt versouck ende aenhouden van Abraham ende Ysaac Franco, mitsgaders Michael Nehemie, Portugeesche Coopluyden, woonende tot Amsterdam, gedaen aen de E.E. Heeren Burgemeesteren ende Regeerderen der Stede van Haerlem, van wegen die van de Portugeesche ende Spaensche Natie, affcoomstich van den Orientaelsche ende Westersche Hebreen ofte Joden, woonende ende professie doende van de Hebreeusche religie in Italien ende verscheyden plaetsen van Turcquije.

1: Is bij Burgemeesteren ende Regeerders voorn. die van de voors. Hebraische Natien toegelaten ende geaccordeert, dat zij met heure huijsgesinnen ende familien binnen Haerlem sullen mogen comen woonen, ende hair aldaer generen mit alder.

No 553 2

FIGURE 9
The city council of Haarlem gave permission in 1605 for Jewish settlement in the city as well as for the construction of a synagogue. The provisions of settlement were never fulfilled, so the synagogue was never built.

permission to establish a synagogue, or else no merchant would come. The City Council took this objection seriously and sent envoys to Van Oldenbarnevelt and Wtenbogaert for advice on this matter. The main problem was that, if the city would allow Jews to have their own prayer houses, Roman Catholics could no longer be prohibited from celebrating their Masses publicly. For the orthodox Calvinists, it was of vital importance that Dutch Reformed Protestantism was the only form of religion that could be exercised publicly. After receiving the replies from the envoys, the City Council decided that Jews could settle in Haarlem and practise their religion freely. However, they could only establish a synagogue if at least 50 wealthy families would settle in this city.

Although the Haarlem episode was rather shortlived, as it was clear that it was impossible to attract 50 wealthy families to Haarlem, it is still an important episode historically, not least because the initiators of this initiative, Abraham and Isaac Franco [Mendes] and Michael Nehemiah did not return into the fold of Jacob Tirado, but established a new community, Neve Shalom, in a house opposite Tirado's.[28] It is generally assumed that Franco and his entourage were more religiously motivated than Tirado's community. This is inferred from the fact that Franco Mendes *cum suis* explicitly asked for a place of public worship in their negotiations with Haarlem. As they did not stay in Haarlem when the agreed number of immigrant families was not met, it may be assumed that their sole motive for settling in Haarlem would have been the establishment of a public synagogue. When it became clear that no public synagogue would be established in Haarlem, there was no reason to leave Amsterdam. Nonetheless Zwarts still assumes that the Amsterdam merchants managed to gain something from this endeavour: shortly after this event, in 1606, the city refuses the *Portuguese Nation* a burial site. According to Zwarts, although no synagogue or burial site was granted, the gain was that they were formally addressed, ergo recognized as a Jewish community. Zwarts assumes that the request for the burial site was made by the community Beth Jacob.[29]

The second important feature of the Haarlem episode is the fact that here for the first time both important historical lines of the *Remonstrantie* intersect. For, as has been shown by Huussen from the personal notes of the Secretary of Haarlem Michiel van Woerden, the Pensionary of Haarlem and its burgomasters explicitly consulted Van Oldenbarnevelt (1547–1619) and probably Wtenbogaert (1557–1644).[30] According to these notes, Van Oldenbarnevelt was not opposed to granting the Jews a synagogue, as long as the City Council of Haarlem could accommodate the local Reformed preachers. Van Oldenbarnevelt and Wtenbogaert were both key figures in the religious and political developments of the first two decades of the 17th century. And possibly due to the fact that these authorities were included in the decision-making of this case, the expected settlement of Jews in Haarlem was something that was talked about, at least in Holland in certain social environments. For the famous scholar Josephus Scaliger mentions the Haarlem episode in his personal notes:

> Les Juifs viendront à Harlem, & y auront Synagogue & privilege de Estats, erit magna in his regionibus commoditas, ils seront plus libres qu'ailleurs, [...].[31]

There seems to be no reason that Scaliger would have been included in the process of making these decisions by either Oldenbarnevelt or Wtenbogaert, which suggests that it was merely a talked-about event.

A third, perhaps obvious point of interest in this episode, lies in the same citation. It has not sufficiently been noted that Scaliger clearly states that Jews will come to Haarlem and that they will have a synagogue and permission from the States. In most literature where this episode is discussed, the presentation of the situation is usually as follows: Franco Mendez came *cum suis* to Haarlem and asked for settlement, freedom of religion and a synagogue. The City Council granted settlement and freedom of religion, but never intended to let the Jews have a synagogue. Although it is never literarily stated as such, the tendency seems to be that the City Council intentionally stated an unattainable number of families in order to prevent the Portuguese from establishing a synagogue.[32] How-

28 Vlessing, "על ראשית יהודי פורטוגאל באמסטרדאם," 84–86.

29 Zwarts follows De Barrios here; see Zwarts, *Eerste rabbijnen*, 52–53. Vlessing vehemently opposes his reading. According to Vlessing, there is no evidence to support the claim that Beth Jacob existed before 1616, when Beth Jacob and Neve Shalom bought the site in Oudekerk together, whereas Neve Shalom already appears in notarial archives as early as 1612; see Vlessing, "על ראשית יהודי פורטוגאל באמסטרדאם," 85–90.

30 Huussen Jr, "De toelating van Sefardische joden in Haarlem in 1605", 51.

31 'The Jews will come to Haarlem and they will have a synagogue and permission from the States, which will be a great advantage in this region, they will have more freedom than anywhere else.' Scaliger, *Scaligeriana*, 185.

32 Bodian interprets the episode differently: 'The Haarlem burgomasters were aware that they would have to offer excellent terms to persuade "Portuguese" merchants to choose their town rather than Amsterdam, and they

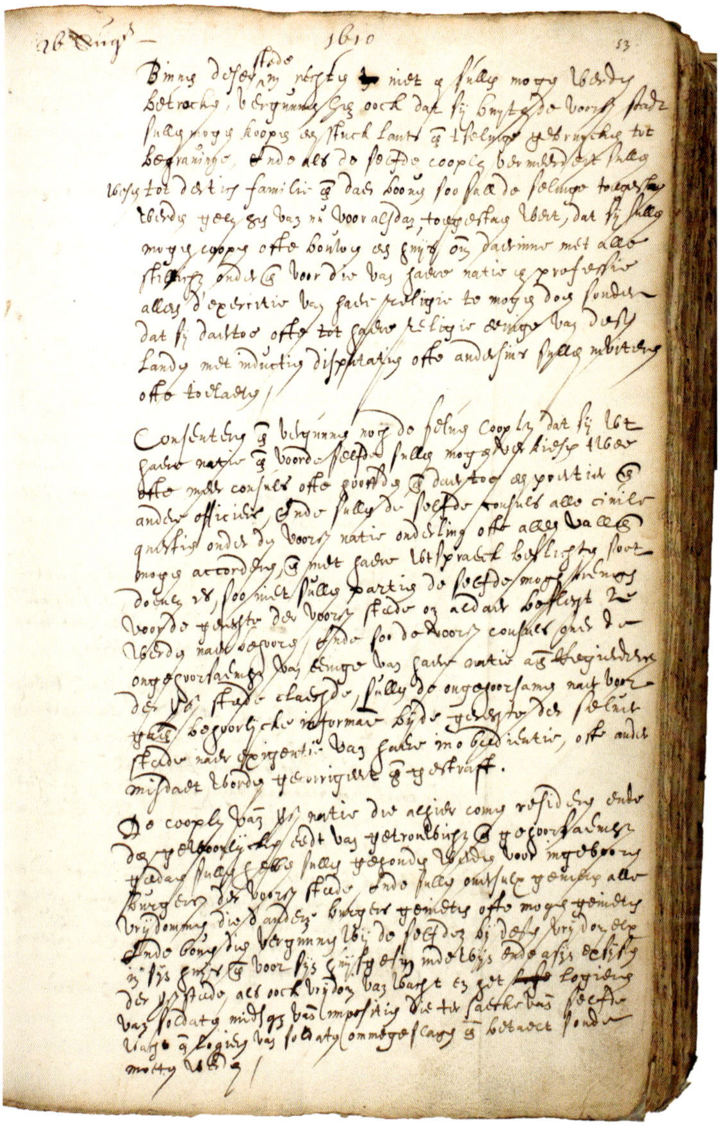

FIGURE 10
The city of Rotterdam allowed Jewish settlement in 1610, provided that thirty wealthy families established themselves there within two years, as seen on line 5.

ever, if Scaliger's notes here are authentic (which remains somewhat problematic, as they had been recorded by admirers and edited a considerable time after his passing away), this statement proves that the Dutch authorities did at least believe that 50 families were a reasonable number and that possibly the Portuguese negotiators had made the same estimation.

A similar endeavour was made at Rotterdam in 1610. Comparable conditions to those of Haarlem were agreed upon, this time with the number of 30 wealthy families that should be residing in Rotterdam within two years. As the Portuguese community of Rotterdam did not manage to grow sufficiently, the agreement was annulled in 1612 and most members returned to Amsterdam.[33] As Elias van Oldenbarnevelt, the younger brother of Johan

did. But in the end, these terms proved insufficient to lure Jews to Haarlem, […]'. Bodian, *Hebrews of the Portuguese Nation*, 58–59.

33 Zwarts, *Eerste rabbijnen*, 61–62.

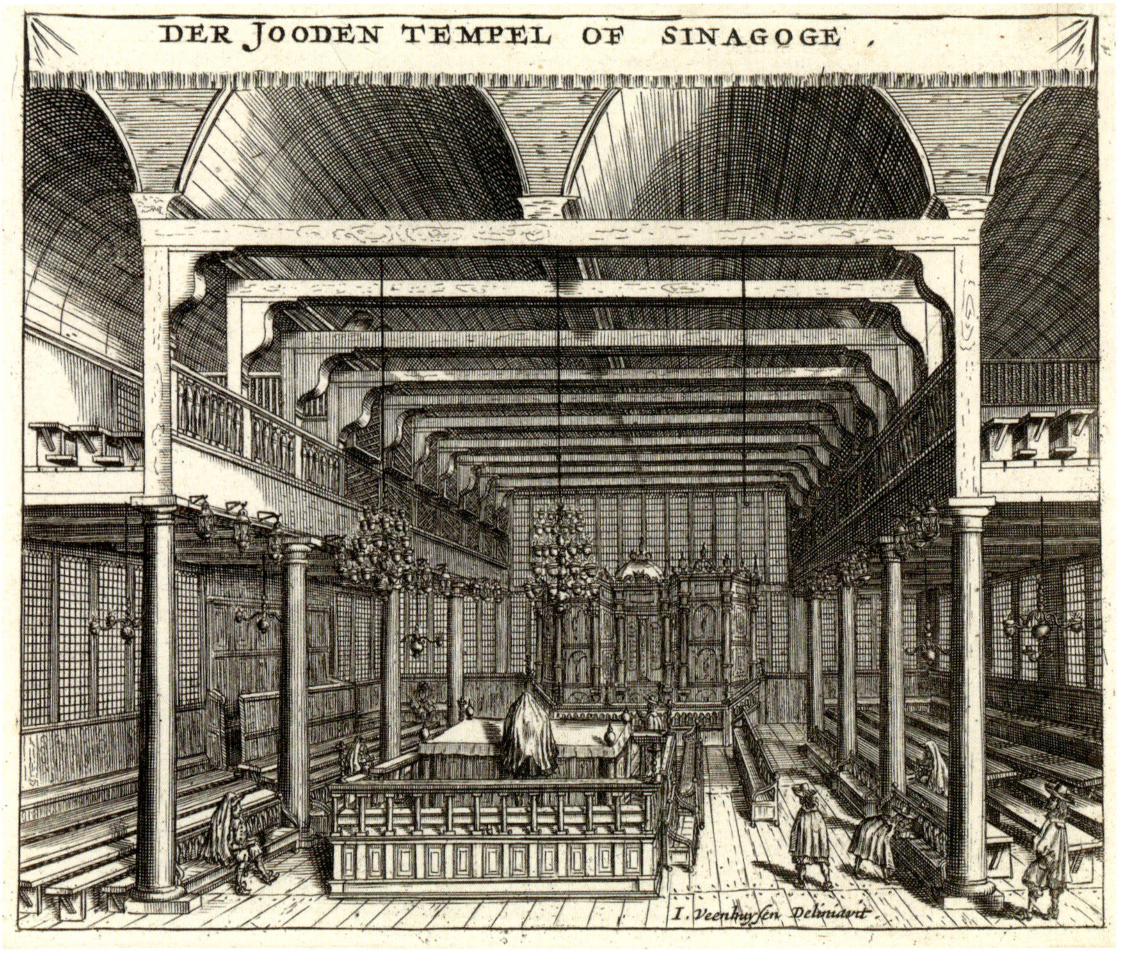

FIGURE 11 The interior of the Synagogue at the Houtgracht in 1664. The Houtgracht no longer exists as it was dammed along with the Leprozengracht in 1882 to create Waterlooplein.

van Oldenbarnevelt, was Pensionary of Rotterdam, it may be supposed that the Land's Advocate was consulted in this matter. And what is more, this is the only case where Hugo de Groot was personally nearly involved—Elias van Oldenbarnevelt died in 1612 and Grotius succeeded him in 1613. It is likely, then, that Grotius had learned of this case from both Van Oldenbarnevelt and the city administration.

Rotterdam was for a while the last attempt of the Portuguese merchants to establish a community outside Amsterdam and to obtain official permission to establish a synagogue. The three attempts are remarkable for at least two reasons. Firstly, the local authorities exhibit a remarkably pragmatic approach to the new immigrants. In contrast to attitudes elsewhere, they seem to be quite welcoming of the idea of Jewish settlement within their cities. They hardly seem worried by the religious differences, as long as certain boundaries are respected. Apparently, the magistrates in particular had high expectations in terms of the economic prosperity these immigrants were supposed to bring with them. Secondly, the Portuguese merchants were apparently well aware of their alleged value and knew how to use it to their advantage, at least to a certain degree. Zwarts's statement that the Amsterdam Jews consciously used the results of their negotiations with Alkmaar, Haarlem and Rotterdam is difficult to prove. On the

FIGURE 12 A Jewish burial at the Ouderkerk cemetery outside Amsterdam around 1675

other hand, it seems clear that the merchants' preference was to stay in Amsterdam. They could easily have moved en masse to Rotterdam and have established a community with a synagogue there. This suggests that they either valued their economic prospects higher than the possibility of having a synagogue and saw their best opportunities in Amsterdam, or they suspected that there was still room for negotiation with the City Council of Amsterdam, or both.

In 1612, one of the communities decided not to wait any longer for official approval and started the building of a synagogue at the Houtgracht. We do not know, of course, whether there was any sort of unofficial approval on the part of the magistrates, but it is known that a carpenter was hired and paid to do the job.[34] However, the orthodox Calvinist faction in the city vehemently opposed this project and created such a stir that the City Council had no option but to prohibit the work.[35] The solution to the problem is probably symptomatic of the pragmatic attitude of the City Council—the house was sold to a member of the Council, Nicolaes van Campen, who rented the house to the community. It seems that this became the designated way of proceeding—not asking for official approval, but simply starting and usually the City Council would

34 As is suggested by Bodian, see: *Hebrews of the Portuguese Nation*, 59.

35 Bodian, 59; Swetschinski, *Reluctant Cosmopolitans*, 11–12.

benignly ignore the complaints from the Calvinist clergy. At least, that is how the Portuguese Nation finally acquired their burial grounds in Ouderkerk aan de Amstel. In 1614 both communities, Beth Jacob and Neve Shalom, jointly bought property for a burial site. When local citizens lodged a complaint with the Amsterdam magistrates, their complaint was simply ignored.

The only instance when the complaints of the Protestant clergy could not be ignored was when Christians converted to Judaism. It was one of the serious stipulations made against the new immigrants that they should never circumcise adults (read: convert non-Jews). There were several rumours about Mennonites who considered conversion or probably had converted already.[36] It is generally assumed that these incidents prompted the States of Holland and West Frisia to draw up a set of rules and regulations for Jewish settlement in the Dutch cities.[37] While waiting for the official regulation, the city of Amsterdam responded by issuing its own decrees, or *keur*, firmly condemning both physical relations between Jews and Christians and any kind of Christian apostasy.[38] It is not impossible that the conversion of the Mennonites was actually the last straw. However, it was known and evident to all that the Portuguese merchants had repeatedly managed to negotiate favourable conditions for settlement and freedom of religion, and obtained a burial site and a synagogue without proper permission from the government. It was probably a combination of these factors that urged the States to take the helm and steer towards a more formalized and restricted policy towards the Jews, without chasing them, and their profitable commerce, away.

It may be noted here that the States of Holland and West Frisia decided in the end not to use the *Remonstrantie* discussed here, but left it to the separate cities to judge for themselves what would be the best regulation, offering as prototypes both the *Keur* of Amsterdam and Grotius's elaborated text.[39]

36 *Infra*, n. 59.

37 'De Pensionarissen van Amsterdam ende Rotterdam zyn ghelast ende ghecommittert, jeghens de naeste Daghvaert een Reglement te beramen, waer naer de Joden (in dese Landen hen onthoudende) tot weeringhe van alle schandalen, ergernisse ende seductie, hen sullen hebben te reguleren. Ende zyn de Gecommitteerde Raden geauthoriseert, met goed-bevinden van de Burgemeesters ende Regeerders van Hoorn, op de gevangene Joden aldaer sulcke ordre te stellen als dienstigh bevonden sal worden.' ['The Pensionaries of Amsterdam and Rotterdam have been ordered and commissioned to draft a regulation before the following session with which the Jews living in these countries will have to comply in order to prevent all scandals, offences and seductions. Furthermore, the *Gecommitteerde Raden* have been authorized, with the approval of the Burgomasters and Regents of Hoorn, to act on the imprisoned Jews there as will be found most beneficient.'] Resolutien van de Heeren Ridderschap, Edelen, ende Gedeputeerden van de Steden van Hollandt ende West-Vrieslandt, Staets-ghewyse genomen in haer Edele Mog. Vergaderinghe gehouden alhier in den Hage, zedert den vierden Maert des Jaers sesthien hondert en vijfthien, ende eyndigende den seventhienden dito daer aen volgende. National Archive, The Hague, Staten van Holland, nummer toegang 3.01.04.01, inventarisnummer 49, p. 6.

38 The text of this *Keur* or regulation can be found in Noordkerk, *Handvesten; ofte Privilegien ende octroyen; mitsgaders willekeuren, costuimen, ordonnantien en handelingen der stad Amstelredam …*, 2:472.

39 'Op het derthiende poinct van de beschyvinge, naer gelesen waren de Concepten van Reglement, eertydts by den Pensionaris Pauw ende de Groot ingestelt, ende daer neffens de Keuren by de Stadt Amsterdam, over die van de Hebreeuwsche Natie aldaer woonende, ghemaeckt, ende den Eedt die sy de selve tot observatie van de Keuren hadden afgenomen, is verstaen dat elck van de Leden die sulcks in den haren noodigh vinden, mede alsulcke Keuren ende Ordre particulier daer op sullen moghen maecken, alsoo tot dienst haerder Stede sullen goedt vinden, sonder men goedt vindt de selve met eenigh kenbaer Teycken te doen uytmunten, stellende de Steden vry die by den anderen te doen woonen ende af-sluyten of niet; zynde aen de Gedeputeerden van Haerlem en Alckmaer gegeven Copie van de voorsz Concepten, Keuren en Eedt, om hen te dienen na behoren.' ['On the 13th point of the agenda it has been decided, after reading the drafts of a regulation, made earlier by the Pensionaries Pauw and Grotius, and the regulations of the City of Amsterdam regarding those of the Hebrew Nation living there, as well as the Oath that was taken from them for the observation of the regulations, that all members who find it nec-

2 The Political Context of the *Remonstrantie*

Hugo de Groot was born in Delft in 1583 to Jan de Groot (1554–1640) and Aeltje Borre van Overschie (1561–1643).[40] His family belonged to the patrician class and had strong ties to the recently established Leiden University—his uncle Cornelis de Groot (1554–1610) was a member of the board of trustees for some time and taught several subjects, among them Law. His father was an alumnus and had been friends with Justus Lipsius (1547–1606). Young Hugo turned out to be an exceptionally gifted child, who absorbed everything he was taught. In 1594, at the age of 11 he matriculated at Leiden University, where he studied Philosophy and Law.[41] However, although Grotius was destined to pursue either a legal career or one in public administration, he had great literary talents as well. He would become a key example of the humanist scholar, who led an active public life and pursued the *studia humanitatis* as a means of leisure. His talents aroused the interest of Josephus Justus Scaliger (1540–1609), who accepted the prodigy child into his personal classroom. The great French scholar had been convinced by Janus Dousa (1545–1604) and others to reside in Leiden, without having an obligation to lecture. All he had to do was associate the radiance of his reputation with the young university. However, Scaliger made an exception for the brightest students, whom he invited to attend his tutorials. These students were to be educated to become the champions of the Republic of Letters.[42] It was probably here that Grotius first met Daniel Heinsius (1580–1655). For a time, the two would be connected in a close friendship and a shared love of writing poetry and pursuing the *studia humanitatis*, until the troubles of the Twelve Years' Truce drove them apart. Grotius's talents developed during these years to a level that he could write complicated occasional Latin poetry *ex tempore* and he could publish his first scholarly edition in 1599.[43]

However, Grotius was not to be educated solely within the walls of Leiden University, which is why he was included in retinue of Johan van Oldenbarnevelt (1547–1619) on a diplomatic mission to France in 1598.[44] This mission has become known for the audience Grotius was granted with the French King Henry IV on 5 April 1598, on which occasion the King is believed to have said: 'Ah, voilà, le miracle de Hollande!'[45] At Orleans, Grotius took a doctoral degree *utriusque iuris*.[46] Upon his return, Grotius soon started working as an advocate in The Hague. Not much is known about how successful he was as a lawyer. He complains in letters about the triviality of his new profession, but at the same time seems to have worked hard on the advancement of his career. At this he succeeded well, for he was appointed Advocate-Fiscal for the provinces of Holland and Zeeland in 1607, a function that saw him having to protect and advance

essary, can each make such regulations and orders, as seems right for the benefit of their Cities, as long as they will not be forced to stand out by any recognizable sign, leaving the Cities free to let them live near the others and to segregate or not; copies of the aforementioned drafts, regulations and Oath have been given to the Deputies of Haarlem and Alkmaar to serve them accordingly.'] Resolutien van de Heeren Staten van Hollande ende West-Vrieslandt, genomen in haer Edele Mog. Vergaderinge gehouden in 's Graven-Hage zedert den negenthienden January des Jaers sesthien hondert negenthien. National Archive, The Hague, Staten van Holland, nummer toegang 3.01.04.01, inventarisnummer 52.

40 For all biographical information on Grotius, see: Nellen, *Hugo Grotius*.

41 Nellen, 33–34.

42 Grafton, *Joseph Scaliger II*, 389–392. On Janus Dousa, see: Dorsten, *Poets, Patrons and Professors*; Heesakkers, *Praecidanea Dousana: Materials for a Biography of Janus Dousa Pater (1545–1604). His Youth*; Heesakkers and Reinders, *Genoeglijk bovenal zijn de muzen: de Leidse Neolatijnse dichter Janus Dousa (1545–1604)*; Lefèvre and Schäfer, *Ianus Dousa*.

43 *Martiani Minei Felicis Capellæ Carthaginiensis viri proconsularis Satyricon, in quo de nuptiis Philologiæ & Mercurij libri duo, & De septem artibus liberalibus libri singulares. Omnes, & emendati, & notis sive februis Hug. Grotii illustrati.*

44 On this mission, see: Tex, *Oldenbarnevelt: II. Oorlog 1588–1609*, 288–321.

45 Tex, 303; Nellen, *Hugo Grotius*, 47.

46 I.e. Roman law and canonical law.

the interests of these provinces at the Courts of Holland and Zeeland and the High Councils of Holland and Zeeland. It was a prestigious and well-paid appointment that he probably earned due to his good relationship with Van Oldenbarnevelt.[47] In 1613, Grotius was appointed as Pensionary of the city of Rotterdam.[48] It was in this function that he became deeply involved with the politics of the States of Holland and West Frisia and worked closely with Van Oldenbarnevelt.

Grotius entered the Dutch political scene at a turbulent time. The young Republic had barely survived the first decades of its existence. The Stadtholder Maurice of Orange had managed with his brilliant strategical insight to expand the territory of the Republic to a defendable area. The cities of Holland and Zeeland had soon recovered from the wars and prospered. Their population grew due to repression of Protestants in the Southern Netherlands, which caused many to seek refuge in the Protestant North. Nonetheless, the Republic desperately needed powerful allies and always tried to forge alliances of Protestant countries against Spain. Important allies were France and England. The French had been engaged in subsequent wars with the Habsburg Empire for many years already and had a strong Protestant faction, at least until the St Bartholomew's Day massacre. However, due to the efforts of the Queen Mother Maria de Medici, France shifted and the Protestant King Henry IV converted to Roman Catholicism. Additionally, the French grew tired of their wars and wanted peace at their southern borders, which estranged them from the Dutch cause. For years, France had contributed financially to Maurice's army and this money was dearly needed. A continuous fear for Holland was that Spain would have its hands free for more, new campaigns in the North.

The other obvious ally was Protestant England. However, England and the Dutch had a difficult relationship as they both sought to expand their influence overseas and often clashed on conflicting interests; nor was England's relationship with France unproblematic as it had supported the Huguenot cause and still held claims on French port towns. Spain, the Northern Netherlands and England were active in overseas trade and England was only lukewarm in its opposition to Spain. This became even worse when James I negotiated a peace treaty with Spain that explicitly excluded Dutch trade.[49] Other important allies were the Protestant German Countries, the Electoral Palatinate in particular, and Sweden.[50]

The internal political situation of the young Republic was an unstable equilibrium of different bodies of power that were all seeking primarily to advance their own interests. The States General was actually the governing body of the whole Republic, in which the separate States, the provinces, each had their own voice, and were largely autonomous. The stadtholdership of Maurice of Orange in fact contained separate stadtholderships of these provinces, each with its own rights and privileges. There was an opposition between Holland and the other provinces, but also between the towns and the Provincial States, between nobility and the towns with their patricians. There was also an opposition between Church and State and the question of authority in religious matters.

These dynamics were more or less controlled and regulated by two persons: Maurice of Orange and Johan van Oldenbarnevelt. Although opposite in character, they managed for a considerable time to overcome their differences and steer the Republic through this maze of challenges. Prince Maurice was very popular with the common people and the army for his strategic talents and the many victories he had secured. It remains a matter of debate whether or not Maurice aspired to a royal title. Van Oldenbarnevelt, on the other hand, was a *landsad-*

47 Huijbrecht, "Hugo de Groot als advocaat-fiscaal".
48 Smit, "De Rotterdamse jaren van Hugo de Groot".

49 Israel, *The Dutch Republic*, 400.
50 Deursen has written a monography about the complex international political situation in which the young Republic had to manoeuver in the early years of the Twelve Years' Truce; see *Honni soit qui mal y pense?*

vocaat or Advocate of Holland, and by virtue of this role very powerful in the States of Holland and, consequently, in the States General. He represents the patrician class that took full advantage of new economic opportunities and investments. It was at Van Oldenbarnevelt's instigation that the VOC, or the Dutch East India Company was created. It was also Van Oldenbarnevelt who wanted an armistice with Spain, whereas Prince Maurice's preference was to continue the war.

Complicated as these situations were, it would be an apparently minor theological moot point that would bring the young Republic to the verge of chaos. From the Republic's inception in the days of William of Orange until quite recent times there had been antithetical views about the actual cause of the so-called Dutch Revolt—was it a matter of religion, namely the liberation of the oppressed Protestants from their Roman Catholic oppressors, or was it a call for sovereignty from towns and nobility in the Northern Netherlands? Evidence of the nature of this clash of views is to be found in the money that the Leiden City Council had produced after the liberation, on which it had printed *haec libertatis ergo* (this [endured siege] was for liberty), whereas a preacher in the city protested that it should have read *haec religionis ergo* (this was for religion)! The regent class in particular felt that the Revolt had liberated the Northern Netherlands from Philips II's centralizing politics and his heavy taxations for wars that were not felt to be immediately in their own interest. Orthodox Calvinists, by contrast, saw the Revolt as an act of God. After the persecutions that they had had to endure, they were finally liberated from papist oppression. Preachers liked to compare the new Republic with the people of Israel—God had liberated them from Pharaoh, but now they needed to obey God's Word, or else they would be punished as the people of Israel (frequently) were during their years in the desert and in the Holy Land.

The orthodox Calvinists had a strong base among the common people. At the Union of Utrecht, it was decided that the Protestant religion would be the official public religion, albeit with citizens being granted freedom of conscience and religion in the private sphere of their homes. Public worship was only allowed for the Dutch Reformed Church. This did not automatically mean that all or most of the population of the Northern Netherlands became professed members of the Dutch Reformed Church. Calvinism was a religion for the elect and only those who were willing to adhere strictly to its principles were allowed to become member. A considerable proportion of the population remained Roman Catholic and continued to attend Mass more or less secretly. There were also groups of Lutherans and Anabaptists. However, it is generally assumed that the majority of the population in the Northern Netherlands sympathized with the Dutch Reformed Church, without immediately feeling the need to become a professed member. But many seem to have attended services and used its facilities for marriage, baptism and burial.

Within the new Dutch Reformed Church different views on orthodoxy evolved. As said above, the dispute would focus on what to modern eyes would appear to be a minor theological question, which came close to causing a civil war. This question can be summarized as whether or not man has his own salvation (partly) in his own hands. In other words, do men have a choice when it comes to living according to the (Calvinist interpretation of) the Bible and, by means of their own endeavours and God's grace, have the possibility of becoming one of the elected? Or did God already know which souls would eligible for salvation even before the creation of the first man and only those who lived decent lives could earn this salvation, whereas the non-elect would never attain salvation, no matter how hard they tried? Although the latter view seems harsh, it was felt to be tantamount to diminution of God's omniscience were the possibility entertained of God not knowing from the beginning of time which souls would be saved at the end of time.

The majority of Calvinist preachers shared the more negative view of man's freedom; only a minority thought man could cooperate with God

FIGURE 13 Symbolic print of the victory of the counter-remonstrants, with portraits of Maurice, Prince of Orange, Johan van Oldenbarnevelt, Franciscus Gomarus, and Jacobus Arminius

for his own salvation. The conflict rose gradually; it seems that John Calvin himself wrote differently about the subject in different places. However, the second-generation Calvinist teachers and preachers developed his thoughts and Beza in particular was very much preoccupied with the subject of predestination.[51] The Dutch preacher Arminius listened to Beza's lectures as student, but devel-

51 White, *Predestination, Policy and Polemic*, chap. 2.

oped his own thoughts. When he was a preacher in Amsterdam, Arminius held several sermons on the subject of predestination, based on Paul's epistle to the Romans. From these sermons much discussion arose among church councils and preachers in Holland and the Republic. Beza's more conservative views had found a place in the *Heidelberg Catechism*, a document that became more and more authoritative. To avoid heterodoxy, aspirant preachers were increasingly asked to sign documents that stated their devotion to the Heidelberg principles.

Conflict broke out in the open when Arminius was appointed as *Professor Theologiae* at Leiden University in 1603. One of the resident professors of Theology in particular, Franciscus Gomarus, fervently proclaimed his objections to his new colleague, questioning Arminius's orthodoxy and demanding clear statements from the latter about his views on predestination.[52] However, the conflict spread and the orthodox Calvinists in particular increasingly refused to share the Lord's Supper with the Arminians and refused to listen to Arminian preachers. As the Arminians were outnumbered by the Gomarists, it became increasingly difficult for them to perform services. In order to arrive at a workable situation, a group of influential followers of Arminius signed a remonstrance, or *Remonstrantie* (1610), asking the States of Holland and West Frisia to intervene and to make sure that Arminians would be accepted again in churches and by the public.[53] Henceforth, the followers of Arminius were known as Remonstrants and their opponents, after signing a counter-petition, Counter-Remonstrants. Arminius did not see the final *Remonstrantie*; he died in 1609.

The growing conflict and the strict refusal of the Counter-Remonstrants to join Remonstrants in services and to listen to Arminian preachers caused considerable public unrest, occasionally leading to riots. With the appeal to the States of Holland and the disturbance of public order, the theological conflict became a concern for the public administration—city councils and provincial states. The administrators of the Dutch Reformed Church were of the opinion that it was not the responsibility of the provincial states to intervene—religious matters were to be dealt with by theologians. As the majority of the Dutch Reformed Church sided with Gomarus, their course of action would be to chide the Remonstrants and to restore orthodox unity in the Church. However, the Remonstrants had many adherents among the regent class. Their call for help appealed to the sense among the regents that the State should have the final say in matters ecclesiastical. The most remarkable spokesman of this view was Van Oldenbarnevelt. Although he was theologically more inclined towards Counter-Remonstrant views, he still felt that the State had to have ultimate authority in these matters, as the Dutch Reformed Church was the national religion.

Grotius was not immediately involved in these religious oppositions. When Arminius died, he still felt that it was mostly a group of hot-headed preachers who were quarrelling about theological trifles. He personally felt more attracted to Arminius, both on account of his mild character and his theological views. However, as the conflict increasingly became a source of public unrest, Grotius had to involve himself in order to restore public order. Grotius accepted Van Oldenbarnevelt's stance, and in the second decade he would increasingly become the spokesman of the Remonstrants. In these years Grotius developed an irenicistic view of religion, which identified him more as a humanist in the Erasmian tradition than as a Dutch Protestant. Grotius advocated one national Church that would encompass all Protestants. The Church would fall under the jurisdiction of the secular government, in the same way as the Church of England does. Members should only have to agree on a minimum set of basic principles that all members could agree on, such as the nature of the Trinity, Resurrection of Christ, sal-

52 Bangs, *Arminius*, chap. 17; Rabbie, "Grotius' denken over kerk en staat", 195; Rohls, "Calvinism, Arminianism and Socinianism in the Netherlands until the Synod of Dort", 12.

53 Not to be confused with Grotius's *Remonstrantie*.

vation, etc. Grotius went to great lengths to prove in his *Ordinum Pietas* that the Remonstrant vision on predestination and his ideas on the relation between Church and state corresponded to the vision of the Fathers of the Early Church and the New Testament.[54]

Grotius wrote his *Ordinum Pietas* in defence of the States of Holland and West Frisia. After the death of Arminius, a new professor of Theology was needed and, in order to preserve a precarious equilibrium, the German Conradus Vorstius was hired. He was reckoned a lenient Calvinist, in the same tradition as the Dutch Remonstrants. It seems that the board of directors of Leiden University acted rather fast, without taking the time to investigate Vorstius's reputation among Calvinists in general and the Counter-Remonstrants in particular. It is also highly possible that the University wanted to make a statement about their independence from ecclesiastical bodies in the appointment of university staff.[55] However, even among Arminians Vorstius was not of unquestionned reputation. Vorstius repeatedly displayed strong leanings towards the theological ideas of the Italian theologian Fausto Sozzini (1539–1614). Sozzini, or Socinus, had questioned the divinity of Christ and the existence of the Holy Spirit, which made him an arch-heretic to any Christian denomination.

The appointment of a professor who was suspected of Socinianistic sympathies was too much for Gomarus, who left the University and instead became a preacher in Middelburg. That was not the end of the conflict, however. The advent of Vorstius created enormous turmoil among Counter-Remonstrants all over the country and orthodox preachers did not hesitate to make their opinion publicly known, both from the pulpit and in pamphlets. The most vehement reaction came from Sibrandus Lubbertus, Professor of Theology at the orthodox University of Franeker. He wrote a lengthy critique of Vorstius's theological thought and claimed that the States of Holland and West Frisia had hired Vorstius in order to introduce Socinianism in the Republic and the Dutch Reformed Church.[56]

The publication of *Ordinum Pietas* aroused an enormous tumult in theological circles. It immediately identified Grotius as a sympathizer of the Remonstrants, although Grotius spoke more on behalf of the States of Holland and his own political and religious views and less of specific Arminian principles. Nonetheless, it was clear that he advocated a tolerant and inclusive irenicistic view rather than an exclusive vision of a purified, orthodox Church and this, combined with his advocacy for strong governmental influence over matters ecclesiastical, identified him in the eyes of the Counter-Remonstrants as their sworn enemy.

It was in this complex situation that Grotius wrote the *Remonstrantie*. The situation in the Dutch Republic was highly explosive and although Grotius himself kept believing in his views and the Remonstrant cause until the very moment of Maurice of Orange's coup d'état in 1618, the situation never looked really favourable for the Remonstrants. The Counter-Remonstrants had a larger adherence and were more resourceful at mobilizing and convincing the public opinion. It is important to realize that Grotius wrote the *Remonstrantie* at a time when he was working and fighting for his and Van Oldenbarnevelt's political survival literally night and day. It was only after the coup that he realized it was not only a political survival he had been fighting for, when Van Oldenbarnevelt was sentenced to death.

In this complex field of tensions, the advent of a handful of Portuguese Jews was the least of Grotius's problems. As far as is known, he hardly set eyes on any of them and only much later would polite correspondence with Menasseh ben Israel evolve. As was the case with many of his contemporaries, he was somewhat interested in the ancient House of Israel, but had no interest whatsoever in contemporary Jews. Nonetheless,

54 Groot, *Ordinum pietas*; Nellen, *Hugo Grotius*, 174.

55 Nellen, *Hugo Grotius*, 137.

56 Lubbertus, *Sibrandi Lubberti commentarii ad nonaginta novem errores Conradi Vorstii*.

FIGURE 14 The well-attended public execution of Johan van Oldenbarnevelt in 1619. Notice the crowd on the roof of the church

the case of the settlement of Jews in the Republic could have entailed several risks for Grotius. Firstly, he had already been accused of Socinianistic leanings by his Gomarist adversaries. He had experienced how hard it could be to battle such an accusation. Grotius had to be very careful not to give his enemies any grounds for adding the accusation of *judaizare*, of sympathizing with Jews, Judaism or (parts of) Jewish faith, to the accusation of Socinianism.[57] Grotius knew that any display of sympathy towards the new immigrants could and would be used against him. On the other hand, Grotius belonged to a social class that was highly interested in the commercial networks of the Portuguese merchants. Grotius had advanced the interests of the Dutch East India Company, the VOC, significantly on various occasions and his *De iure praedae* (1604) was in fact a legitimation of the Dutch overseas enterprises.[58] It was this social class that tried to attract considerable numbers of Portuguese merchants to their respective cities, for the expansion of their trades.

Conversely, the Counter-Remonstrants were not at all indifferent to Jewish settlement—they strongly objected to it. Time and again Calvinist spokesmen complained to the Amsterdam Burgo-

57 Rabbie, "Hugo Grotius and Judaism", 99.

58 Ittersum, *Profit and Principle*, liii–lxi *et passim*.

masters about the settlement of the Jews, the public display of their religion, the building of a synagogue and the contacts between Jews and Christians. It was especially this last point that was feared most, for it could both lead to illicit sexual relations and to apostasy. It is generally assumed that it was the latter, namely the conversion of several Mennonites to Judaism, that convinced the States of Holland that some sort of regulation had to be made to avoid further unrest, as the Calvinists were upset by these conversions.[59]

The assignment for drafting up a regulation concerning the settlements of Jews in the Dutch Republic was given to Grotius and Pauw—Grotius representing the Remonstrants, whereas Pauw represented the orthodox Calvinists. It is unclear whether there was any input from Pauw. It may be that his text has not survived, or it may be that Grotius's text already contains Pauw's input.[60] In any case, the result is a text that can only be understood against the complex background of these years. In what follows, the text will be examined closely from several directions, but first we will turn to Grotius's technique as a humanist.

59 Alexander van der Haven made an interesting study of the most famous conversion case that is generally assumed to have stirred the States of Holland into action, the three converts of Hoorn. The States were intensively consulted by the various parties in this matter and possibly as the States felt that sufficient legislation was lacking, they ordered Grotius and Pauw to provide regulation. Haven shows that this case in Hoorn was not only used by the Counter-Remonstrants to demonstrate the lacking orthodox standards of the Remonstrant magistrates of the City of Hoorn, but probably even more by the magistrates to let the Remonstrant secular powers prevail in a religious domain, see Haven, "Conversion on Trial"; Haven, "Predestination and Toleration". Nonetheless, the fact is that the Counter-Remonstrants were very annoyed with Jewish (visible) presence, as can be learned from Amsterdam Protestant Church Archives, in which complaints are made on conversions, a synagogue and Jewish-Christian relations; see Zwarts, *Eerste rabbijnen*, 121–122; Groot, *Remonstrantie*, 48–51 (esp. n. 88).

60 Van der Haven assumes that the Amsterdam regulation of 1616 reflects (much of) Pauw's input; see Haven, "Predestination and Toleration", 194.

3 Grotius's Method

The *Remonstrance* is a text that has posed permanent problems for interpretation. The text consists of three parts with very different content. The main text, the regulations, are usually positively judged, as they contain the relatively favourable conditions for new immigrants. The third part, Grotius's own commentary, or *annotationes*, is usually ignored. Here, it will receive ample attention in the next chapter. The introduction, by contrast, usually receives most attention, as this is the most problematic part. This is the part that is most mined to find proof of Grotius's opinions about Jews. However, as the text was written in a period when Grotius was under enormous strain, particularly from the Counter-Remonstrant side, it is difficult to assess only from this introduction what Grotius's opinions were. It may be useful, however, to assess Grotius's writing on Church, state and religion in the years before his writing was influenced by the political realities he had to deal with daily. This may help us to find out which parts of the *Remonstrance* are most congruent with his thinking and writing in his other works and which parts are not. We shall see that the second and the third parts in particular fit in very well with Grotius's writing, and that the introduction remains something of a *Fremdkörper*.[61] The work that will be discussed here to demonstrate Grotius's method is the *Meletius* (written in 1611/12, but never published).[62]

3.1 *Meletius*

The *Meletius, sive De iis quae inter Christianos conveniunt epistola*, was probably written shortly after the States had ordered both Remonstrants and Counter-Remonstrants to cease their quarrels.[63]

61 This does not automatically mean that these parts are more positive towards Jews, as will be seen from the next chapter.

62 Groot, *Meletius, sive, De iis quae inter Christianos conveniunt epistola*.

63 Nellen, *Hugo Grotius*, 137.

It was written at a time when Grotius was not yet fully involved in the conflict between these two groups. We know from his letters that Grotius was reluctant at first to take sides, although he disliked Franciscus Gomarus and probably felt more aligned with the Remonstrant views. Jacobus Arminius had died in 1609 and Grotius had written an obituary poem that betrayed his irenicistic inclinations. However, as the appointment of Vorstius complicated and exacerbated the conflict, Grotius decided to write a treatise that would explain that Christians should focus on what connects them instead of on dogmatic details that caused endless strife. To give the treatise a harmless format Grotius put his ideas into the mouth of Meletius Pegas (1549–1601), patriarch of Alexandria, whom Johannes Boreel (1577–1629) had met on his travels and whose praises he had sung to Grotius. Apparently, the patriarch had complained to Johannes Boreel about the dissension in the Christian world and how Christians were spending their energy on fighting each other, whereas they should be focusing on conquering and converting gentiles.[64]

The work had a twofold purpose. Firstly, it points out which principles define Christianity. It was Grotius's belief that agreement on these principles should overcome most differences in the Christian world. It may of course be assumed that he primarily meant the differences of opinion between the Remonstrants and Counter-Remonstrants. However, he seems also to have thought that larger distances could be bridged by agreeing on these principles, even between Protestants and moderate Catholics.[65] Secondly, the work intends to lead the theological discussions away from a focus on religious dogma and the differences these caused and instead reformulate the basic principles of Christianity in rationally acceptable ethical prescriptions. 'And since ethical rules are mostly plainer and less complicated, it stands to reason that people most readily agree on precepts.'[66]

The text has been written in a persuasive style, and its argument appeals mainly to common sense, using arguments from classical philosophers either to contrast or to underscore the line of argumentation. Consequently, the *Meletius* is not a highly developed theological or philosophical text, but more a blueprint or vantage point for a process that should lead to ecclesiastical peace and tolerance. For example, when Grotius discusses the necessary existence of divine retribution and afterlife, he starts his discussion as follows:

> Let us now turn to the subject proper. As is the case with everything that happens according to free choice, it is necessary first to inquire about ends. What is perfect aims at perfection, and religion surpasses everything in perfection. Therefore, what religion aims at is simply the best, or the supreme good. But in what the supreme good, in other words human happiness consists, has long been most fiercely disputed among philosophers. Christianity agrees with right reason that the supreme good of man consists in enjoying to the fullest extent what is intrinsically the supreme good, and this is God.[67]

If Grotius had intended to enter the theological or philosophical arena with this text, we should probably have to conclude that he would have entered ill-equipped and insufficiently armed. Complex theological and philosophical concepts

64 Groot, *Meletius, sive, De iis quae inter Christianos conveniunt epistola*, 17–24.

65 Groot, 24.

66 Groot, 24. Cited from the text, *Meletius* 89.8 (Latin text) and p. 133 (translation).

67 'Veniamus ad propiora et, ut omnibus quae fiunt κατὰ προαίρεσιν, necesse est finem primo investigemus. Finis rei optimae optimus, at est religio res omnium optima. Finis igitur eius simpliciter optimus sive summum bonum. Quod autem sit summum bonum sive beatitudo hominis, inter philosophos diu summis contentionibus certatum. Christiana religio idem quod recta ratio monstrat, summum hominis bonum esse quam perfectissime frui eo qui per se est summum bonum, id autem est Deus.' Groot, para. 13.

from apparently different schools and periods are easily connected to sum up the purpose of human life. The term κατὰ προαίρεσιν, according to free choice, seems Aristotelian, although Plato uses it as well.[68] The idea of the human soul striving for the highest transcendental goal, the Supreme Good, seems Platonic. The identification of the Supreme Good with God has been made by Augustine and others.

In the next paragraph, Grotius elaborates on the striving of the soul to God as the ultimate purpose, or the Supreme Good and contrasts this view with certain philosophers, who define this purpose as a life of virtue for the sake of virtue itself. This makes no sense, according to Grotius, for great hardship is often connected to the pursuit of virtue, and why would anyone suffer this hardship if there was no retribution in afterlife?[69] Grotius then proceeds:

> From this it also follows that those too err who, even though they posit an afterlife, find their greatest happiness in food and drink, like the Talmudic Jews, or in sexual indulgence, like the Mohammedans, while Christians exclude both from a life of happiness as signs of an insatiable appetite, 'for true happiness knows no needs'. Food and sex may be good for cattle, for man they are certainly not, for, since in him the soul is superior to the body, he must, to achieve true happiness, assimilate body to soul, not soul to body, and become a spiritual body instead of a bodily spirit. Aristotle perceived something of this, since in the 'Eudemian Ethics' he states: 'Therefore whatever mode of choosing and of acquiring things good by nature will promote the contemplation of God better than goods of body or wealth or friends or the other goods, that is the best mode, and that standard is the finest; and any mode of choice and acquisition that through excess hinders us from serving and from contemplating God—that is a bad one. This is how it is for the spirit, and this is the best spiritual standard—to be as far as possible unconscious of the other, inferior part of the spirit, as such.'[70]

This second citation shows the same characteristics as the previous. The line of reasoning is superficial for a theological or philosophical discourse. The argument of the prevalence of spirit over body is substantiated only with a citation from the *Nicomachaean Ethics*, whereas Grotius's characterization and refutation of Jews and Muslims lacks any proof. At the same time, Grotius hardly adduces any positive arguments from Christian sources. He either speaks of philosophers in general or of

68 Maria C. Pantelia, "Προαίρεσις, -εως, Ἡ."

69 'Indeed, their one basic assumption is false, that virtue should be sought after for its own sake, a tenet that is unmistakably refuted by reason. For virtue is chiefly concerned with trouble. And no one will accept trouble unless for the sake of something else. Hence other philosophers declared, with better reason, that the certainty of afterlife is proved beyond possibility of doubt by the fact that in this life most often the good fare ill and the bad fare well.' ('Falsum enim est illud quo solo nituntur, expetendam propter se virtutem, quod certissima ratio refellit. Versatur enim virtus circa molesta maxime. At molestias nemo suscipit nisi propter aliud; unde rectius alii hoc ipso certissime probari dixere, vitam post hanc esse alteram, quia in hac vita plerumque bonis male, malis bene est.') Groot, *Meletius, sive, De iis quae inter Christianos conveniunt epistola*, para. 15.

70 'Sequitur etiam hinc falli et eos, qui vitam quidem statuunt alteram, sed summam beatitudinem collocant aut in victu potuque, ut Iudaei thalmudici, aut in veneris usu, ut Mahumetistae, cum Christiani et hoc et illud e vita beata eximant, ut indigentiae signa; τὸ δὲ εὐδαῖμον ἀνενδεές. Pecudum ista forte bona sunt, hominis neutiquam, in quo cum sit animus corpore praestantior, ut vera contingat felicitas, corpus animo assimilari, non animus corpori debet, et fieri σῶμα πνευματικόν (*corpus spirituale*), non πνεῦμα σωματικόν (*spiritus corporalis*). Vidit hoc partim Aristoteles, qui in Eudemicis inquit: *Quae igitur possessio electioque eorum quae naturaliter bona sunt magis id efficit ut consuleretur Deus, quam aut corpus aut pecuniae aut amici aut bona coetera: haec sane optima est isque terminus pulcherrimus. Quod si qua talis est quae per copiam impediat Deum colere atque considerare; haec vero mala est. Id vero ad animam pertinet, isque animae praestantissimus finis: quam minimum sentire alteram illam atque inferiorem animae partem, qua talis est.*' Groot, para. 16.

Christians. It is left to the knowledge and imagination of the reader to guess whether the arguments stem from classical philosophy, the New Testament, Augustine or medieval philosophers and theologians. It is tempting to question whether Grotius was sufficiently knowledgeable and capable of treating this subject.

The answer to this question has nothing to do with Grotius's abilities and capabilities. The answer lies in his perception of his world in general and of knowledge in particular. Grotius can be characterized as a typical exponent, or maybe even protagonist, of the humanist discourse that was dominant at that time in the circles around Leiden University. The discourse of the Leiden humanists was the local variant of the Republic of Letters as it had come into existence in the previous century. It had been laid at the roots of this university when it was founded in 1575 by Janus Dousa (1545–1604), who had been infused with the ideals of the Italian Renaissance and the Republic of Letters by Jean Dorat (1508–1588) during the years that he studied in Paris. It had been cultivated first by Justus Lipsius (1547–1606), who had made sure that a sound humanist curriculum stood at the basis of the new university. It was somewhat differently continued by Joseph Scaliger, who had been attracted from France to vouch for the university's standing. Scaliger was attracted on the condition that he only had to reside in Leiden, being free from any teaching obligation. He did, however, lecture small groups of carefully selected students. Among them were Hugo Grotius and his friend Daniel Heinsius. Scaliger was regarded as one of the most important authorities in the Republic of Letters. The fact that students like Grotius were introduced by Scaliger into the scholarly community was of great significance for their careers.

This humanist discourse can best be characterized by its orientation towards the classical world. What the exact boundaries of this classical world were could vary, but generally it meant a very strong identification with the cultures of classical Rome and Greece. Humanists such as Grotius and Heinsius saw themselves as the heirs of classical civilization. This meant that they imitated Greek and Roman authors in language, style and content. They made extensive use of classical imagery and they adapted their classical examples to their situations. A typical way of addressing a problem or a situation for these humanists was looking for possible answers in the works of their examples and subsequently elaborating a solution from their classical examples. And that is exactly what Grotius is doing here. For the style Grotius uses here greatly resembles the style of Cicero in his philosophical works.[71] It is a conversant style, wherein an all-knowing author tells his audience his philosophical truths, adducing citations from famous Greek philosophers to underscore or contrast the line of argumentation.

The obvious contradiction for a modern reader is of course the pagan character of the classical philosophers and their adherents, whereas the humanists were Christians. This contradiction was solved by stating beforehand that Christianity was both the completion and perfection of classical civilization. The humanists saw themselves as the re-embodiment of classical civilization, only with the potentiality of reviving it on a higher level, enriched by Christian insights and religion. It may be understood that not all contemporaries of Grotius shared this vision, as we shall see later on. This point is nicely illustrated by the following passage from the *Meletius*:

71 'In my [i.e. Posthumus Meyjes's] opinion, the significance of their works [i.e. of the classical authors] for the nature and the content of the *Meletius* can hardly be overestimated. Ever since his youth Grotius was familiar with Seneca. [...] The same goes for Cicero, of whose works Grotius had a very thorough knowledge, as is even proved by his choice of words. Certain passages from the *Meletius* are almost unintelligible unless read in conjunction with Cicero. That, for example, is the case with the passage on the supreme good, the intention of which only becomes clear by comparing it with Cicero's *De finibus*. It certainly looks as if Grotius had this work next to him when he was writing the passage, but he does not mention it.' Groot, 68.

> There is another thing worth our attention, namely that those things that are separately considered to be the highest good by the individual people, are collectively contained in the highest good of the Christians. For irrespective of whether you look for it in pleasure, either that which exists in passivity and is called freedom from pain, as does the philosopher Hieronymus, or, with the school of Aristippus, that which lies in activity, both are present in the Christian religion, absence of any suffering as well as the highly pleasurable experience by which the soul, not the body (since this only impedes the soul), is moved to joy and delight; or whether you place the highest good in virtue, with the Stoics, this is also truly present here, in addition to the good fortune of a perfect life, which Aristotle links with virtue.[72]

The passages cited here from the *Meletius* illustrate how Grotius's work from the period when he was not yet fully absorbed by the conflict between the Remonstrants and the Counter-Remonstrants can best be understood if we see him as an exponent of the Leiden humanist discourse. The most important feature of this discourse, which cannot be overemphasized, is the identification with antiquity which permeates every scholarly endeavour of these humanists. However, this discourse will gradually change under the pressure of an orthodox Calvinist discourse.[73] In the case of Grotius, this means that he somehow has to adapt to this Calvinist discourse, when it becomes apparent that the humanist discourse is not accepted in the Republic outside the circles of the Leiden humanists.

However, before we continue with the *Remonstrantie*, it is worthwhile looking at how Judaism is portrayed in the *Meletius*. Judaism in the *Meletius* has little to do with actual Jews Grotius met in the Republic, although he mentions their immigration in the introduction, but more to do with the portrayal of Jews, painted in various classical and post-classical sources.[74] In the text, Judaism is principally portrayed as an intermediary step on the scale from irreligious amorality to Grotius's version of Christianity. This scale runs from denial of religion in general to natural religions and polytheism, to the monotheistic religions of Judaism and Islam till the perfection of Christianity.[75]

72 'Illud quoque animadversione non indignum, quae alii singula singuli summum esse bonum voluerunt, ea in summo Christianorum bono cuncta reperiri. Nam sive voluptatem quaeras, aut eam quae in statu est et indolentia vocatur, cum Hieronymo philosopho, aut cum Cyrenaicis, eam quae in motu est, utrunque hic est et doloris omnis vacuitas, et suavissimus, non corporum—id enim animum impedit—sed animorum motus gaudiumque et laetitia; seu cum Stoicis virtus placet, et hic vera est, addita insuper ea, quam virtuti Aritoteles coniungit perfectae vitae prosperitate.' Groot, para. 17.

73 I have described this discursive change in Foucauldian terms in my dissertation, "Clashes of Discourses". It has been discussed in a different framework by Marc Somos, who sees the Leiden humanists as forerunners in the process of secularization. We do, however, share the identification of the Leiden humanists as a distinctive group (I prefer to focus on their discourse, the implicit and explicit expression of [parts of] their shared values as can be found in their textual expressions) that flourished until the coup d'état of Maurice of Orange: 'After its memorable foundation in 1575, Leiden University became the hothouse of secularising thought until 1618–1619, when the Calvinist purge destroyed this experiment, and exiled or executed the leading figures of Dutch secularisation.' Somos, *Secularisation and the Leiden Circle*, 8. See also Otterspeer, *Het bolwerk van de vrijheid*, 281–288.

74 'At si aut Indos illos, ad quos felicissime navigamus, aut quibus tu vixisti Turcas, aut qui nunc se nobis inserunt Iudaeos respicere liberet, deberemus vel illorum comparatione in animum revocare oblitam prope necessitudinem.' ('Yet, if we were willing to consider the people of the Indies, to whom we send our ships so successfully, or the Turks among whom you, [= J. Boreel] have lived, or the Jews who are now settling among us, we should be obliged to remember our almost forgotten kinship, even if only by comparing ourselves with them.') Groot, *Meletius, sive, De iis quae inter Christianos conveniunt epistola*, para. 2.

75 'Habet igitur hoc primum in se christianitas, quod religione utitur commune quidem cum multis, non tamen cum omnibus. Impii enim et quos ἀθέους dicimus hoc limite arcentur.' ('The first characteristic that Christianity has in common with many [movements] though

Judaism and Islam are consequently mentioned several times in one sentence. As Judaism is somewhere below perfection on Grotius's scale, it may be understood that Judaism fares negatively in the comparison. For example, Grotius considers Judaism an ethnocentric religion:

> We should now go into the question who has access to the forgiveness we spoke about. The Christian religion teaches that it is attainable for all mankind, as against the intolerance of the Jews who want to reserve that hope all for themselves to the exclusion of all other peoples.[76]

and:

> But nature persuades him that these people [i.e. the barbarians] too are humans and therefore should be considered brothers. How fatally the Jews err now and erred in the past in this respect is clearly indicated by these verses of Juvenal: Not to show the way to anybody but co-religionists, / to lead only the circumcised to the well they asked for. And in the words of Tacitus: among themselves there is a steadfast faithfulness and spontaneous compassion, but toward all others hostile hatred.[77]

Naturally Grotius is criticizing champions of Jewish and Muslim religion, both Mohammed and the Messias, whom he considers to be men of weaponry and violence, whereas Christ is a better example for imitation, full of piety, charity and patience.[78] And the Jewish religion is too full of cumbersome rites, whereas religion should have its place in the quiet mind.[79] Summarizing, it may be said that Grotius's portrait of Judaism in the *Meletius* hardly consists of fierce criticism. The negative evaluation stems primarily from the comparison with Christianity, which Grotius regards as a superior religion. Nonetheless, the only stereotype the reader encounters is the saying that Jews are eager for food and drink and Muslims have a great sexual appetite, as quoted above. Grotius mentions no source for this observation.

---

not with all, is that it is a religion. The impious, therefore, and those we call atheists, fall outside this scope.') Groot, para. 6. And later: 'Haec illa sunt principia quae communia habet christiana religio et cum falsis omnibus, et cum veris quidem, sed minus perfectis, qualis est primum naturalis religio, inde mosaïca.' ('These are the principles which the Christian religion has in common with all religions, the false ones and the true but less perfect ones, such as, in the first place, natural religion, and, next, the Mosaic religion.') Groot, para. 12.

76 'Venia autem haec de qua diximus, cui pateat videndum nunc est. Eam christiana religio docet patere toti humano generi, contra quam statuit Iudaeorum invidentia, qui omnes praeter se gentes ab ea spe exclusas volunt.' Groot, *Meletius, sive, De iis quae inter Christianos conveniunt epistola*, para. 50.

77 'Sed naturae credit hos quoque esse homines, ac proinde habendos fratrum loco, in quo Iudaei quam pernitiose ut nunc labantur et lapsi sint olim, Iuvenalis versus facile indicant *Non monstrare vias eadem nisi sacra colenti, / Qaesitum ad fontem solos deducere verpos*. Et Tacitus: *apud ipsos fides obstinata, misericordia in promptu, sed adversus omnes alios hostile odium.*' Groot, para. 69.

78 'At Christiani eum sibi proponunt imitandum, cuius nulla culpa argui potest; cuius tota vita plena est non violentiae et armorum, ut Mahumetis et sperati Iudaeis Messiae, sed pietatis, charitatis mansuetudinis, patientiae.' ('Christians, however, take as their example him who can be accused of no crime at all; whose life, unlike that of Mohammed or the hoped-for Messiah of the Jews, is full not of violence and the din of arms, but of mercy, charity, gentleness and patience.') Groot, para. 56.

79 'Rursus et hoc cavet christiana religio, ne Deus operose et per innumeros ritus colatur, qua parte non veterum modo gentium religiones antecellit, quae multos ritus comminiscebantur Deo iniussos ideoque ingratos, sed ipsam quoque iudaicam, plenam et ipsam sumtuosis et molestis caeremoniis. Hoc autem praeter quod pars magna est libertatis et insigne Dei beneficium, etiam monet nos, praecipuum Dei cultum in mente consistere.' ('In this respect it is superior not only to the religions of the peoples of antiquity who devised many rites which were not commanded by God and therefore were disagreeable to Him, but even to the Jewish religion, which is also replete with sumptuous and cumbersome ceremonies. Apart from the fact that it greatly enhances our freedom and is an extraordinary gift from God, it also reminds us that the cult of God principally takes place in the mind.') Groot, para. 64.

It is worthwhile emphasizing two points here. The first is that this text was not meant as a text for or about Jews. It is a text for and about Christianity and aims at inner-Christian tolerance. To that end it contrasts Christianity with non-Christian religions and philosophies. Secondly, the image depicted here of Judaism, not to mention Islam, creates a very meagre impression. It seems to be based only on a few classical sources. Even biblical references seem absent. It is an impression that will linger during the discussion of the *Remonstrantie* in the following chapters; Grotius had no special sympathy for Jews and Judaism, nor did he have much first-hand knowledge of Jews and Judaism.

4 The Multifaceted Appearance of the *Remonstrantie*

Unconventionally, the discussion of the *Remonstrantie* here will start with the third part of the text, for it is this last part of the *Remonstrantie* in particular that closely resembles in its style and method the *technique* discussed in the previous chapter. It consists of a commentary on the 49 rules that constitute the main part of the text. As is not uncommon with commentaries, it surpasses the main text in length, here about twice its size. The appearance of this commentary poses all sorts of questions. The first question is why Grotius deemed it necessary to add a commentary to a draft text of public rulings. Was it necessary to convince members of the States of Holland and West Frisia? Was he already anticipating a publication of the text? As the public collections in the Netherlands show, it was not uncommon to publish a *Remonstrantie* as a pamphlet.[80] These were, however, usually texts that either aimed at public impact or had to factor it in. These remonstrances were usually written in Dutch and consisted of a main text, sometimes followed by supporting texts, for example copied letters or excerpts from texts that could corroborate the claims made in the main text.

To name some examples, around 1608 there appeared a pamphlet with the title *Discours, by forme van Remonstrantie; vervatende de nootsakelijckheyt vande Oost-Indische Navigatie* [...].[81] The text, sometimes assigned to Willem Usselincx (1567–1647), intends to convince the Dutch government or the governing bodies of the provinces that constituted the Republic that it was necessary and profitable to engage in the East Indian trade. The text is printed on one quire in quarto, seven pages of which contain the *Discours*, the last page being left blank. The long title explains the purpose of the text, and what follows is a description of the East Indies.[82] No supporting

80 See "Dutch Pamphlets Online—BrillOnline Primary Sources".

81 "Discours, by forme van remonstrantie; vervatende de nootsakelijckheyt vande Oost-Indische navigatie." The text can be accessed via https://archive.org/stream/ned-kbn-all-00014914-001#page/n5/mode/1up.

82 'Discours, by forme van Remonstrantie; vervatende de nootsakelijckheyt vande Oost-Indische Navigatie, by middel vande welcke de vrye Nederlandtsche Provincien apparent zijn te gheraecken totte hoochste Prosperiteyt, in't stuck vande alder-rijckste ende costelijckste Waren vande gheheele Werelt. Waer uyt consequentelick sal volghen, dat de voorsz. vrye Nederlandtsche Republijcke, t'allen tyden soo sal wesen ghequalificeert, in't stuck vande Equipagie ter Zee, soo om de Caep, als deur de Straet van Maghellaen, dat sy sich van geen uytheemsche macht lichtelijck aenghevochten te werden, sullen hebben te vreesen; Maer ter contrarie (met Gods hulpe) op hare Inlandsche, ende naebuerighe Bont-ghenooten saken goede ordre ghestelt hebbende, inde uyterste deelen, maer oock lief-tael, wel bemint, ende van vele der selver gheacht, ende ontsien sullen wesen, &c. Ende dit alles tot groote vercleeninghe, jae in eenige quartieren gantsche vernietinghe der groote aensienlijcke heerschappye vande Spaensche ende Portugesche Natien, in de selve quartieren.' ('Discourse, by means of Remonstrance on the necessity of navigating the East Indies, by means of which the free Provinces of the Low Countries are likely to reach the highest Prosperity, concerning the richest and costliest goods of the whole world. From which will follow consequently that the aforementioned free Dutch Republic, at all times will be qualified as such, concerning the equipage at sea, both around the Cape, and through the Strait of Maghellaen, that she will not

texts have been added, no sources are referred to, and even details on author, date and place of publishing and intended addressees have been omitted. Also printed in quarto, on two quires, is the *Remonstrantie* by Casper Coolhaas (1534–1615).[83] As the title suggests, the text aims at motivating the magistrates to purge the public space of all Roman Catholic reminiscences. The text was written in Dutch and supporting evidence from other sources has been added in another typecast in the main text, largely citations from the Bible. The reason that it appears in print seems evident: the pamphlet is not addressed to one clearly defined addressee, but aims at motivating anyone in charge, as it were. By disseminating the text in print the author is maximizing the chances of his text reaching its intended audience. As a final example, the *Remonstrantie by de zes colloquenten* may be introduced.[84] This remonstrance works somewhat differently, as it appeared in print *after* it had been submitted to the addressee, here the States of Holland and West Frisia. The text stems from the final phase of the conflict during the Twelve Year's Truce (1609–1621), where the orthodox Calvinists, the Counter-Remonstrants are clearly getting the upper hand and are aiming for a national synod where the question of the legitimacy of the Remonstrants will be settled. Representatives of the Remonstrants have offered their conditions to the States of Holland and West Frisia, on which grounds they will agree to attending this synod. In its printed form this text, ascribed to Wtenbogaert, is not necessarily meant for its stated addressee, for the members of the States had heard and possibly received the text already. The target readership is probably the Remonstrants' support base, namely Remonstrants, sympathizers and non-outspoken Counter-Remonstrants. The text is in Dutch and the only appendices are supportive statements from several communities that agree to be represented by the six *colloquenten*. The text is much longer than the previous remonstrances, seven quires in quarto.

The examples show, that it was not uncommon to have a remonstrance printed. It is conceivable that Grotius had an edition of his remonstrance in mind when he took pains to write quite an extensive introduction and commentary. What has become clear from these examples, however, is that it was by no means common to have a document meant for solving a practical situation be accompanied by a lengthy commentary. Indeed, the presentation of the text leads the reader towards the realm of the humanist discourse. As mentioned earlier, one important characteristic of the humanist discourse was the edition of classical texts complete with commentary, usually called *notae* or *adnotationes*. Naturally, within the confines of the Republic of Letters, these texts were written in Latin and reflected on the classical world. However, as we shall see, Grotius actually does the same thing here with a practical legal text in the public realm. Of course, the text has been adapted to the context and its

have fear to be attacked lightly by any foreign power; But contrarily (with God's help) having put in order her domestic affairs and those with her neighbours, she will be well liked and loved, regarded and respected in the remotest parts and by the very richest and faraway great powers of the world, etc. And all of this will lead to the diminishing, and even in some parts complete annihilation of the great esteemed masteries of the Spanish and Portuguese Nations in the same regions.') "Discours, by forme van remonstrantie; vervatende de nootsakelijckheyt vande Oost-Indische navigatie", A1.

83 Coolhaas, *Remonstrantie aen zijne prinslijcke excellentie, ende de edele … zeer vermogende Heeren Staten ende Steden der vereenighde ende gereformeerde neder-Landen, in dewelcke (onder verbeteringe) aenghewezen wordt 't ghene, dat nootlijck naer eysch der Heyligher Godlijcker Schriftuer … met kleyne moyte verbetert zal konnen werden.* ('Remonstrance to his princely excellence, and the honourable and powerful Lords of the States and Towns of the United and Reformed Low Countries, in which is indicated what should be improved with little effort according to the demands of the Holy and Divine Scripture.') The text can be accessed at: https://books.google.nl/books?id=XKxpAAAAcAAJ&hl=nl&pg=PP1#v=onepage&q&f=false.

84 Wtenbogaert, *Remonstrantie by de zes colloquenten vander remonstranten weghen in de Haeghsche conferentie bekent … Waer in sy hare bedenckinghen openen over het houden der synoden.*

readership, and the text has been written in Dutch. But the scheme introduction, text and commentary betray Grotius as a scholar working in the public arena.

In fact, we know from Grotius himself that he strove for an implementation of his humanist ideals in the public arena. In a letter from 1604 to the Palatine diplomat Georg Michael Lingelsheim (1556–1636), the young advocate bravely writes that he has adjusted to the harsh reality of the real world:

> As for me, I spend virtually all my time in court. But you do not have to feel sorry for me: already my soul has adjusted to this unpleasant and harsh reality. There is even in this trade some use for knowledge, I believe, and erudition, even though it is unknown to most: it begins however to shine forth more and more, although it has to be concealed to a certain extent […].[85]

And:

> And so, I spend as much energy as I can, both when I am working on my cases—for I receive quite a few interesting cases—and in leisure time in developing my [scholarly and rhetorical—DK] skills, lest I would be regarded as belonging to the common people.[86]

Grotius clearly tried to make his theoretical knowledge useful in his daily work. This should not be regarded as some play for the intellectually gifted, although a certain amount of playfulness had its place in the humanist discourse, again in imitation of the classical examples. The humanist mindset, however, was directed at re-establishing the classical world in an ameliorated sense in his own society. This improved version of the classical world could however only be found by constantly looking at the ancient Greek and Roman examples, to see what answers were found in antiquity to given problems and whether their solutions could be implemented in the 17th century, or needed modification. And that is exactly what Grotius does in his career. He, and the other Leiden humanists, were consciously trying to re-enliven as much as they could of the classical world in their own society.

It is from this discourse that the third part of the *Remonstrantie* can be understood. It shows Grotius consistently referring for his judgement to classical sources, in this case mostly Roman Law. The legal collections of the Roman emperors Theodosian and Justinian were still important reference points for legal decision-making. However, Grotius seems to give these collections more authority and centrality than contemporary legalists. Many legal humanists were occupied with the question of how Roman law functioned and developed within the developments of ancient Roman civilization and the emendation of the transmitted legal texts. Grotius was probably influenced by his uncle, Cornelis de Groot, who taught Law at Leiden University (intermittently from 1583–1610). He taught his students to relate and reduce contemporary economic and social principles to the principles of Roman Law.[87] Besides, it is interesting to look at the personal notes of the Haarlem secretary Michiel van Woerden, where an historical substantiation for the *nihil obstat* against a synagogue is very briefly mentioned:

> […] it may be noted that from ancient times onwards the Christian emperors such as Constantine, Theodosius, Antonine and others as well as the popes have allowed the Jews their synagogues and the free practice of their reli-

85 'Ego quidem paene totus in foro sum. Nec te misereat mei: occaluit iam animus ad illa inamoena et aspera. Est etiam in his artibus usus sapientiae sentio et litterarum, ignotus plerisque: sed hoc magis elucescit, etsi adhibenda est dissimulatio, […].' Grotius to Lingelsheim, 25 January 1604.

86 'Ego igitur et cum in causis versor—affluunt autem non paucae et satis illustres—et ubi quid otii est, exercitando me, quantum licet, operam do, ne censear ex plebe rabularum.' Grotius to Lingelsheim.

87 Otterspeer, *Het bolwerk van de vrijheid*, 358.

> gion. It may be noted as well, that also the most famous theologians and preachers of the Protestant religion with sound and concise reasons sustain and conclude that Jews are to be tolerated under the Christians and their synagogue and practice of religion to be allowed; it can also be seen that they have not only been allowed in the Papal Countries in Italy and other parts, but also by the Lutherans in Germany and by those of the Reformed religion in Emden as well; [...][88]

The partakers of the discussion on the admission of public Jewish religious practice in Haarlem not only looked at the *Corpus Iuris*, but also mentioned both Roman and canonical law, and this is the part Grotius elaborates on. However, Van Woerden's notes also speak of Protestant theologians and contemporary legislation. There may be various reasons why Grotius chose not to include these examples; one reason, however, is that Grotius's own mind was strongly fixed on classical Rome.

There is in fact one chapter of the *Corpus Iuris Civilis* that seems to be the backbone of Grotius's commentary. The *Corpus* has one section devoted to regulations pertaining to Jews and pagans (*De Iudaeis et caelicolis*), and it is this section in particular to which Grotius is referring in his commentary. For example, the sixth article from the *Remonstrantie* states that Jews should be allowed to settle and live freely and will enjoy the same rights as any other citizen as long as they keep to the specific regulations for Jews, as they appear in this text. No additional taxation or tribute will be demanded from them.[89] This is of course an important point, for in one article of Grotius's regulation a huge difference with almost all other regulations becomes visible. In many contemporary and earlier charters, Jews were forced to live in ghettos,[90] were certainly not free to choose their profession[91] and always had to pay for protection from the lord of the land.[92]

The reason Grotius provides for this point is that it was a Roman Catholic (read: medieval?) measure to impose taxes on Jews, inspired by a taste for tyranny and avarice:

> The custom of making Jews pay a tax for their freedom of religion was introduced by the popes, which exposes their tyranny and greed. The ancient emperors never imposed such a tax, but treated the Jews like all other citizens. Furthermore the free commerce by Jews is explicitly dealt with in art. 1.9.9 of the Corpus Iuris Civilis.

Here Grotius is referring to a regulation from the emperors Arcadius and Honorius from the year 396, which can be found in the aforementioned chapter:

88 '[...] gemerct van allen ouden tijden bijden Christelicken Keysers als Constantine, Theodosio, Anthonino ende anderen als oock bij den Pausen de Joden haer Sinagogen ende vrije exercitie van haer religie toegelaten is geweest. Gemerct oock de vermaerste Theologanten ende predicanten vande Gereformeerde religie oock met goede ende bondige redenen sustineren ende concluderen datmen den Joden onder den Christenen behoort te tollereren ende haere Sinagoge ende exercitie van religie toe te laeten; gelijckmen oversulcx oock syet dat dezelve nyet alleene int Pausdom in Italien ende andere quartieren, maer oock bij de Evangelische in Duijtschlant ende bij die van vande Gereformeerde religie oock tot Embden toegelaten werden; [...].' Huussen Jr, "De toelating van Sefardische joden in Haarlem in 1605", 59.

89 '6. That Jews are to live freely in their places of residence and engage in trade, retailing or local industry as they see fit, and that they shall enjoy the same liberties, exemptions and privileges enjoyed by other citizens and residents without having a special tax imposed on them, provided they adhere to the following rules.' See pp. 105 and 205.

90 Ravid, "The Venetian Government and the Jews"; Israel, *European Jewry in the Age of Mercantilism, 1550–1750*, 19.

91 During the Middle Ages, Jews in Northern Europe had been confined to a limited choice of professions, as most crafts had been organized in guilds, and consequently been forbidden for Jews. In many cases they were explicitly allowed to engage in moneylending. In Southern Europe and the Mediterranean, the situation was altogether different; see Yeivin and Ben-Sasson, "Crafts".

92 The so-called *Judenschütz* (Jews' protection).

> No one who does not belong to the Jewish religion shall set prices for Jews when their goods are put out for sale. For it is just to commend each to his own. Therefore, the provincial governors shall permit no one to be your auditor or regulator. If someone other than you and your elders should dare to arrogate this office to himself, they shall hasten to punish him as if he were usurping the possession of others.[93]

It is tempting to read this quote as a proof of Grotius's benevolent attitude towards Jews. For he abolishes a long-established praxis of the Middle Ages, by expounding a minor article from the *Corpus Iuris Civilis*. What is more, Grotius ends in two lines a 1,000-year-old restriction on the freedom of profession. Jews were not allowed to be members of any guilds and were therefore very limited in their means of income. They were traditionally confined to professions that were not united in guilds, e.g. trade, finance and banking, and medicine. Both the abolishment of special taxation and the freedom of profession are remarkable deviations from other European regulations and are very different from the rights Jews had in the Low Countries during the Middle Ages. These ameliorations had been negotiated earlier in the Alkmaar, Haarlem and Rotterdam charters. Grotius, however, relates these measures solely to classical sources, e.g. the transmitted texts of the Roman Law. For the eighth article in the *Remonstrantie* deals with prayer houses:

> Namely, they shall designate to the city authorities one, two or three or more of their own houses or of those they occupy, where they will be permitted to gather in order to perform their religious duties at certain fixed hours.[94]

He explains this ruling as follows:

> The emperors traditionally allowed Jews to establish their synagogues, which was thereafter restricted insofar as they were permitted to repair their old synagogues, but not build new ones. Cod. 1.9.18(19), Cod. Th. 16.8.22 and 16.8.25. The reason appears to have been that their religion seemed to be endorsed too much by being allowed to build in public spaces. In this country, too, the understanding has always been that there should only be one public religion, so that it is actually better not to allow the Jews the exercise of their religion in public places but in private houses, which is also less noticeable for the people.[95]

The cited passages from the *Codex Theodosianus* read:

> No new synagogues shall be erected, the old ones shall remain in their present state.[96]

And:

> What we have decided lately about Jews and their synagogues, remains fixed: namely that they will neither under any circumstance be allowed to build new synagogues, nor that they have to fear that the old ones will be taken from them. They should know that any other prohibitions should be observed, as the recently expanded constitution declares.[97]

93 'Nemo exterus religionis iudaeorum iudaeis pretia statuet, cum venalia proponentur. Iustum est enim sua cuique committere. Itaque rectores provinciarum vobis nullum discussorem aut moderatorem esse concedent. Quod si quis sumere sibi curam praeter vos proceresque vestros audeat, eum velut aliena appetentem supplicio coercere festinent.' Krueger et al., *The Codex of Justinian*, 231–232.

94 See pp. 107 and 205.

95 See pp. 147 and 210.

96 'Synagogae de cetero nullae protinus extruantur, veteres in sua forma permaneant.' *Cod.Th. 16.8.25.2* (Grotius's reference to 22 seems to be a scribal error.)

97 'Quae nuper de iudaeis et synagogis eorum statuimus, firma permaneant: scilicet ut nec novas umquam synagogas permittantur extruere nec auferendas sibi veteres pertimescant. Cetera vero vetita in posterum sciant

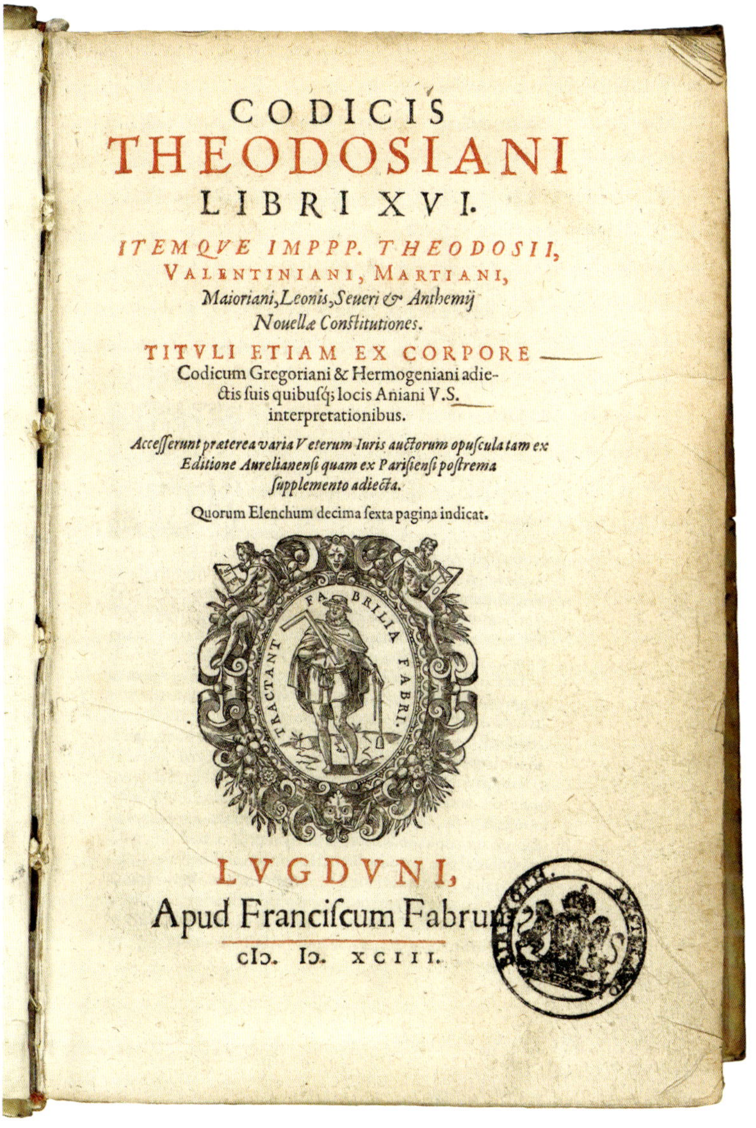

FIGURE 15
The title page of Codex Theodosianus, a book of law used by the Christian emperors of the Roman Empire, referenced by Grotius

The cited article of the *Codex Justinianus* reads:

> By this law, which shall endure for all time, We decree that no Jew, to whom all offices and ranks are forbidden, shall hold the office of defender of the city, nor do We permit them to seize the office of father (of the city), lest fortified by the authority of the office that they have acquired, they should have any power of judging or pronouncing against Christians and even the bishops of the sacred religion themselves, as if insulting our faith. 1. Censuring this, too, with equal consideration of reason, We command that no Jewish synagogue may rise up in a new construction, but permission is granted for propping up those in danger of collapse. 2. Therefore whoever either receives the insignia (of office) shall not obtain the positions sought; or if he sneaks into offices forbidden him, he shall be utterly expelled from them; or if he constructs a synagogue, he shall know that he has

esse servanda, quemadmodum nuper constitutionis latae forma declarat.' *Cod.Th. 16.8.27*

> laboured to the benefit of the Catholic Church. And he who infiltrates honours and rank shall, as before, be considered of the lowest status, even if he illicitly was granted an honorary rank; and he who undertakes the construction of a synagogue not in the interest of repairing it shall be cheated of the effect of his daring with the loss of 50 pounds of gold. 3. He who overwhelms the faith of another by his perverse teaching shall see his property confiscated and himself then destined for a penalty exacted in libel.[98]

Although Grotius must have known this text well, he clearly modifies the sense to make it fit to the situation at hand. Firstly, the Roman emperors are quite outspoken on why they did not want any new synagogues erected—they were considered as an insult against Christianity. The explanation as to why Jews were allowed to repair their synagogues seems evident from the last citation—to prevent them from collapsing, which would have resulted in public disorder. The emperors probably considered new buildings as an efficient means of propaganda, not unlike the emperor Augustus did; by monopolizing the right to erect prayer houses, the Jews were denied this kind of manifestation. Grotius draws on the main part of the law, namely the interdiction of building synagogues, albeit based on a different foundation. In fact, he uses two reasons why Jews should have no synagogues, namely: a) there is only one public Church and only the public Church should be entitled to public prayer houses; and b) synagogues might be offensive to the public eye. Contrary to the former regulation on taxes and profession, Grotius's imitation of his classical example does not result in the most progressive regulation for the Jews. For even in the Middle Ages they were often free to build synagogues, albeit with certain restrictions. What is more, even the recent charters of Alkmaar, Haarlem and Rotterdam had, sometimes conditionally, granted the right of erecting a public synagogue. What should be kept in mind, however, is that Roman Catholics were denied public prayer houses as well. It would be hard to defend Jews being permitted to have synagogues while Catholic churches remained forbidden. This last argument, though, has no place in Grotius's written text, where he only refers to the text of the Roman Law.

Grotius used other parts of the *Corpus* as well, as well as some contemporary legal texts. For example, he discusses at quite some length the question of whether Jews should be allowed to have a separate legal system. Grotius's own conclusion is very clear—Jews answer to the same legal bodies as any other citizen:

> All Jews shall furthermore be subject to the same rights, decrees and customs, taxes, levies, judiciary and jurisdiction to which all other citizens of these lands are also subjected, to equal punishments like the others, in particular they shall also be subject to the laws regulating the interest on lent money.[99]

98 '*Impp. Theodosius et Valentinianus* AA *Florentio pp.* Hac victura in omne aevum lege sancimus neminem iudaeum, quibus omnes administrationes et dignitates interdictae sunt, nec defensoris civitatis fungi saltem officio nec patris honorem adripere concedimus, ne adquisiti sibi officii auctoritate muniti adversus christianos et ipsos plerumque sacrae religionis antistites velut insultantes fidei nostrae iudicandi vel pronuntiandi quamlibet habeant potestatem. 1. Illud etiam pari consideratione rationis arguentes praecipimus, ne qua iudaica synagoga in novam fabricam surgat, fulciendi veteres permissa licentia, quae ruinam minantur. 2. Quisquis igitur vel infulas ceperit, quaesitis dignitatibus non potiatur, vel si ad officia vetita subrepserit, his penitus repelletur, vel si synagogam extruxerit, compendio catholicae ecclesiae noverit se laborasse: et qui ad honores et dignitates inrepserit, habeatur, ut antea, condicionis extremae, etsi honorariam illicite promeruerit dignitatem: et qui synagogae fabricam coeperit non studio reparandi, cum damno auri quinquaginta librarum fraudetur ausibus suis. 3. Cernat praeterea bona sua proscripta, mox poenae sanguinis destinandus, qui fidem alterius expugnavit perversa doctrina. *D. prid. k. Febr. Constantinopoli Theodosio A. xvii et Festo conss.* [a. 439].' *Cod.*1.9.18. English: Krueger et al., *The Codex of Justinian*, 237.

99 See pp. 181, 183 and 207–208.

Grotius finds this regulation evident, as this same law applied to Jews in the Roman Empire:

> It is evident from Roman law the Jews are subject to the general laws with respect to matrimonial laws; the same also applies to general taxes. Cod. 1.9.3, Cod. 1.9.7, Cod. 1.9.5 and Cod. 1.9.10.[100]

The laws cited here, are:

> We desire that the Jews and their elders and patriarchs be informed that, if anyone after this law should dare to assail anyone with stones or some other manner of fury (which We have learned is now being done) who has fled their deadly sect and turned to the worship of God, the assailant shall be consigned to the flames and burned with all his accomplices.[101]

And:

> No Jew shall observe his custom in contracting marriage, nor any Jewess be given in marriage according to their law, nor may one enter into different marriages at the same time.[102]

And:

> The order with which men of Jewish status flatter themselves, whereby immunity from curial charges was given to them, shall be rescinded.[103]

And:

> Whosoever of the Jews is proven to belong to a curia shall be delivered up to it.[104]

The quoted citations all speak of limitation of the jurisdiction of the traditional rabbinical courts, whether it concerns punishing apostates or cases of private and maybe even criminal law. The emperors apparently did not want to allow for a parallel judicial system, even if it would only be used by consenting parties, as may be supposed in the case of a marriage. This example again shows how Grotius prefers the regulations of the Roman emperors over well-known customs from the Middle Ages that were continued to be used in his own time all over Europe. For the Jewish community in a town was often allowed to settle disputes among themselves by means of a traditional religious court, a *Beth Din*. Grotius could have left it at this, but he continues:

> Some scholars were of the opinion that the Jewish laws should prevail for Jews among themselves, both in matrimonial affairs, in inheritances, as well as in other matters, and that they should be tried by Jewish judges, but this is reprehensible and is not covered by the legal code.[105]

Here Grotius is referring to the Italian legal scholars Johannes Andreae (c. 1270–1348), Baldus de Ubaldis (1327–1400) and Petrus de Ancharano (c. 1333–1416) 'and others', who according to him 'judged wrongly and not in accordance with the

100 See pp. 181 and 214.

101 '*Imperator Constantinus*. Iudaeis et maioribus eorum et patriarchis volumus intimari, quod, si quis post hanc legem aliquem, qui eorum feralem fugerit sectam et ad dei cultum respexerit, saxis aut alio furoris genere, quod nunc fieri cognovimus, ausus fuerit attemptare, mox flammis dedendus est et cum omnibus suis participibus concremandus.' *Cod.* 1.9.3. English: Krueger et al., *The Codex of Justinian*, 229.

102 '*Imperatores Valentinianus, Theodosius, Arcadius*. Nemo iudaeorum morem suum in coniunctionibus retinebit nec iuxta legem suam nuptias sortiatur nec in diversa sub uno tempore coniugia conveniat.' *Cod.* 1.9.7. English: Krueger et al., 231.

103 '*Imperatores Gratianus, Valentinianus, Theodosius*. Iussio, qua sibi iudaeae legis homines blandiuntur, per quam eis curialium munerum dabatur immunitas, rescindatur.' *Cod.* 1.9.5. English: Krueger et al., *The Codex of Justinian*; Scott, "The Civil Law". Krueger translates here for *munera* 'liturgies', whereas I have followed Scott, who has 'charges'. This seems to fit better in Grotius's text.

104 '*Imperatores Arcadius, Honorius*. Quicumque ex iudaeis obnoxii curiae comprobantur, curiae mancipentur.' *Cod.* 1.9.10. English: Krueger et al., *The Codex of Justinian*, 233.

105 See pp. 181–183 and 214.

text of the laws'.[106] To make his point clearer, Grotius explicitly says, that

> The Jewish community solely exists in its religion and not in any other sense. As such they cannot establish institutions on their own initiative, using their own laws.[107]

Remarkable as this citation is in itself, it may refer to an actual situation. For the charter made between the Portuguese merchants and the city of Rotterdam had allowed for a house that could be used for religious purposes, and was managed by *consuls*. Zwarts assumes that the Rotterdam community had asked for and obtained permission for a consular house from where the Portuguese nation could be governed by its *consuls*. This was apparently the way the Portuguese community in Antwerp had been governed during the 16th century.[108] Again according to Zwarts, it was about the same issue that a conflict had risen in Amsterdam when the first synagogue was build, as it was possibly intended as consular house and not only as a synagogue in the confined sense of the word.[109]

Until this point, both the regulations of Grotius and his explanation of the regulations display a very neutral attitude towards Jews and Judaism. The regulation about the synagogues, namely that only in private houses gatherings for religious services could be held, could be explained very well from the point of view that Roman Catholics were subjected to the same regulation and that it would not be right to let the Jews have a public prayer house and the Catholics not. What is more, Grotius could substantiate this point with similar regulations from the *Codex*. However, when we follow Grotius's argumentation and he comes to speak of moneylending and interest, he strikes a different key:

> With respect to usury, this has greatly increased because recently, Christian rulers did not impose any restrictions on the Jews so that they could reap the benefits from the Jews bleeding the poor dry. The law of Moses allows the Jews to lend money at exorbitant interest rates to accursed peoples, towards whom they are allowed to express every hostility. See Deut. 23:20. As Ambrose very rightly observed: you may demand interest from whom it is no crime to kill him. Where the law of war reigns, reigns the law of usury. A Christian city government, however, cannot allow such hostility to be exercised against its citizens, as it is contrary to the principle of natural equality, of which the Jews themselves are also sufficiently convinced in their conscience. See Ps. 15:6. and Ez 18:8.[110]

Although the majority of the explanations of the regulations follows the scheme mentioned earlier, namely extrapolated from codices of Roman Law, the last example is not the only exception to this rule. A striking example is regulation no. 16, which reads:

> Furthermore, Jews in this country will be permitted to own, use and also cause all books to be printed, with the exception of those containing any blasphemies or profanities, as indicated above. This on pain of banishment from the country with confiscation of possessions of those who would have such books printed; and the punishment for those who own and use these books is confiscation of the books and a fine of 50 guilders at the first offence, 100

106 See pp. 181 and 214.

107 'De gemeenschap van de Joden bestaet puijrelijck in de religie, ende nijet daer buijten. Oversulcx en moghen zij geen Universiteiten maecken op haer selven, quae suis legibus utatur.' pp. 183 and 214.

108 Zwarts, *Eerste rabbijnen*, 63–65.

109 Zwarts, 71.

110 See pp. 183–185 and 214–215. For Ambrosius on usury, see *Sancti Ambrosii, Mediolanensis Episcopi, opera omnia ... editio prae aliis omnibus completa*, 816–817; Swift, "St. Ambrose on Violence and War", 534; Stein, "Moneylending".

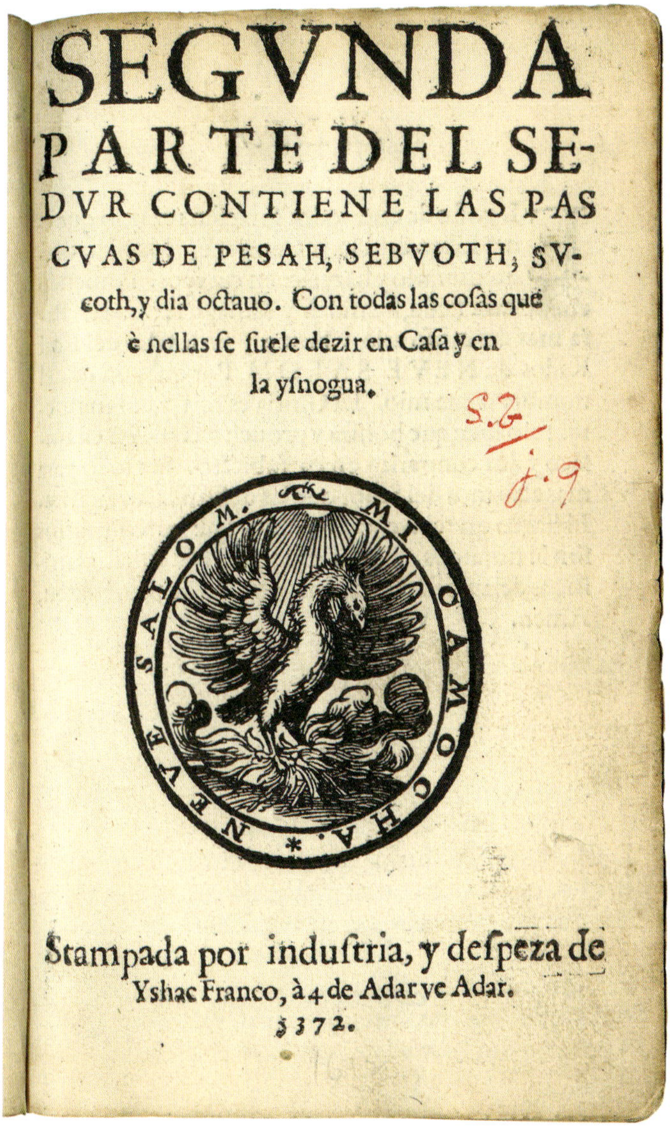

SEGVNDA
PARTE DEL SE-
DVR CONTIENE LAS PAS
CVAS DE PESAH, SEBVOTH, SV-
coth, y dia octauo. Con todas las coſas que
è nellas ſe ſuele dezir en Caſa y en
la yſnogua.

Stampada por induſtria, y deſpeza de
Yshac Franco, à 4 de Adar ve Adar.
5372.

FIGURE 16
The *Segunda parte del Sedur* was printed in 1612 by Isaac Franco, and is an example of the Jewish books being printed in Amsterdam around the time Grotius wrote his *Remonstrantie*.

> guilders at the second, 200 guilders at the third, and a penalty to be imposed by the judge thereafter.[111]

Although this regulation in itself does not seem particularly surprising, when one supposes that it is directed at outspoken anti-Christian polemic texts, Grotius seems to have had a less restricted definition of blasphemous texts:

> Jurisprudence allows Jews to read the Holy Writ of the Old Testament, both in the original language and in translation. They are forbidden the use of the Talmud, which contains numerous blasphemies against Christians; similarly the Talmud was also burnt by the popes of Rome. Nov. 146 and Hostiensis, Commentaria to X 3.34.8.[112]

111 See pp. 113–115 and 206.

112 See pp. 151 and 211.

The *Novella* quoted here by Grotius bears the title *That it be allowed to Jews to read the Holy Scripture in Greek and Latin and any other language* [...].[113] The text is too lengthy to quote in full, but is very strict on the use of the Bible. Emperor Justinian allows Jews to read and teach the text of the Bible, without using or adding any commentary. There is no mention of the Talmud, which is not surprising as the law dates from 553 CE, and the redaction of the (Babylonian) Talmud is generally assumed to have been around 700 CE. However, Grotius clearly interpreted the *No permission is given to the interpreters among them, who use only the Hebrew language, to corrupt it as they wish, covering up their badness through the ignorance of the many* as referring to the Talmudic text.[114] Nothing is said about other Jewish texts, such as the *midrashim*, philosophical and mystical works.

The references to the canonical law are curious, for the text of Innocence IV only mentions the burning of the Talmud as an example that the Pope holds jurisdiction over all people, Jews included:

> In the same way, the Pope can judge the Jews if they act contrary to law of the Gospel in their moral behaviour, if their own religious leaders do not punish them. And also, if they invent heresies relating to their law and it was on this ground that Gregorius and Innocentius ordered the burning of these books, which contain many heresies and they ordered that those who followed or taught these heresies be punished.[115]

113 'Ut liceat Hebraeis secundum traditionem legere sacras scripturas latine vel graece vel alia lingua [...]'

114 'et non fiduciam esse his qui apud eos sunt expositoribus solam Hebraicam tradentibus malignari hanc, quemadmodum voluerint, multorum ignorantia suam eis abscondentes malam consuetudinem.' *Nov.* 146.

115 'Item iudeos potest iudicare papa si contra legem evangelii faciunt in moralibus si eorum prelati eos non puniant. Et eodem more si hereses circa suam legem inveniant et hac ratione motus Greg. et Inno. mandaverunt comburi libros talium in quo multae obtinebantur hereses et mandaverunt puniri illos qui predictas hereses sequerentur vel docerent.' Innocentius IV, *Apparatus*, 164v.

The interpretation of this article remains ambiguous, as on the one hand it can be argued that Grotius has founded this article firmly within the confines of the Roman Law, by clearly relating his text to Justinian's *Novella*, but on the other hand he stands firmly in the medieval tradition of the condemnation of the Talmud as a hostile text and actually explicitly approves the orders issued by the Roman Catholic Popes to burn the Talmud.

However, the most curious article in Grotius's commentary is actually the first. It explains the first regulation, which reads:

> That all Jews of the nation and the religion, who are now in this country or will come later, shall declare their names one by one within eight days of the publication [of these decrees—DK] or after their arrival to the Magistrate of the residence; for parents however it will suffice that they submit the names of their younger children, under 14 years old. All this subject to a penalty of 50 guilders.[116]

In itself this rule quite straightforward—if a government wants to implement regulations that include quota, it is necessary to keep track of the new immigrants. According to Grotius, the reason for this rule lies in the following:

> Registering names is very useful to monitor people of a different religion. Here is an example from Livy, 4th Decade, Book 9, which deals with the cult of Bacchus. If any person considered such worship to be ordained by tradition or to be necessary, and believed that he could not omit it without sin and atonement, he was to make a declaration before the city praetor.[117]

This is in itself still comprehensible and Meijer rightly notes:

116 See pp. 101 and 205.

117 See pp. 141–143 and 210.

> Grotius considers the Bacchus-cult in Rome analogous with the position of the Jews in the Netherlands. At least as far as the Bacchus-cult as well can be seen as a community that in closed community could constitute a danger to the state. The parallelization characterizes the humanist.[118]

However, it is the context of this sentence that casts this explanation of the first regulation in a completely different light. For the Bacchus-cult that Grotius is referring to here has a very negative connotation. The story is told by Livy in Book 39, chapters 8–19 and relates how a fake cult was introduced in Italy, 'by an ignoble Greek, coming first to Etruria, […] a priest of occult and nocturnal rites'.[119] This must have happened somewhere around 188 BCE, for in 186 the consul Sp. Postumius Albinus learned from questioning that the cult had been introduced two years before. At that time, the new cult had attracted several thousands of initiates, who committed criminal and illicit acts of every kind.[120] Before the consul starts the inquisition and persecution of the adherents, he makes a public speech in which he vividly describes how the cult has secretly spread to such an extent that it can only be contained by public force. The people should not be disturbed by a public campaign against a cult, not even from denouncing the names of citizens who were followers, for the Roman religion cleansed them from any religious guilt:

> Nothing is more deceptive in appearance than a false religion. When the authority of the gods is put forward as a defence for crime, there steals upon the mind a fear lest in punishing human misdeeds we may violate something of divine law which became mixed up with them. From this scruple, innumerable edicts of the pontiff, decrees of the senate, and finally responses of the haruspices free you. How often, in the times of our fathers and our grandfathers, has the task been assigned to the magistrates of forbidding the introduction of foreign cults, of excluding

118 'Grotius beschouwt de dienst van Bacchus te Rome analoog met de positie der Joden in Nederland. Voorzover althans ook bij de Bacchus-dienst sprake is van een gemeenschap, die in nauwer groepsverband een gevaar zou kunnen worden voor de staat. De parallellisering is kenmerkend voor een humanist.' Groot, *Remonstrantie*, 122, n. 7.

119 'Graecus ignobilis in Etruriam primum venit, […] occultorum et nocturnorum antistes sacrorum.' Livius, *Ab urbe condita*, para. XXXIX.8.3. For an interesting introduction and an extensive bibliography about these *Bacchanalia* in Livy's text, see Briscoe, *A Commentary on Livy*, 230–250.

120 'There were initiatory rites which at first were imparted to a few, then began to be generally known among men and women. To the religious element in them were added the delights of wine and feasts, that the minds of a larger number might be attracted. When wine had inflamed their minds, and night and the mingling of males with females, youth with age, had destroyed every sentiment of modesty, all varieties of corruption first began to be practised, since each one had at hand the pleasure answering to that to which his nature was more inclined. There was not one form of vice alone, the promiscuous matings of free men and women, but perjured witnesses, forged seals and wills and evidence, all issued from this same workshop: likewise poisonings and secret murders, so that at times not even the bodies were found for burial. Much was ventured by craft, more by violence. This violence was concealed because amid the howlings and the crash of drums and cymbals no cry of the sufferers could be heard as the debauchery and murders proceeded.' Livy, *History of Rome, Volume XI*, 241–243. 'Initia erant quae primo paucis tradita sunt, deinde uolgari coepta per uiros mulieresque. Additae uoluptates religioni uini et epularum, quo plurium animi inlicerentur; cum uinum animos ⟨movisset⟩ et nox et mixti feminis mares, aetatis tenerae maioribus, discrimen omne pudoris exstinxissent, corruptelae primum omnis generis fieri coeptae, cum ad id quisque, quo natura pronioris libidinis esset paratam uoluptatem haberet. Nec unum genus noxae stupra promiscua ingenuorum feminarumque erant, sed falsi testes, falsa signa testamentaque et indicia ex eadem officina exibant, uenena indidem intestinaeque caedes, ita ut ne corpora quidem interdum ad sepulturam exstarent. Multa dolo, pleraque per uim audebantur; occulebat uim quod prae ululatibus tympanorumque et cymbalorum strepitu nulla uox quiritantium inter stupra et caedes exaudiri poterat.' Livius, *Ab urbe condita*, para. XXXIX.8.5–8.

> dabblers in sacrifices and fortune tellers from the Forum, the Circus, and the City, of searching out and burning books of prophecies, and of annulling every system of sacrifice except that performed in the Roman way. For men, wisest in all divine and human law used to judge that nothing was so potent in destroying religion as where sacrifices were performed, not by native but by foreign ritual.[121]

The episode ends with the rounding up of all enthusiasts, and the execution of most of them. Only a few ancient altars were allowed to remain and only a few were allowed to celebrate the cult of Bacchus. Those who felt they had to fulfil an obligation in this regard were required to register with Praetor Urbanus, which is Grotius's cue.

It may be assumed that Grotius was well aware of the context of his citation. The context gives a strange view of his perception of Jews and the place of a new religion in Dutch society. The first thing that is remarkable, is that for his regulation Grotius again refers to a Roman rule, this time not a law from the Christian Roman Emperors, but from the Roman Senate in 186 BCE. If Livy's text is not sufficient proof of the existence of such a text, the same text was found in an inscription on bronze in Calabria in 1640, and features a number of *senatus consulta* regarding the Bacchanalia.[122] But Livy's text was probably sufficiently reliable for Grotius's taste.

What triggered the comparison is presumably the introduction of a new religion.[123] But from there it is hard to imagine how Grotius saw the comparison between the immigrant merchants and the Bacchic enthusiasts. The context suggests that Grotius saw the new immigrants as a potentially dangerous group who could be dangerous for the moral standards of the Republic and could pose some serious danger for the state by illegal activities. The registration of names, which seemed straightforward in a policy that focused on regulating the quota of immigrants, has a completely different function in Livy's text: the prosecutors needed the names of the followers of the Bacchic cult in order to trace them and arrest them. When the few allowed followers later needed to sign up, it was again to keep the cult under very close surveillance.

This bleak view is underscored by the citation from the consul's speech. It is of course debatable whether or not Grotius had this part of the relatively long episode in his mind, but it is interesting to see that much of it fits in very well with Grotius's views on Church and state. The idea that only one religion should be allowed dovetails with Grotius's idea of a Church encompassing all Christianity and uniting against foreign religions, such Judaism and Islam. The seeking out and burning of heretical texts can easily be read as second approbation of the burnings of the Talmud.

In conclusion, it may be said that the third part of the *Remonstrantie*, Grotius's justification of his regulations, is remarkably consistent in its methods of presentation and argumentation. Grotius, true to his humanist *Bildung*, refers as much as he can to classical sources. It is easy to understand why the *Corpus Iuris Civilis* is his most inten-

121 Livy, *History of Rome, Volume XI*, 265. 'Nihil enim in speciem fallacius est quam praua religio. Vbi deorum numen praetenditur sceleribus, subit animum timor ne fraudibus humanis uindicandis diuini iuris aliquid inmixtum uiolemus. Hac uos religione innumerabilia decreta pontificum, senatus consulta, haruspicum denique responsa liberant. Quotiens hoc patrum auorumque aetate magistratibus negotium est datum uti sacra externa fieri uetarent, sacrificulos uatesque foro circo urbe prohiberent, uaticinos libros conquirerent comburerentque, omnem disciplinam sacrificandi praeterquam more Romano abolerent! Iudicabunt enim prudentissimi uiri omnis diuini humanique iuris nihil aeque dissoluendae religionis esse quam ubi non patrio sed externo ritu sacrificaretur.' Livius, *Ab urbe condita*, para. XXXIX.16.6–9. [Sage reads 'iudicabant' instead of 'iudicabunt', as does Welsh.]

122 Briscoe, *A Commentary on Livy*, 233.

123 I cannot help wondering whether Grotius was thinking of Euripides' *Bacchae*, which also tells of the introduction of a new religion, but with a completely different ending for enthusiasts and persecutors!

sively used source in his commentary. Firstly, the *Codex* has a comprehensive set of regulations in one chapter. Secondly, the source fitted well as an antique point of reference, even if it was assembled in the fifth century, for the *Corpus* was a collection of older Roman rulings. What was most convenient, however, is that most (if not all) of the regulations in the *Codex* were written by Christian emperors. They provided Grotius with a set of rules that he could use very well without having to fear religious inconsistencies. Finally, it should not be forgotten that Roman Law was still applicable in cases where no contemporary rulings, the so-called *ius proprium*, existed.[124]

5 Tolerance and the *Remonstrantie*

If there is one thing the Dutch presently take pride in, it is their supposed tolerance of different lifestyles and religions. This supposed national characteristic is usually seen as a result of the Spanish oppression and the following Revolt. As we have experienced oppression ourselves and have had to struggle for our freedom of conscience, we know how important freedom of conscience is for others, or so the argument generally goes. However, the validity of tolerance as a national characteristic has come under some strain, both presently in the public sphere and historically in a more academic atmosphere.[125] Although the concept of tolerance in the present-day public sphere lies beyond the scope of this work, the *Remonstrantie* provides an interesting touchstone for comparing competing views on tolerance in the early Dutch 17th century.

A positive view of tolerance in the Dutch Republic is expressed by Frijhoff. According to him, Dutch tolerance evolved gradually from an aversion to an oppressing Roman Catholic Church and a centralizing Habsburg Empire to a decentralized Republic, where power was relegated to the provinces and from there to the towns. According to Frijhoff, it was partly due to the adherence of the magistrates to decentralized bases of power that a strong centralized Church was unable to rise. The towns had replaced the Church as units of identification, creating their own myths, heroes and rituals.[126] Thus it was possible for citizens of various Christian denominations to coexist more or less peacefully. This was a necessary step, for by no means all citizens of the Northern Netherlands had become enthusiastic followers of either the Dutch Reformed Church or Protestantism in general. There was no sufficient base to establish the Dutch Reformed Church as a single official Church that could unite all citizens. Toleration in this context meant the primacy of the Dutch Reformed Church in the public domain with freedom of conscience in the domestic sphere (within certain limits), and legislative and executive power in the hands of the magistrates.[127]

124 I thank Prof. Dr Marc de Wilde for bringing this aspect of the *Corpus Iuris Civilis* to my attention.

125 A concise overview of the development of this idea of 'Dutch tolerance' can be found in Kaplan, "'Dutch' Religious Tolerance: Celebration and Revision".

126 'The desire for a single Church encompassing all the people was transferred to the secular community which had to be closely knit. By stripping the urban (and rural) landscape of its religious elements, the town itself, in its role as body politic, became the new sacred community, with its own history, its legends, and its symbolism and ritual which ensured a civic peace that went beyond differences of convictions.' And: 'It is the combination of both these characteristics that made the United Provinces unique: a tacit toleration of religious diversity that was allowed to flourish as long as necessary concord between the believers did not endanger the unity of the body politic and the civic community. Rather than the concept of unity it is, effectively, that of *concordia*, which was at the center of the religious policy of the United Provinces; [...]. It is this pragmatic concept of toleration that provides the supranational political foundation of a socio-religious practice of toleration, already well established in the United Provinces [...]'. Frijhoff, "Religious Toleration in the United Provinces", 31–32.

127 Along the same line of thought: Mout, "A Comparative View of Dutch Toleration", 45–46. and Tracy, "Erasmus, Coornhert and the Acceptance of Religious Disunity in the Body Politic: A Low Countries Tradition?", 60–62.

Jonathan Israel questions the tolerance in the Dutch Republic. There certainly were influential advocates of tolerance, the words of whom were and are regularly cited, but it is questionable to what extent they reflected a majority view. The first example is William of Orange, who strongly advocated freedom of religious practice. Although, according to Israel, Orange's idealism stemmed from a practical need to unite adherents of different denominations, he was also influenced by contemporary thinkers such as Sebastian Castellio.[128] This plea for tolerance was most famously and radically voiced by Dirck Volkerszoon Coornhert. However, according to Israel, the majority of Dutch and political leadership felt more at ease with the views of Justus Lipsius and Simon Stevin, both of whom advocated unity and uniformity for the sake of a strong coherent republic.[129]

It is not easy to assess the particular tolerance of the *Remonstrantie* in its time. However, we can compare Grotius's text with the other contemporary local charters, which will reveal its peculiarity on this scale of tolerance. Although it would be very interesting to compare this charter with many others, only a few will be adduced here. Naturally we will compare the text of Grotius with the other charters negotiated by the Portuguese merchants in the Dutch Republic, namely those of Alkmaar, Haarlem and Rotterdam. The most remarkable charter is that of Alkmaar in 1604, for it allowed for complete freedom to all Jewish immigrants, whether Portuguese or not. The only discriminatory rule was that Jews were not allowed to partake in the city guard and had to pay an additional tax instead. The fact that this charter did not result in an overwhelming rise in immigration, suggests that religious freedom was an important, but not the only argument for migration.

5.1 *The Haarlem Charter*

The second charter, that of Haarlem in 1605, is much longer and more detailed—the Alkmaar Charter is in fact only one long sentence. The Haarlem Charter was exclusively made for the Portuguese merchants, and actually only for a very specific group of these: *oriental* and *occidental* Hebrews or Jews, who live and profess the Jewish religion in Italy and in several places in Turkey.[130] It may well be that *occidental Jews* refers to the

128 'For William not only evinced a powerful aversion to religious persecution and preference for religious freedom, but actively sought to introduce political and legal guarantees, based in part on recent German and French precedents for freedom of religious practice at least for the main established churches, the Catholic and Lutheran, as well as the Reformed. His was an unabashedly *politique* stance, rooted in his assessment of the international and local political realities with which he had to cope. But it was certainly not without an intellectual component. In his political propaganda, Orange made use of the writings of Sebastian Castellio and other recent advocates of "religious peace". [...] The freedom of religious practice urged by Orange and some others seemed too radical and too risky, to city governments, concerned above all with minimizing the disruptive consequences of the bitter political and religious divisions in society and restoring a semblance of political, religious and social stability.' Israel, "The Intellectual Debate about Toleration in the Dutch Republic", 4.

129 'It is evident then that the dominant view among the Dutch political and academic leadership at the close of the sixteenth century, with regard to toleration approximated much more to that of Justus Lipsius than it did to the passionate plea for freedom of religious practice, and of expression, of Coornhert. Lipsius assigned a very high value to freedom of conscience, and freedom of thought, and was fully aware that these were indispensable assets not least for the humanist scholar such as himself. But the freedom which Lipsius was anxious to protect was essentially a private matter, an inward freedom detached from any right to freedom of outward expression. [...] Because, in his view, there could be no freedom for the individual without the restoration of stability and order, Lipsius rejected toleration on principle, seeing it as incompatible with the political and institutional uniformity which he considered vital if the new kind of (preferably monarchial) state which he wished to see was to succeed its task. No contemporary thinker reflected better than Lipsius the tension, even contradiction, in the contemporary context, between liberty of conscience and full toleration.' Israel, 6–7.

130 '[...] van wegen die van de Portugeesche ende Spaensche Natie, afcompstich van den Orientaelsche ende Westersche Hebreen ofte Joden, woonende ende professie doende van de Hebreeusche religie in Ital-

Hebrew word *Sephardim* and *occidental Jews* is a translation of *Ponentine Jews*, the specific term in Venice for Jews and New Christians who had fled from the Iberian Peninsula. In Venice, the Levantine Jews (from the Middle East), the Ponentine Jews and the long-time settled so-called German Jews, *Tedeschi*, lived uncomfortably together in the Venetian ghettos. The Levantine and Ponentine Jews, however, had been very successful in establishing a trade route from Constantinople via Split to Venice.[131] Apparently, the representatives of the Amsterdam Portuguese merchants offer the city of Haarlem a piece of this Venetian cake, or at least in the trade from the Middle and Far East via Constantinople and Italy, for Venice is not mentioned explicitly.

Both the Haarlem Charter and Grotius's text deal firstly with the relation between immigrants and the city administration—new immigrants are to be registered. The city of Haarlem asks for letters of recommendation from the Jewish communities from which the new immigrants are departing. On the other hand, the *Remonstrantie* explicitly states that the registration should be completed within eight days and adds a fine for failing to comply with this rule. The Haarlem text then immediately proceeds with the religious freedom—the Portuguese merchants are allowed to have synagogue and a burial site, they can keep the Sabbath and all Jewish holidays, and if they are obstructed or insulted or maltreated, then the perpetrator(s) will be prosecuted. They are free to dress as they please, they can hire Christian maids and midwives, as long as no carnal relations evolve and no Christians are induced to adopt the Jewish faith. They also can have a kosher butcher and are free to bring and print books in Hebrew or any other language, as long as they contain no blasphemies against Christianity.

All these points can be found in the *Remonstrantie* as well, with the conspicuous difference being the allowing of a synagogue. Grotius would only allow for one, two or three *private* houses in the towns in which Jews were allowed to live, where they could meet for religious purposes. To this point, however, the City Council of Haarlem had added the condition that it would only be effected if 50 families had come to live in Haarlem:

> All these freedoms can be enjoyed immediately upon arrival at Haarlem by the members of the aforementioned nation, except the use of a public synagogue and the open and free practice of their religion, which will be enjoyed only when 100, 80, 60 or at least 50 respectable families, being persons of a certain esteem and wealth, have come to live within the city of Haarlem and have taken their Domicilium, permanent housing and residence there.[132]

The Haarlem Charter clearly defines the jurisdictional borders—the new immigrants are subject to all regular laws, customs and regulations as any other citizen of Haarlem. They are also subject to the same taxes as other citizens. Disputes between Jews and Christians are to be settled in the sheriffs' courtroom. Conflicts between Jews are to be settled by the *parnassim* and *mamonim* (i.e. the synagogue board). The verdict of the *parnassim* and *mamonim* is to be brought to the sheriffs' courtroom and will be confirmed there as if it had been decided by the sheriffs' courtroom. If one of the conflicting parties does not agree with the verdict of the *parnassim* and *mamonim*, he may bring the

iën ende verscheyden plaetsen van Turkuye.' Wolff, *Geschiedenis der joden te Haarlem*, 57; Groot, *Remonstrantie*, 40.

131 Ravid, "The Third Charter of the Jewish Merchants of Venice, 1611".

132 'Alle welcke vrijdommen die van de voors. natie terstont zullen genyeten tot Haerlem comende, uijtgesondert het gebruyck van heure publycke Synagoge ende open ende vrije exercitie van heure religie, twelcke zij eer nyet zullen genyeten dan als hondert, tachtig, tsestich, ofte ten minsten vijftich treffelijcke van heure familien, wesende luyden van sorte, aensien ende van vermogen binnen Haerlem metter woon gecomen zullen zijn ende haere Domicilium vaste woninge ende residentie aldaer genomen zullen hebben.' Wolff, *Geschiedenis der joden te Haarlem*.

case in the sheriffs' courtroom. Religious matters are only decided by the *parnassim* and *mamonim*, and they may excommunicate members if that is deemed necessary. Grotius, following Roman Law, does not recognize a Jewish court. He does not speak of *parnassim* and *mamonim*, but leaves the excommunication of unruly members in the hands of 'their teachers, or others appointed by them for this task'. Internal conflicts between Jews may be settled by Jews who have been appointed as arbiters.[133]

The most interesting part of this comparison, however, is the fact that two documents with a comparable set of rulings are at the same time two completely different textual artefacts. For the Haarlem Charter, although most rules are comparable to Grotius's text, is clearly the result of a dialogue. This can be concluded not only from the fact that we know that the Portuguese petitioners had objected to the first draft, but all the more from the text itself. This can be concluded *i.a.* from the terminology used, e.g. the clear definition of the group for whom this charter is meant (the Levantine and Ponentine Jews), the use of the terms *parnassim* and *mamonim* for the synagogue board. It is, however, even more evident from the rules that regulate contact and relations between Jews and Christians. Whereas Grotius only sets rules for Jews having sexual relations with Christians and for Jews inducing Christians to convert to Judaism, the Haarlem Charter treats both directions—equal punishment is set for Jewish men seducing Christian women and vice versa. Likewise, Jews are forbidden to circumcise Christians, and Christians are not allowed to baptize Jews against their will, on pain of equal fines. Grotius's text shows no sign of negotiation with the objects of his rulings.[134] It is a text largely based on existing rulings from Roman Law and, of course, it is known that Grotius used the Haarlem Charter. It is remarkable that Grotius dismissed some of the favourable rulings for Jews, which could easily have been granted, for example those quoted here on Jewish-Christian relations. By contrast, Grotius elaborates on rulings that protect Christianity from blasphemy as well as on rules that protect baptized Jews.

These differences lead to the question of whether the *Remonstrantie* is only Grotius's work, or the result of his cooperation with Adriaen Pauw. For both Grotius and Pauw had been ordered to write a document regulating Jewish life in the Northern Netherlands. The choice of these two men is understandable—Pauw was a protagonist of the Counter-Remonstrants and Grotius of the Remonstrants. By naming these two champions the States hoped to obtain a result that would be acceptable to all parties. Besides, Pauw and Grotius were Pensionaries of Amsterdam and Rotterdam respectively, two cities that had been making regulations for Jewish settlement. It is generally assumed that Pauw's text either was never submitted or has been lost.[135] However, Grotius's text emphasizes Christian concerns to a greater extent than would be expected. This can be explained partly (as was

133 'De Joden zullen bij haere Leeraeren, ofte anderen by hemluijden daer toegestelt, ter saecke van quaed leven ofte quaede leere mogen werden geexcommuniceert, ofte afgesneden van haere vergaderinge; midts dat de gene dije hem zoude willen beclaeghen t' onrechte geexcommuniceert te zijn, t' zelve zal doen voor den Magistraet van de plaetze, dije daer van kennisse sall nemen ende wijsen nae de Wetten begrepen in t' Oude Testament.' And: 'De Joden sullen oock tusschen de Joden genomen mogen werden tot arbiters, midts dat van haer arbitraige sall moghen werden geprovoceert bij maniere van reductie, gelijck van het arbitragie van anderen'.

134 Though there is an anonymous letter from a Portuguese Jew, addressed to the States of Holland and West Frisia, which pleads for generous and fair treatment. It is, however, unclear when the letter was written and by whom. It was sold in the auction of Grotius's legacy in 1864, which makes it probable that it was in Grotius's possession either when he wrote the *Remonstrantie* or received it as a reaction to his text. The letter, written in Portuguese and Dutch, can be found in the Bibliotheca Rosenthaliana, in the Special Collections of the Amsterdam University Library, MS Ros. 350/1. The Dutch version is printed and discussed in Groot, *Remonstrantie* 98–101; 141–143.

135 Alexander ten Haven assumes that the Keur of Amsterdam is actually the text of Pauw; see no. 59.

done in Chapter 2) by Grotius's extensive use of the Roman Code of Civil Law, which was composed by, or ordered by, Roman Christian emperors whose concerns were primarily Christian. Nonetheless, these pronounced concerns may also imply that Grotius either had adapted his text to make it more acceptable to Pauw's faction of orthodox Calvinists, or that this text is the result of Grotius incorporating Pauw's critique on an earlier version.

5.2 *The Rotterdam Charter*

A comparison of the *Remonstrantie* with the Rotterdam Charter of 1610 can only lead to the conclusion that the Rotterdam Charter was the best possible outcome, allowing almost the same liberties as Alkmaar. The charter was directed specifically at the Portuguese merchants, clearly stating in the first sentence that they were admitted to the city for the advancement of commerce.[136] The merchants were allowed to settle, to practise their religion and buy land for a cemetery. If more than 30 families were to settle, then they would be allowed to build or buy a house to use for religious purposes, as long as they would refrain from proselytizing. The most conspicuous ruling is that the merchants were allowed to elect a board of two or more consuls, who were to rule the community of Portuguese merchants.[137] In this aspect, the Rotterdam Charter radically differs from the other contemporary charters in Holland and it clearly exhibits a different vision on the position of the Portuguese Jews in the Dutch Republic than Grotius had. This becomes especially apparent in the terms the Rotterdam Charter uses, as *consul* and *natie* (nation). The Rotterdam Charter describes the relationship between the merchants and the city as mutually beneficent contact. The Portuguese Jews are strangers who apparently feel no need to become anything other than strangers and both parties prefer a situation where the Portuguese merchants took care of themselves and settled their differences among themselves, hence the consuls were to be installed. Only if differences were not able to be settled within the community would recourse to the regular courts be permissible. The Rotterdam Charter makes no single reference to religion or to relations between Christians and Jews, or to what Jews are allowed to say or to read or to print.

This is diametrically opposed to Grotius's view on the position of Jews in the Netherlands. Grotius explicitly did not want the Jewish community to form a republic within the Republic. The new immigrants were to become normal citizens, who fell under normal jurisdiction. We do not know

136 '… dat wij tot vordering van de trafique ende negotiatie binnen desen Stadt dienstich vinden de coopluyden van de Poortugaelsche natie met eenige privilegien ende vrijheden te inviteren omme binnen de voorschreven stede te coomen resideren …' ('… that we saw it as right to invite the merchants of the Portuguese nation with certain privileges and concessions to come and reside in the aforementioned city …'). Groot, *Remonstrantie*, 45.

137 'Consenteren ende vergunnen noch de selven coopluyden, dat sij uut haere natie ende voor de selfde sullen mogen verkiesen twee ofte meer consuls ofte hoofden ende daartoe een poertier ende ander officier. Ende sullen de selfde consuls alle civile questien onder den voorschreven natie onderling ofte alleen vallende mogen accorderen ende met haere uutspraeck beslichten soot doenlijk is, soo niet sullen partien de selfde mogen brengen voor de gerechte der voorschreven stede om aldaer beslecht te werden naer behooren. Ende soo de voorschreven consuls over de ongehoorsaemheyt van eenige van haere natie aen de Regierders der voorschreven stede claechde, sullen de ongehoorsamen naer voorgaende behoorlijcke informatie bij de gerechte der selver stede naer exigentie van haere inobedientie ofte ander misdaet worden gecorrigeert ende gestraft.' ('The aforementioned merchants may choose from their midst two or more consuls or heads and further a porter and an additional officer. The said consuls may decide on all internal civil cases of the aforementioned nation insofar as they are sufficiently competent to do so; if not, the parties will defer the case to the court of the aforementioned town, to be properly judged there. If the aforementioned consuls file a complaint regarding the insubordination of anyone of their nation with the governors of the aforementioned town, the disobedient will be punished and corrected after thorough investigation by the court of the aforementioned town in accordance with their disobedience or other crime.') Groot, 45.

what Grotius's internal motivations were, but for the purposes of his argumentation he uses references to Roman Law. The fact that Grotius wants to proceed a step further on the path of integration could seem to be a form of advancement, of an emancipation of Jews in society. However, this integration means a significant diminishment of autonomy of the communal organization and de facto constitutes closer surveillance of the internal dynamics of the Jewish community.

It may be worthwhile taking a moment to reflect on what the consequences of both rulings could have meant. It could very well be that the Rotterdam Charter was again the result of extensive negotiations between the City Council and representatives of the Portuguese Jews. It is an ideal construction for strangers, who are used to taking care of themselves and have access to sufficient organizational resources to take care of their lives and the lives of their families. The Portuguese, who had managed to survive inquisitions and expulsions and yet had managed to maintain their trades and their networks, were self-sufficient and would probably be able to agree wholeheartedly to the Rotterdam Charter. From the point of view of communal preservation, the Rotterdam Charter provides maximum freedom. From a certain point of view, it even provides a maximum degree of tolerance—all parties leave each other be and only practical boundaries are set.

By contrast, Grotius almost denies the existence of communal independence. His regulation greatly diminishes the traditional forms of Jewish self-government within the Jewish communities. However, for those members of the Jewish communities who did not want to be ruled by a government in a republic within a Republic, Grotius's rulings offer more perspective. From the point of view of personal freedom, Grotius offers an easier escape for all those who did not want to be ruled by communal boards. Again, we do not know what Grotius's motivations were. In the context of the *Remonstrantie*, it seems as if Grotius wanted to diminish the influence of the Jewish boards in order to facilitate an easy conversion for Jews. This view can be underscored by his introduction to the *Remonstrantie*, where he clearly speaks about the advantages of Jews living together with Christians within a Christian society, namely that they may more readily convert. It can also be proven by some regulations of the *Remonstrantie*, which are intended to strengthen the position of those newly converted to Christianity.[138] On the other hand, these regulations that diminish the influence of communal structures fit well in Grotius's views on religious and secular power. During the conflict between the Remonstrants and the Counter-Remonstrants in the Dutch Republic, he consequently advocated a broad national Church, which would encompass all Christians in the said Republic and which was ultimately ruled by the secular powers of the Republic, not unlike the situation in the Church of England.[139] Grotius was clearly weary of strongly independent ecclesiastical boards. However, as was said earlier, it may also very well be that Grotius simply preferred the Roman Civil Code.

Finally, it is time to discuss the most difficult part of the *Remonstrantie*, the introduction. The aim of the introduction is, as Grotius writes, to discuss whether Jews should be allowed in Holland and West Frisia at all; and if they are to be allowed, whether they should be granted freedom to exercise religion; and if that is to be granted, how adverse influence on the Christian society can be prevented. The question of whether Jews should be allowed in Holland and West Frisia is not treated lightly in this introduction. According to Grotius, there is no question that Jews hate Christians and that they gladly hurt them when they can. Grotius cites proof for this thesis from numerous sources, from antiquity to his own days. And although he is prepared to admit that not all these cases have been properly investigated, the overwhelming quantity of evidence leaves no other

138 Namely the articles 34–37.

139 Nellen, "Een tweespan voor de arminiaanse wagen: Grotius en Wtenbogaert", 175–176.

conclusion than that there must some truth in it. Hence the question naturally is: why admit Jews at all?

Grotius answers this question with some remarkable arguments. Firstly, it happens from time to time that Jews convert to Christianity. This is a process that should be encouraged. But how are they to be converted if they don't live between Christians? And they should of course be converted to the right brand of Christianity, which happens to be exercised in the Low Countries; hence it is necessary that Jews are allowed here. Secondly, it is written in Holy Scripture that at the end of times, all Jews shall convert to Christianity. Again, there must be Jews living among Christians then to make that event come about. And possibly the Dutch Protestants could even advance this process a little by demonstrating to the Jews how good Christians live and act. For until now, Jews have mostly been exposed to the idolatry of the papists, hence it is hardly surprising, and even laudable, that so few of them have embraced Christianity. Grotius adds that it is probably the case that not all measures taken by Christian rulers have been helpful in giving the Jews a positive impression of Christianity and the Christians. Thirdly, Jewish settlement can be useful for scholars to learn Hebrew. And last but not least, the settlement of Jews among Christians may offer the Christians a good example of perseverance, for how long have the Jews been resisting conversion?[140]

After establishing that Jews are to be allowed in Holland and West Frisia, the second question follows more or less automatically. For being Jewish is, in Grotius's view, already one step in the right direction, on the scale from godlessness to righteousness. Forcing Jews to stop exercising religion, would move them one step down on this scale. And the only way up on this scale is converting to Protestantism. However, the Dutch Protestants are very outspoken that conversion cannot be forced, but has to be reached by conviction. This means that, as long as they resist baptism, they can best follow their own religion. Grotius is not afraid of detrimental effects on the Christian population, as he is of the opinion that the majority would sooner be misled by Christian sects and heresies than by an altogether different religion. Grotius ends the introduction with the third question: now that we have decided that Jews can reside here and are allowed to exercise their religion, how do we prevent any harm coming to our state or to the Christians living here? That is why a set of regulations has been drawn up, so they may experience our Christian benevolence … *Selah*.

It is this part of the *Remonstrantie* that is usually read and quoted as evidence for Grotius's opinion on Jews.[141] Marc de Wilde has recently ventured the interesting theory that this introduction does not represent Grotius's own convictions, but serves to provide building blocks in a legal defence, by first summing up all the possible objections and ending with the preferable alternative.[142] In conclusion, the observation may be added that the *Remonstrantie* has been introduced here as a cultural crossroads. The intersecting roads that were mentioned were the Portuguese merchants and the Dutch humanist tradition. Another intersection is that of the humanist tradition with the

140 In fact, Grotius also refers to natural law, that the banished should be received willingly. This point is discussed in detail in Wilde, "Offering Hospitality".

141 'Hugo Grotius erhielt im Jahre 1615 von den Staaten von Holland den Auftrag, ein Gutachten über die rechtliche Stellung der portugiesischen Juden zu verfassen. Er nutzte die Gelegenheit zu einer grundsätzlichen Debatte über die Rolle der Juden in der christlichen Gesellschaft, die auch die theologischen Aspekte ausdrücklich mit einbezog. Aus heutiger Sicht erscheinen mehrere seiner Aussagen als widersprüchlich. Für Grotius selber bestand dieser Widerspruch jedoch nicht. Die Juden seien zwar die Feinde der Christen, aber die Hoffnung auf ihre Bekehrung dürfte man nicht aufgeben. […] Die suggestiven Bemerkungen des Hugo Grotius über das Thema des Ritualmordes haben in der Literatur Bestürzung ausgelöst. Deuten sie tatsächlich auf ein antijüdisches Ressentiment des großen Gelehrten hin?' Peterse, "Hugo Grotius und sein Gutachten über die rechtliche Stellung der in Holland (1615)", 232.

142 Wilde, "Offering Hospitality".

social, political and economic reality of the 1610s. The urban elite, to which Grotius belonged, had much to gain from the intensivization of overseas trade. It is hard to imagine that this document was not drafted with the interests of a mercantile elite in mind. By contrast, it is highly conceivable that representatives of this mercantile elite would have lobbied for settlement of the Portuguese merchants. On the other hand, as an important exponent of the humanist discourse, Grotius had certainly absorbed all opinions on Jews both from classical antiquity and the early Church, none of them favourable. Finally, the option should not be ruled out that Grotius adapted his text to make it more acceptable in orthodox Calvinist eyes.

There is no solution to the question of Grotius's real opinion. Nonetheless, it is highly possible to regard the *Remonstrantie* as a piece of cultural evidence of the second decade of the 17th century. Stephen Greenblatt has emphasized on various occasions the importance of valuing any scrap of evidence of a certain era. It is impossible to make complete historical descriptions and we cannot know what people think or thought, but we can regard historical (in Greenblatt's case especially: literary) artefacts as phenomena that reflect, as it were, the cultural dynamics of a certain time. This undoubtedly incomplete analysis of the *Remonstrantie* has shown how it can be regarded as such an artefact, offering a prismaic view of social and cultural tendencies and crossroads of the beginning of the 17th century in the Dutch Republic, which combined pragmatic mercantilism with dominant Calvinism and profound humanist learning.[143]

143 Greenblatt, *Renaissance Self-Fashioning*, chap. Introduction.

CHAPTER 2

Facsimile of the Original Text with Transliteration and Modern Dutch Translation

Transliteration by Adri K. Offenberg
Translation by Marijke J. Blankman

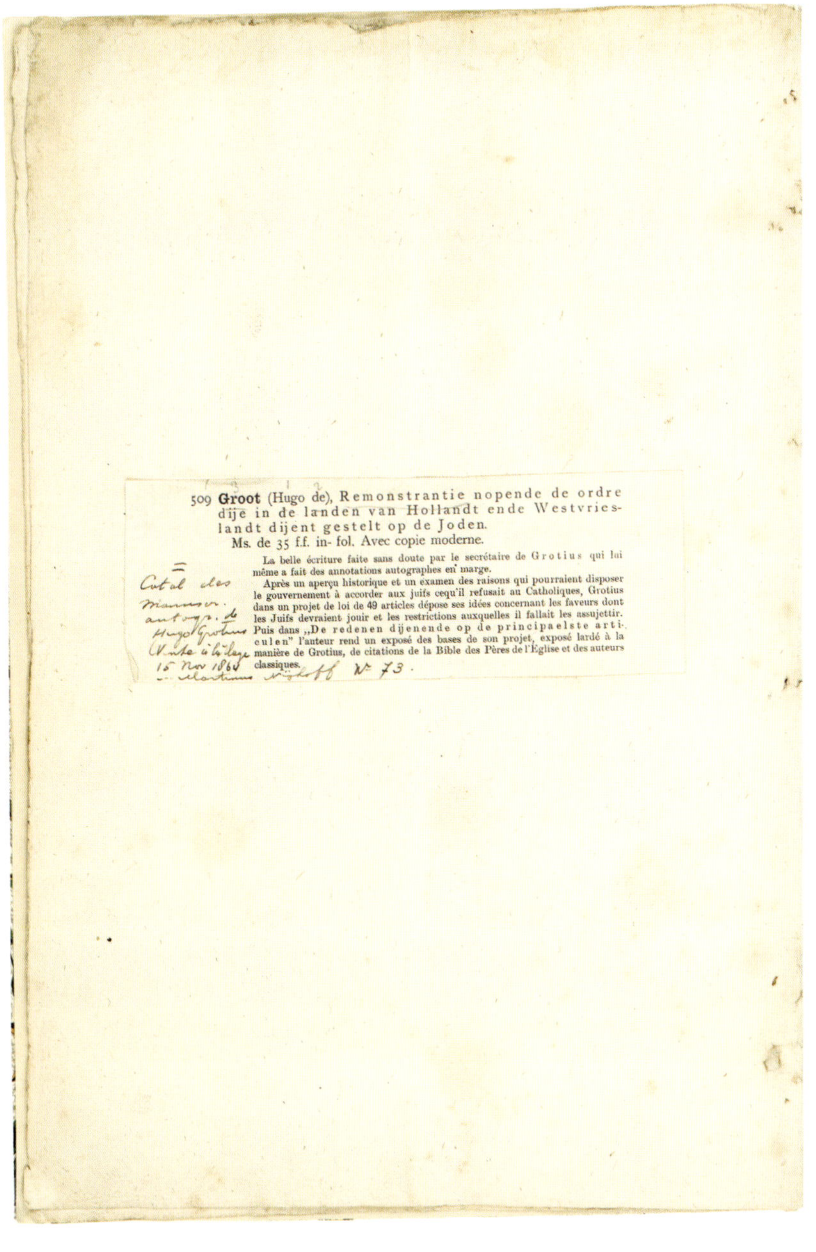

509 **Groot** (Hugo de), Remonstrantie nopende de ordre dije in de landen van Hollandt ende Westvrieslandt dijent gestelt op de Joden.
Ms. de 35 f.f. in- fol. Avec copie moderne.

La belle écriture faite sans doute par le secrétaire de Grotius qui lui même a fait des annotations autographes en marge.
Après un aperçu historique et un examen des raisons qui pourraient disposer le gouvernement à accorder aux juifs cequ'il refusait au Catholiques, Grotius dans un projet de loi de 49 articles dépose ses idées concernant les faveurs dont les Juifs devraient jouir et les restrictions auxquelles il fallait les assujettir. Puis dans „De redenen dijenende op de principaelste articulen" l'auteur rend un exposé des bases de son projet, exposé lardé à la manière de Grotius, de citations de la Bible des Pères de l'Église et des auteurs classiques.

Flyleaf of the *Remonstrantie*, upon which is pasted the catalogue description for the auction by Vita Israel and Lamed in Amsterdam, 1899. See Notes on This Edition, page 1.

1r

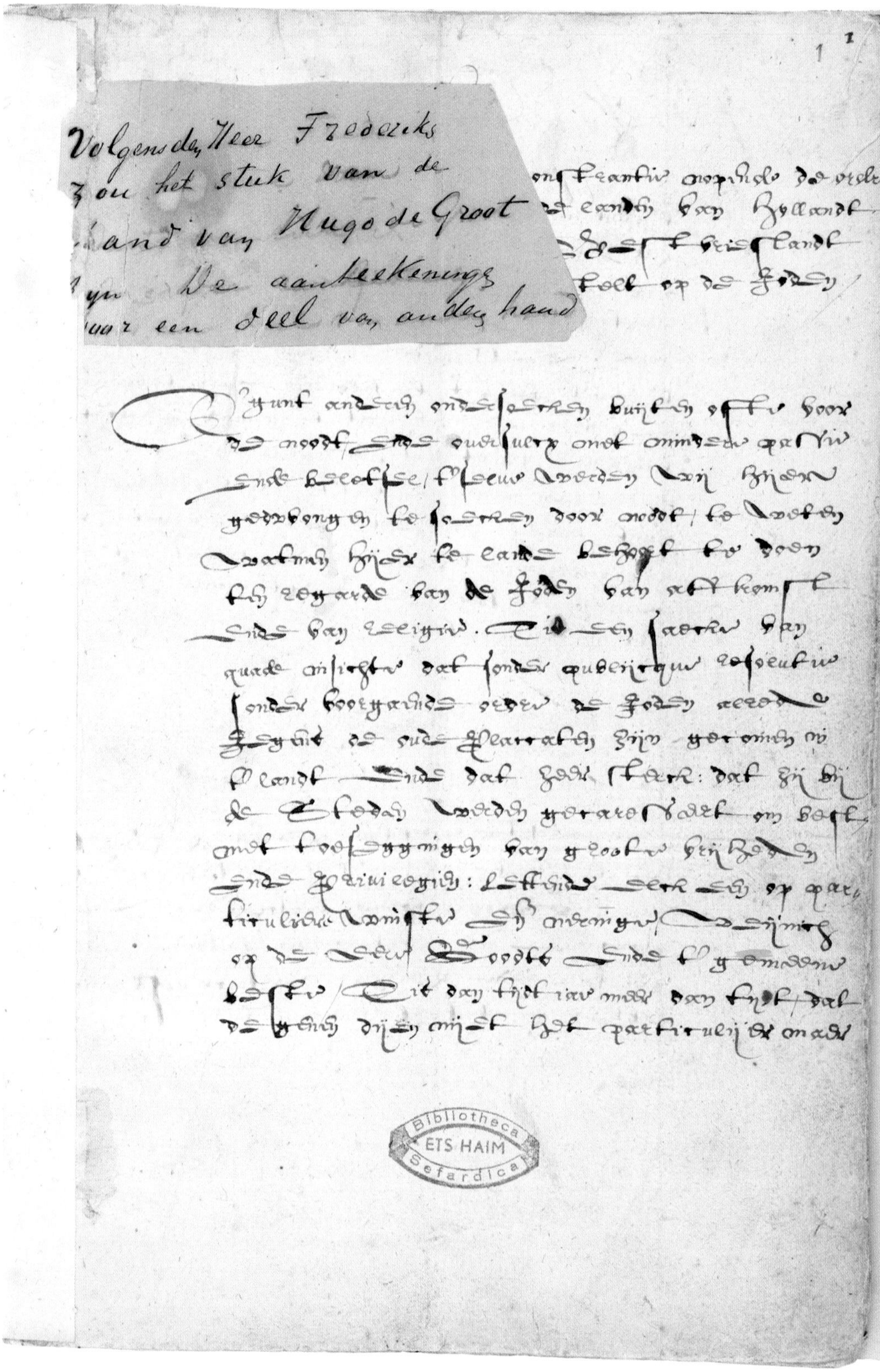
Volgens den Heer Fredericks
zou het stuk van de
hand van Hugo de Groot
zyn. De aanteekenings
waar een deel van ander hand

Remonstrantie nopende de ordre dije in de landen van Hollandt ende Westvrieslandt dijent gestelt op de Joden.

T' gunt anderen ondersoecken buijten ofte voor de noodt / ende oversulcx met mindere passie ende beletsel / t' selue werden wij hijer gedwongen te soecken door noodt / te weten watmen hijer te lande behoort te doen ten regarde van de Joden van affkomst ende van religie. T' is een saecke van quade insichte dat sonder publijcqe resolutie sonder voorgaende ordre de Joden alrede Jegens de oude Placcaten zijn gecomen in t' landt ende dat zeer sterck: dat zij bij de Steden werden gecaresseert om best met toeseggingen van groote vrijheden ende Privilegien: lettende elck een op par= ticuliere winste en*de* neringe / weynich op de eere Goodts ende 't gemeene beste / T is dan tijdt iae meer dan tijdt / dat de genen dijen nijet het particulijer maer

Remonstrantie betreffende de regelgeving die in Holland en West-Friesland moet worden opgesteld ten aanzien van joden.

Wat anderen minder gemotiveerd, onnodig en voorbarig onderzoeken, dwingt ons zelf te onderzoeken, te weten, wat men hier te lande moet doen met de joden, zowel die van afkomst als van religie. Het is een kwalijke zaak, dat zonder publiek besluit, zonder voorafgaande regelgeving de joden in strijd met de oude verordeningen, reeds in groten getale het land zijn binnengekomen, en dat zij door de steden met de grootste voorkomendheid zijn behandeld, met toezeggingen van grote vrijheden en privileges: waarbij een ieder is gericht op particuliere winst en handel, maar weinig gericht op Gods eer en op wat het beste is voor het algemeen belang.

Het is dus de hoogste tijd dat degenen die niet het persoonlijk maar

1v

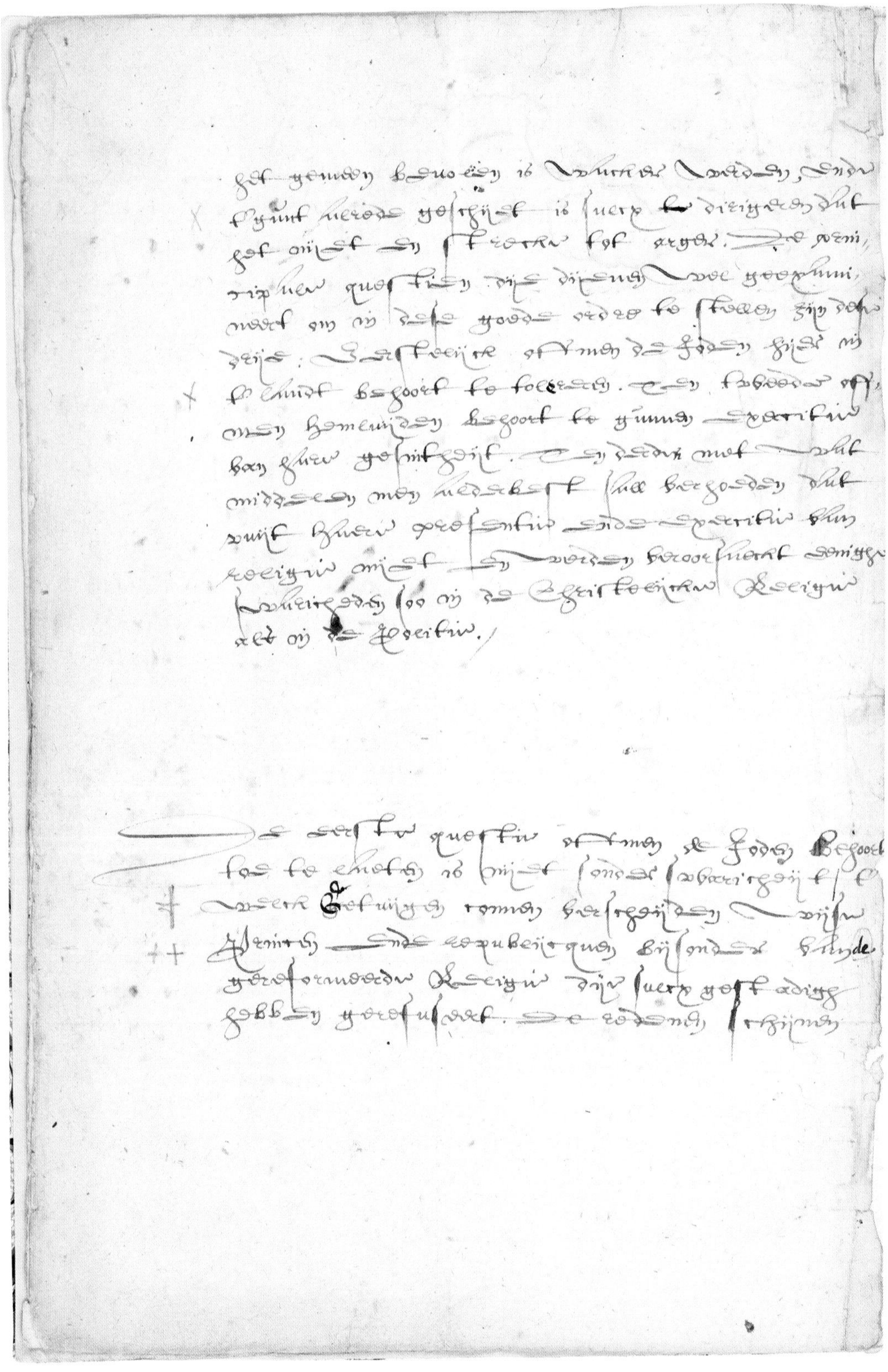

het gemeen beuolen is wacker werden, ende t' gunt alrede geschijet is sulcx te dirigeren dat het nijet en strecke tot arger. De prin=cipale questien dije dijenen wel geexami=neert om in dese goede ordre te stellen zijn dese drije: Eerstelijck offmen de Joden hijer in t' landt behoort te tolereren. Ten tweede off men hemluijden behoort te gunnen exercitie van hare gesintheijt. Ten derden met wat middelen men alderbest sall verhoeden dat vuijt hare presentie ende exercitie van religie nijet en werden veroorsaeckt eenighe swaricheden soo in de Christelijcke Religie als in de Politie. /

De eerste questie off men de Joden behoort toe te laeten is nijet sonder swarigheijt / t' welck getuijgen connen verscheijden wijse Princen ende republijcqen bijsonder van [de] gereformeerde Religie dije sulcx gestadigh hebben gerefuseert. De redenen schijnen

het algemeen belang te behartigen hebben, wordt aangeraden wakker te worden en dat wat al is gebeurd, zo in goede banen te leiden dat het niet slechter wordt.

Om hierin orde op zaken te stellen zijn de belangrijkste kwesties die onderzocht moeten worden de drie volgende:

Ten eerste of men de joden hier in het land moet toelaten.

Ten tweede of men hen de uitoefening van hun godsdienst moet toestaan.

Ten derde met welke middelen men het best kan voorkomen, dat problemen worden veroorzaakt door hun aanwezigheid en godsdienstuitoefening, zowel wat betreft de christelijke religie als de openbare orde.

De eerste kwestie, of men de joden moet toelaten, is niet zonder problemen. Verschillende wijze vorsten en staten kunnen hiervan getuigen, in het bijzonder die van de gereformeerde religie, die dit voortdurend hebben afgewezen.

De redenen lijken

2r

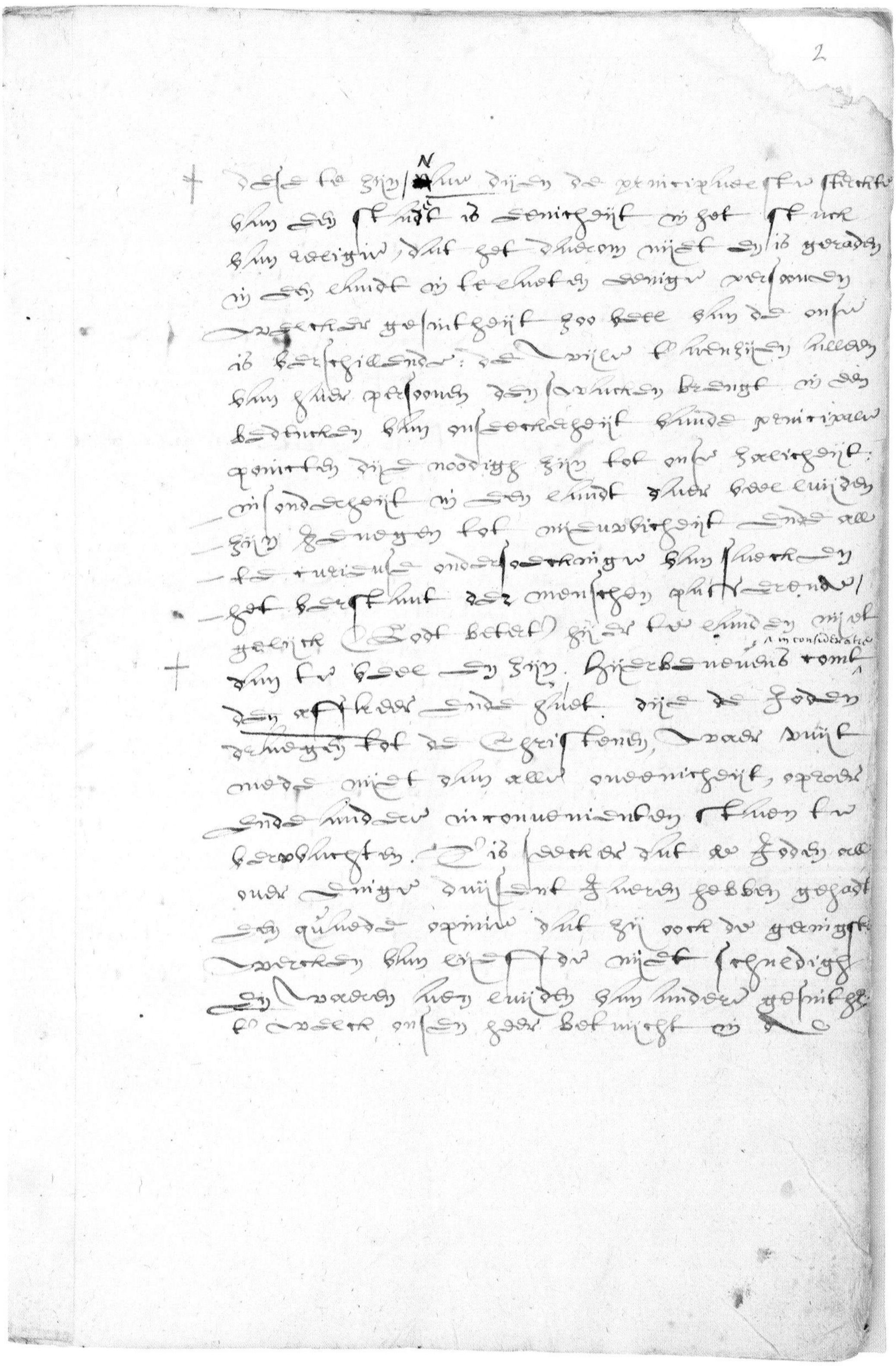

dese te zijn / Na dijen de principaelste sterckte van den sta~~d~~et is eenicheijt in het stuck van religie, dat het daerom nijet en is geraden in een landt in te laeten eenige persoonen welcker gesintheijt zoo veel van de onse is verschillende: de wijle t' aenzijen alleen van haer persoonen den swacken brengt in een bedencken van onseeckerheijt vande principale poincten dije noodigh zijn tot onze zalicheijt: insonderheijt in een landt daer veel luijden zijn genegen tot nijeuwicheijt ende all te curieuse ondersoeckinge van saecken het verstant der menschen passserende / gelijck (God betert) hijer te landen nijet dan te veel en zijn. Hijer benevens comt in consideratie den afkeer ende haet dije de Joden draeghen tot de Christenen, waer vuijt mede nijet dan alle oneenicheijt, oproer ende andere inconvenienten staen te verwachten. T' is seecker dat de Joden all over enige duijsent Jaeren hebben gehadt een quaede opinie dat zij oock de geringste wercken van lijeffde nijet schuldigh en waeren aen luijden van andere gesinthe*den* t' welck onsen heer betuijcht in de

deze te zijn:

Aangezien eenheid op het gebied van religie de grootste kracht is van een sterke staat, is het niet raadzaam mensen in het land op te nemen van wie de religie zo veel van de onze verschilt. Omdat immers alleen al de aanblik van deze mensen de zwakken van geest aan het twijfelen brengt omtrent de belangrijkste zaken die nodig zijn voor onze zaligheid. Dat geldt in het bijzonder in een land waar veel mensen geneigd zijn tot nieuwigheden en al te nieuwsgierig zijn naar zaken die het verstand van de mens te boven gaan en waarvan er hier te lande—God betere het—maar al te veel zijn.

Hierbij dienen in overweging genomen te worden de afkeer en de haat van de joden ten opzichte van de christenen, waaruit alleen allerlei onenigheid, oproer en andere moeilijkheden zijn te verwachten.

Het staat vast dat de joden al enige duizenden jaren de boosaardige opvatting koesterden, dat zij niet ook maar de geringste daden van liefde verschuldigd waren aan mensen van andere religies, waarvan onze Heer getuigt in de

2V

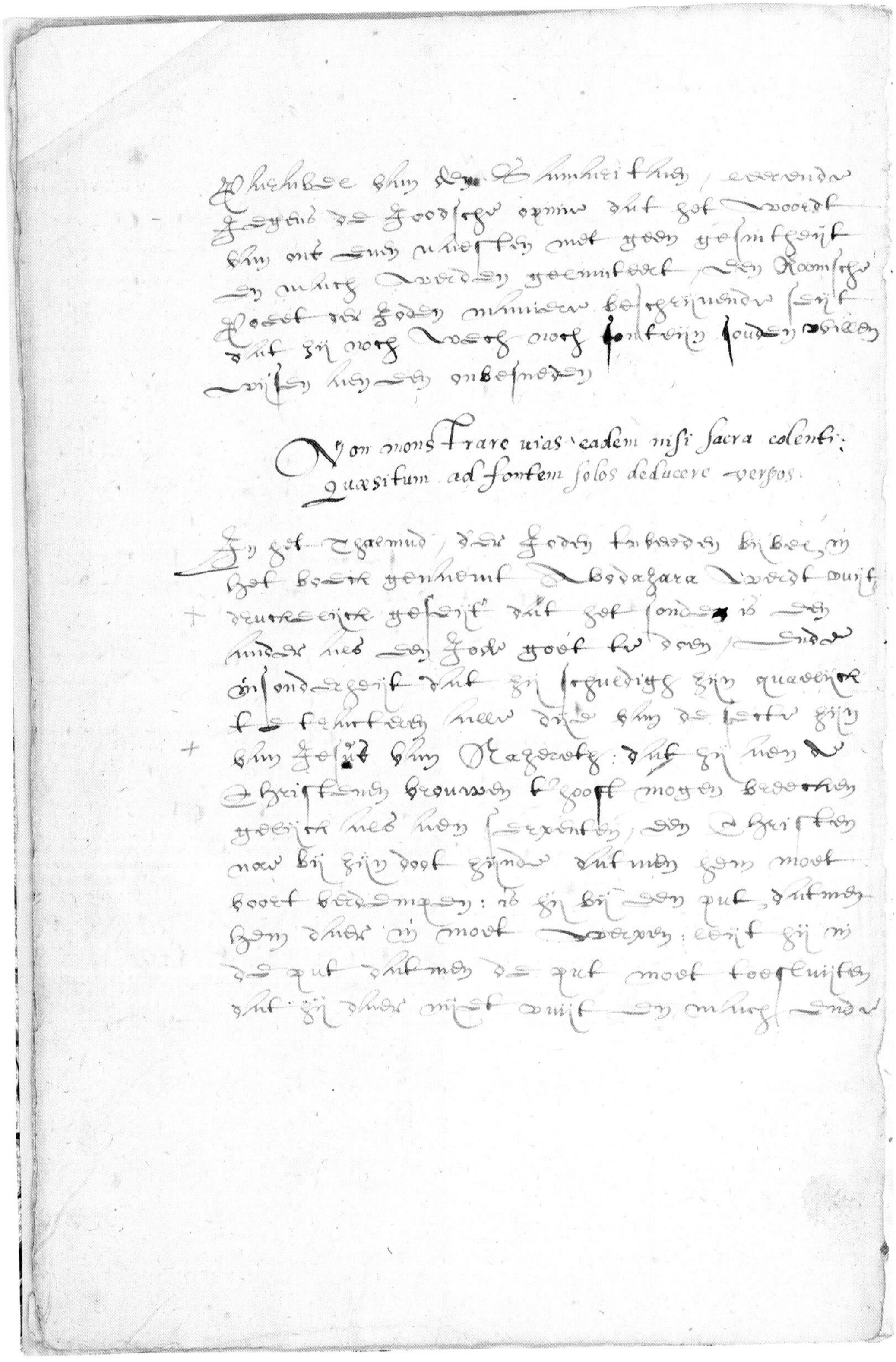

Non monstrare vias eadem nisi sacra colenti:
Quaesitum ad fontem solos deducere verpos.

Parabel van den Samaritaen / leerende Jegens de Joodsche opinie dat het woordt van ons even naesten met geen gesintheijt en mach werden gelimiteert / een Roomsche Poeet der Joden maniere beschrijvende seijt dat zij noch wech noch fonteijn souden willen wijsen aen een onbesneden

Non monstrare vias eadem nisi sacra colenti
quaesitum ad fontem solos deducere verpos.

In het Thalmud / der Joden tweeden bijbel, in het boeck genaemt Abodazara werdt vuijt=druckelijck geseijt dat het sonde is een ander als een Jode goet te doen / ende insonderheijt dat zij schuldigh zijn quaelijck te tracteren alle dije van de secte zijn van Jesūs van Nazareth: dat zij aen de Christenen vrouwen t' hooft mogen breecken gelijck als aen serpenten, een Christen nae bij zijn doot zijnde datmen hem moet voort verdempen: is hij bij een put, datmen hem daer in moet werpen: leijt hij in de put datmen de put moet toesluijten dat hij daer nijet vuijt en mach ende

gelijkenis van de Samaritaan, die leerde, in tegenstelling tot de joodse opvatting, dat de uitdrukking 'onze naasten' niet mag worden beperkt tot de aanhangers van dezelfde godsdienst. Een Romeins dichter, die de joodse gebruiken beschreef, zei dat zij noch de weg noch een fontein zouden willen wijzen aan een onbesnedene.

… [*leert hij van buiten en volgt nauwgezet*
de Wet der Joden, elk verbod dat Mozes
in zijn geheime wetboek heeft beschreven,]
zoals de weg aanwijzen aan een man
die andere riten eert, of niet-besneden
dorstige lieden iets te drinken geven.[1]

In de Talmoed, de tweede bijbel van de joden, in het traktaat genaamd *Avoda Zara*, wordt uitdrukkelijk gesteld, dat het een zonde is om goed te zijn voor een ander dan een jood, en in het bijzonder dat zij verplicht zijn al degenen van de sekte van Jezus van Nazareth slecht te behandelen;

dat zij christelijke vrouwen het hoofd mogen breken, net zoals slangen;

dat zij een christen die stervende is, moeten verstikken;

is hij dichtbij een put, dan moeten zij hem erin werpen;

ligt hij in een put, dan moeten zij de put afdekken, zodat hij er niet meer uit kan,

en

1 Juvenalis, *De Satiren*, 180.

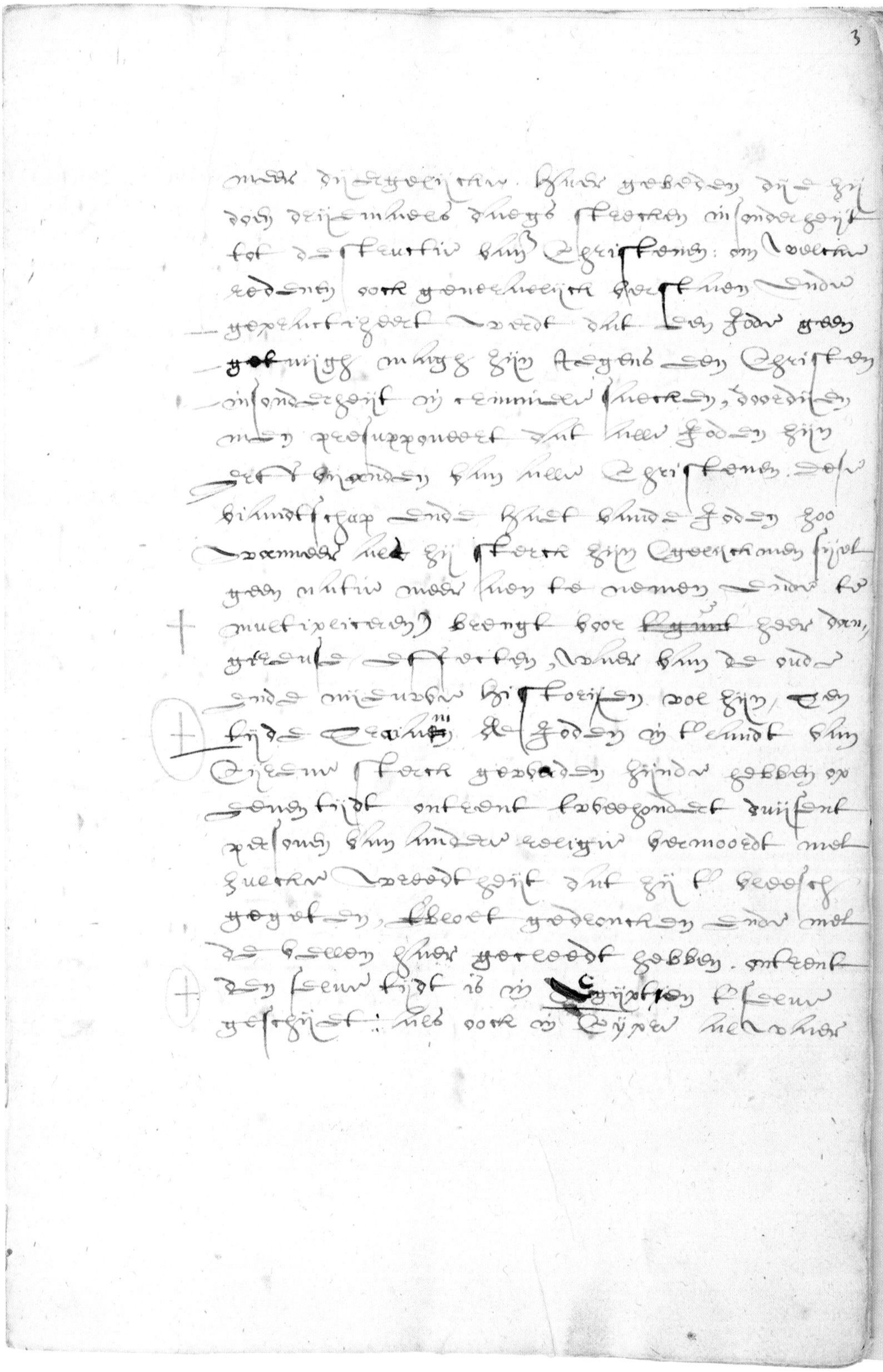

3r

meer dijrgelijcke. Haer gebeden dije zij doen drijemaels daegs strecken insonderheijt tot destructie van*de* Christenen: om welcke redenen oock generaelijck verstaen ende gepractizeert werdt dat een Jode geen getuijgh magh zijn tegens een Christen insonderheijt in criminele saecken, doordijen men presupponeert dat alle Joden zijn erffvijanden van alle Christenen. Dese viandttschap ende haet vande Joden zoo wanneer als zij sterck zijn (gelijckmen sijet geen natie meer aen te nemen ende te multipliceren) brengt voor ~~t' gunt~~ zeer dan= gereuse effecten, waer van de oude ende nijeuwe historijen vol zijn / Ten tijde Traia~~ne~~ni de Joden in t' landt van Cyrene sterck geworden zijnde hebben op eenen tijdt ontrent tweehondert duijsent personen van andere religie vermoordt met zulcke wreedtheijt dat zij t' vleesch gegeten, t' bloet gedroncken ende met de vellen haer gecleedt hebben. ontrent den selve tijdt is in Egijpten t' selve geschijet, als oock in Cijpre alwaer

meer van dergelijke zaken.

De strekking van hun driemaal daags uitgesproken gebeden is vooral dat de christenen vernietigd mogen worden. Om deze reden wordt dan ook algemeen aangenomen en in praktijk gebracht dat een jood niet mag getuigen tegen een christen, in het bijzonder in strafzaken, omdat men ervan uitgaat dat alle joden erfvijanden zijn van alle christenen.

Deze vijandschap en haat van de joden zorgt, vooral wanneer zij sterk zijn (men ziet immers dat er geen volk is dat sterker groeit en zich vermenigvuldigt) voor zeer gevaarlijke gevolgen, waarvan de oude en nieuwe geschiedschrijving vol zijn.

Ten tijde van Trajanus, toen de joden in het land van Cyrene meer macht hadden gekregen, hebben zij op een gegeven moment ongeveer 200.000 andersdenkenden vermoord, met zo'n wreedheid, dat zij het vlees gegeten, het bloed gedronken en zich met de huiden hebben aangekleed. Ongeveer tegelijkertijd is dit ook gebeurd in Egypte en ook op Cyprus, waar

3v

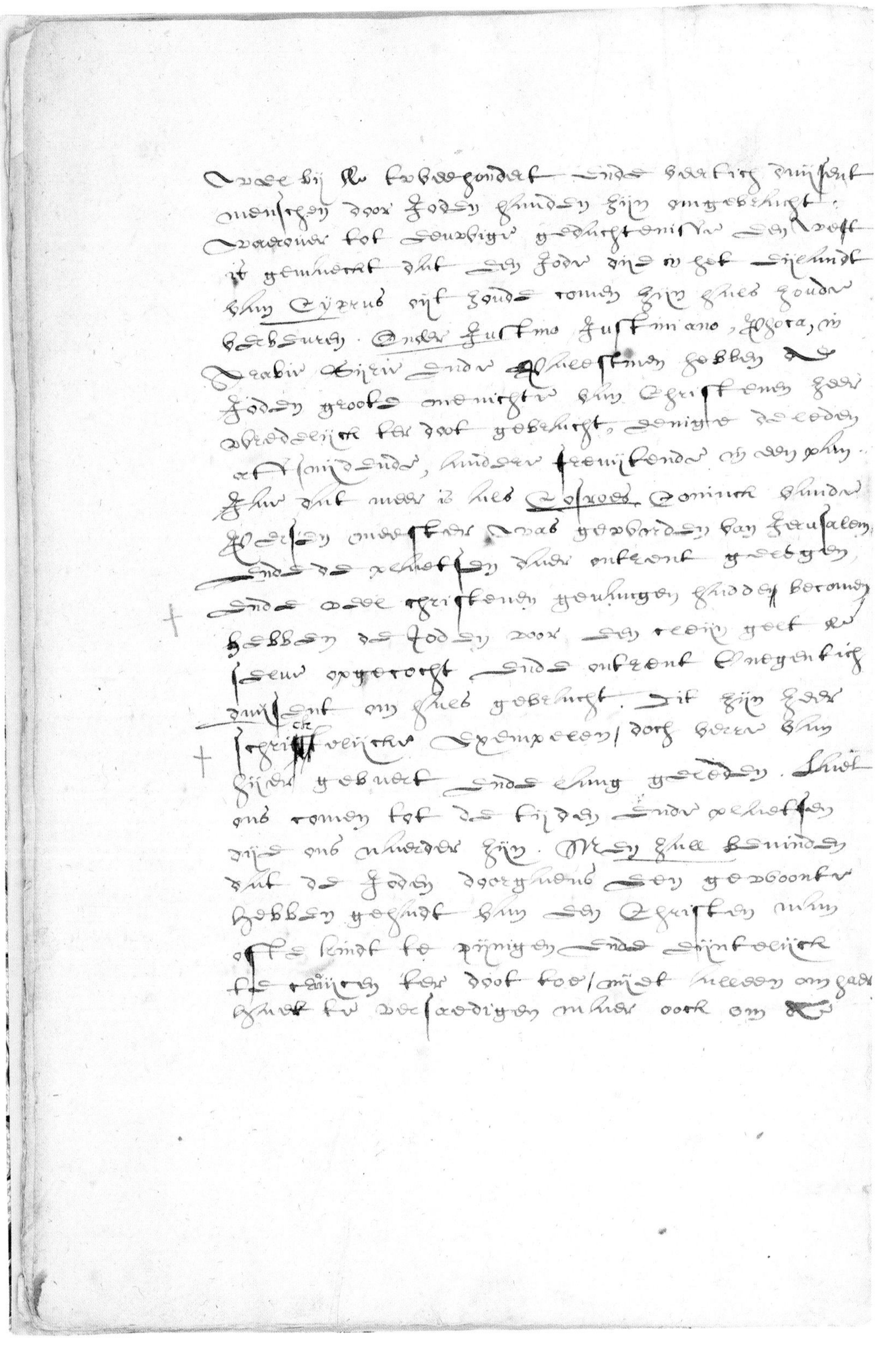

wel bij de tweehondert ende veertigh duijsent menschen door Joden handen zijn omgebracht. waerover tot eeuwige gedachtenisse een wett is gemaeckt dat een Jode dije in het eijlandt van Cijprus oijt zoude comen zijn hals zoude verbeuren. Onder Justino, Justiniano, Phoca, in Arabie, Sijrie ende Palestinen hebben de Joden groote menichte van Christenen zeer wredelijck ter doot gebracht, eenige de leden afsnijdende, anderen freuijtende in een pan. Jae dat meer is als Cosroes, Coninck vande Persen meester was geworden van Jerusalem ende de plaetsen daer ontrent gelegen, ende veel christenen gevangen hadden becomen hebben de Joden voor een cleijn gelt de selve opgecocht ende ontrent t' negentich duijsent om hals gebracht. Dit zijn zeer schristckelijcke exempelen / doch verre van hijer gebeurt ende lang geleden. Laet ons comen tot de tijden ende plaetsen dije ons naerder zijn. Men zall beuinden dat de Joden doorgaens een gewoonte hebben gehadt van een Christen man ofte kindt te pijnigen ende eijntelijck te cruijsen ter doot toe / nijet alleen om haer haet te versaedigen maar oock om de

bijna 240.000 mensen door joodse handen zijn omgebracht. Ter eeuwige herinnering hieraan is een wet opgesteld dat een jood, die ooit nog op Cyprus zou komen, zou worden terechtgesteld.

Onder Justinus, Justinianus en Phocas hebben de joden in Arabië, Syrië en Palestina grote groepen christenen wreed ter dood gebracht, waarbij van sommigen de lichaamsdelen werden afgesneden en anderen werden gebraden in een pan. Ja, en meer nog, toen Chosroes, koning van Perzië, Jeruzalem en de omliggende steden had overmeesterd en veel christenen gevangen had genomen, hebben de joden deze voor weinig geld opgekocht en er ongeveer 90.000 gedood.

Dit zijn verschrikkelijke voorbeelden, maar ver hier vandaan en lang geleden gebeurd. Laten wij het nu hebben over tijden en plaatsen die ons meer nabij zijn.

Men zal constateren dat de joden doorgaans de gewoonte hadden, een christelijke man of kind te pijnigen en uiteindelijk te kruisigen tot de dood erop volgde, niet alleen om hun haat te bevredigen, maar ook om de

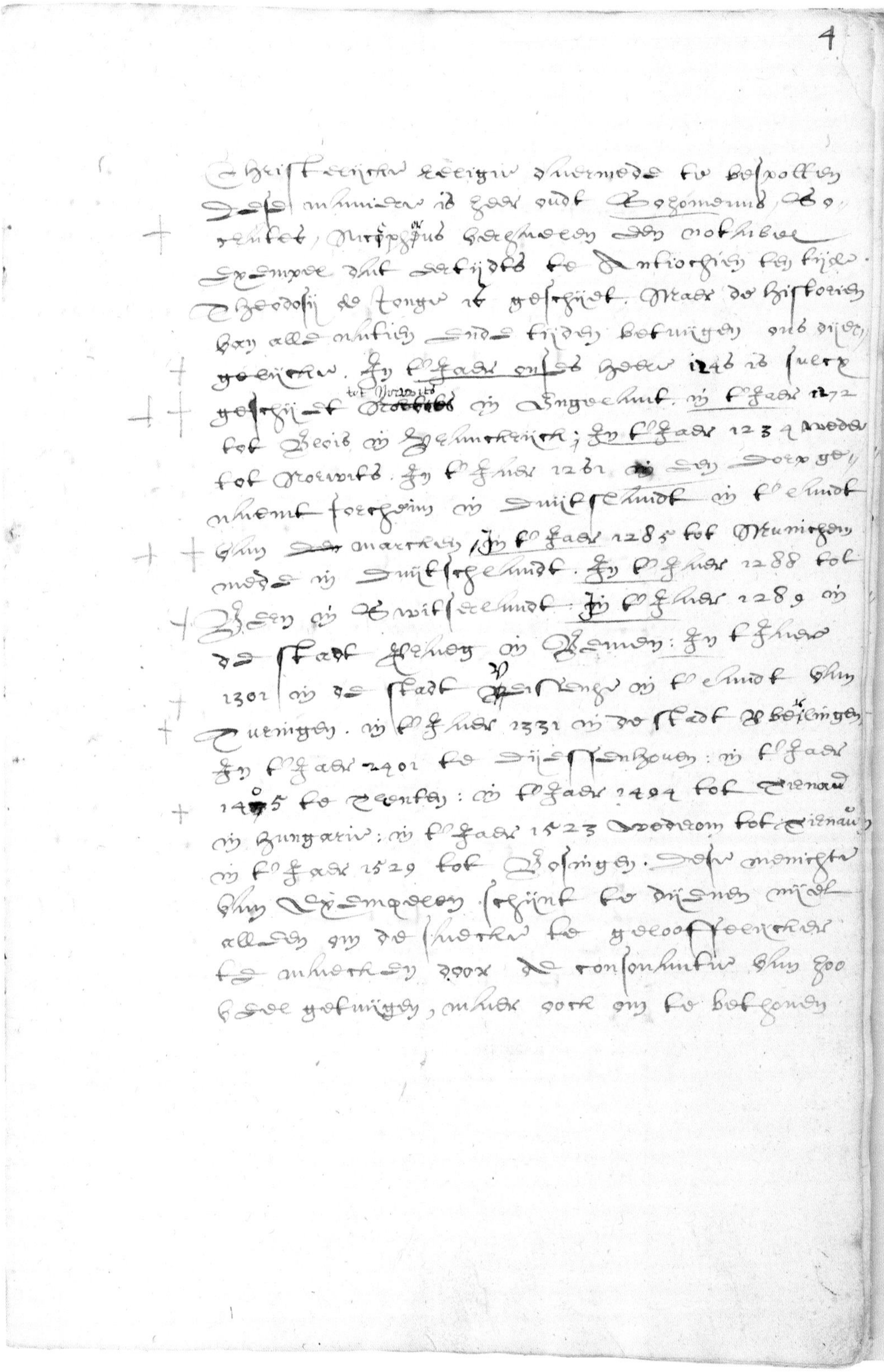

4r

Christelijcke religie daermede te bespotten Dese maniere is zeer oudt Sozomenus, So=crates, Nicoepheorus verhaelen een notabel exempel dat eertijdts te Antiochien ten tijde Theodosij de Jonge is geschijet. Maer de historien van alle natien ende tijden betuijgen ons dijer=gelijcke. In 't Jaer onses Heere 1246 is sulcx geschijet tot ~~Norvids~~ Norwits in Engelant. in t' Jaer 1272 tot Blois in Vranckrijck; In 't Jaer1234 weder tot Norwits. In 't Jaer 1262 in een dorp ge=naemt Forcheim in Duijtslandt in t' landt van den marcken / In t' Jaer 1285 tot Munichem mede in Duijtschlandt. In t' Jaer 1288 tot Bern in Switserlandt: In t' Jaer 1289 in de stadt Praeg in Bemen: In t' Jaer 1302 in de stadt ~~U~~Vessenge in t' landt van Turingen. In t' Jaer 1331 in destadt Uberlingen. In t' Jaer 1402 te Dijessenhouen: in t' Jaer $14^{0}5$ te Trenten: in t' Jaer 1404 tot Tirnnauw in Hungarie: in t' Jaer 1523 wederom tot Tirnauw in t' Jaer 1529 tot Bosingen. Dese menichte van exempelen schijnt te dijenen nijet alleen om de saecke te gelooffelijcker te maecken door de consonantie van zoo veel getuijgen, maer oock om te bethonen

christelijke religie daarmee te bespotten. Dit gebruik is zeer oud.

Sozomenus, Socrates en Nicephorus verhalen van een opmerkelijk gebeurtenis, die zich destijds in Antiochië ten tijde van Theodosius de Jongere heeft voorgedaan. Maar de verhalen van alle volken en uit alle tijden getuigen van hetzelfde.

In het jaar des Heren 1146 is dit gebeurd in Norwich in Engeland; in 1272 in Blois in Frankrijk; in 1234 opnieuw in Norwich; in 1262 in een dorp genaamd Forcheim in Duitsland, in het land van Marken; in 1285 in München, eveneens in Duitsland; in 1288 in Bern te Zwitserland; in 1289 in de stad Praag in Bohemen; in 1302 in de stad Vessenge in Thüringen; in 1331 in de stad Überlingen; in 1402 in Diessenhofen; in 1405 te Trente;[2] in 1404 de stad Tirnau in Hongarije; in 1523 opnieuw in Tirnau; in 1529 in Bösing.

Dit grote aantal voorbeelden kan de zaak niet alleen geloofwaardiger maken, door het overeenstemmen van zoveel getuigen, maar ook benadrukken

2 Hier is in de tekst het jaartal gecorrigeerd. In Trente vond een bloedbeschuldiging plaats in 1475.

4v

dat de selve effecten nijet en moeten toegeschreven werden aen eenighe particu= lijere oorsaecken, maer alleen aen den ge= neraelen onuersoenlijcken haet van de Joden tot de Christenen: t' welck voorwaer wel staet te considereren. Want ~~W~~waerom zijn de Joden gebannen vuijt Franck= rijck / vuijt Engelant, vuijt Hungarije, vuijt Spagnie ende Portugael iae selfs vuijt de nederlanden / daer zij soo langen tijdt geresideert ende de Princen groote profijten ingebracht hadden / als om dese ende dijergelijcke oor= saecen? Desе natuijre vande Joden is ons oock bij de heijlighe schrift claerlijck aenge= wesen / al waer zij genoemt werden hardtneckinghe / onbesneden van harten, Prophe= tenmoorders, addergebroet /daer geseijt werdt dat haer vader is den duijvel dije vanden beginne aen een moorder is: / dat zij de maet van haere voorouders veruullen: Ende wat alle Christenen van hemluijden te wachten hebben werdt pertinentelijck aengewesen als onsen heer seijt. Den vader des huijsgesins hebben zij Beelzebub genoemt. wat zullen de huijsgenoten doen / Den Discipel en is nijet beter als zijn meester. Sijet nae de

dat deze identieke gevolgen niet moeten worden toegeschreven aan enkele specifieke oorzaken, maar alleen aan de onverzoenlijke haat van de joden jegens de christenen: dit dient zeker in overweging genomen te worden.

Want waarom zijn de joden verbannen uit Frankrijk, uit Engeland, uit Hongarije, uit Spanje en Portugal, ja zelfs uit de Nederlanden waar zij zo lange tijd hadden gewoond en de vorsten groot voordeel hebben gebracht, behalve vanwege deze en soortgelijke oorzaken?

De aard van de joden is ons ook door de Heilige Schrift duidelijk gemaakt, waar zij genoemd worden: hardnekkig, onbesneden van hart, profetenmoordenaars, addergebroed; van wie gezegd wordt dat hun vader de duivel is, die vanaf het begin een moordenaar was, dat zij handelen net zoals hun voorouders.

En wat alle christenen van hen te verwachten hebben, is nadrukkelijk aangetoond wanneer onze Heer zegt: De vader van het huisgezin hebben zij *Beëlzebub* genoemd. Wat zullen de huisgenoten doen? De leerling is niet beter dan zijn meester. Kijk naar de

5r

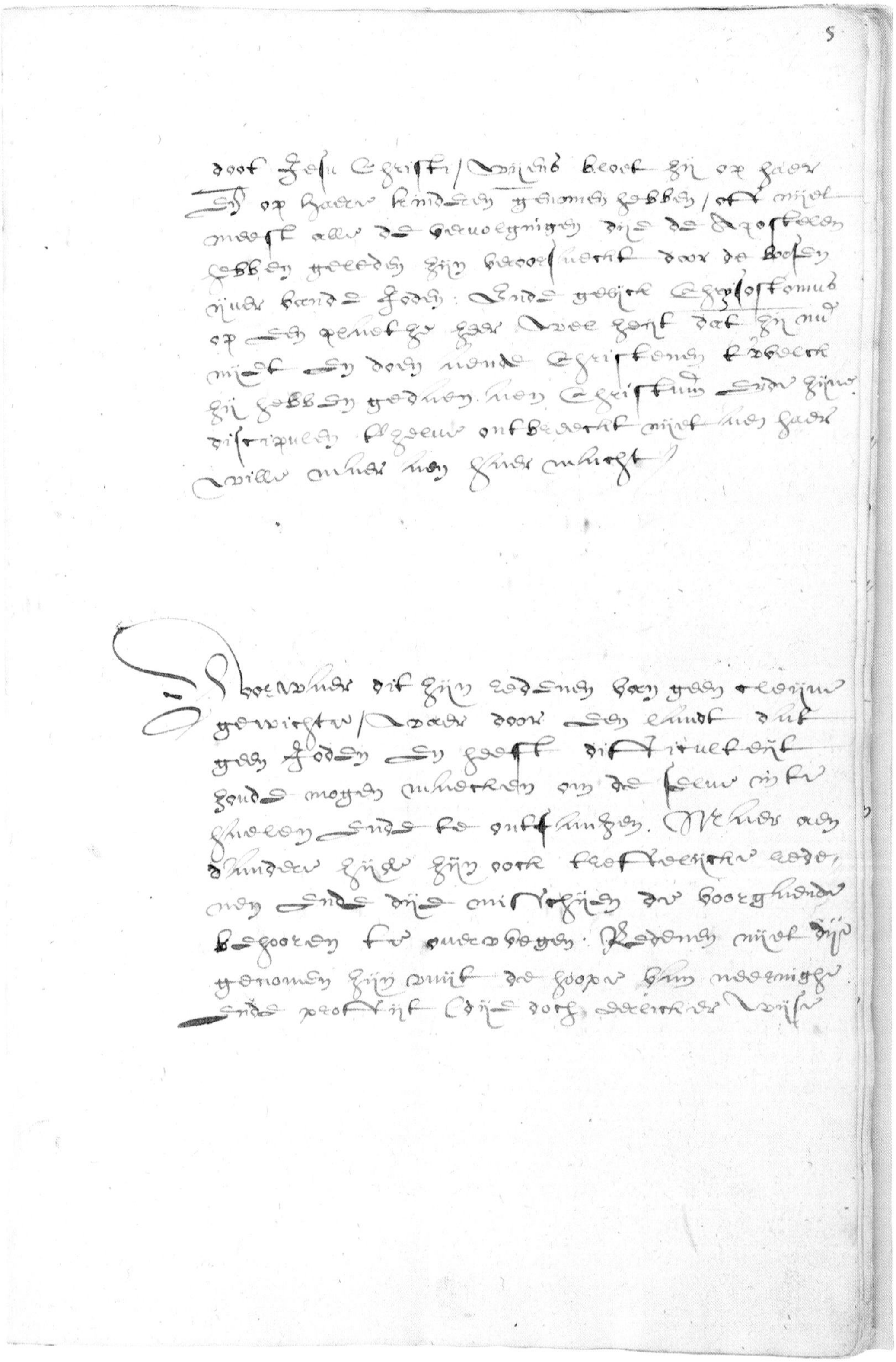

doot Jesu Christi / wijens bloet sij op haer
en*de* op haere kinderen genomen hebben / off nijet
meest alle de veruolgingen dije de Apostelen
hebben geleden zijn veroorsaeckt door de boosen
ijuer van de Joden: Ende gelijck <u>Chrysostomus</u>
op een plaetze zeer wel zeijt dat zij nu
nijet en doen aende Christenen t' welck
zij hebben gedaen aen Christum ende zijne
discipulen t' zelue ontbreeckt nijet aen haer
wille maer aen haer macht.

Voorwaer dit zijn redenen van geen cleijne
gewichte / waer door een landt dat
geen Joden en heeft difficulteijt
zoude mogen maecken om de selue in te
haelen ende te ontfangen. Maer aen
d'andere zijde zijn oock treffelijcke rede=
nen ende dije misschijen de voorgaende
behooren te ouerwegen: Redenen nijet dije
genomen zijn vuijt de hoope van neeringhe
ende proffijt (dije doch eerlicker wijse

dood van Jezus Christus, wiens bloed zij op zich en hun kinderen hebben genomen. En of niet de meeste vervolgingen waaronder de apostelen hebben geleden, zijn veroorzaakt door de slechte bedoelingen van de joden. En zoals Chrysostomus het ergens zeer goed verwoordt: dat zij de christenen nu niet aandoen wat zij Christus en zijn discipelen hebben aangedaan, komt niet omdat het hun ontbreekt aan wil, maar aan macht.

Welnu dit zijn geen onbelangrijke redenen, waarom een land, dat geen joden heeft, bezwaar zou kunnen maken deze binnen te halen en te ontvangen.

Maar aan de andere kant zijn er ook voortreffelijke argumenten en deze behoren misschien de voorgaande te overtreffen: argumenten, die niet voortkomen uit de hoop op handel en profijt (die toch eerlijkerwijs

5v

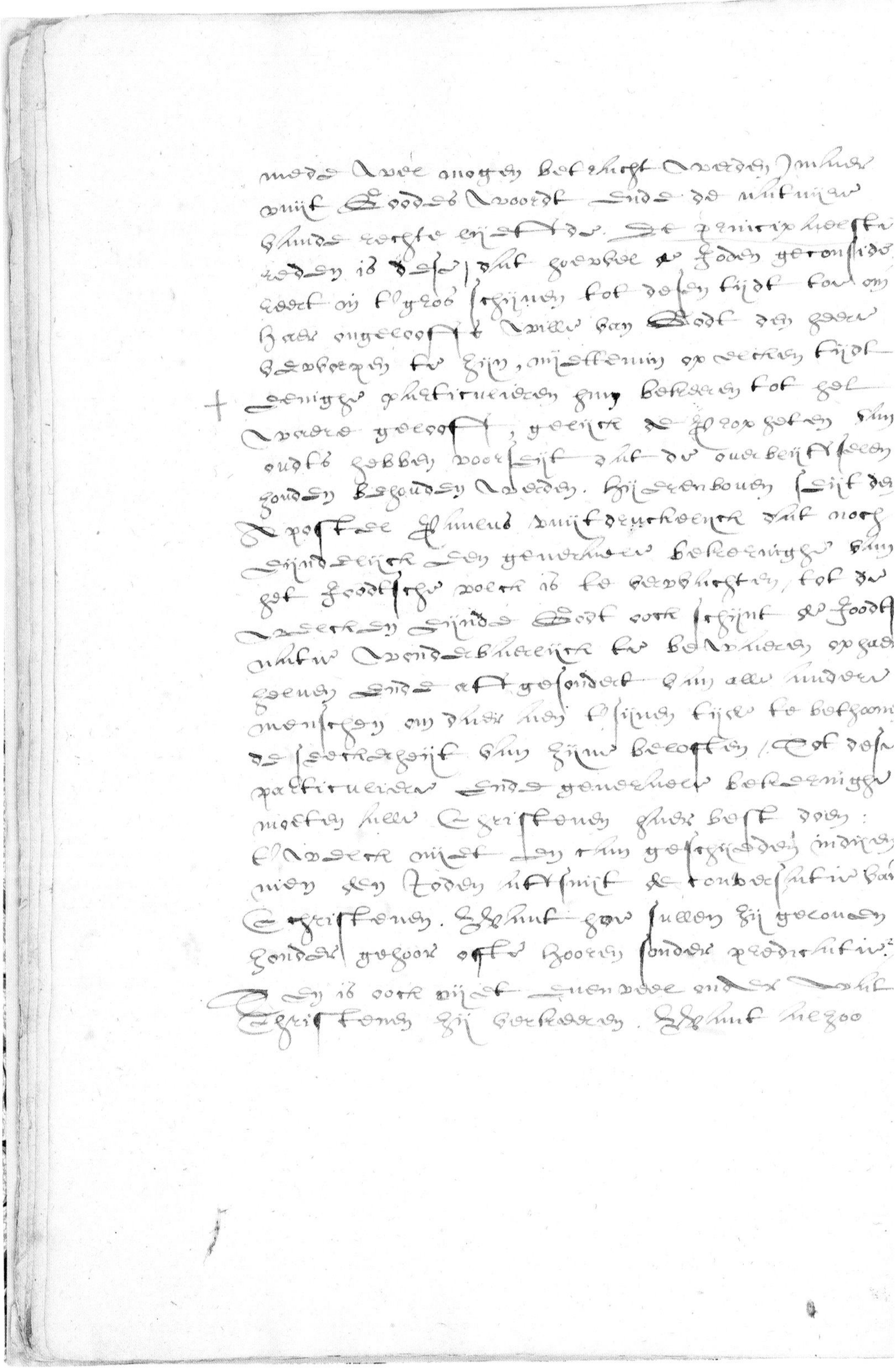

mede wel mogen betracht werden) maer vuijt Goodes woordt ende de natuijre vande rechte lijeffde. De principaelste reden is dese / dat hoewel de Joden geconside= reert in t' gros schijnen tot desen tijdt toe om haer ongelooffs wille van Godt den heere verworpen te zijn, nijettemin op elcken tijdt eenighe particulieren hun bekeeren tot het waere gelooff, gelijck de Propheten van oudts hebben voorseijt dat de ouerblijffselen zouden behouden worden. Hijerenbouen seijet den Apostel Paulus vuijtdruckelijck dat noch eijndelijck een generaele bekeeringhe van het Joodtsche volck is te verwachten / tot de welcken eijnde Godt oock schijnt de Joodtsche natie wonderbaerlijck te bewaeren op haer zeluen ende affgesondert van alle andere menschen om daer aen t'sijnen tijde te bethoonen de seeckerheijt van zijne beloften /. Tot dese particuliere ende generaele bekeringhe moeten alle Christenen haer best doen: 't welck nijet en can geschijeden indijen men den Joden affsnijt de conversatie van*de* Christenen. Want hoe sullen zij geloven zonder gehoor ofte hooren sonder predicatie? T en is oock nijet evenveel onder wat Christenen zij verkeeren. Want alzoo

eveneens in aanmerking genomen mogen worden), maar uit Gods woord en uit natuurlijke oprechte liefde. De belangrijkste reden is dat, hoewel de joden in het algemeen tot op heden om hun ongeloof door God verworpen schijnen te zijn, in iedere tijd niettemin enkelen zich tot het ware geloof bekeren, zodat, naar de profeten vroeger hebben voorspeld, de overigen behouden zullen worden. Bovendien zegt de apostel Paulus nadrukkelijk, dat uiteindelijk een totale bekering van het joodse volk valt te verwachten, tot welk doel God het joodse volk op wonderbaarlijke wijze schijnt te bewaren, op zichzelf en afgezonderd van alle andere mensen, om daarmee te zijner tijd blijk te geven van de betrouwbaarheid van zijn beloften. Voor deze persoonlijke en algemene bekering moeten alle christenen hun best doen, wat niet kan gebeuren indien men de joden uitsluit van de omgang met christenen: Want hoe kunnen zij geloven zonder te horen of horen zonder prediking? En het is ook niet onbelangrijk onder welk soort christenen zij verkeren. Want aangezien

6r

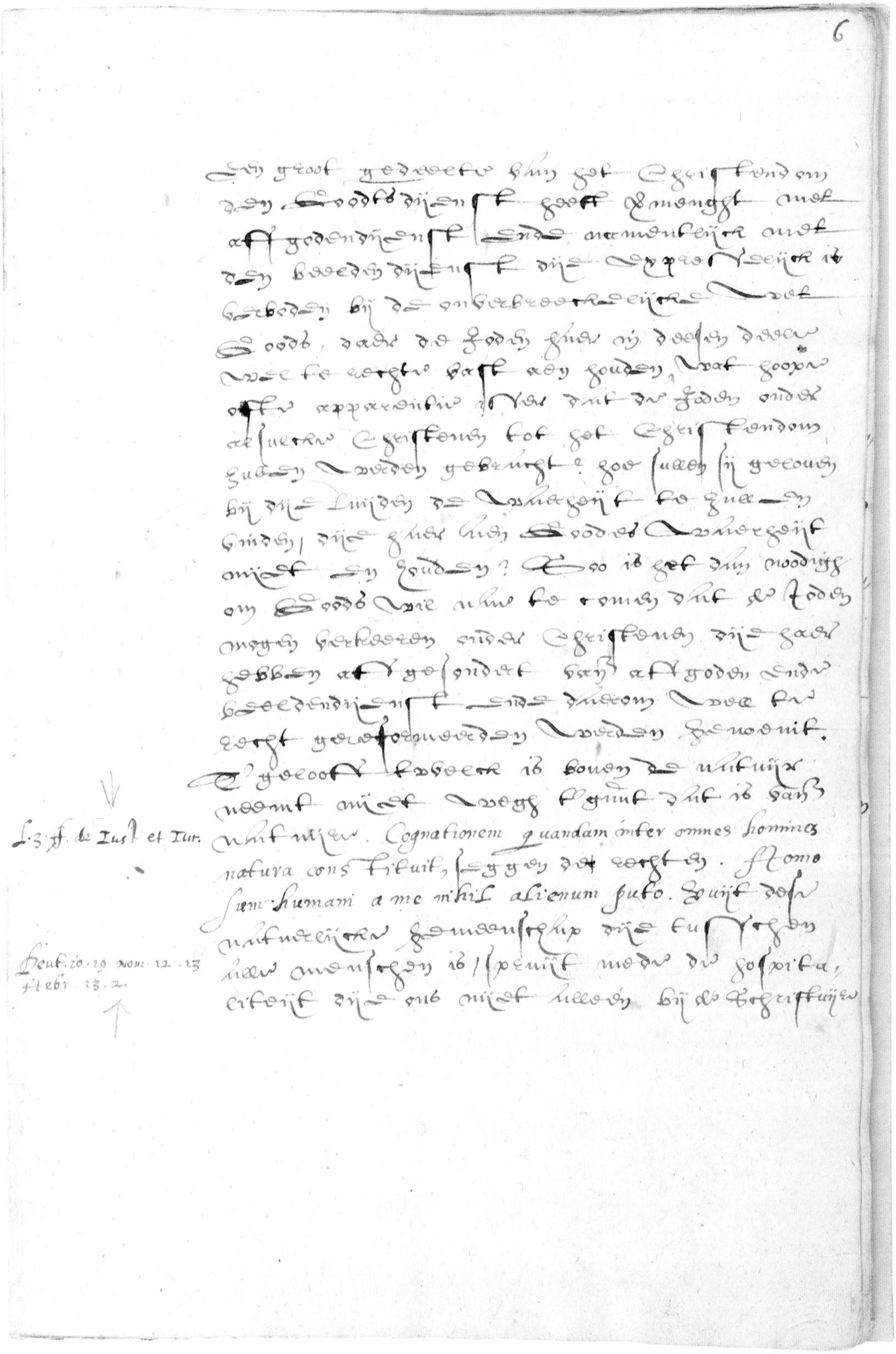
6
L. 3 ff. de Iust. et Iur.
Cognationem quandam inter omnes homines natura constituit,
Homo sum humani a me nihil alienum puto.
Deut. 10.19 Rom. 12.13 Hebr. 13.2.

een groot gedeelte van het Christendom den Goodtsdijenst heeft *ver*menght met affgodendijenst ende namentlijck met den beeldendijenst dije expresselijck is verboden bij de onverbreeckelijcke wet Goods, daer de Joden haer in deesen deele wel te rechte vast aen houden, wat hoope ofte apparentie isser dat de Joden onder alsulcke Christenen tot het Christendom zullen werden gebracht? hoe sullen sij gelouen bij dije Luijden de waerheijt te zullen vinden / dije haer aen Goodes waerheijt nijet en houden? Soo is het dan noodigh om Goods wil nae te comen dat de Joden mogen verkeeren onder Christenen dije haer hebben affgesondert van*de* affgoden ende beeldendijenst ende daerom well te recht gereformeerden werden genoemt. T' geloof twelck is bouen de natuijr neemt nijet wegh t'gunt dat is van*de* natuijre. *Cognationem quandam inter omnes homines** *natura constituit*, seggen de rechten. *Homo sum. humani a me nihil alienum puto*. Vuijt dese natuerlijcke gemeenschap dije tusschen alle menschen is / spruijt mede de hospita=† liteijt dije ons nijet alleen bij de Schriftuijre

* ⟨*L.3. ff. de Inst. et Iur.*⟩

† ⟨*Deut. 10. 19 Nom. 12. 13*[3] *Hebr. 13. 2*⟩

een groot gedeelte van het christendom de godsdienst heeft vermengd met afgodendienst en met name met de aanbidding van beelden, wat uitdrukkelijk is verboden door de onverbrekelijke wet Gods, waaraan de joden zich in dezen terecht vasthouden. Welke hoop of waarschijnlijkheid is er dat de joden onder zulke christenen tot het christendom zullen worden gebracht? Hoe kunnen zij geloven, dat zij bij die mensen de waarheid zullen vinden, die zichzelf niet aan Gods waarheid houden?

Daarom is het van belang, om Gods wil te volgen, dat de joden kunnen verkeren onder de christenen die zich hebben afgekeerd van de afgoden en de beeldendienst en daarom met recht gereformeerden worden genoemd. Het geloof, dat boven de natuur staat, neemt niet weg wat door de natuur gegeven is. *De natuur heeft een soort verwantschap gevestigd tussen alle mensen*, zeggen de juristen.[4] *Ik ben een mens, niets menselijks is mij vreemd.*[5] Uit deze natuurlijke verwantschap, die tussen alle mensen geldt, komt ook de gastvrijheid voort, die ons niet enkel door de Schrift,[6]

3 Nom. *lees* Rom.

4 In kantlijn: ⟨*L.3. ff. de Inst. et Iur.*⟩ (= Dig. 1.1.3).

5 Citaat uit toneelstuk van Terentius, *De zelfkweller*, r. 77.

6 In kantlijn: ⟨*Deut. 10. 19 Nom* [lees: Rom.]. *12. 13 Hebr. 13. 2*⟩.

6v

Quod genus hoc hominum, quaeve hunc tam barbara morem
Permittit patria? hospitio prohibemur arenae.

maer oock bij de heijdensche schrijuers werdt
gerecommandeert. de welcke bestaet
in het ontfangen ende wel tracteren van
vremdelingen. De natien dije de vremde=
lingen van haer hebben geweert werden
ouer all gescholden voor Barbaren ende on=
natuijrlijcke menschen.
Quod genus hoc hominum, quœue hunc tam barbara morem
Permittit patria? hospitio prohibemur arenœ
Als den apostel Paulus will dat wij
goet zullen doen aen alle personen, insonderheijt
aen de huijsgenoten des gelooffs, zoo stelt
hij wel een naerder trap van lieffde
tusschen de gelouigen / maer sluijt nochtans
de ongelouigen nijet buijten de lijeffde.
Onsen heer selue daer hij de Joden berispt
geeft hij ons instructie wat wij behooren
te doen / onder t' exempel vanden Samaritaen
ons lerende dat alle menschen oock van and*e*re
ges*in*theijt ons euen naesten zijn. Doet, seijt
hij / gelijck uwen Vader dije laet sijne sonne
schijnen ende sijnen regen daelen ouer goeden
ende quaeden. Soo moeten wij dan mede
aen alle personen bethoonen de gemene wercken
~~en~~vande natuijrlijcke lijeffde / sonder ijemant

maar ook door de heidense auteurs wordt aanbevolen, die bestaat uit het ontvangen en goed behandelen van vreemdelingen. De volken, die vreemdelingen hebben geweerd, worden overal uitgemaakt voor barbaren en onnatuurlijke mensen.

Wat voor soort mensen leeft hier? Welk land accepteert deze zeden:
men houdt ons af van het gastvrije strand [...].[7]

Als de apostel Paulus wil dat wij goed zijn voor alle mensen, in het bijzonder voor geloofsgenoten, veronderstelt hij wel een inniger liefde tussen gelovigen, maar sluit nochtans de ongelovigen niet buiten de liefde. Onze Heer zelf geeft, waar hij de joden berispt, ons instructie wat wij behoren te doen, door de gelijkenis van de Samaritaan, die ons leert dat alle mensen, ook van andere gezindten, onze naasten zijn. "Doet", zegt hij, "zoals uw Vader, die laat zijn zon schijnen en zijn regen dalen over de goeden en de kwaden."

Zo moeten wij ook aan alle mensen de gewone werken van de natuurlijke liefde betonen, zonder iemand

7 Vergilius, *Aeneas*, 59.

7r

daer buijten te sluijten. Bannissement strijt met de natuijre als affsnijdende de ge= meenschap dije de natuijre instelt e*nde* is daerom een straffe dije nijet en behoort te geschijeden dan nae voorgaende delict. In t' regard vande Joden vallen noch particuliere consideratien meer als in t' regard van andere ongeouigen. Sij zijn de kinderen Abrahams Isaacs ende Jacobs / de Israeliten der welcker is de aenneminge tot kinderen / de heerlickheijt, de verbonden, de wetgeuinge / de Goodsdijenst ende de beloften: der welcker zijn de voorvaderen: en*de* vuuijt de welcken Christus selffs is nae den vleesche de rechte de bloetverwanten van*de* Aposte= len *en* eerste leeraers van ~~eerste~~ onse religie: Jae de genen aen de welcken Godts Oraculen zijn vertrouwt. Als wij disputeren wat boecken Canonijck zijn~~de~~ in het oude Testament t' is op de Joden dat wij ons beroepen. Sij moeten ons zijn / als den Apostel zeijt, wel vianden zoo veel het euangelie belangt, maer beminden om der voorvaderen wille dije van Godt sonderling zijn verkoren / De Heijdenen hebben valsche Goden: De Ma= Humetisten een valsche Profeet. De Joden hebben eenichsints den rechten Godt ende de rechte Propheten. de substantie van haer gelooff gelooуen wij mede / ende t' gunt

buiten te sluiten. Verbanning is in strijd met de natuur, omdat dit de gemeenschap afsnijdt van de natuur en is daarom een straf die niet behoort te worden gegeven dan nadat een delict is begaan. Ten opzichte van de joden gelden deze specifieke overwegingen nog meer dan ten opzichte van andere ongelovigen. Zij zijn de kinderen van Abraham, Isaac en Jacob, de Israëlieten, die zijn aangenomen als kinderen, de heerlijkheid, de verbondsgenoten, de wetgeving, de godsdienst en de beloften. Zij zijn de voorouders waaruit Christus is geboren, zij zijn de bloedverwanten van de apostelen en de eerste leraren van onze religie. Ja, aan hen zijn Gods voorspellingen toevertrouwd.

Als wij beargumenteren welke boeken canoniek zijn in het Oude Testament beroepen wij ons op de joden. Zoals de Apostel zegt, zij moeten wel onze vijanden zijn voor zover het het evangelie betreft, maar beminden om wille van de voorouders, die in het bijzonder door God zijn uitverkoren. De heidenen hebben valse Goden. De Mohammedanen een valse Profeet. De joden hebben in ieder geval de ware God en de ware Profeten.

De essentie van hun geloof geloven wij ook, en datgene wat

7v

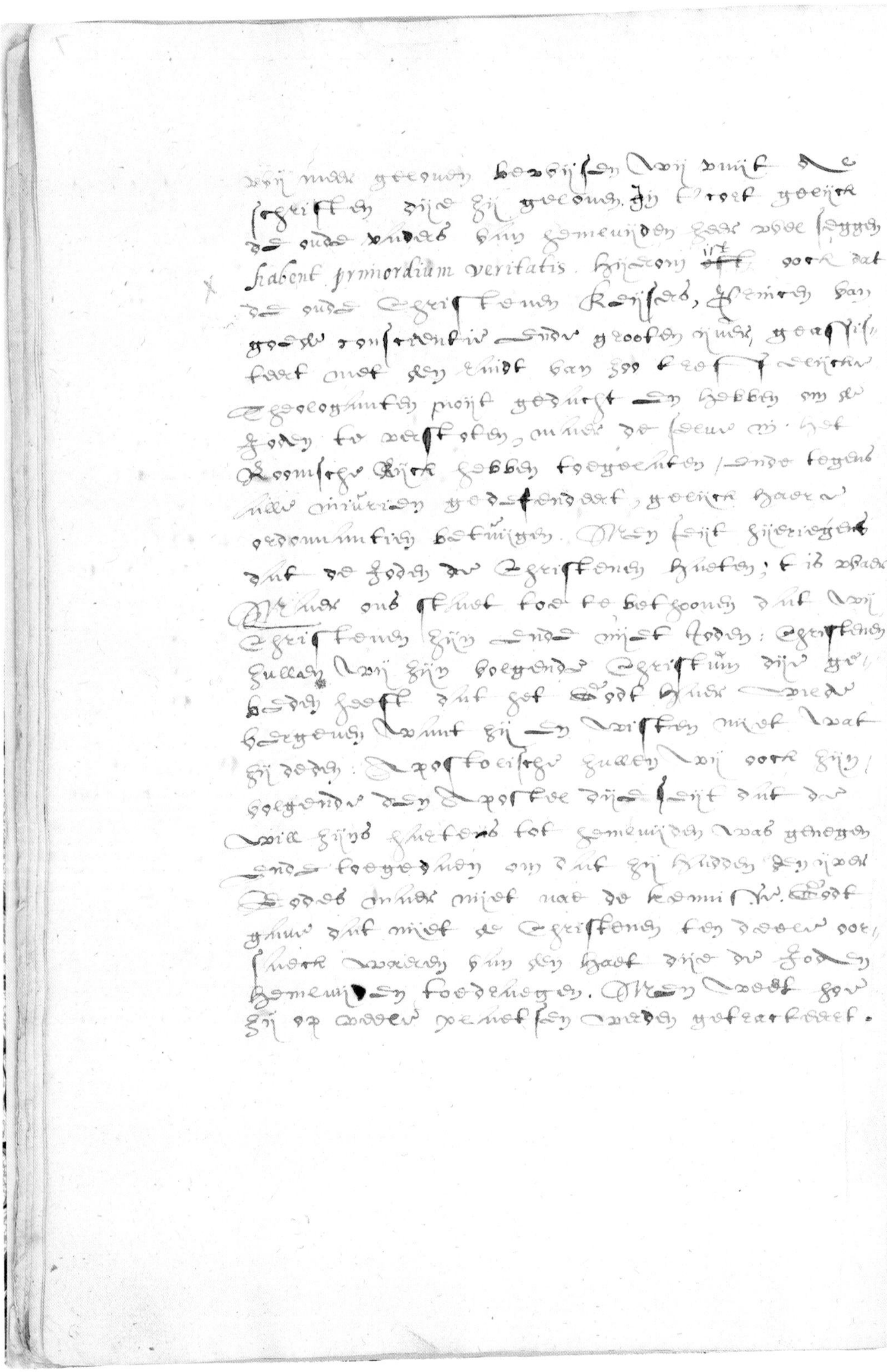

wij meer gelouen bewijsen wij vuijt de schriften dije zij gelouen. In t' cort gelijck de oude vaders van hemluijden zeer wel seggen *habent primordium veritatis*. Hijerom ~~ost~~ ist oock dat de oude Christenen Keijsers, Princen van goede conscientie ende grooten ijuer, geassis=teert met den raidt van zoo treffelijcke Theologanten noijt gedacht en hebben om de Joden te verstoten, maer de selue in het Roomsche Rijck hebben toegelaten / ende tegens alle iniurien gedefendeert, gelijck haere ordonantien betuijgen. Men seijt hijer iegens dat de Joden de Christenen haeten; t is waer. Maer ons staet toe te bethoonen dat wij Christenen zijn ende nijet Joden: Christenen zullen wij zijn volgende Christum dije ge=beden heeft dat het Godt haer wilde vergeven want zij en wisten nijet wat zij deden: Apostolische zullen wij ook zijn / volgende den Apostel dije seijt dat de will zijns hartens tot hemluijden was genegen ende toegedaen om dat zij hadden den ijver Godes maer nijet nae de kennisse. Godt gaue dat nijet de Christenen ten deele oor=saeck waeren van den haet dije de Joden hemluijden toedraegen. Men weet hoe zij op veele plaetsen werden getracteert.

wij nog meer geloven, bewijzen wij uit de geschriften waarin zij geloven. Kortom, zoals de Oude Vaders over hen zeer terecht zeggen: *Zij hebben de oorsprong van de waarheid.* Daarom hebben de eerste christelijke keizers en vorsten met een goed geweten en grote ijver, bijgestaan door de raad van voortreffelijke theologen, er nooit aan gedacht de joden te verstoten, maar hebben hen in het Romeinse Rijk toegelaten en hen tegen alle onrecht verdedigd, waarvan hun verordeningen getuigen. Men brengt hier tegenin, dat de joden de christenen haten. Dat is waar. Maar het past ons te tonen dat wij christenen zijn en geen joden. Wij zullen christenen zijn, in navolging van Christus, die gebeden heeft, dat God het hen wilde vergeven, want zij wisten niet wat zij deden. Verkondigers zullen wij ook zijn, in navolging van de Apostel, die zegt, dat zijn hart hen was toegedaan, omdat zij Godsijver hadden maar geen Godskennis. God geve, dat de christenen niet deels de oorzaak zijn van de haat die de joden hen toedragen. Men weet hoe zij op veel plaatsen worden behandeld.

8r

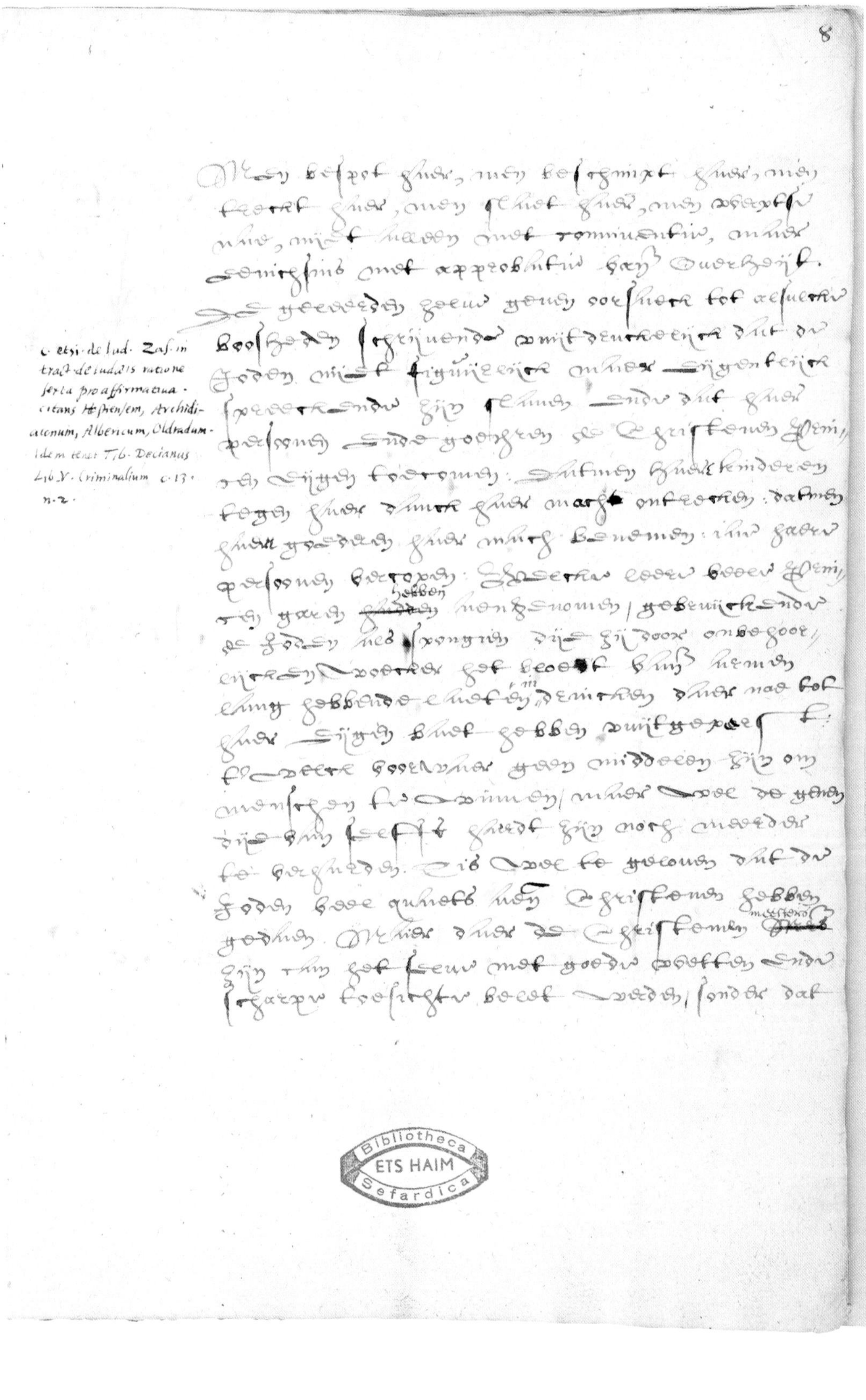

8

c. etsi. de Iud. Zas. in
tract. de Iudaeis ratione
sexta pro affirmativa.
citans Hostiensem, Archidi-
aconum, Albericum, Oldradum.
Idem tenet Tib. Decianus
Lib. V. Criminalium c. 13.
n. 2.

Men bespot haer, men beschipt haer, men treckt haer, men slaet haer, men werptse nae, nijet alleen met conniuentie, maer eenichsins met approbatie van*de* Ouerheijt. De geleerden zelue geuen oorsaeck tot alsulcke* boosheden schrijuende vuijtdruckelijck dat de Joden nijet figuijrlijck maer eijgentlijck spreeckende zijn slauen ende dat haer persoonen ende goe[de?]ren de Christenen Prin= cen eijgen toecomen: datmen haere kinderen tegen haer danck haer mach ontrecken: datmen haer goederen haer mach benemen: iae haere persoonen vercopen: Welcke leere veele Prin= cen garen ~~hadden~~ hebben aengenomen / gebruijckende de Joden als spongien dije zij door onbehoorlijcken woecker het bloedt van*de* armen lang hebbende laeten [in] drincken daer nae tot haer eijgen baet hebben vuijtgeperst: t'welck voorwaer geen middelen zijn om menschen te winnen / maer wel de genen dije van selffs hardt zijn noch meerder te verharden. Tis wel te gelouen dat de Joden veel quaets aen*de* Christenen hebben gedaen. Maer daer de Christenen ~~Mees~~ meesters zijn can het selue met goede wetten ende scharpe toesichte belet werden / sonder dat

* *c. etsi. de Iud. Zas. in tract. de Iudaeis ratione sexta pro affirmativa. citans Hostiensem, Archidi- aconum, Albericum, Oldradum. tenet Tib. Decianus Lib. v. Criminalium c. 13. n. 2.*

Men bespot ze, men beschimpt ze, men trekt aan ze, men slaat ze, men werpt dingen naar ze, niet enkel met medeweten maar zelfs met toestemming van de overheid.

De geleerden zijn zelf de oorzaak van zulke boosaardigheden, zij schrijven uitdrukkelijk dat de joden niet figuurlijk, maar letterlijk slaven zijn, en dat zij zelf en hun bezit de christelijke vorsten zelf toebehoren. Dat men ze hun kinderen tegen hun wil mag afnemen. Dat men hun bezit in beslag mag nemen, ja, henzelf mag verkopen.[8] Veel vorsten hebben met graagte deze opvatting gehuldigd en gebruikten de joden als sponzen, die zij het bloed van de armen lange tijd door onbehoorlijke woeker hebben laten opzuigen en daarna, tot hun eigen voordeel, hebben uitgeperst; hetgeen voorwaar geen middelen zijn om de mensen voor zich te winnen, maar wel om diegenen die van zichzelf hard zijn, nog verder te verharden.

Het is juist om te geloven, dat de joden de christenen veel kwaad hebben gedaan. Maar omdat de christenen de meesters zijn kan dit met goede wetten en scherp toezicht worden voorkomen, zonder dat het

8 In de kantlijn: *c. etsi. de Iud. Zas. in tract. de Iudaeis ratione sexta pro affirmativa. citans Hostiensem, Archidiaconum, Albericum, Oldradum. tenet Tib. Decianus Lib. v. Criminalium c. 13 n. 2*. Grotius verwijst hier naar het canoniek recht. Zie ook noot 23 op blz. 153 naar het canoniek recht.

8v

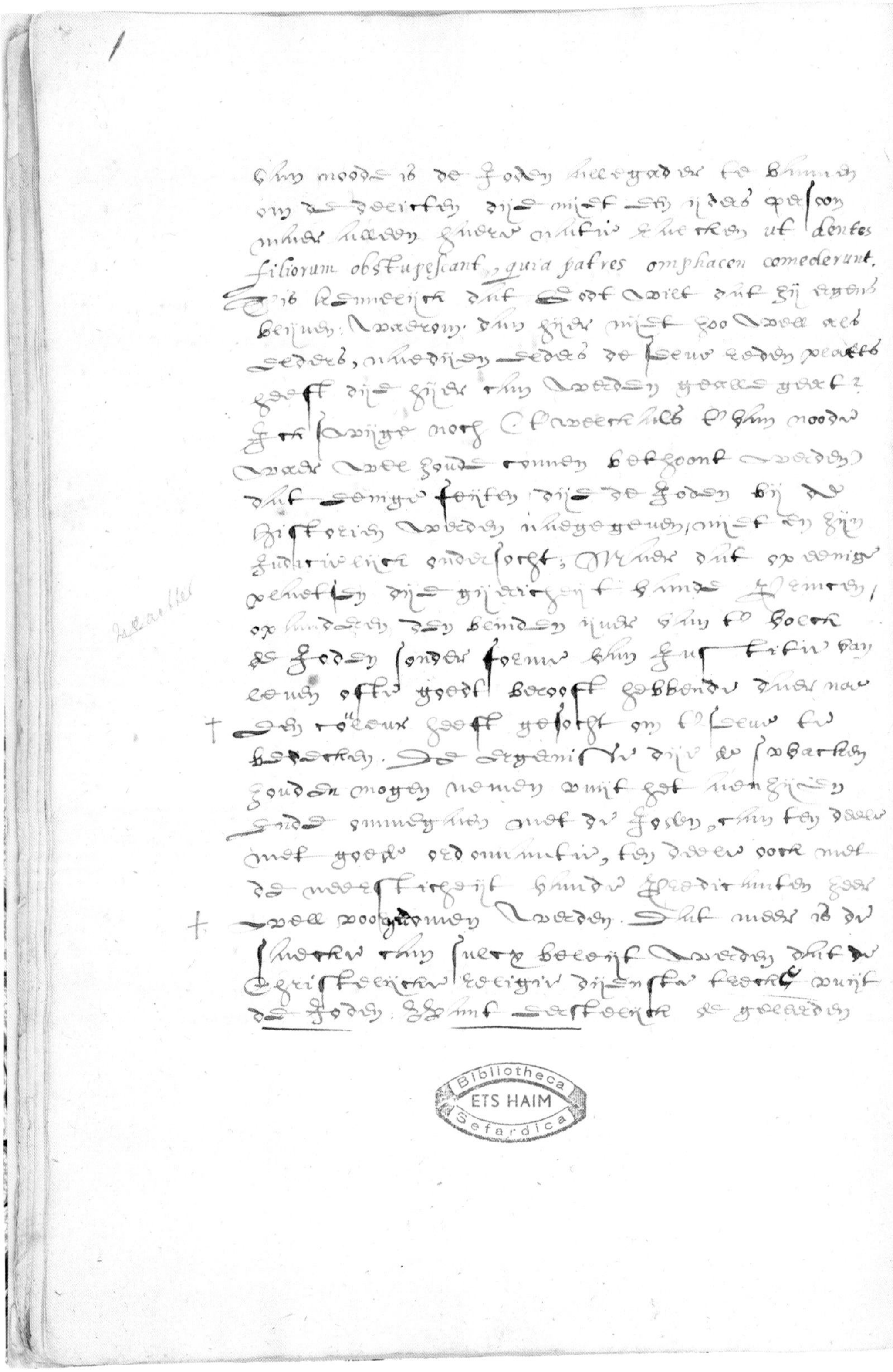

ut dentes filiorum obstupescant, quia patres omphacem comederunt.

van noode is de Joden allegader te bannen om de delicten dije nijet een ijders persoon maer alleen haere natie raecken *ut dentes filiorum obstupescant, quia patres omphacen comederunt*.

T'is kennelijck dat Godt wilt dat zij ergens blijven: waerom dan hijer nijet zoo wel als elders, nadijen elders de selue reden plaets heeft dije hijer can werden geallegeert? Ick swijge noch (t'welck als t' van noode waer wel zoude bethoont werden) dat enige feijten / dije de Joden bij de historien werden naegegeven / nijet en zijn Judicielijck ondersocht; Maer dat op eenige plaetsen dije gijericheijt vande Princen / op anderen den blinden ijuer van t' volck de Joden sonder forme van Justitie van leven ofte goedt berooft hebbende daer nae den couleur heeft gesocht om t' selue te bedecken. De ergernisse dije de swacken zouden mogen nemen vuijt het aenzijen ende ommegaen met de Joden, can ten deele met goede ordonantie, ten deele oock met de neersticheijt vande Predicanten zeer well voorgecomen werden. Dat meer is de saecke can sulcx beleijt werden dat de Christelijcke religie dijenste trecke vuijt de Joden: Want eerstelijck de geleerden

nodig is de joden allen te verbannen om strafbare feiten die niet het individu maar enkel het volk betreffen *Zoals de tanden van de zonen stomp worden, omdat de vaders iets onrijps hebben gegeten*.[9] Het is duidelijk dat God wil dat zij ergens verblijven. Waarom dan niet hier, zo goed als elders, aangezien elders hetzelfde argument bestaat, dat hier ook kan worden beweerd?

Dan zwijg ik nog (dat als het nodig is, zeer goed benadrukt kan worden) over enkele feiten, die de joden volgens de geschiedenis worden verweten, die niet juridisch zijn onderzocht; maar die in enkele bronnen worden vermeld, dat door de hebzucht van de vorsten ten opzichte van anderen het fanatisme van het volk de joden zonder vorm van rechtspraak van leven of bezit heeft beroofd, en dat daarna de vorsten een manier hebben gevonden om dit te verbergen. Als de zwakken van geest zich zouden ergeren aan het zien van en de omgang met de joden kan dit, deels met goede regelgeving en deels met inspanning van de predikanten, zeer goed worden voorkomen.

Als dat vaker het geval is, zou het van groter belang zijn, dat de joden de christelijke religie tot nut zijn. Ten eerste, de geleerden

9 Ezechiel 18:2 (omphacen komt van het Griekse ὄμφακα).

9r

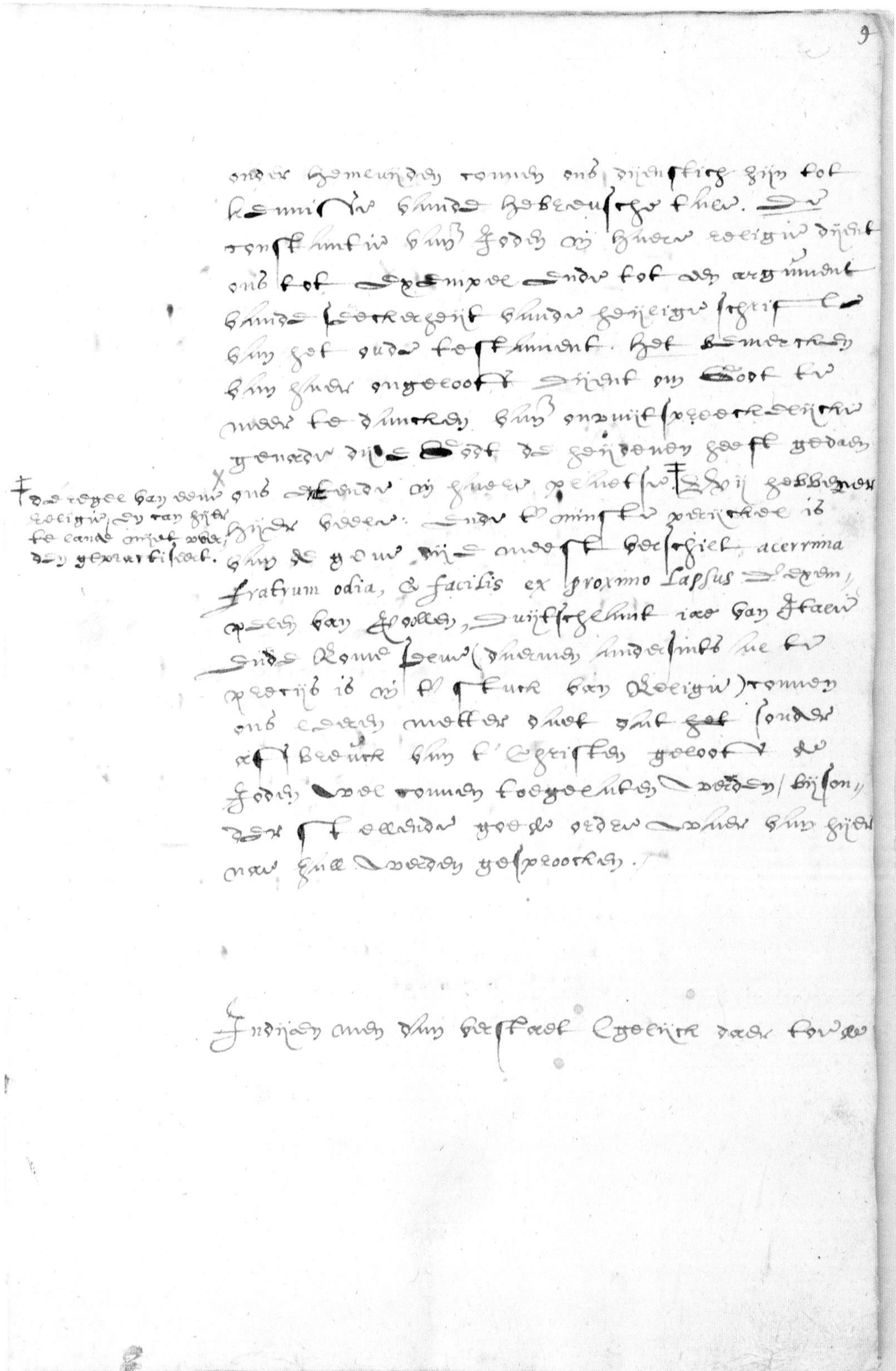
acerrima fratrum odia, & facilis ex proximo lapsus

onder hemluijden connen ons dijenstich zijn tot kennisse vande hebreuse tale. De constantie van*de* Joden in haere religie dijent ons tot exempel ende tot een argument vande seeckerheijt vande heijliige schrift van het oude testament. Het bemercken van haer ongelooff dijent om Godt te meer te dancken van*de* onvuijtspreeckelijcke genade dije Godt de heijdenen heeft gedaen ons entende in haere plaetse. ↑Wij hebbener* hijer veele: ende t' minste perijckel is van de gene dije meest verschilt: *acerrima fratrum odia, & facilis ex proximo lapsus*. D' exem= pelen van Poollen, Duijtechlandt iae van Italie ende Rome selue (daermen andersints al te precijs is in 't stuck van Religie) connen ons leeren metter daet dat ~~het~~ sonder affbreuck van t' Christen geloof de Joden wel connen toegelaten werden / bijson= der stellende goede ordre waer van hijer nae zal werden gesprooken.

Indijen men dan verstaet (gelijck daer toe de

* ↑ De regel van eene religie / en can hijer te lande nijet wer= den gepractiseert.

onder hen kunnen ons van nut zijn met hun kennis van de Hebreeuwse taal. De standvastigheid van de joden in hun religie dient ons tot voorbeeld en als argument van de waarheid van de Heilige Schrift van het Oude Testament. Het benoemen van hun ongeloof dient om God des te meer te danken voor de onuitsprekelijke genade, die God de heidenen heeft geschonken, ons in hun plaats te stellen.

In dit land kan de wetgeving niet slechts voor één religie gelden.[10] Wij hebben hier vele religies; en het geringste probleem veroorzaakt de religie welke het meeste verschilt: *Het bitterst is de haat onder broeders, en het vallen van dichtbij ligt voor de hand.*[11] De voorbeelden van Polen, Duitsland, ja, van Italië en van Rome zelf (waar men anderszins al te precies is op het gebied van religie) kunnen ons in de praktijk leren dat, zonder afbreuk te doen aan het christelijke geloof, de joden wel kunnen worden toegelaten, namelijk door goede verordeningen op te stellen waarover hierna zal worden gesproken.

Indien men dan begrijpt (waartoe de

10 Deze zin is ingevoegd vanuit de kantlijn.

11 Op Tacitus gebaseerde tekst met verwijzing naar de godsdiensttwisten in de Republiek. Zie: Kaplan, *Muslims in the Dutch Golden Age*, 11–12.

9v

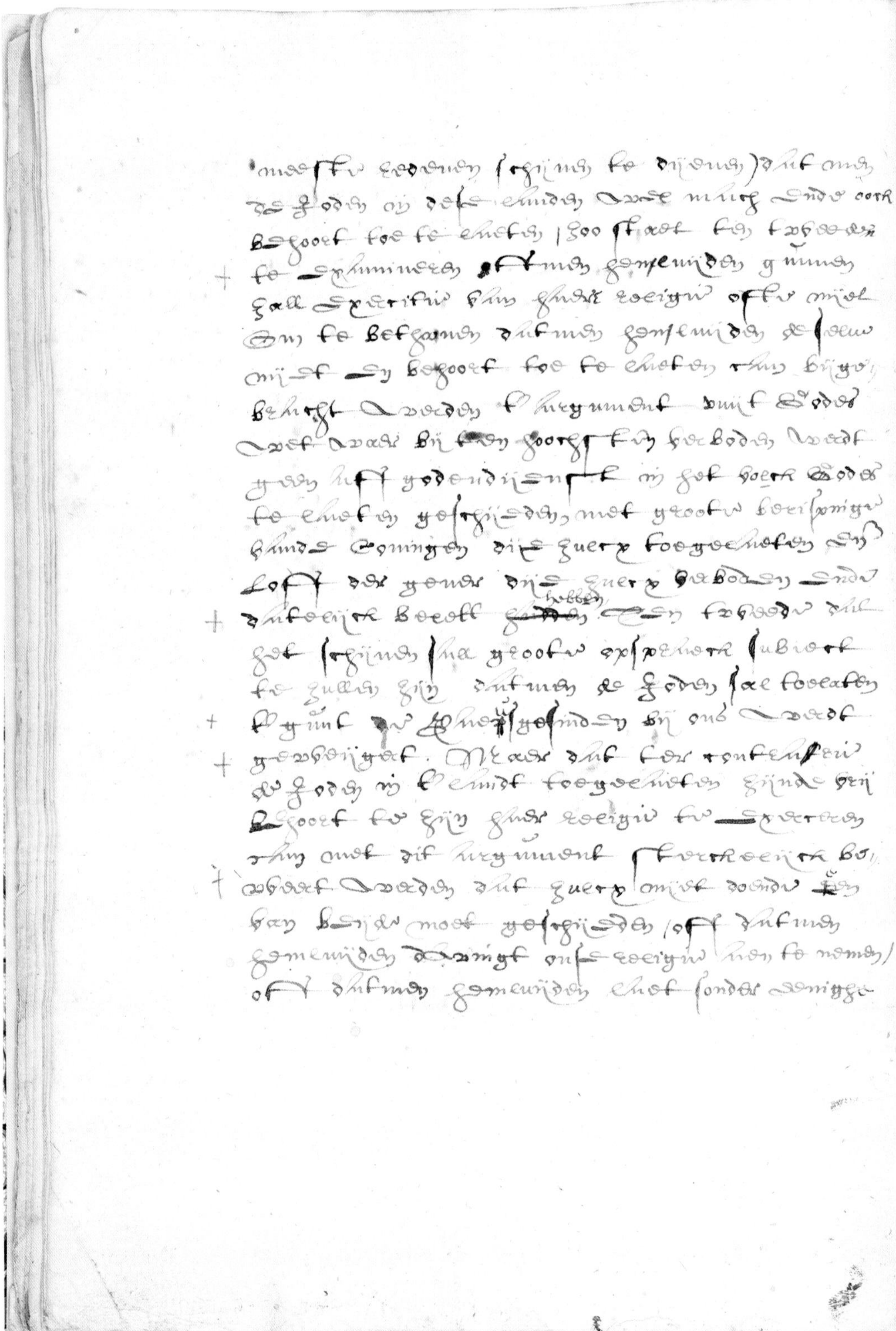

meeste redenen schijnen te dijenen) dat men de Joden in dese landen wel mach ende oock behoort toe te laten / zoo staet ten tweeden te examineren off men he~~m~~nluijden gunnen zall exercitie van haere religie ofte nijet Om te bethonen datmen he~~m~~nluijden de selue nijet en behoort toe te laeten can bijge=bracht werden t' argument vuijt Godes wet waer bij ten hoochsten verboden werdt geen affgodendijenst in het volck Godes te laeten geschijeden, met groote berispinge vande Coningen dije zulcx toegelaten en*de* loff der gener dije zulcx verboden ende datelijck belett ~~hadden~~ hebben. Ten tweede dat het schijnen sall groote opspraeck subiect te zullen zijn datmen de Joden sal toelaten t' gunt de Paeusgesinden bij ons werdt gewijgert. Maer dat ter contra~~t~~rie de Joden in t' landt toegelaeten zijnde vrij behoort te zijn haer religie te exerceren can met dit argument sterckelijck be=weert werden dat zulcx nijet doende een van beijde moet geschijeden / off datmen hemluijden dwingt onse religie aen te nemen / off datmen hemluijden laet sonder eenighe

meeste genoemde argumenten schijnen te leiden), dat men de joden mag en ook behoort toe te laten in deze landen, dan moet men in de tweede plaats onderzoeken of men hun wel de uitoefening van hun religie zal toestaan of niet.

Om aan te geven dat men hun dit niet behoort toe te staan, kan het argument uit Gods wet worden gebruikt, dat ten strengste werd verboden afgodendienst in Gods volk te laten plaatsvinden, waarbij de vorsten die dit toelieten, streng werden berispt en degenen geprezen die dit hebben verboden en feitelijk hebben voorkomen.

Ten tweede, dat het waarschijnlijk onderwerp zal zijn van grote ophef, als men de joden zal toestaan wat bij ons de rooms-katholieken werd geweigerd. Maar dat het daarentegen de joden, die in het land zijn toegelaten, vrij behoort te staan hun godsdienst uit te oefenen, kan met dit argument krachtig worden beweerd. Dat, als men dat niet doet, een van beide moet gebeuren: ofwel dat men hen dwingt onze religie aan te nemen of dat men hen zonder enige

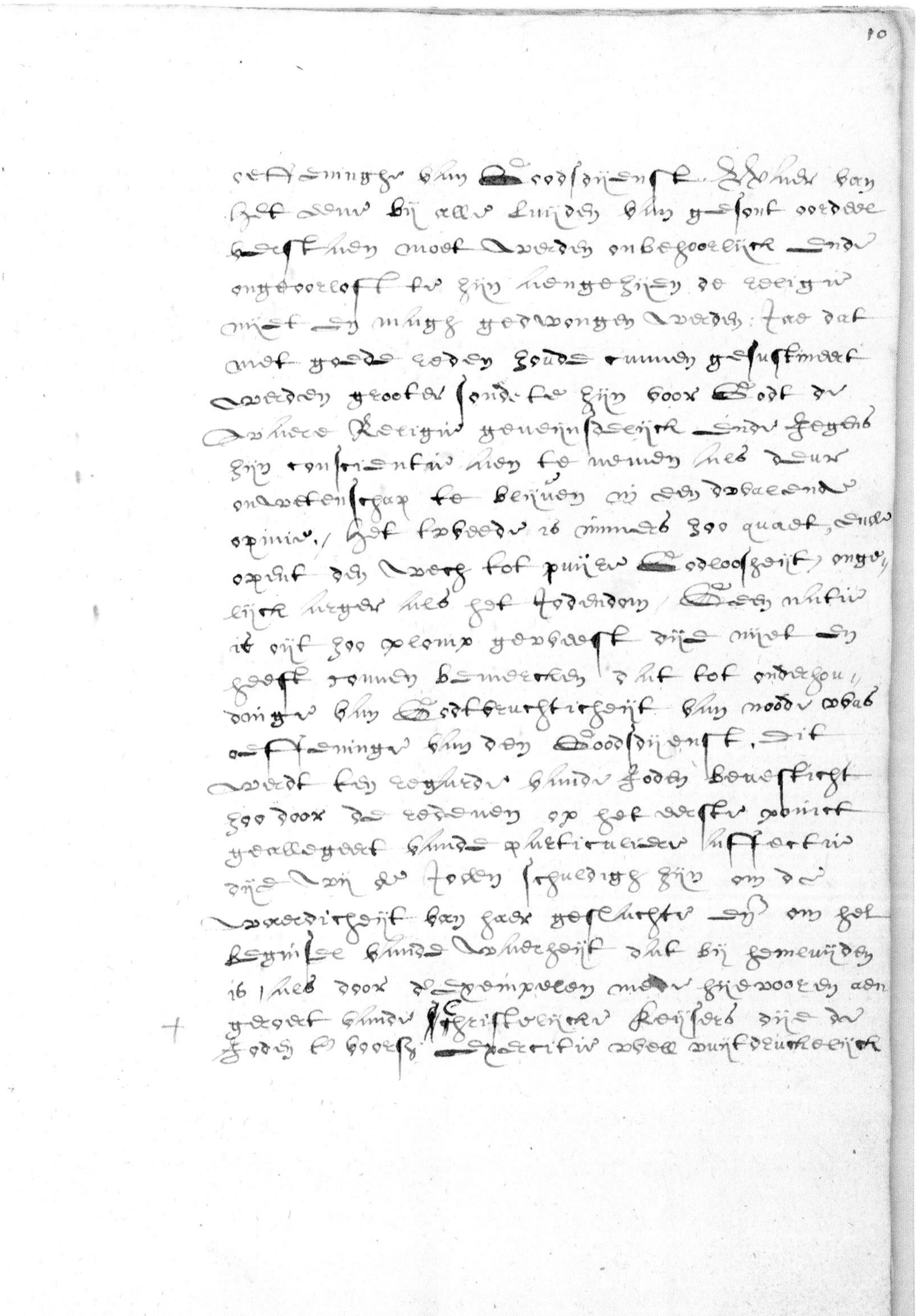

10r

oeffeninghe van ~~G~~goodsdijenst. Waer van het eene bij alle luijden van gesont oordeel verstaen moet werden onbehoorlijck ende ongeoorloft te zijn aengezijen de religie nijet en magh gedwongen werden: Jae dat met goede reden zoude cunnen gesustineert werden grooter sonde te zijn voor Godt de waere Religie geueijnsdelijck ende Jegens zijn conscientije aen te nemen als deur onwetenschap te blijuen in een dwalende opinie. / Het tweede is immers zoo quaet, ende opent den wech tot puijre ~~G~~godloosheijt, onge= lijck arger als het Jodendom / Geen natie is oijt zoo plomp geweest dije nijet en heeft connen bemercken dat tot onderhou= dinge van Godtvruchticheijt van noode was oeffeninge van den Goodsdijenst. Dit werdt ten regarde vande Joden beuesticht zoo door de redenen op het eerste poinct geallegeert vande partculiere affectie dije wij de Joden schuldich zijn om de waerdicheijt van haer geslachte end*e* om het beginsel vande waerheijt dat bij hemluijden is / door de exempelen mede hijervooren aen geroert vande cChristelijcke Keisers dije de Joden t' voorsz. exercitie well vuijtdruckelijck

godsdienstoefening laat.

Waarvan het eerste door alle mensen met gezond verstand moet worden gezien als onbehoorlijk en ongeoorloofd, aangezien religie niet opgedrongen mag worden: Ja, dat met goede reden aangevoerd kan worden dat het een grotere zonde is voor God de ware religie te veinzen en tegen zijn geweten aan te nemen, dan onwetend te blijven in een verkeerde opvatting.

Het tweede is immers net zo verkeerd en opent de weg naar pure goddeloosheid, wat nog veel erger is dan het jodendom. Geen volk is ooit zo lomp geweest dat het niet heeft kunnen bemerken dat de uitoefening van godsdienst noodzakelijk was tot het onderhouden van godvruchtigheid.

Dit werd ten aanzien van de joden bevestigd, zowel door de aangevoerde argumenten ten aanzien van het eerste punt, de bijzondere genegenheid die wij de joden verschuldigd zijn vanwege de waardigheid van hun afkomst en het beginsel van de waarheid dat bij hen aanwezig is, als ook vanwege de voorbeelden die hiervoor al aangevoerd zijn, van de christelijke keizers die de joden de genoemde uitoefening uitdrukkelijk

10v

hebben toeghestaen. Ghelijck besnijdinge, offerhanden
dien niet alleen de Joden toelieten, haere sij-
nagoghen te houden, maer oock den ijder verbieden
gemeijnschap daerin te moeten, gonnende oock
hen de tienden ende offeren, onder den Jode-
schen dignitijt ende authoriteijt. Daer-
nement mijt het verbot van den Godts-
dienst [illegible] ieghens [illegible].
Want weest soo en is den Joden dienst
van het godendienst, maer een dienst
Godes, doch ghemenght met ongeloof:
[illegible] ende haere oude ceremonien [illegible],
uijtgenomen de besnijdinge, den Sabbath,
ende [illegible] verboden spijsen.
Voorts soo en is oock de voorseijde wet
die den volcke van Israel is gegeven
[illegible] niet dat de selve [illegible] op haere
volcken ende tijden. Want die wet
is gegeven hen [illegible] volck commende van
de selve ouders, [illegible] in deser
[illegible], [illegible] [illegible] oock niet sichtbaer
[illegible] ende [illegible] van [illegible]
[illegible] [illegible] [illegible]: [illegible]
[illegible] van [illegible] en geeft [illegible] meest
alle de volckeren van desen tijdt: behalven
noch dat de Christelijcke sachtmoedicheijt

hebben toegestaen. T' selue betuijgen de wetten
dije nijet alleen de Joden toelaeten haer Sij=
nagogen te houden / maer oock een ijder verbijeden
hemluijden daerin te molesteren, geuende oock
aen de Leeraers ende ouersten onder den Joden
seeckere digniteijt ende authoriteijt. T' ar=
gument vuijt het verboth van een Affgoden=
dijenst can hijer iegens nijet opereren.
Want eerst zoo en is der Joden dijenst
geen affgodendijenst, maer een dijenst
Godes / doch gemenght met ongeloof:
Selfffs al haer oude cerimonien cesseren,
vuijtgenomen de besnijdinge, den Sabbath,
ende t' abstineren van verboden spijsen.
Voorts zoo en is oock de voorschreuen wet
dije den volcke van Jsrael is gegeven
sulcx nijet dat de selue past op alle
volcken ende tijden. Want dije wet
is gegeuen aen een volck comende van
de selue Ouders, opgevoet all in eene
religie, wecke religie oock met sighttbare
Miraculen ende gauen van Propheten
dageelijcx wijerd beuesticht: t' welck
alles geen plaets en heeft in meest
all de volckeren van desen tijdt: behalue
noch dat de Christelijcke sachtmoedicheijt

hebben toegestaan. Hetzelfde blijkt uit de wetten, die niet alleen de joden toestaan hun synagogen te hebben, maar ook iedereen verbieden hen daarin te molesteren en die ook aan de leraren en de opperste leiding van de joden in zekere zin waardigheid en autoriteit verlenen. Het argument betreffende het verbod van afgodendienst kan hiertegen niet gelden. Want ten eerste is de dienst van de joden geen afgodendienst, maar een dienst aan God, echter vermengd met bijgeloof: zelfs als haar oude ceremoniën komen te vervallen, behalve de besnijdenis, de Sabbat en het zich onthouden van verboden spijzen. Verder is ook de wet, die het volk van Israël is gegeven niet zodanig, dat deze toepasbaar is op alle volkeren en in alle tijden.

Want deze wet is gegeven aan een volk afkomstig van dezelfde voorouders, opgevoed in een religie die ook met zichtbare wonderen en gaven van profeten dagelijks wordt bevestigd: hetgeen alles niet meer voorkomt bij tegenwoordige volken, behalve dat de christelijke zachtmoedigheid

11r

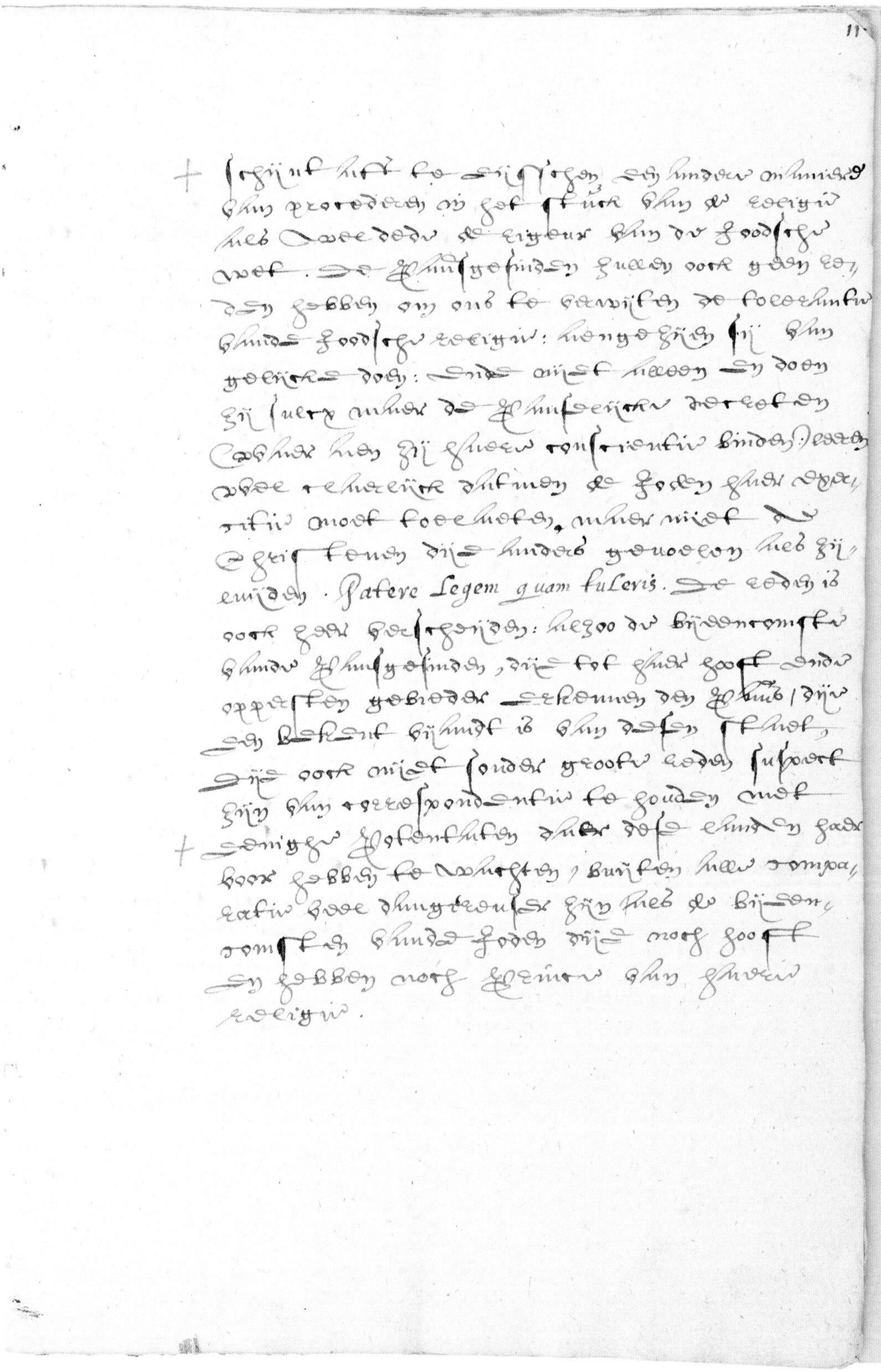

Patere Legem quam tuleris.

schijnt aff te eijsschen een andere maniere van procederen in het stuck van de religie als wel dede de rigeur van de Joodsche wet. de Pausgesinden zullen oock geen re= den hebben om ons te verwijten de tolerantie vande Joodsche religie: aengezijen sij van gelijcke doen: ende nijet alleen en doen zij sulcx maer de Pauselijcke decreten (waer aen zij haere conscientie binden:) leeren wel claerlijck datmen de Joden haer exer= citie moet toelaeten, maer nijet de Christenen dije anders geuoelen als zij= luijden. *Patere legem quam tuleris*, de reden is oock zeer verscheijden: alzoo de bijeencomste vande Pausgezinden, dije tot haer hooft ende oppersten gebieder erkennen den Paus / dije een bekent vijandt is van desen staet, dije oock nijet sonder groote reden suspect zijn van correspondentie te houden met eenighe Potentaten daer dese landen haer voor hebben te wachten, buijten alle compa= ratie veel dangereuser zijn als de bijeen= comsten vande Joden dije noch hooft en hebben noch Prince van haere religie.

een andere wijze van optreden op het gebied van religie schijnt te vereisen dan de onverbiddelijkheid van de joodse wet.

De rooms-katholieken zullen ook geen reden hebben om ons tolerantie van de joodse religie te verwijten, aangezien zij hetzelfde doen: en niet alleen doen zij dit ook, maar de pauselijke besluiten (waaraan zij hun geweten verbinden) geven zeer duidelijk aan, dat men de joden de uitoefening moet toestaan, maar niet de christenen die anders van opvatting zijn dan zijzelf. *Accepteer de wet die je (zelf) hebt gemaakt.*[12] De reden is ook zeer verschillend. Aldus zijn de bijeenkomsten van de rooms-katholieken die tot hun leider en opperste gebieder de Paus erkennen, die als erkend vijand van deze staat, niet zonder belangrijke reden verdacht wordt van het communiceren met enige machthebbers waar dit land zich voor moet hoeden, onvergelijkelijk veel gevaarlijker dan de bijeenkomsten van de joden, wier religie noch een leider noch een vorst heeft.

12 Volgens Romeins recht; voor de herkomst van deze uitpraak, zie: Wilks, *The Problem of Sovereignty in the Later Middle Ages*, 216, n. 1.

11V

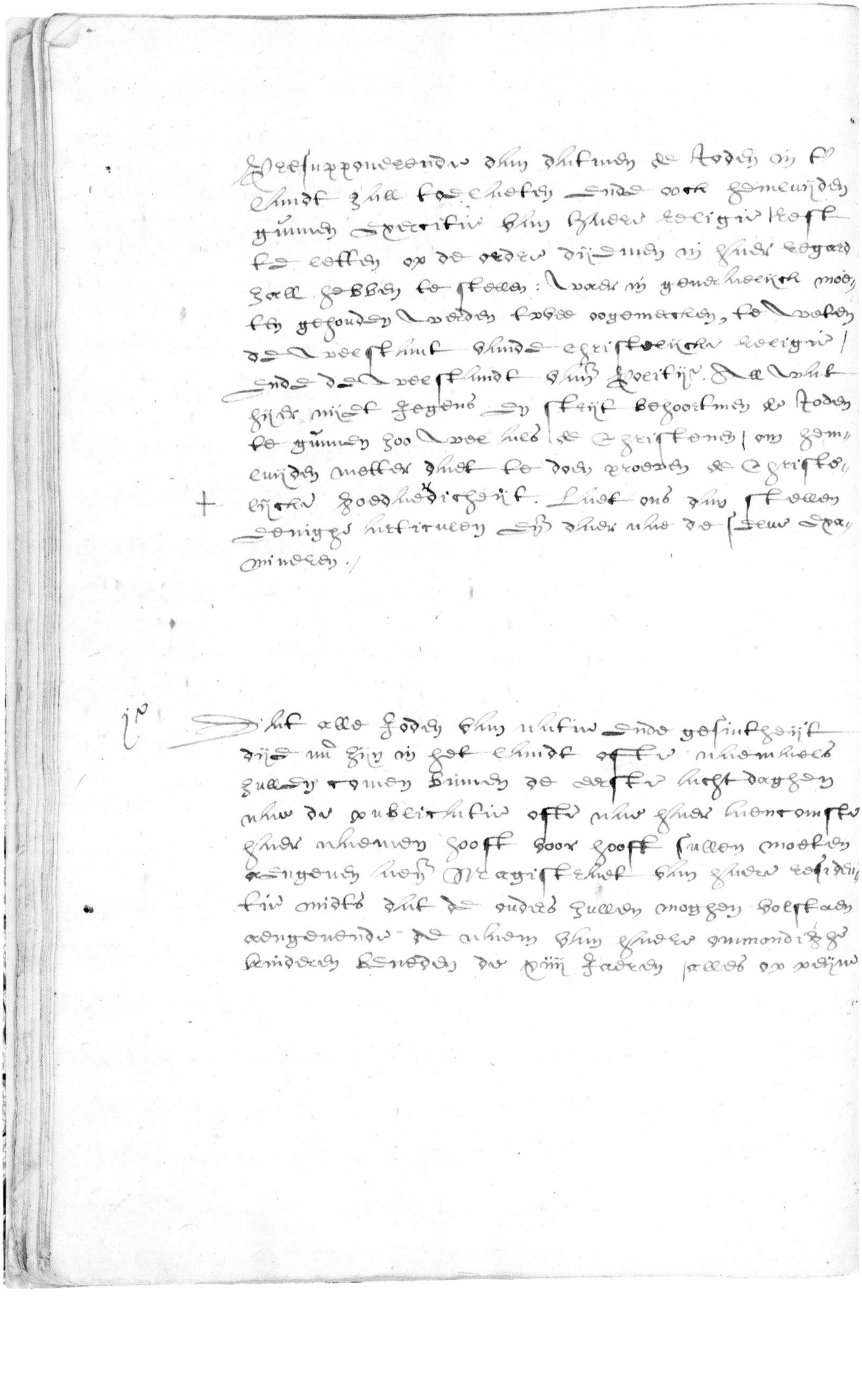

Presupponerende dan datmen de Joden in t'
landt zal toelaten ende oock hemluijden
gunnen exercitie van Haere religie / treft
te letten op de ordre dijemen in haer regard
zall hebben te stellen: waer in generaelijck moe=
ten gehouden werden twee oogemercken, te weten
de welstant vande christelijcke religie /
ende de welstandt van*de* Politije. All wat
hijer nijet Jegens en strijt behoortmen de Joden
te gunnen zoo wel als de Christenen / om hem=
luijden metter daet te doen proeven de Christe=
lijcke goedaerdicheijt. Laet ons dan stellen
eenighe articulen en*de* daer nae de selue exa=
mineren. /

j[e] Dat alle Joden van natie ende gesintheijt
dije nu zijn in het landt ofte naemaels
zullen comen binnen de erste acht daghen
nae de publicatie ofte nae haer aencomste
haer naemen hooft voor hooft sullen moeten
aengeuen aen*de* Magistraet van haere residen=
tie midts dat ouders zullen moghen volstaen
aengeuende de naem van haere ommondighe
kinderen beneden de xiiij jaeren / alles op peijne

Veronderstellende dan, dat men de joden in het land zal toelaten en hen ook de uitoefening van hun religie toestaat, dan zal men moeten letten op de regelgeving, die men ten opzichte van hen dient op te stellen,

waarbij in het algemeen twee doeleinden van belang zijn, te weten:

het welvaren van de christelijke religie en het welvaren van de staat. Alles wat hiermee niet in strijd is, behoort men de joden toe te staan, evenals de christenen, om hen daarmee in de praktijk de christelijke liefde te laten ondervinden.

Laten wij dus enkele artikelen opstellen en die vervolgens onderzoeken.

1. Dat alle joden zowel van afkomst als geloof, die nu aanwezig zijn in het land of later zullen komen, binnen de eerste acht dagen na deze kennisgeving of na hun aankomst, per hoofd hun naam moeten aangeven bij het stadsbestuur van hun woonplaats, de ouders zullen echter mogen volstaan de namen van hun minderjarige kinderen onder de 14 jaar aan te geven. Dit alles op straffe

12r

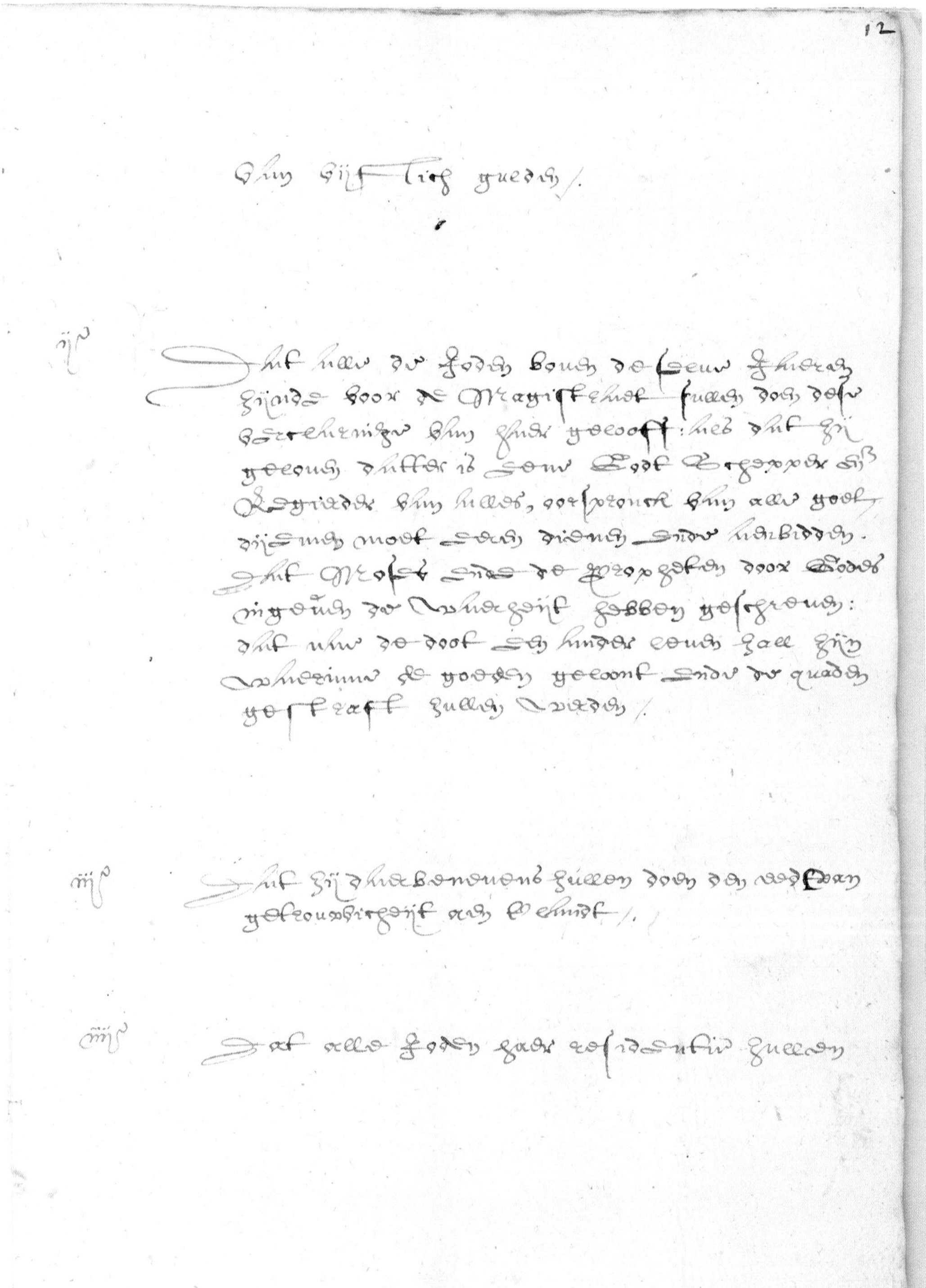

van vijftich gulden /.

ij[e] Dat alle de Joden boven de selue Jaeren zijnde voor de Magistraet sullen doen dese verclaeringe van haer gelooff: als dat zij gelouen datter is eene Godt Schepper en*de* Regierder van alles, oorspronck van alle goedt / dije men moet eeren dienen ende aenbidden. Dat Moses ende de Propheten door Godes ingeuen de waerheijt hebben geschreuen: dat nae de doot een ander leuen zall zijn waerinne de goeden geloont ende de quaden gestraft zullen werden /.

iij[e] Dat zij daer beneuens zullen doen eed van getrouwicheijt aen t' landt /.

iiij[e] Dat alle Joden haer residentie zullen

van vijftig gulden.

2. Dat alle joden boven de 14 jaar voor het stadsbestuur de volgende verklaring van hun geloof zullen afleggen: Dat zij geloven dat er één God bestaat, de schepper en regeerder van alles wat bestaat, de oorsprong van al het goede, die men moet eren, dienen en aanbidden. Dat Mozes en de Profeten, door Gods inspiratie, de waarheid hebben geschreven; dat er na de dood een ander leven zal zijn, waarin de goeden beloond en de kwaden gestraft zullen worden.

3. Dat zij daarbij tevens een eed van trouw aan het land zullen afleggen.

4. Dat alle joden zich moeten vestigen

12V

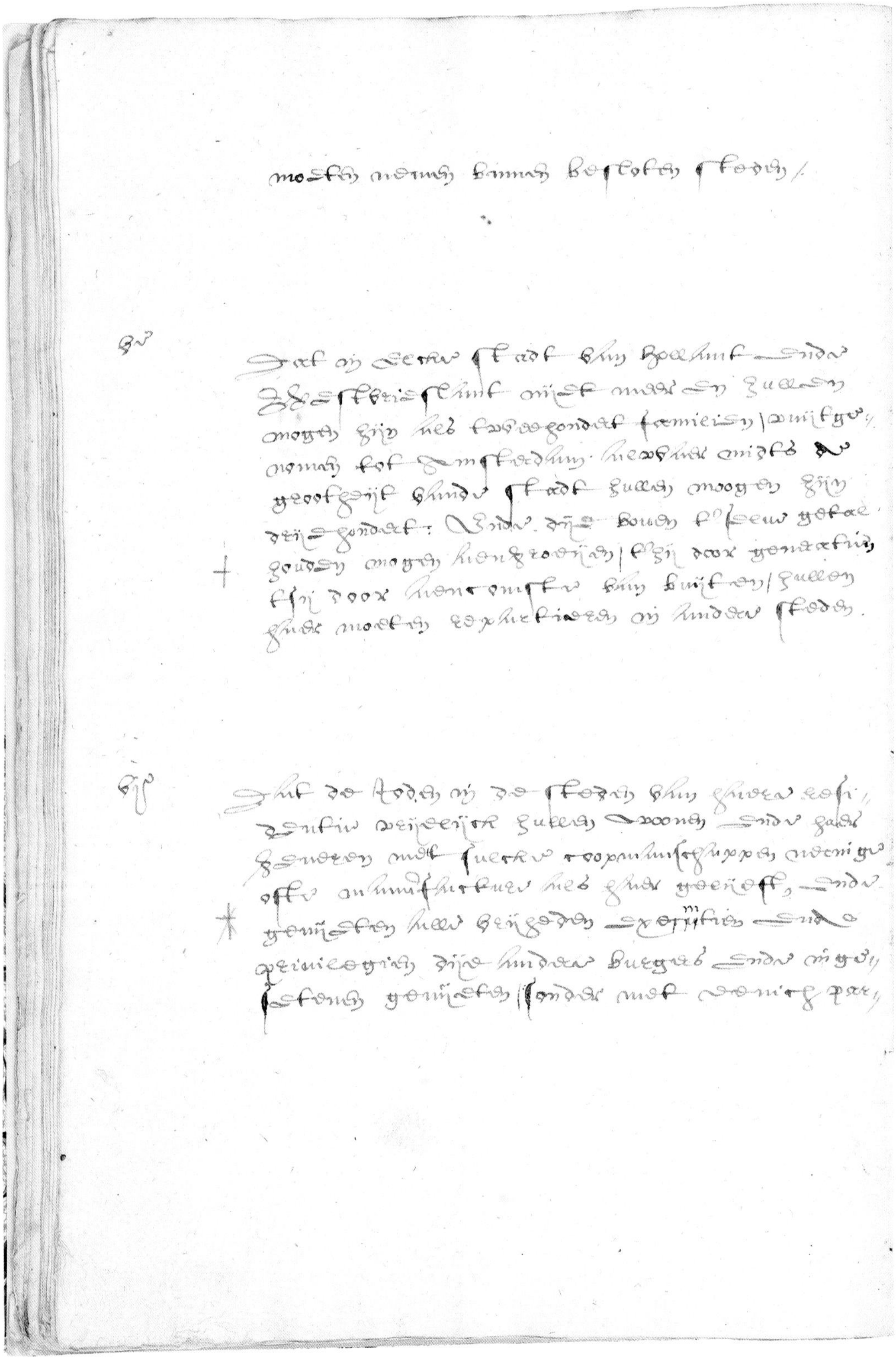

moeten nemen binnen besloten steden /.

v^e Dat in elcke stadt van Hollant ende
Westvrieslant nijet meer en zullen
mogen zijn als tweehondert Familien / vuijtge=
nomen tot Amsterdam. alwaer midts de
grootheijt vande stadt zullen moogen zijn
drijehondert: Ende dije bouen t' selue getal
zouden mogen aengroeijen / t' zij door
generatien
t' sij door aencomste van buijten / zullen
haer moeten repartieren in andere steden.

vi^e Dat de Joden in de steden van haere resi=
dentie vrijelijck zullen woonen ende haer
generen met sulcke coopmanschappen neringe
ofte manufacture als haer gelijeft, ende
genijeten alle vrijheden exemtien ende
priuilegien dije andere burgers ende inge=
setenen genijeten / sonder met eenich par=

binnen ommuurde steden.

5. Dat in elke stad van Holland en West-Friesland niet meer dan tweehonderd families zullen mogen verblijven, uitgezonderd in Amsterdam waar er, vanwege de grootte van de stad, driehonderd mogen verblijven. En dat zij indien dit aantal zou toenemen, hetzij door eigen aanwas of door aankomst van buiten, moeten vertrekken naar andere steden.

6. Dat de joden vrijelijk mogen wonen in hun woonplaatsen en zich bezighouden met de koophandel, kleinhandel of nijverheid zoals zij willen, en dat zij dezelfde vrijheden, ontheffingen en privileges die andere burgers en ingezetenen genieten zonder met enig

13r

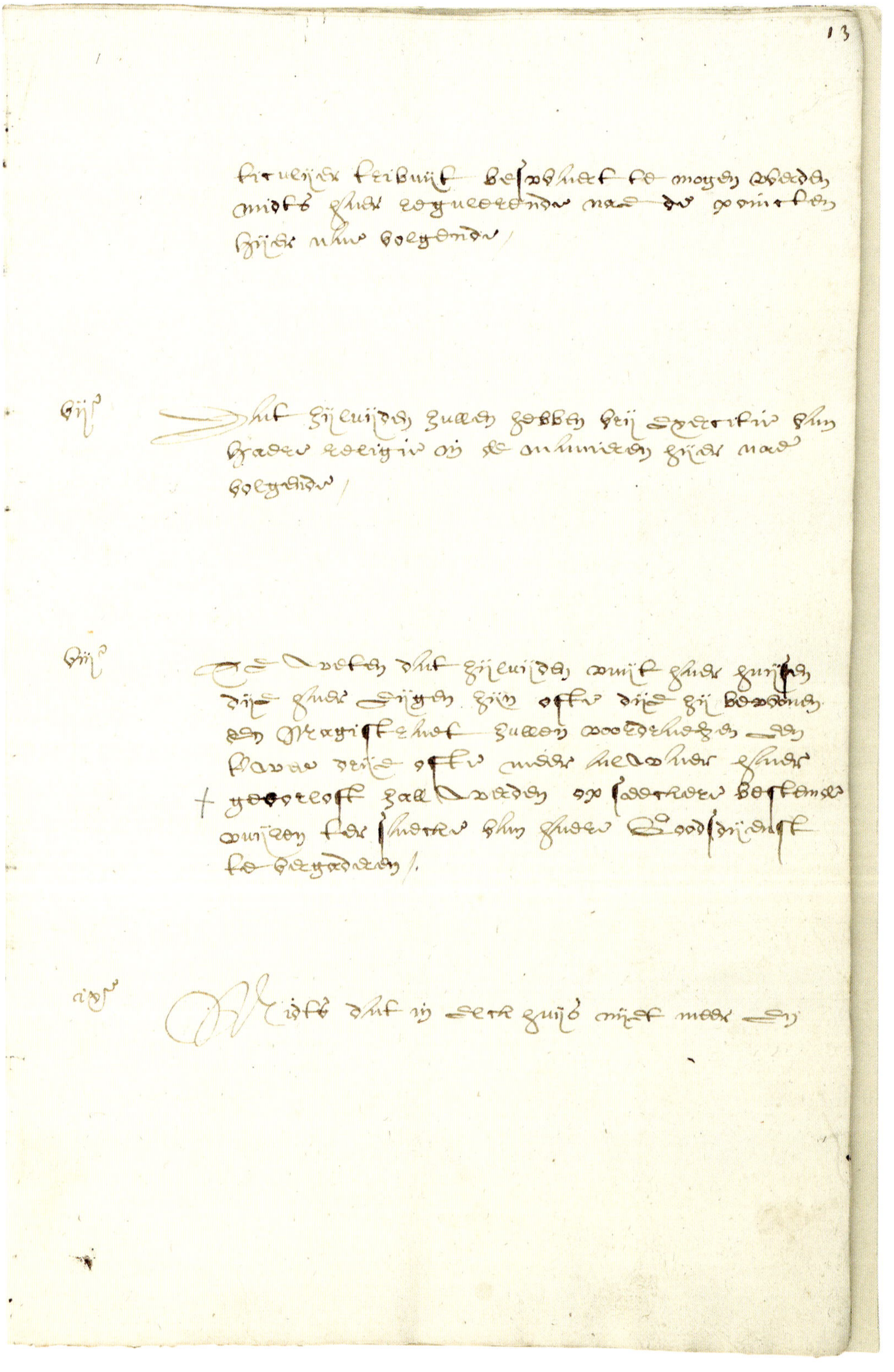

ticulijer tribuijt beswaert te mogen werden midts haer regulerende nae de poincten hijer nae volgende /

vii^{e} Dat zijluijden zullen hebben vrij exercitie van haere religie in de manieren hijer nae volgende /

viii^{e} Te weten dat zijluijden vuijt haer huijsen dije haer eijgen zijn ofte dije zij bewonen den Magistraet zullen voordraegen een twee drije ofte meer alwaer haer geoorloft zall werden op seeckere bestemde vuijren ter saecke van haere Goodsdijenst te vergaderen /.

ixe Midts dat in elck huijs nijet meer en

bijzondere heffing belast te worden, mits zij zich houden aan de volgende regels.

7. Dat zij vrije uitoefening van hun geloof mogen hebben op de volgende wijze.

8. Te weten, dat zij van hun eigen woningen of die zij bewonen er één, twee of drie of meer bij de stedelijke overheid zullen aanwijzen, waarin het hun op bepaalde vaste uren geoorloofd zal zijn bijeen te komen ter zake van hun godsdienst.

9. Onder voorwaarde dat in elke woning niet meer dan

13v

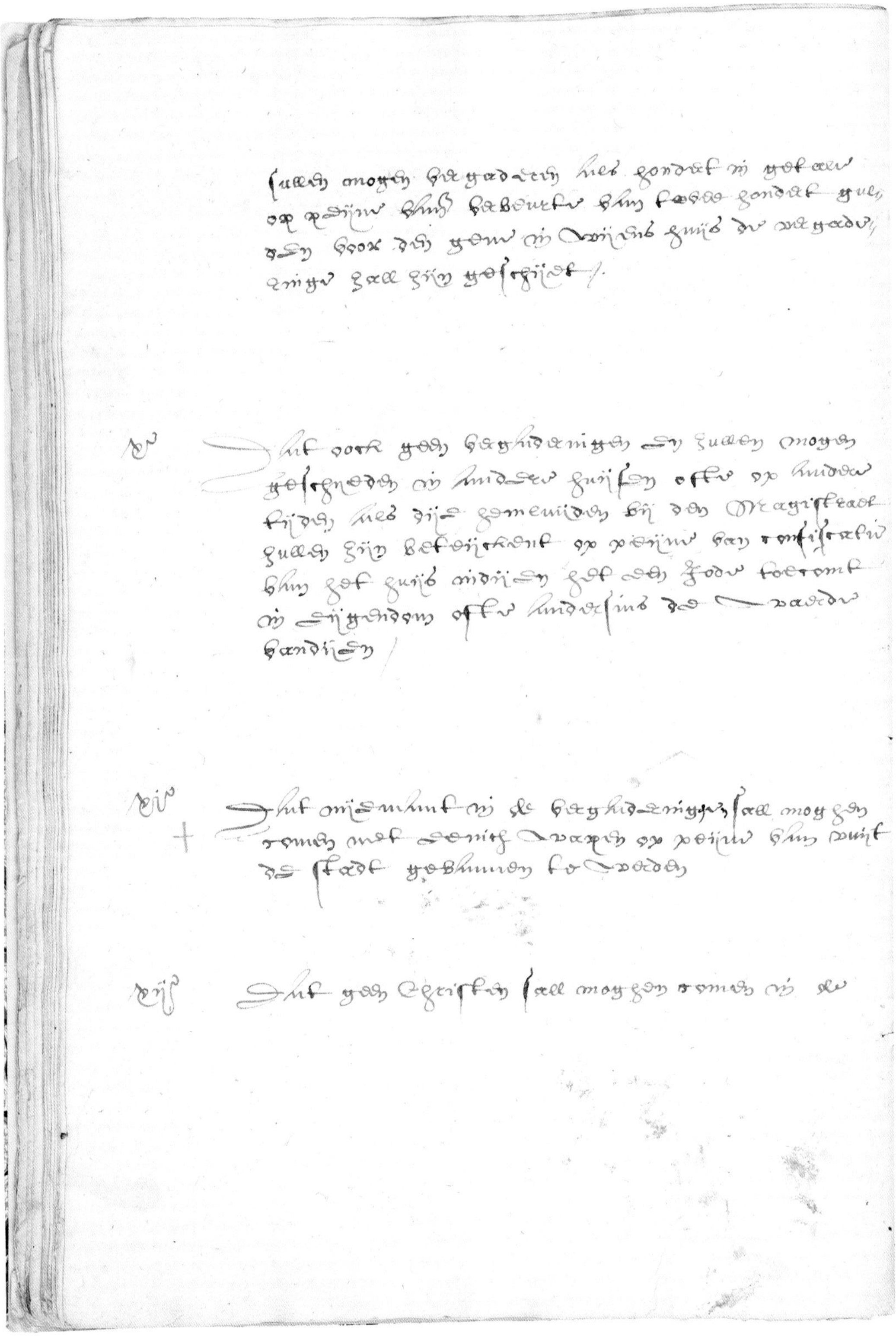

sullen moghen vergaderen als hondert in getale
op peijne van*de* verbeurte van twee hondert gul=
den voor den gene in wijens huijs de vergade=
ringe zall zijn gescheijet /.

xe Dat oock geen vergaderingen en zullen mogen
geschijeden in andere huijsen ofte op andere
tijden als dije hemluijden bij den Magistraet
zullen zijn beteijckent op peijne van confiscatie
van het huijs indijen het een Jode toecomt
in eijgendom ofte andersins de waerde
vandijen /

xie Dat nijemant in de vergaderingen sall mogen
comen met eenich wapen op peijne van vuijt
de stadt gebannen te werden

xiie Dat geen Christen sall moghen comen in de

honderd in getal bijeen zullen mogen komen, op straffe van tweehonderd gulden, te betalen door diegene in wiens huis de bijeenkomst wordt gehouden.

10. Dat ook geen bijeenkomsten zullen mogen plaatsvinden in andere woningen en op andere tijden dan die hun door de overheid zijn toegestaan, op straffe van confiscatie van de woning, wanneer deze het eigendom is van een jood en zo niet, bedraagt de boete de tegenwaarde van het huis.

11. Dat niemand gewapend de bijeenkomst mag bijwonen, op straffe van verbanning uit de stad.

12. Dat geen christen de

14r

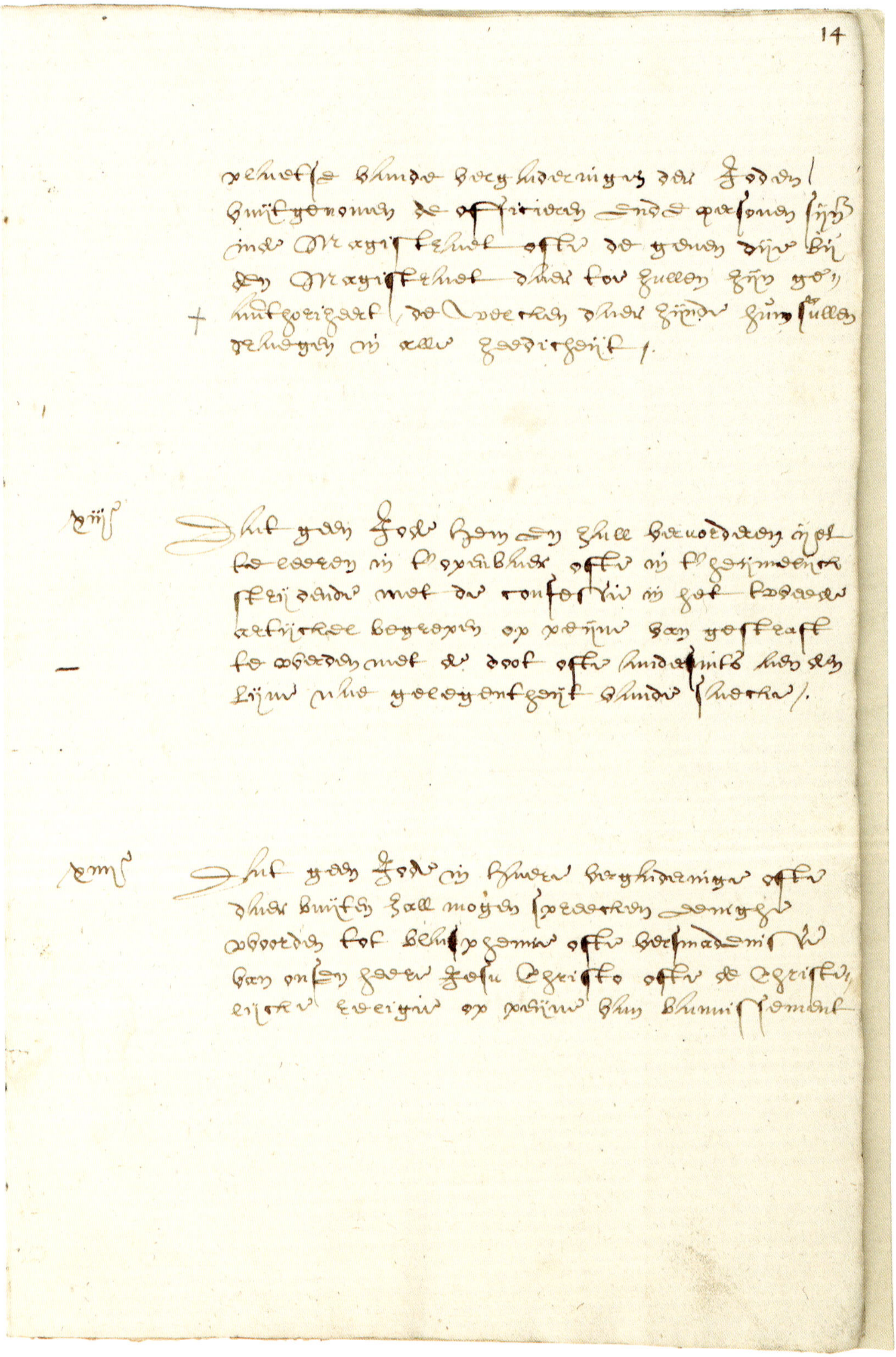

plaetse vande vergaderingen der Joden /
vuijtgenomen de officieren ende personen sijn*de*
inde Magistraet ofte de genen dije bij
den Magistraet daer toe zullen zijn ge=
authorizeert / de welcken daer zijnde hun sullen
draegen in alle zeedicheijt /.

xiii^{e} Dat geen Jode hem en zall veruorderen ijet
te leeren in t' openbaer ofte in t' heijmelijck
strijdende met de confessie in het tweede
artijckel begrepen op peijne van gestraft
te werden met de doot ofte andersints aen den
lijue nae gelegenthheijt vande saecke /.

xiv^{e} Dat geen Jode in Haere vergaderinge ofte
daer buijten zall mogen spreecken enighe
woorden tot blasphemie ofte versmadenisse
van onsen heere Jesu Christo ofte de Christe=
lijcke religie op peijne van bannissement

locatie van de bijeenkomst van de joden mag betreden, behalve de officieren en de leden van het stadsbestuur of diegenen die door de overheid daarvoor toestemming hebben, en dat zij zich daar tijdens hun verblijf ingetogen zullen gedragen.

13. Dat geen jood zich zal verstouten, in het openbaar of in het geheim, iets te verkondigen dat in strijd is met de geloofsbelijdenis van het tweede artikel, op straffe van de dood of anderszins een lijfstraf, afhankelijk van de kwestie.

14. Dat geen jood, tijdens hun bijeenkomst of daarbuiten, godslasterlijke opmerkingen of verwensingen van onze heer Jezus Christus of van de christelijke religie zal mogen uitspreken, op straffe van verbanning

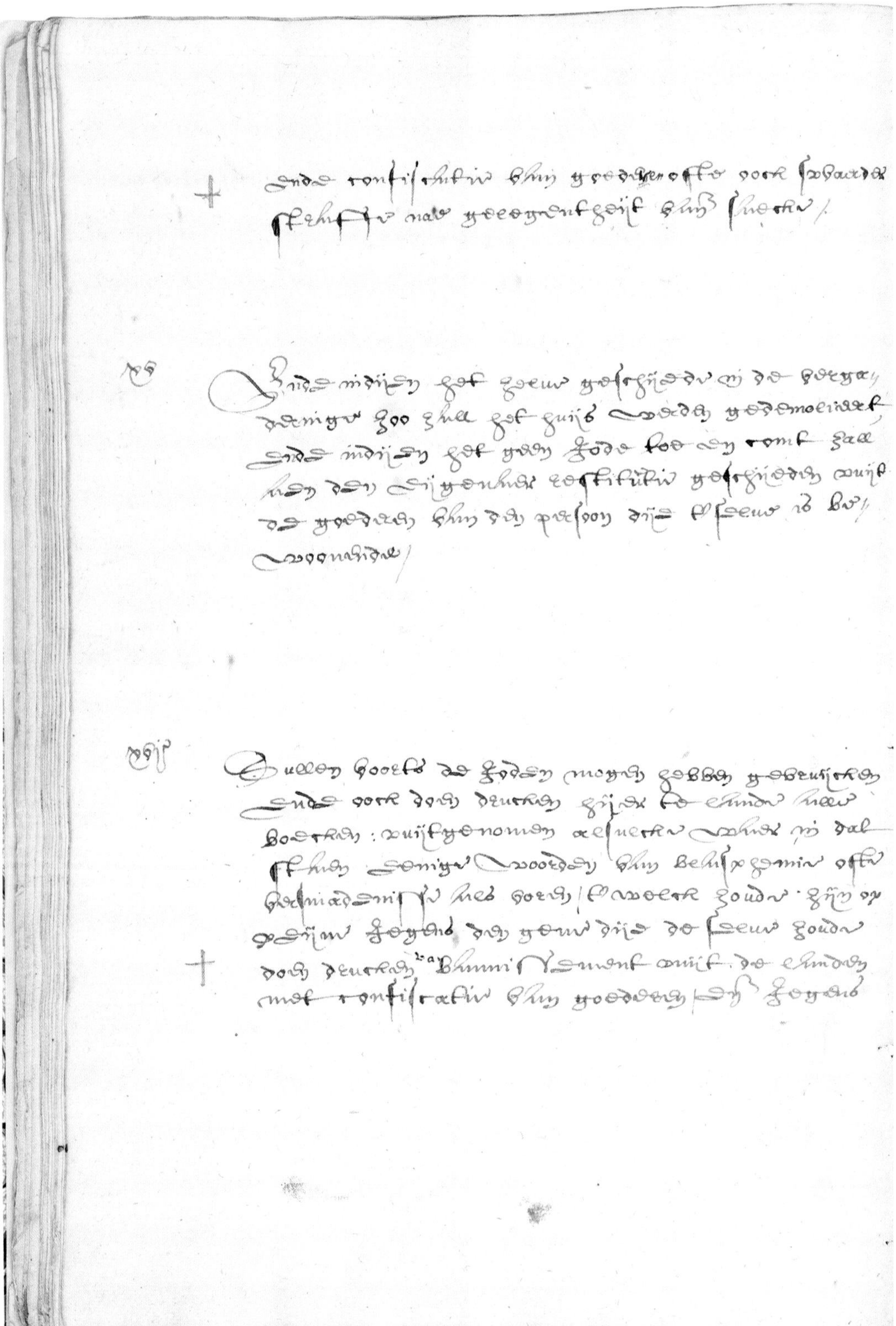

14v

ende confiscatie van goederen ofte oock swaerder
straffe nae gelegentheijt van*de* saecke /.

xv[e] Ende indijen het zelue geschijede in de verga=
deringe zoo zall het huijs werden gedemolieert,
ende indijen het geen Jode toe en comt zall
aen den eijgenaer restitutie geschijeden vuijt
de goederen van den persoon dije t' selve is be=
woonende /

xvj[e] Sullen voorts de Joden mogen hebben gebruijcken
ende oock doen drucken hijer te lande alle
boecken: vuijtgenomen alsulcke waer in dat
staen eenige woorden van blasphemie ofte
versmadenisse als voren / t' welck zoude zijn op
peijne Jegens den genen dije de selue zouden
doen drucken [van] banissement vuijt de landen
met confiscatie van goederen / en*de* Jegens

en confiscatie van bezittingen, of een zwaardere straf, afhankelijk van de kwestie.

15. En indien hetzelfde gebeurt in de bijeenkomst, zal het huis worden gesloopt, en indien het niet toebehoort aan een jood, zal de eigenaar compensatie ontvangen uit de bezittingen van de persoon die het huis bewoont.

16. Voorts zullen de joden in dit land alle boeken in bezit mogen hebben, gebruiken en ook laten drukken, uitgezonderd die waarin enige godslasterlijke uitdrukkingen of verwensingen voorkomen, zoals hiervoor aangeduid. Dit op straffe van verbanning uit het land met confiscatie van bezittingen van degene die dit zou laten drukken; en

15r

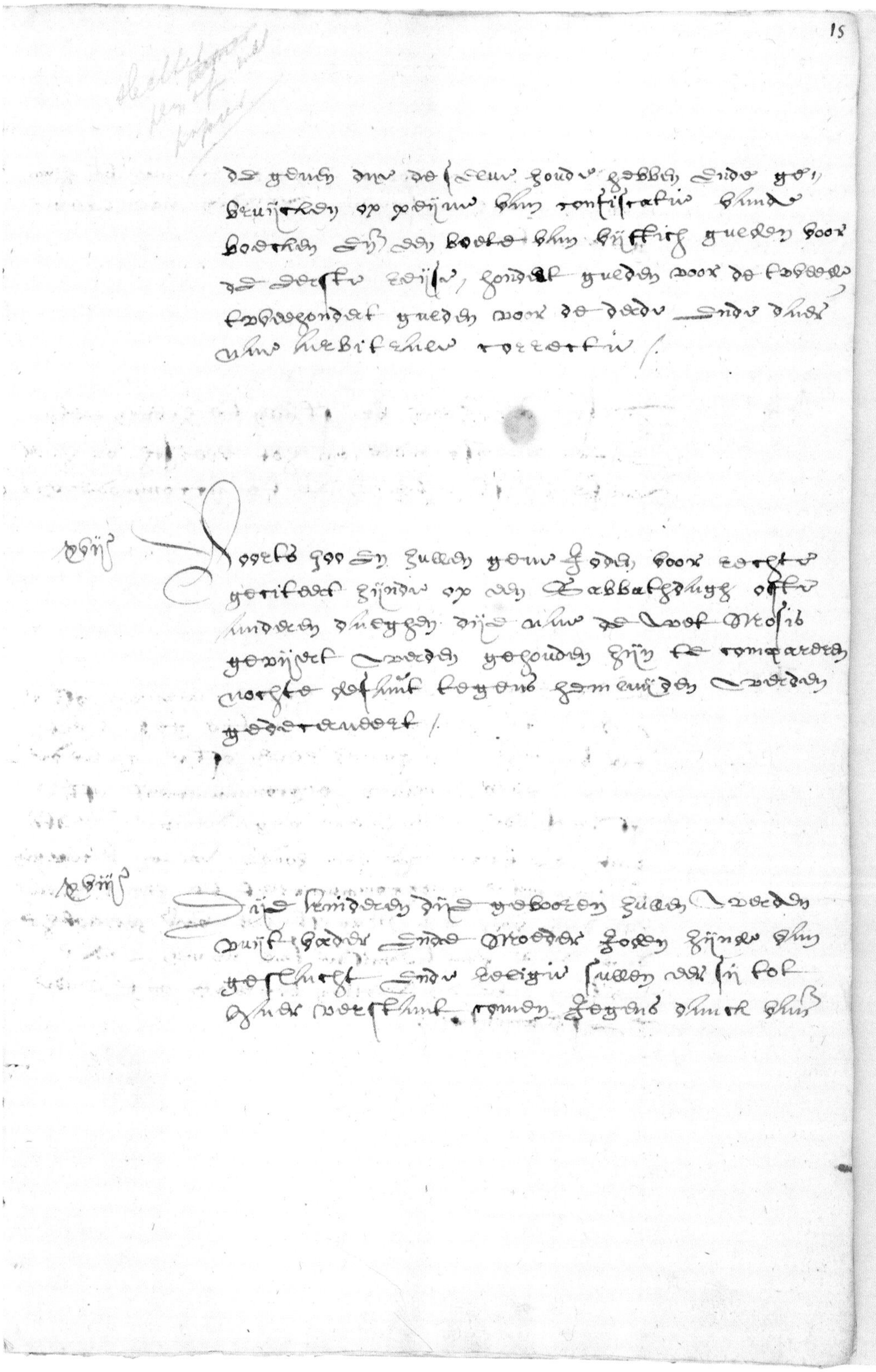
15

de gene die deselve houden hebben ende ge-
bruijcken op pene van confiscatie vande
boecken ende een boete van vijftich gulden voor
de eerste reijse, hondert gulden voor de tweede
tweehondert gulden voor de derde ende daer
naer arbitrale correctie /

xvij Voorts hoe en sullen geene Joden voor rechte
geciteert zijnde op den Sabbathdach ofte
andere daegen die aen de Wet Mosis
gewijet werden gehouden zijn te compareren
[illegible] tegens hemluijden werden
geantwoort /

xviij Die kinderen die geboren sullen werden
wiens vader ende moeder Joden zijnde van
geslachte ende religie sullen [illegible] tot
haer weeshuijs comen tegens danck van

den genen dije de selue zouden hebben ende ge= bruijcken op peijne van confiscatie vande boecken en*de* een boete van vijftich gulden voor de eerste reijse, hondert gulden voor de tweede, tweehondert gulden voor de derde ende daer nae arbitrale correctie /.

diegenen die deze boeken in bezit hebben en gebruiken zullen worden gestraft met confiscatie van de boeken en een boete van vijftig gulden voor de eerste keer, honderd gulden voor de tweede keer, tweehonderd gulden voor de derde keer, en daarna een door de rechter vastgestelde strafmaat.

xvij^{e} Voorts zoo en zullen gene Joden voor rechte geciteert zijnde op een Sabbathdagh ofte andere daeghen dije nae de wet Mosis gevijert werden gehouden zijn te compareren nochte defaut tegens hemluijden werden gedecerneert /.

17. Voorts zullen joden, die voor het gerecht worden gedaagd op een sabbatdag of een andere dag die volgens de wet van Mozes wordt gevierd, niet verplicht zijn te verschijnen en niet bij verstek worden veroordeeld.

xviij^{e} Dije kinderen dije geboren zullen werden vuijt vader ende moeder Joden zijnde van geslacht ende religie sullen eer sij tot haer verstant comen Jegens danck van*de*

18. Die kinderen, die geboren worden uit een joodse vader en moeder, van afkomst en religie, zullen voordat zij volwassen zijn, niet tegen de wil van de

15v

Kinders niet gedoopt worden, maer bij heurluyden mogen besneden worden nae haere gewoonte/.

xix Tsal den Joden vrij staen te hebben een eygen vleeshouder om het vleesch op haer wijse te slachten ende te accommoderen/.

xx De Joden sullen bij haere leeraeren offte anderen bij gemeenden daer toe gestelt tot saecke van quaed leven offte quaede leere mogen werden geexcommuniceert offte afgesneden van haere vergaderinge: Midts dat de gene die hem soude willen beclagen te onrechte geexcommuniceert te zijn tselve sal doen voor den Magistraet van Haerlem die daer van kennisse sal nemen ende wijsen nae de wetten begrepen int Oude Testamente/.

Ouders nijet gedoopt werden maer bij hem=luijden moghen besneden werden nae haere gewoonte /.

ouders worden gedoopt, maar door hen worden besneden zoals het bij hen gebruikelijk is.

xix^{e} T'sall den Joden vrij staen te hebben een eijgen vleijschouder om het vleijsch op haer wijse te slachten ende te accomoderen /.

19. Het zal de joden toegestaan zijn een eigen slager te hebben om het vlees op hun wijze te slachten en uit te snijden.

xx^{e} De Joden zullen bij haere Leeraren ofte anderen bij hemluijden daer toe gestelt ter saecke van quaed leuen ofte quaede leere mogen werden geexcommuniceert ofte afgesneden van haere vergaderinge: Midts dat de gene dije hem zoude willen beclaegen t' onrechte geexcommuniceert te zijn t' zelue zal doen voor den Magistraet van*de* plaetze dije daer van kennisse sall nemen ende wijsen nae de wetten begrepen in t' Oude Testament /.

20. De joden zullen door hun leraren of anderen die daartoe zijn aangesteld, in het geval van slecht gedrag of verkeerde opvattingen mogen worden geëxcommuniceerd of uitgesloten van hun bijeenkomsten; met dien verstande dat diegene die zich zou willen beklagen dat hij ten onrechte geëxcommuniceerd is, hetzelfde zal doen bij het stadsbestuur, dat daarvan kennis zal nemen en zal verwijzen naar de wetten zoals deze zijn vermeld in het Oude Testament.

16r

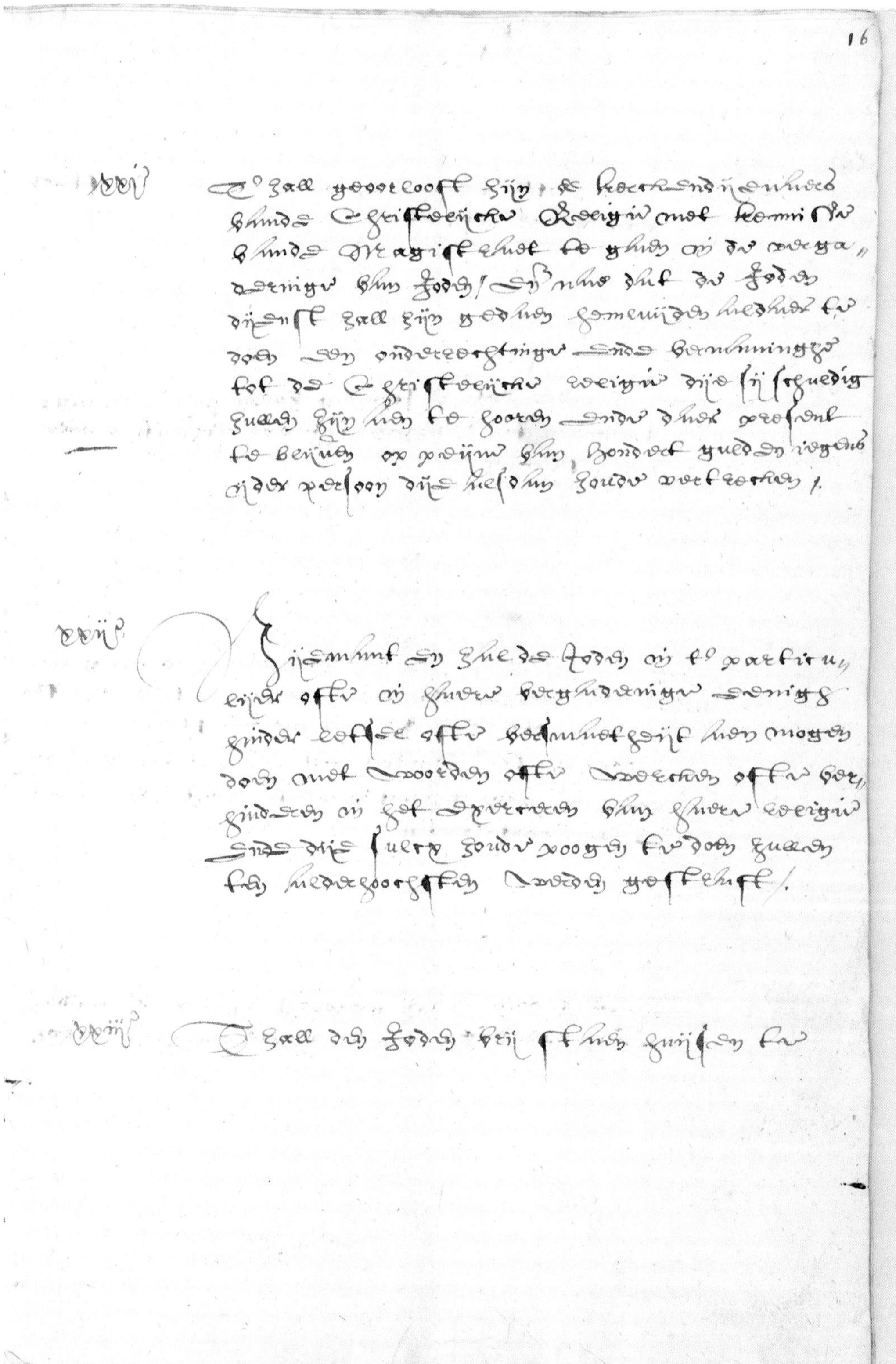
16

xxij Jtem zall voortaen zijn [illegible]
[illegible] Christelicke religie met [illegible]
[illegible] Magistraet te gaen in de verga-
deringe van Joden / ende naer dat de Joden
dienst zall zijn gedaen gemeenlijck hebben te
doen een ondersoeckinge ende vermaninge
tot de Christelicke religie die sij schuldich
zullen zijn te hooren ende daer present
te blijven op peyne van hondert gulden iegelick
ider persoon die hem daer zoude onttrecken /

xxiij Niemant van den Joden in het particulier
ofte in haere vergaderinge eenighe
[illegible] ofte [illegible] mogen
doen met woorden ofte wercken ofte ver-
hinderen in het spreken van haere religie
ende die sulcx zoude voorts te doen zullen
[illegible] worden gestraft /

xxiiij Jtem zall den Joden vrij staen huysen te

xxje T' zall geoorlooft zijn de Kerckendijenaers vande Christelijcke Religie met Kennisse vande Magistraet te gaen in de verga=deringe van Joden / en*de* nae dat de Joden dijenst zall zijn gedaen hemluijden aldaer te doen een onderrechtinge ende vermaninghe tot de Christelijcke religie dije sij schuldig zullen zijn aen te hooren ende daer present te blijuen op peijne van hondert gulden iegens ijder persoon dije alsdan zoude vertrecken /.

xxije Nijemant en zal de Joden in t' particu=lijer ofte in hare vergaderinge eenigh hinder letsel ofte versmaetheijt aen mogen doen met woorden ofte wercken ofte ver=hinderen in het exerceren van haere religie ende dije sulcx zoude poogen te doen zullen ter alderhoochsten werden gestraft /.

xxiije T' zall den Joden vrij staen huijsen te

21. Het zal de kerkdienaren van de christelijke religie geoorloofd zijn, met goedkeuring van het stadsbestuur, de bijeenkomsten van de joden te bezoeken en nadat de dienst van de joden is gehouden, hen aldaar een onderrichting en preek te geven over de christelijke religie, die zij verplicht zijn aan te horen en daarbij aanwezig te blijven, op straffe van honderd gulden voor iedereen, die dan zou vertrekken.

22. Niemand zal de joden in hun persoonlijk leven of tijdens hun bijeenkomsten, enig hinder of letsel mogen aandoen of smadelijk bejegenen, met woorden of door handelingen, of hen hinderen in het uitvoeren van hun religie. Zij die dat pogen te doen zullen ten strengste worden gestraft.

23. Het zal de joden vrij staan huizen te

16v

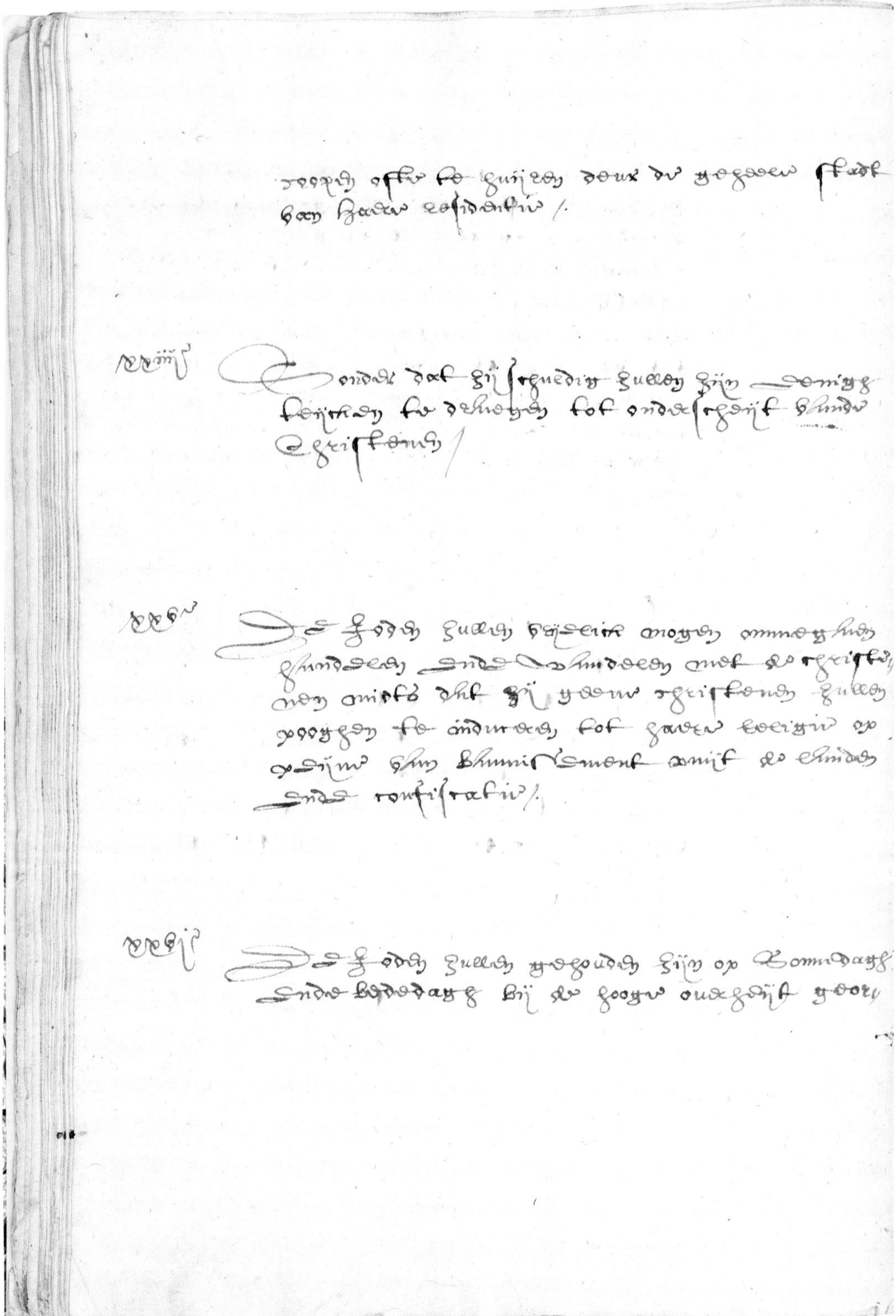

wesen ofte te huijsen daer de gegeven stadt
van haer residentie /

xxiiij Voorts dat zij schuldich sullen zijn [illegible]
[illegible] te [illegible] tot onderscheijt vande
Christenen /

xxv Die Joden sullen geensins moghen ommeghaen
[illegible] ende [illegible] met de christenen,
noch mede dat zij geene christenen sullen
moghen te [illegible], tot haren dienst op
peijne van bannissement ende [illegible]
ende confiscatie /

xxvj Die Joden sullen gehouden zijn op Sonnendach
ende heijlichdach bij de hooge overheijt voor

coopen ofte te huijren deur de geheele stadt van Haere residentie /.

kopen of te huren in hun gehele woonplaats.

xxiiij^{e} Sonder dat zij schuldig zullen zijn eenigh teijcken te draegen tot onderscheijt vande Christenen /

24. Zonder dat zij verplicht zullen zijn enig teken te dragen ter onderscheiding van de christenen.

xxv^{e} De Joden zullen vrijelick mogen ommegaen handelen ende wandelen met de christe= nen midts dat zij geene christenen zullen pooghen te induceren tot haere religie op peijne van bannissement vuijt de landen ende confiscatie /.

25. De joden zullen vrijelijk mogen omgaan, handelen met en verkeren met de christenen, mits zij geen christenen zullen pogen te bekeren tot hun religie, op straffe van verbanning uit het land en confiscatie.

xxvj^{e} De Joden zullen gehouden zijn op Sonnedagh ende bededagh bij de hooge ouerheijt geor=

26. De joden zullen verplicht, op zondag en op door de overheid veror-

17r

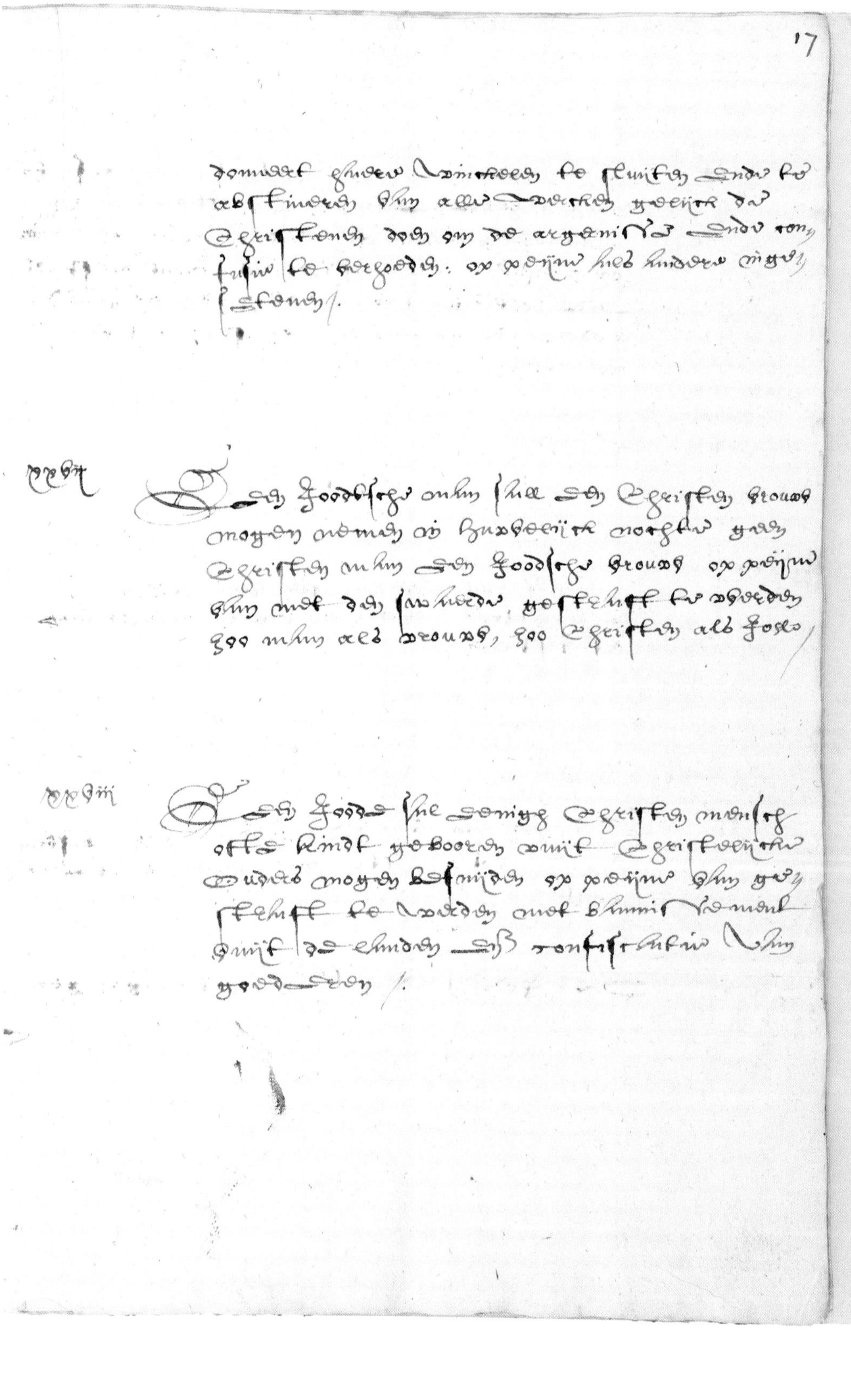

doneert haere winckelen te sluijten ende te abstineren van alle wercken gelijck de Christenen doen om de argernisse ende con=fusie te verhoeden: op peijne als andere inge=setenen /.

donneerde gebedsdagen, hun winkels te sluiten en zich te onthouden van alle arbeid, zoals de christenen, om ergernis en verwarring te voorkomen, op straffe zoals andere ingezetenen.

xxvij^{e} Geen Joodsche man sall een Christen vrouw mogen nemen in Huwelijck nochte geen Christen man een Joodsche vrouw op peijne van met den swaerde gestraft te werden zoo man als vrouw, zoo Christen als Jode /

27. Geen joodse man zal een christelijke vrouw mogen huwen, noch een christelijke man een joodse vrouw, op straffe van met het zwaard gestraft te worden, zowel de man als de vrouw, zowel de christen als de jood.

xxviij^{e} Geen Joode sal eenigh Christen mensch ofte kindt gebooren vuijt Christelijcke Ouders mogen besnijden op peijne van ge=straft te werden met bannissement vuijt de landen en*de* confiscatie van goederen /.

28. Geen jood mag een christelijke volwassene of kind, geboren uit christelijke ouders, besnijden, op straffe van verbanning uit het land en confiscatie van bezittingen.

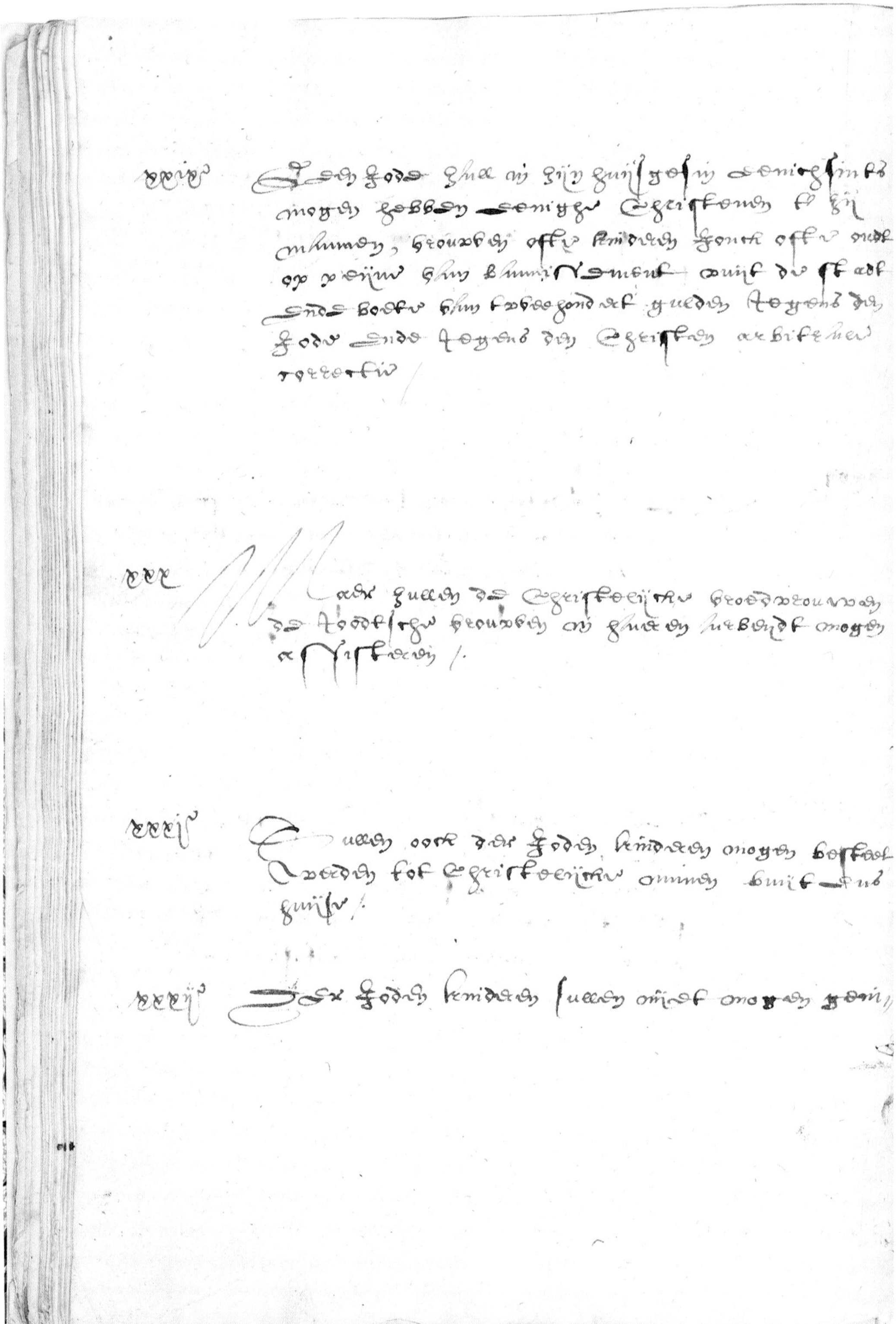

17v

xxix^{e} Geen Jode zal in zijn huijsgesin eenichsints
mogen hebben eenighe Christenen t' zij
mannen, vrouwen ofte kinderen Jonck ofte oudt
op peijne van bannissement vuijt de stadt
ende boete van tweehondert gulden jegens de
Jode ende jegens den Christen arbitrale
correctie /

xxx^{e} Maer zullen de Christelijcke vroedvrouwen
de joodtsche vrouwen in haeren arbeijdt mogen
assisteren /.

xxxj^{e} Sullen oock der Joden kinderen moghen besteet
werden tot Christelijcke minnen buijtens
huijse /.

xxxij^{e} Der Joden kinderen sullen nijet mogen gein=

29. Geen jood zal in zijn huisgezin op enigerlei wijze christenen mogen hebben, hetzij mannen, vrouwen of kinderen, jong of oud, op straffe van verbanning uit de stad en met een boete van tweehonderd gulden voor de jood en voor de christen een door de rechter vastgestelde strafmaat.

30. Maar christelijke vroedvrouwen zullen de joodse vrouwen bij hun bevalling mogen assisteren.

31. Ook mogen de kinderen van joden worden uitbesteed bij christelijke minnen buitenshuis.

32. De kinderen van joden zullen niet onder-

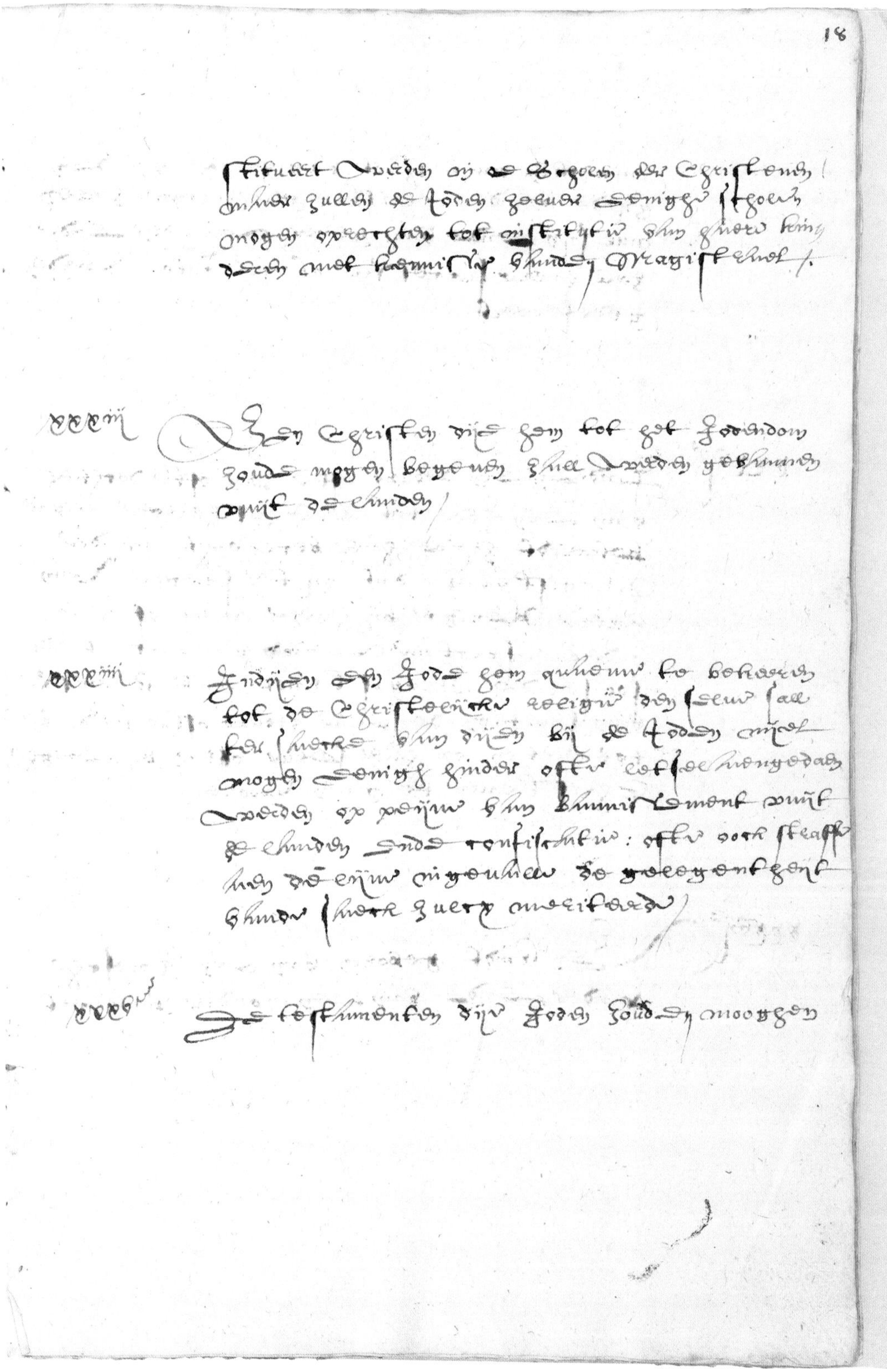

18r

stitueert werden in de Scholen der Christenen maer zullen de Joden zelver eenighe scholen mogen oprechten tot institutie van haere kin=deren met kennisse vanden Magistraet /.

xxxiij^{e} Een Christen dije hem tot het Jodendom zoude mogen begeuen zall werden gebannen vuijt de landen /

xxxiiij^{e} Jndijen een Jode hem quaeme te bekeeren tot de Christelijcke religie den selue sall ter saecke van dijen bij de Joden nijet mogen eenigh hinder ofte letsel aengedaen werden op peijne van bannissement vuijt de landen ende confiscatie: ofte oock straffe aen de*n* lijve ingeualle de gelegentheijt vande saeck zulcx meriteerde /

xxxv^{e} De testamenten dije Joden zouden mooghen

wezen mogen worden op christelijke scholen, maar de joden zullen zelf enkele scholen mogen oprichten, om hun kinderen te onderwijzen, met kennisgeving aan de overheid.

33. Een christen die zich tot het jodendom bekeert, zal worden verbannen uit het land.

34. Indien een jood zich bekeert tot het christelijk geloof, zal hem hierover geen hinder of letsel mogen worden aangedaan, op straffe van verbanning uit het land en confiscatie, of ook een lijfstraf indien de zaak ernstig genoeg is.

35. De testamenten die de joden zouden

18v

maecken want het van ghene kinderen
zijnde onder de Christelijcke religie zullen
nu sijn ende van joode ouders ende
zal haere successie ab intestato worden
gheobserveert /

xxxvj Geduijrende een vrouwe offte soon offte dochter
van een Jode tot de Christelijcke religie
bekeert zijnde haer beclaeght tegen de
Magistraet dat sij ter sterkte van
haere religie bij haren man offte
ouders verspottinge worden gemoeit, sal
soo sullen de Magistraet met kennisse
van saecken de selve vrouwe offte kinderen
toelaten op haer selven offte bij eenighe
Christenen te gaen woonen /

xxxvij Een kindt gheboren van een Joodsche
vader ende van een moeder bekeert

maecken vuijt Haet van haere vrunden zijnde vande Christelijcke religie zullen nul sijn ende van gener waerden . ende zall haere successie *ab intestato* werden gedefereert /.

xxxvj^{e} Jndijen een vrouw ofte zoon ofte dochter van een Jode tot de Christelijcke religie bekeerdt zijnde haer beclaeght aende Magistraet dat zij ter saecke van Haere Religie bij haere man ofte ouders respectiue werden gemolesteert soo sal de Magistraet met kennisse van saecken de selue vrouw ofte kinderen toelaeten op haer selue ofte bij enighe Christenen te gaen woonen /

xxxvij^{e} Een kindt geboren van een Joodsche vader ende van een moeder bekeert

maken uit haat tegen hun verwanten van christelijke religie, zullen van nul en generlei waarde zijn, en er zal hun successie *ab intestato* worden opgelegd.[13]

36. Indien een vrouw, zoon of dochter van een jood, die zich tot de christelijke religie heeft bekeerd, zich beklaagt bij de overheid, dat hun vanwege hun religie door hun man of respectievelijke ouders kwaad wordt aangedaan, dan zal de overheid, die op de hoogte is, deze vrouw of kinderen toestemming geven zelfstandig of bij christenen te wonen.

37. Een kind geboren uit een joodse vader en uit een moeder die zich bekeerd heeft

13 Successie ab intestato: zonder dat er een testament bestaat.

19r

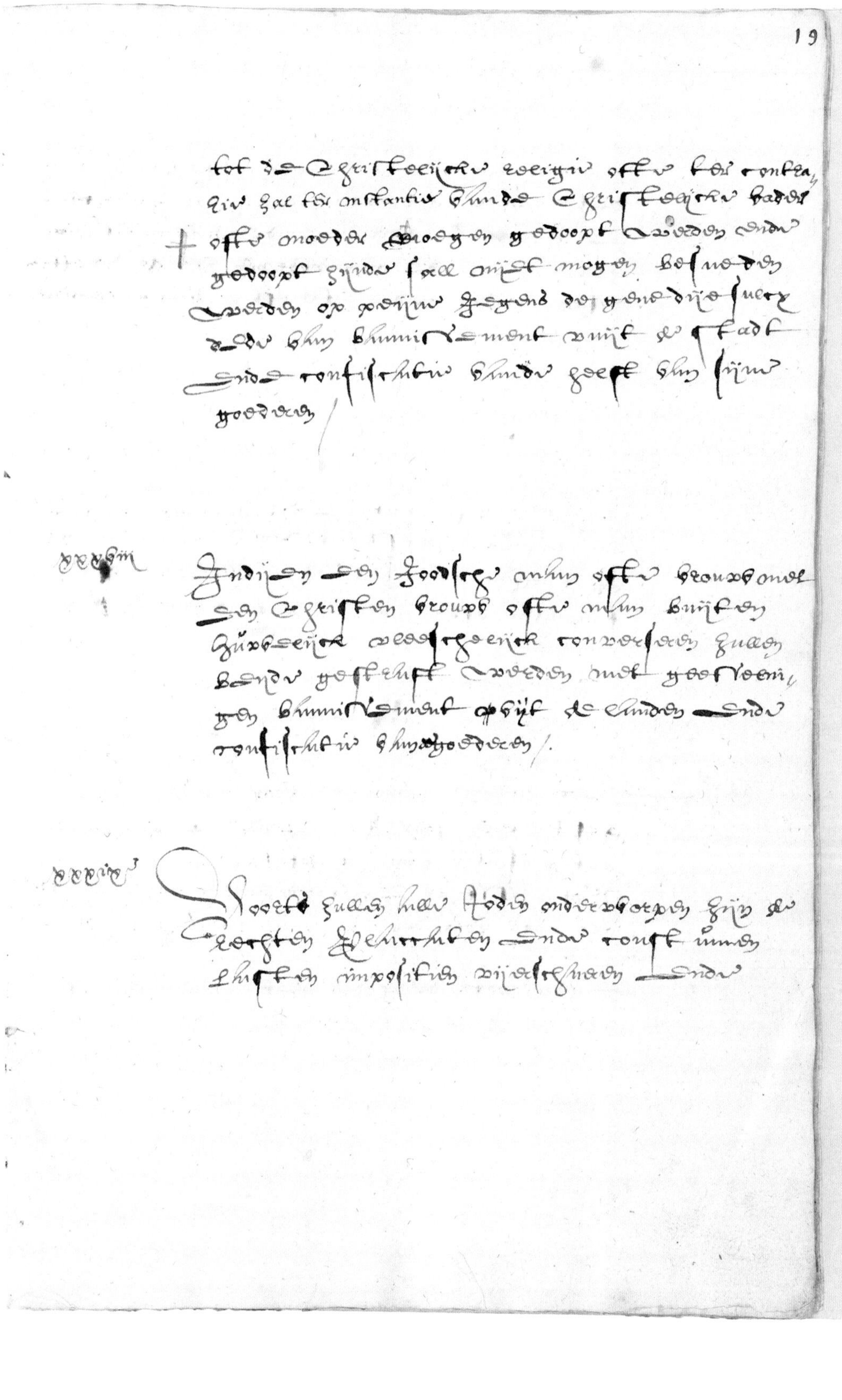

19

tot der christelicke religie ofte ter contra-
rie zal ter instantie vande christelicke vader
ofte moeder, voogden gedoopt worden ende
gedoopt zijnde zal niet mogen besneden
worden op peyne [illegible]
ende van bannissement uuyt der stadt
ende confiscatie vande helft van sijne
goeden /

xxxviii Indien een Joodsche man ofte vrouwe met
een christen vrouwe ofte man buyten
huwelick vleeschelick converseren zullen
bevonden geweest worden met [illegible]
ten bannissement opt lijf de Joden ende
confiscatie van hun goeden /

xxxix Voorts zullen hem Joden onderwerpen zijn de
rechten [illegible] ende contributien
lasten impositien [illegible] ende

tot de Christelijcke religie ofte ter contra=rie zal ter instantie vande Christelijcke vader ofte moeder moegen gedoopt werden ende gedoopt zijnde sall nijet mogen besneden werden op peijne Jegens de gene dije sulcx dede van bannissement vuijt de stadt ende confiscatie vande helft van sijne goederen /

xxxviij^{e} Jndijen een Joodsche man ofte vrouw met een Christen vrouw ofte man buijten Huwelijck vleeschelijck converseren zullen beijde gestraft werden met geesselin=gen bannissement vijt de landen ende confiscatie van goederen /.

xxxix^{e} Voorts zullen alle Joden onderworpen zijn de rechten Placcaten ende coustumen lasten impositien vijerschaeren ende

tot de christelijke religie of omgekeerd, zal op verzoek van de christelijke vader of moeder gedoopt mogen worden, en gedoopt zijnde zal het niet besneden mogen worden, op straffe van diegene die dit uitvoert met verbanning uit de stad en confiscatie van de helft van zijn bezittingen.

38. Indien een joodse man of vrouw met een christelijke man of vrouw buiten het huwelijk gemeenschap heeft, dan zullen beiden met geseling worden gestraft en worden verbannen uit het land met confiscatie van bezittingen.

39. Verder zullen alle joden onderworpen zijn aan de rechten, verordeningen en gebruiken, belastingen, heffingen, justitie en

19v

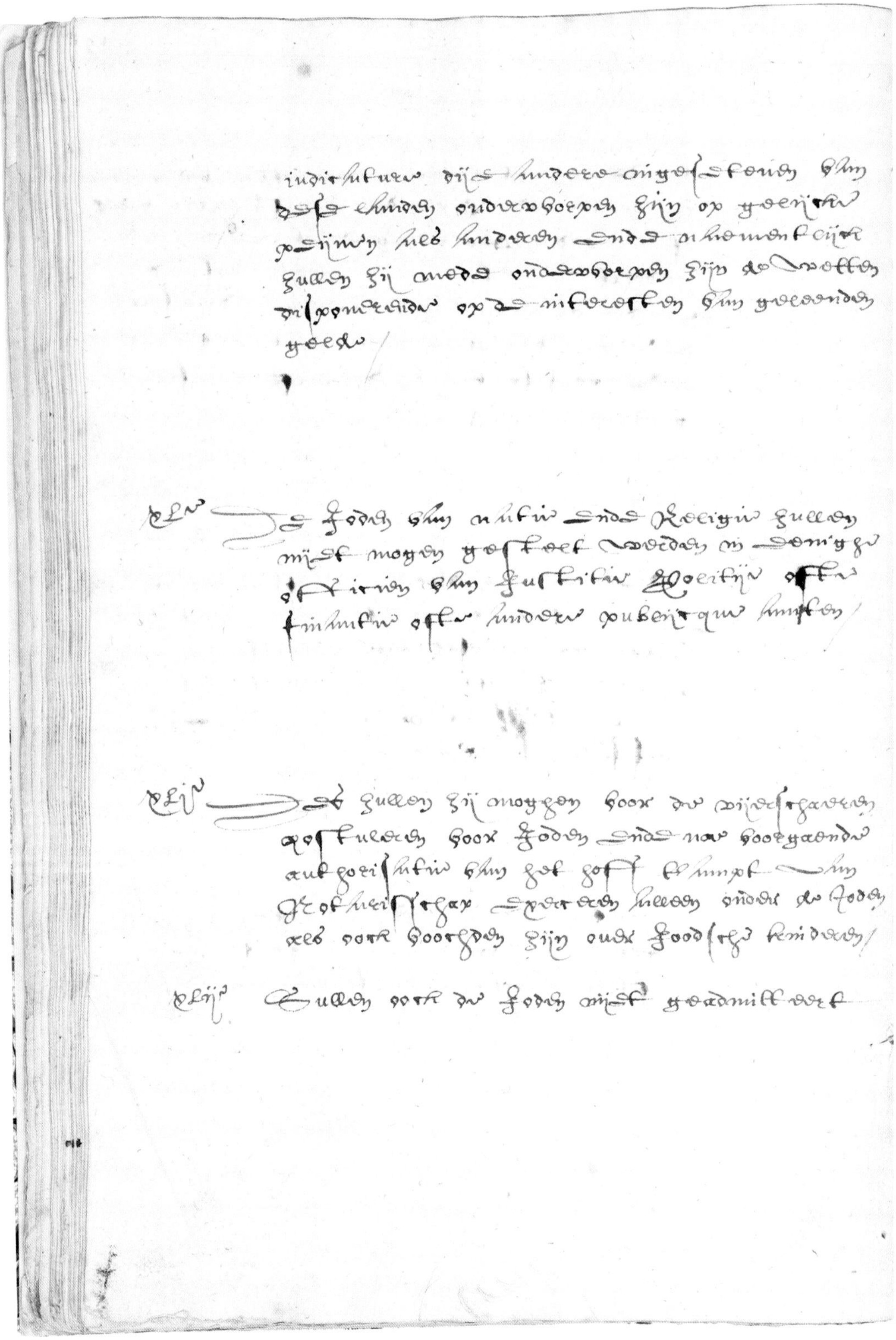
indistin[illegible] bij andere [illegible] van
dese landen onderworpen zijn op geestelijke
persoonen het anderen ende alhoewel dat
zullen zij mede onderworpen zijn de wetten
dispositien op de [illegible] van [illegible]
goede /

xlv De joden van [illegible] ende [illegible] zullen
niet mogen gestelt werden in eenighe
officien van justitie politie ofte
finantie ofte ander publicque ampten /

xlvi Dat zullen zij mogen voor de [illegible]
[illegible] voor joden ende nae voorgaende
authorisatie van het hoff [illegible]
[illegible] spreken [illegible] onder de joden
het oock voorsien zijn onder joodsche kinderen /

xlvii Zullen oock de joden niet geadmitteert

iudicature dije andere ingesetenen van dese landen onderworpen zijn op gelijcke peijnen als anderen ende naementlijck zullen zij mede onderworpen zijn de wetten disponerende op de interessen van geleenden gelde /

xl^{e} De Joden van natie ende Religie zullen nijet mogen gestelt werden in eenighe officien van Justitie Politije ofte finantie ofte andere publijcque ampten /

xlj^{e} Des zullen zij moghen voor de vijerschaeren postuleren voor Joden ende nae voorgaende authorisatie van het hoff t' ampt van Notarisschap exerceren alleen onder de Joden als oock voochden zijn ouer Joodsche kinderen /

xlij^{e} Sullen oock de Joden nijet geadmitteert

rechtspraak waaraan ook andere ingezetenen van deze landen zijn onderworpen, op gelijke straffen als de anderen, met name zullen zij ook onderworpen zijn aan de wetten die de rente op geleend geld regelen.

40. Joden van afkomst of religie zullen niet aangesteld mogen worden in functies bij Justitie, Politie of Financiën of andere publieke ambten.

41. Daarom zal het hen toegestaan zijn in de rechtbank op te treden voor joden en, na voorafgaande toestemming van het Hof, het ambt van notaris uitsluitend onder de joden uit te oefenen en tevens om als voogd op te treden van joodse kinderen.

42. Joden zullen ook niet toegelaten

20r

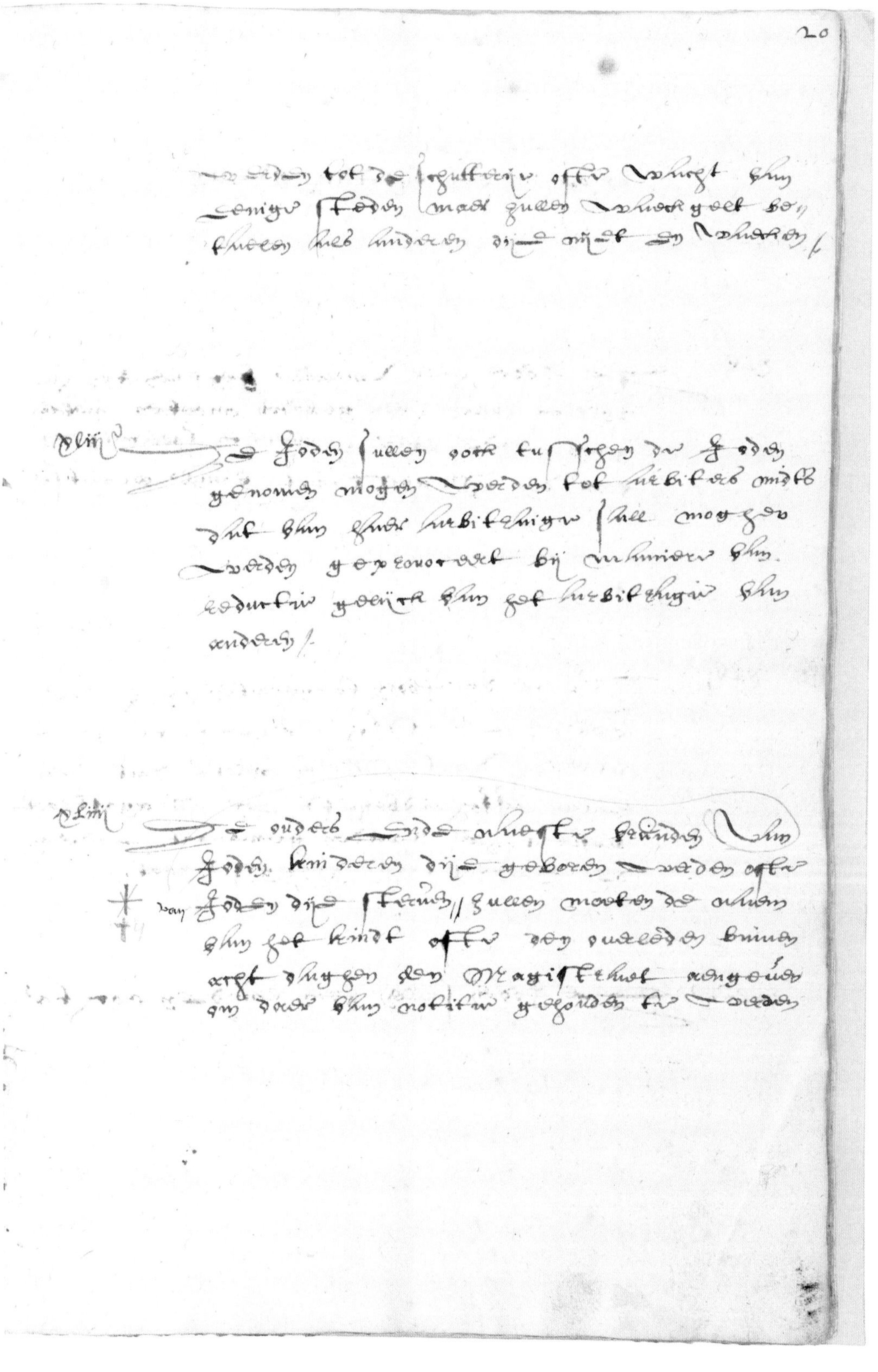

werden tot de schutterije ofte wacht van eenige steden maer zullen waeckgelt be= taelen als anderen dije nijet en waecken /.

worden tot de schutterij of de bewaking van de steden, maar zullen wachtgeld betalen, net zoals anderen die geen wacht lopen.

xliij^{e} De Joden sullen oock tusschen de Joden genomen mogen werden tot arbiters midts dat van haer arbitraige sall moghen werden geprouoceert bij maniere van reductie gelijck aen het arbitragie van anderen /.

43. Joden zullen ook als bemiddelaars tussen joden aangesteld mogen worden, mits dat bij deze rechtspraak hoger beroep mogelijk zal zijn, net zoals bij de rechtspraak door anderen.

xliiij^{e} De ouders ende naeste vrunden van Joden kinderen dije geboren werden ofte van Joden dije steruen // zullen moeten de naem van het kindt ofte den ouerleden binnen acht daghen den Magistraet aengeuen om daer van notitie gehouden te werden

44. De ouders en naaste bloedverwanten van joodse kinderen die worden geboren of van joden die sterven, moeten de naam van het kind of van de overledene binnen acht dagen aangeven bij de overheid, zodat daarvan aantekening kan worden gemaakt,

20V

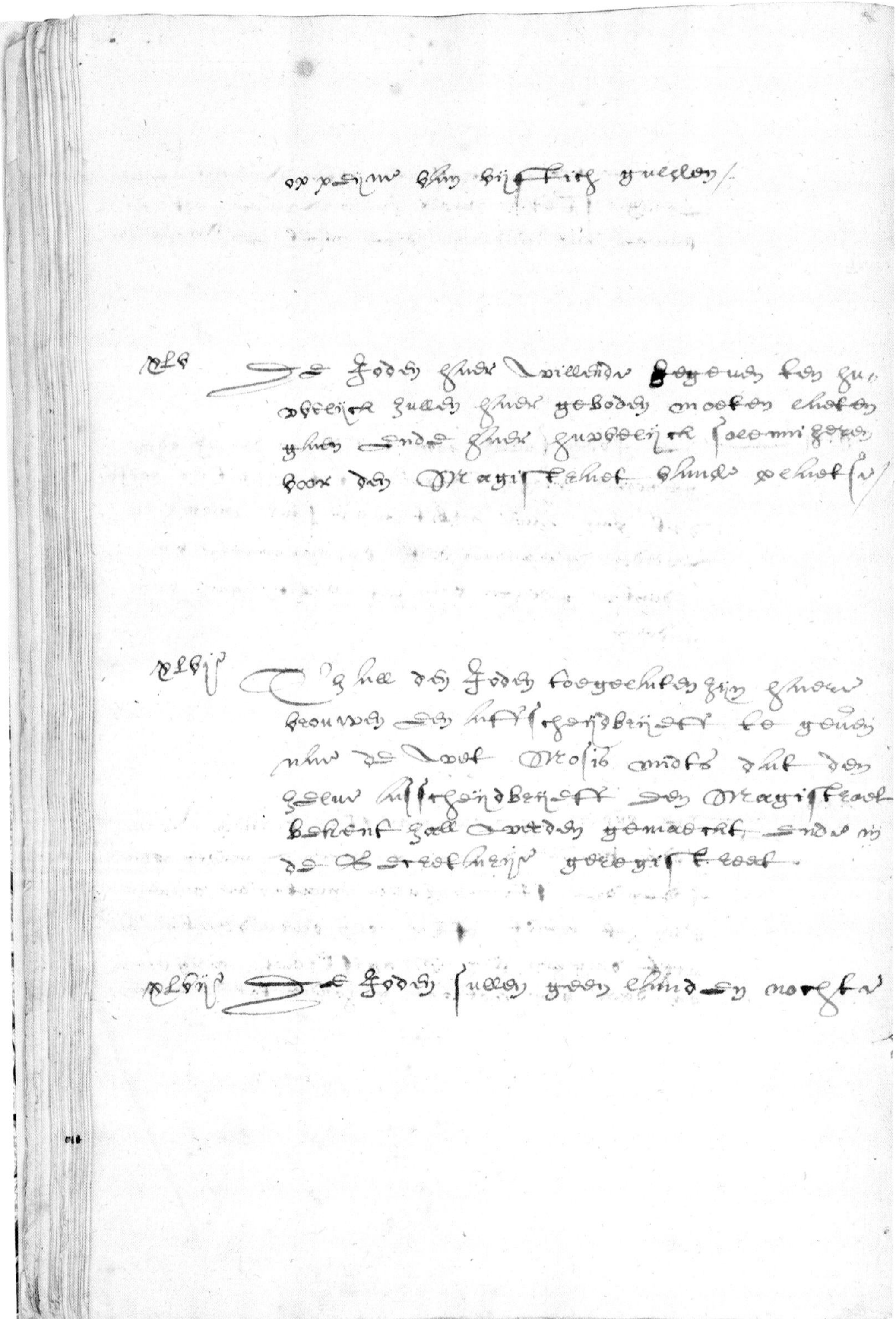

op peijne van vijftich gulden /.

op straffe van vijftig gulden.

xlv De Joden haer willende begeuen ten hu=welijck zullen haer geboden moeten laeten gaen ende haer huwelijck solemnizeren voor den Magistraet vande plaetse /

45. Joden die willen huwen, zullen hun afkondigingen hiervan bekendmaken en het huwelijk formeel laten bevestigen bij de stedelijke overheid.

xlj^{e} T' zall den Joden toegelaten zijn haere vrouwen een affscheidjbrijeff te geuen nae de wet Mosis midts dat den zelue affscheijdbrijeff den Magistraet bekent zall werden gemaeckt ende in de Secretarije geregistreert.

46. Het zal de joden toegestaan zijn hun vrouwen een scheidingsbrief te geven volgens de wet van Mozes, mits deze scheidingsbrief bij het stadsbestuur wordt aangegeven en bij de Secretarie in het stadhuis wordt geregistreerd.[14]

xlij^{e} De Joden sullen geen landen nochte

47. Joden zullen geen land of

14 Bedoeld is de zogenoemde *Get*, een rabbinaal document waarmee een man van zijn vrouw kan scheiden.

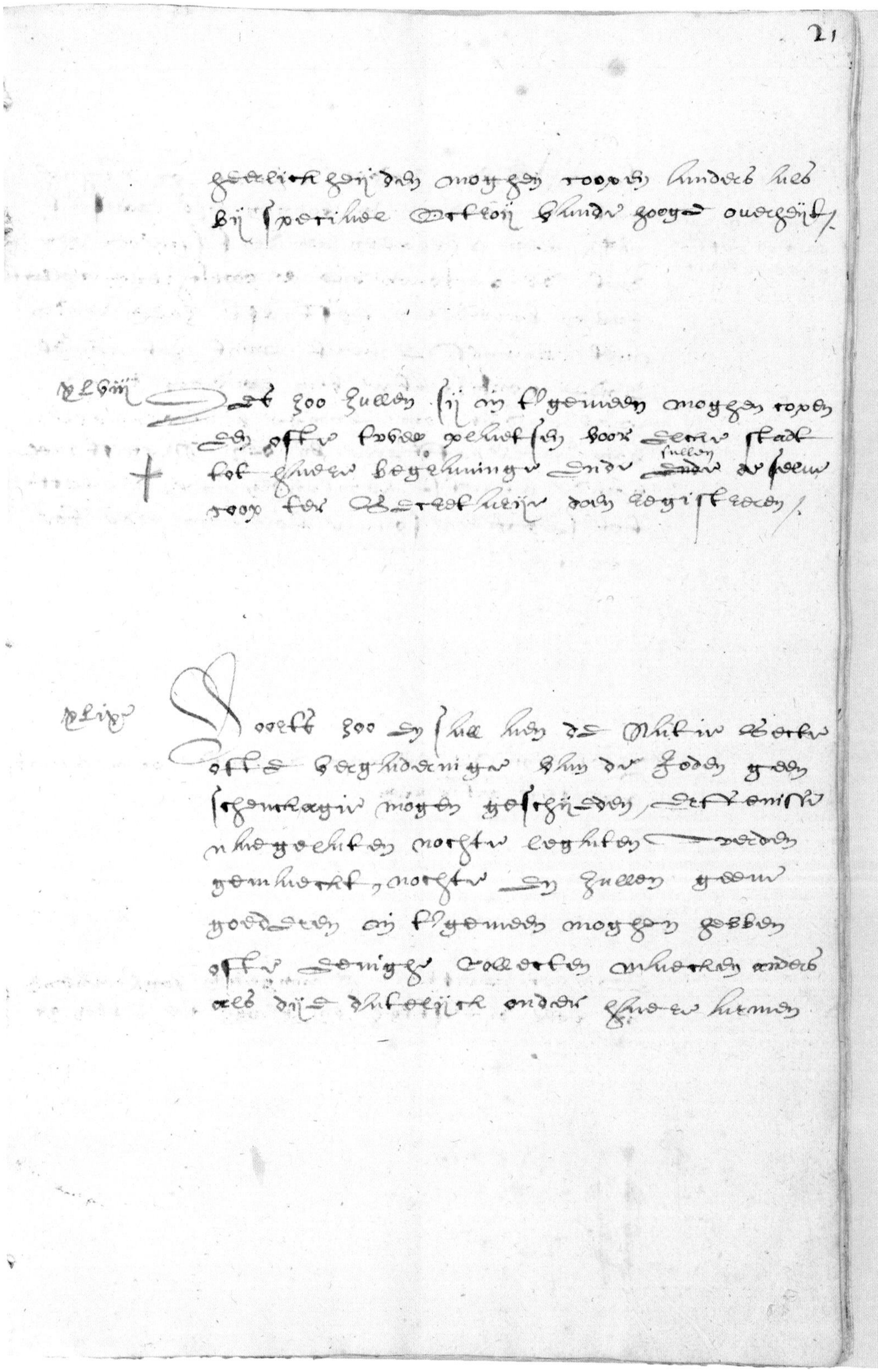

21r

heerlickheijden moghen coopen anders als bij speciael Octroij vande hooge ouerheijt /.

xlviij^{e} Des zoo zullen sij in t' gemeen moghen cope een ofte twee plaetsen voor elcke stadt tot haere begrauinge ende ~~ende~~ sullen deselue coop ter Secretarije doen registreren /.

xlix^{e} Voorts zoo en sall aen de Natie Secte ofte vergaderinge van de Joden geen schenckagie mogen geschijeden, erffenisse naegelaten nochte legaten werden gemaeckt, nochte en zullen geene goederen in t' gemeen moghen hebben ofte eenighe collecten maecken anders als dije datelijck onder haere armen

heerlijkheden mogen kopen tenzij met speciale toestemming van het hoogste gezag.[15]

48. De joden mogen gemeenschappelijk een of twee stukken grond in elke stad kopen voor een begraafplaats en deze koop laten registreren bij de stedelijke Secretarie.

49. Verder zullen aan het volksdeel, de groepering of het volk van de joden geen schenkingen mogen plaatsvinden, erfenissen nagelaten, noch mogen legaten worden verstrekt, noch zullen zij gemeenschappelijke bezittingen mogen hebben of inzamelingen mogen houden anders dan die direct onder hun armen

15 Hiermee wordt bedoeld de Staten van Holland.

21V

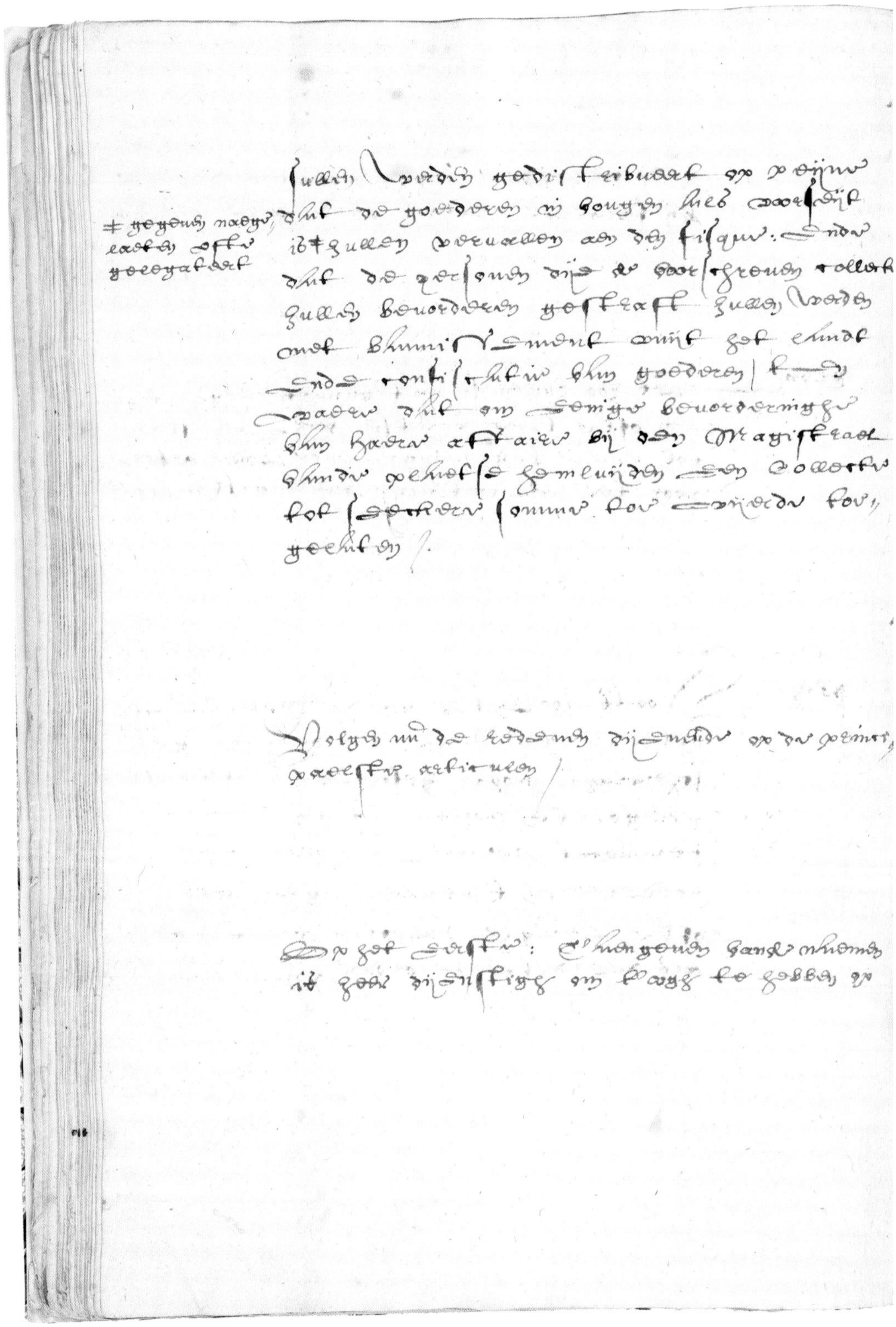

sullen werden gedistribueert op peijne dat de goederen in vougen als voorseijt is ↑ zullen veruallen aen den fisque: ende* dat de personen dije de voorschreuen collecten zullen beuorderen gestraft zullen werden met bannissement vuijt het landt ende confiscatie van goederen / t' en waere dat om eenige beuorderinghe van haere affaire bij den Magistraet vande plaetse hemluijden een collecte tot seeckere somme toe wijerde toe= gelaten /.

Volgen nu de redenen dijenende op de princi= paelste articulen /

Op het eerste: T' aengeuen vande naemen is zeer dijenstigh om t' oogh te hebben op

* ↑gegeven naege= laeten ofte gelegateert

worden verdeeld, op straffe van het vervallen aan de fiscus van de voornoemde bezittingen, nagelaten of gelegateerd; en de personen die de eerder genoemde inzamelingen stimuleren, zullen bestraft worden met verbanning uit het land en met confiscatie van bezittingen, tenzij ter bevordering van de zaak door de stedelijke overheid een inzameling tot een bepaald bedrag is toegestaan.

Volgen hieronder de verklaringen betreffende de belangrijkste artikelen.

Ad Artikel 1.
Het aangeven van de namen is zeer nuttig om zicht te hebben op

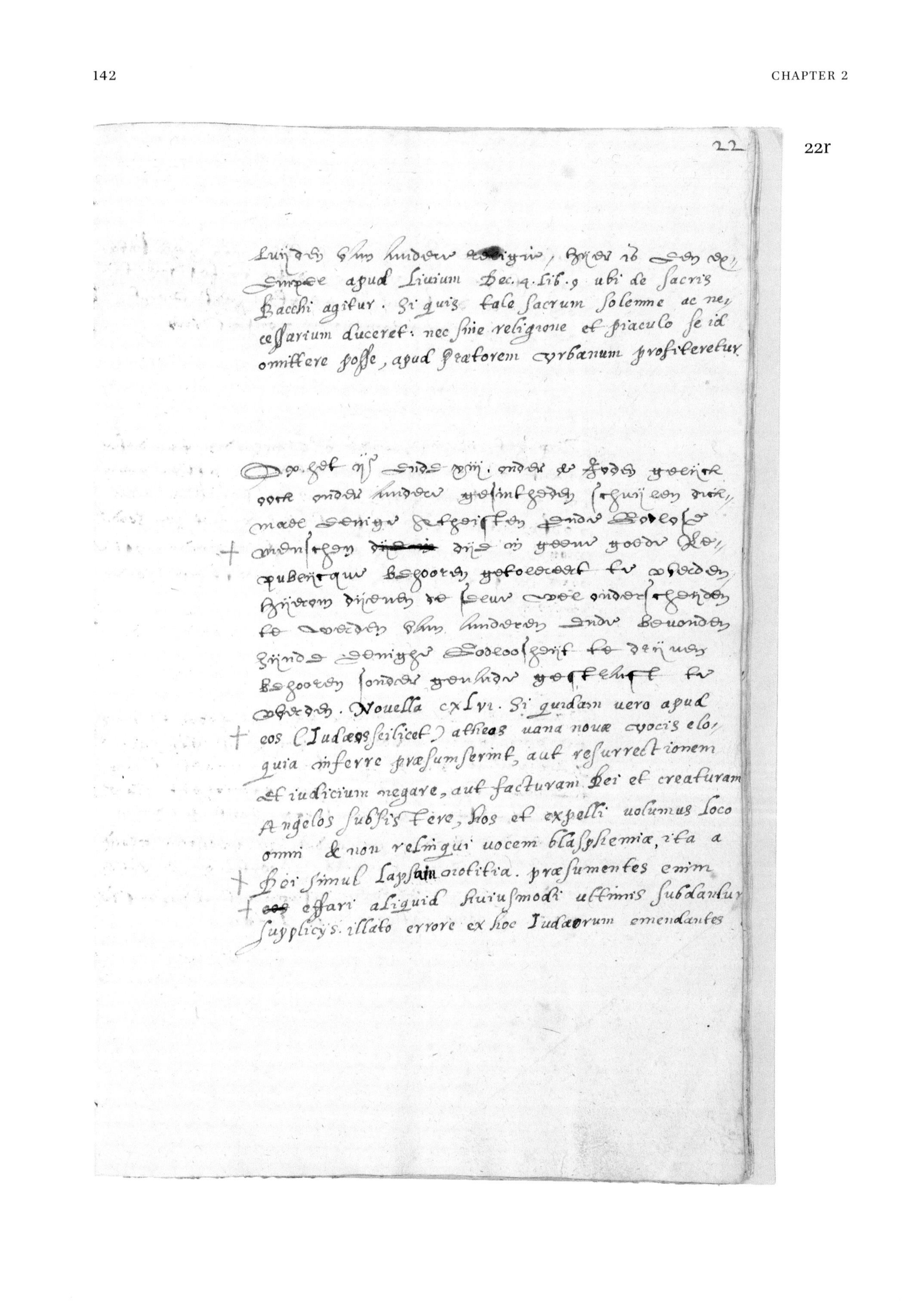

22r

22

[illegible], [illegible]
[illegible] apud Liuium Dec. 4. lib. 9 ubi de sacris
Bacchi agitur. Si quis tale sacrum solemne ac ne-
cessarium duceret: nec sine religione et piaculo se id
omittere posse, apud praetorem urbanum profiteretur

[illegible]
[illegible]. Nouella cxlvi. Si quidam uero apud
eos (Judaeos scilicet) atheas uana nouae uocis elo-
quia inferre praesumserint, aut resurrectionem
et iudicium negare, aut facturam Dei et creaturam
Angelos subsistere, hos et expelli uolumus loco
omni & non relinqui uocem blasphemiae, ita a
Dei simul lapsam notitia. praesumentes enim
~~eos~~ effari aliquid huiusmodi ultimis subdantur
supplicijs. illato errore ex hoc Judaeorum emendantes

Luijden van andere religie / Hijer is een ex= empel *apud Liuium Dec. 4. Lib. 9 ubi de sacris Bacchi agitur. Si quis tale sacrum solemne ac ne= cessarium duceret: nec sine religione et piaculo se id omittere posse, apud Praetorem Vrbanum profiteretur.*

Op het ij^e^ ende xiij. onder de Joden gelijck oock onder andere gesintheden schuijlen dick= mael eenige Atheisten ende Godlose menschen ~~dije in~~ dije in geene goede Re= publijcque behooren getolereert te werden / Hijerom dijenen de selue wel onderscheijden te werden van anderen ende beuonden zijnde eenighe Godloosheijt te drijuen behooren sonder genade gestraft te werden. *Nouella cxlvi. Si quidam uero apud eos (Iudæos scilicet) atheos uana nouæ vocis elo= quia inferre præsumserint, aut resurrectionem et iudicium negare, aut facturam Dei et creaturam Angelos subsistere, hos et expelli uolumus loco omni & non reliqui uocem blasphemiæ, ita a Dei simul lapsam notitia. præsumentes enim ~~eos~~ effari aliquid huiusmodi ultimis subdantur supplicijs. illato errore Iudæorum emendantes*

mensen met een andere religie. Hier is een voorbeeld *bij Livius, 4^e^ decade, boek 9, waar het gaat over de Bacchus-dienst. Als iemand zou menen dat een dergelijke eredienst gebruikelijk en noodzakelijk is en deze niet achterwege kan laten zonder rituele tegenprestatie, zou hij zich bij het stadsbestuur moeten aangegeven.*[16]

Ad Artikel 2 en 13.

Onder de joden, even als onder andere gezindheden, zijn dikwijls enige atheïsten en goddeloze mensen aanwezig, die in een goede republiek niet getolereerd behoren te worden. Daarom dienen deze goed onderscheiden te worden van anderen, en diegenen die enige goddeloosheid vertonen, behoren zonder genade gestraft te worden.

'Als er echter onder hen lieden zijn die proberen goddeloze drogredenen te introduceren, waarbij zij of de Opstanding of het Laatste Oordeel of dat de engelen een maaksel en schepping van God zijn, loochenen, willen Wij dat de betrokkenen worden verjaagd uit iedere plaats en dat zij geen taal spreken die godslasterlijk is en totaal weggegleden is van de kennis zelf omtrent God. Want in het geval dat zij zo iets trachten te verkondigen, onderwerpen Wij hen aan de zwaarste van alle straffen en zuiveren aldus het joodse volk van de daaruit bij hen geïntroduceerde dwaling.'[17]

---

16 Livius, *Ab urbe condita*, bk. XXXIX.18.8. Deze passage uit Livius heeft een wat vreemde connotatie—het fragment, dat De Groot hier citeert, komt uit een langere passage waarin het *laissez-faire* van een ongeautoriseerde cultus een ontwrichtende uitwerking op de Romeinse samenleving kreeg en er uiteindelijk hard moest worden ingegrepen. Het is eigenlijk niet denkbaar dat De Groot deze negatieve connotatie van dit fragment niet in zijn achterhoofd had toen hij dit opschreef.

17 Nov. 146. Spruit et al., *Corpus iuris civilis: tekst en vertaling.*, XII. Novellen 115–168:289.

22V

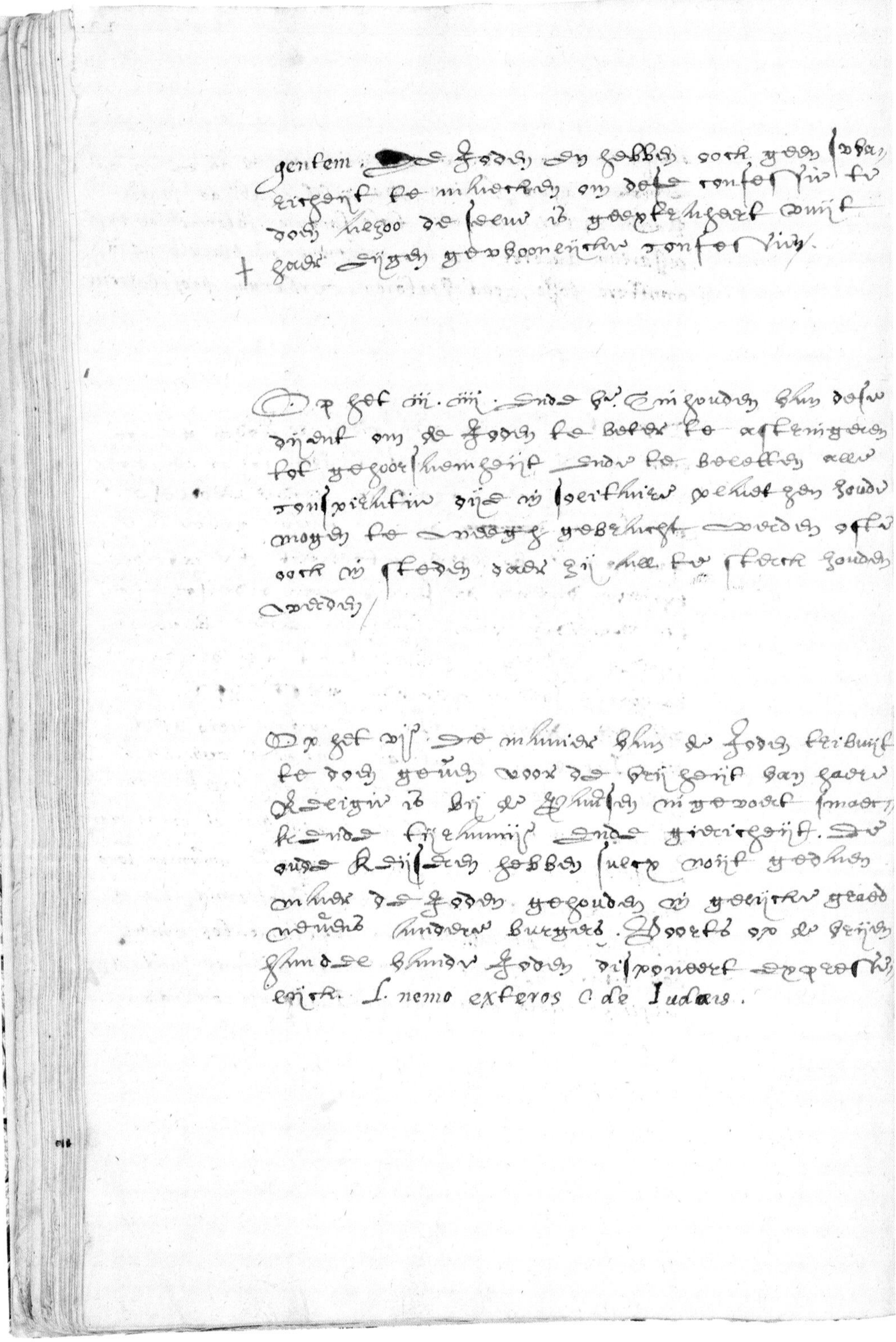

gentem. De Joden en hebben oock geen swa=richeijt te maecken om dese confessie te doen alzoo de selue is geextraheert vuijt haer eijgen gewoonlijcke confessien /.

Op het iij. iiij. ende v^{e}. T inhouden van dese dijent om de Joden te beter te astringeren tot gehoorsaemheijt ende te beletten alle conspiratie dije in solitaire plaetzen zoude mogen te weegh gebracht werden ofte oock in steden daer zij all te sterck zouden werden /

Op het vj^{e}. De manier van de Joden tribuijt te doen geuen voor de vrijheijt van haere Religie is bij de Pausen ingevoert smaec=kende tijrannije ende giericheijt. De oude Keijseren hebben sulcx noijt gedaen maer de Joden gehouden in gelijcke graed neuens andere burgers. Voorts op de vrijen handel vande Joden disponeert expresse=lijck *L. nemo exteros C. de Iudæis*.

De joden hebben ook geen problemen om deze getuigenis af te leggen, omdat deze is overgenomen uit hun eigen gebruikelijke getuigenissen.

Ad Artikel 3, 4 en 5.
Het inhouden hiervan dient om de joden te verplichten tot grotere gehoorzaamheid en ook om alle samenzweringen te voorkomen die op afgezonderde plaatsen zouden kunnen worden gesmeed of ook in steden, als zij al te talrijk zouden worden.

Ad Artikel 6.
De manier om de joden tribuut te laten betalen voor hun vrijheid van hun godsdienst, is door de Pausen ingevoerd, wat tirannie en hebzucht betekent. De oude keizers hebben dat nooit gedaan, maar de joden op dezelfde wijze behandeld als de andere burgers. Verder beschikt over de vrije handel van de joden uitdrukkelijk artikel 1.9.9 van het Corpus Iuris Civilis.

23r

33

Op het selve de keijseren van outs hebben
de Joden verboden haer Synagogen te
maecken: Ende alhier is het seer [illegible],
geset dat sij oude Synagogen mochten
repareren maer geen nieuwe maecken
L. ult. C. de Judaeis & L. 22. et L. 27. Codice Theo-
dosiano eodem titulo. De Joden schijnt ge-
weest te sijn om dat haere religie
schijnt te hebben gelijckheijt te wesen
met het [illegible] van publicque predicatien:
Ende nochtans schijnt de [illegible] niet
versekert is datter maer eene publicque
religie en behoort te wesen / soo schijnt
dat het verboth is de Joden maer
en publicque maer in particuliere huijs
[illegible] haer exercitie toe te laten: Waerom
oock minder loopt in de ogen van't volck.

Op het vi. vii. viii. Articule sonder
bij consequentie is haer verboth gedaen
maer te trouwen, op dat alle [illegible]

Op het viij^{e} de Keijseren van outs hebben de Joden toegelaten haere Sijnagogen te maecken: daer nae is het selue gerestrin=geert dat zij oude Sijnagogen mochten repareren maer geen nijeuwe maecken *L. ult. C. de Judæis & L. 22. et L 27. Codice Theo=dosiano eodem titulo*. De reden schijnt ge=weest te zijn om dat haere religie scheen te zeer geauthorizeert te werden met het opbouwen van publijcque plae^{t}sen: Ende alzoo hijer te lande altijdt verstaen is datte^{r} maer eene publijcque religie en behoort wesen / zoo schijnt dat het alderbest is de Joden nijet in publicque maer in particuliere huij=sen haer exercitie toe te laeten: t' welck oock minder loopt in d' oogen van t' volck /.

Op het ix^{e} x^{e} xj^{e} xij^{e} T' getal vande bijeencomste is zeer oorboir gedefi=nieert te werden, op dat alle oploop

Ad Artikel 8.
De keizers hebben vanouds de joden toegestaan hun synagogen te stichten, daarna is dit beperkt, zodat zij wel de oude synagogen mogen repareren, maar geen nieuwe bouwen.[18] De reden schijnt geweest te zijn dat hun godsdienst te zeer leek te worden goedgekeurd door het bebouwen van de openbare ruimte. En ook hier in dit land is altijd aangenomen dat er maar één algemene godsdienst behoort te zijn, zodat het maar beter is om de joden niet in openbare gebouwen maar in particuliere huizen hun uitoefening van hun godsdienst toe te staan, hetgeen ook minder zichtbaar is voor de bevolking.

Ad Artikel 9, 10, 11, 12.
Het is van belang het aantal van de bijeenkomsten te omschrijven, zodat opstootjes

18 Cod. 1.9.18(19), Cod. Theod. 16.8.22 en 16.8.25.

23v

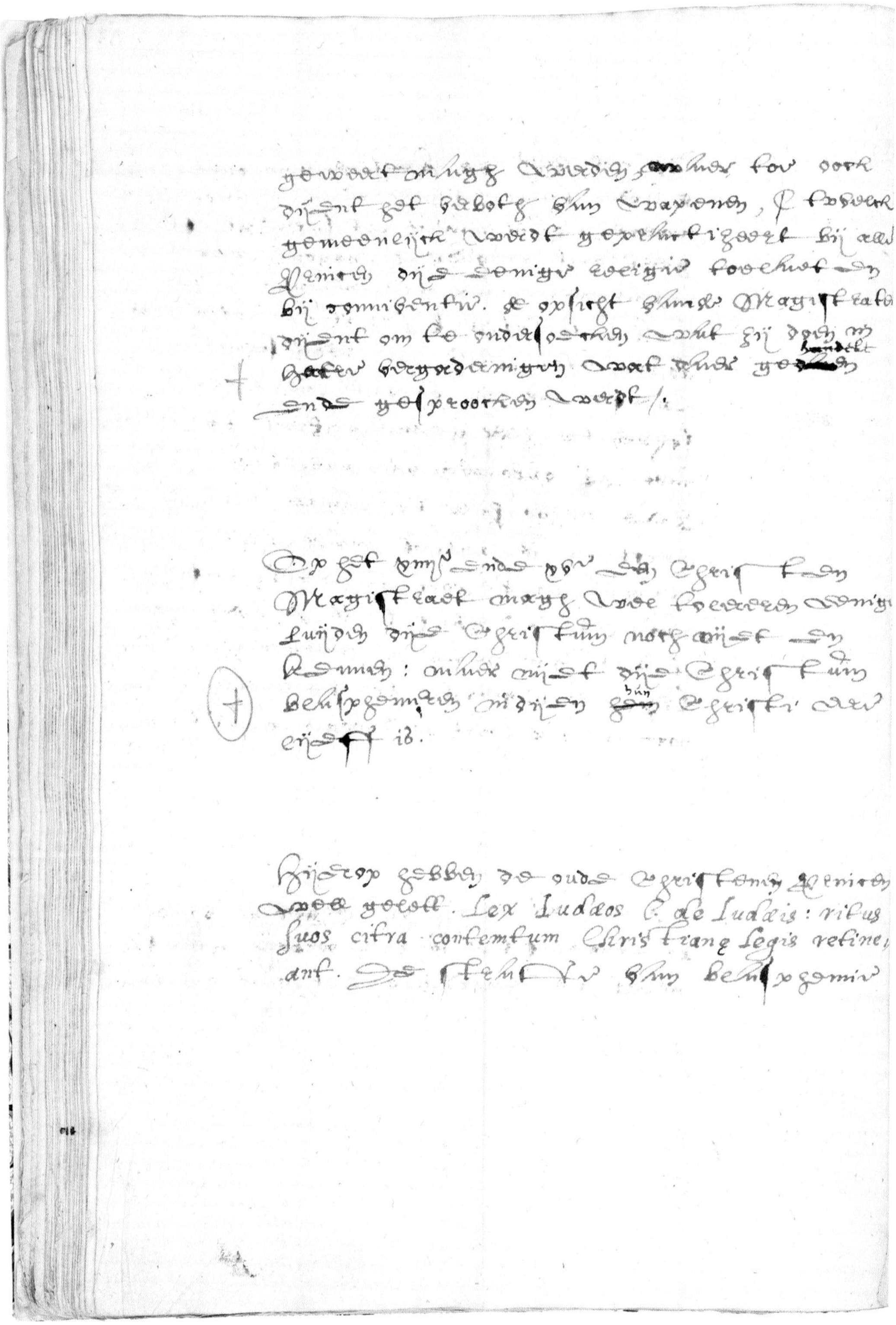

geweert magh werden waer toe oock dijent het verboth van wapenen, ~~C~~ twelck gemeenlijck werdt gepractizeert bij alle Princen dije eenige religie toelaeten bij conniventie. de opsicht vande Magistraten dijent om te ondersoecken wat zij doen in haere vergaderingen wat daer ge~~daen~~handelt ende gesproocken werdt /.

Op het xiiij^{e} ende xv^{e} een Christen Magistraet magh wel tolereren eenige Luijden dije Christum noch nijet en kennen: maer nijet dije Christum blasphemeren indijen ~~hem~~ hun Christi eere lijeff is.

Hijerop hebben de oude Christenen Princen well gelett. *Lex Iudæos C. de Iudæis: ritus suos citra contemtum Christianę legis retine=ant.* De straffe van blasphemie

kunnen worden geweerd. Daartoe dient ook het wapenverbod, dat in het algemeen wordt toegepast door alle heersers die een godsdienst oogluikend toestaan. Het toezicht van het stadsbestuur dient om te onderzoeken wat zij doen in hun bijeenkomsten, waarover het gaat en wat er besproken wordt.

Ad Artikel 14 en 15.
Een christelijk stadsbestuur kan wel enkele mensen tolereren die Christus nog niet kennen, maar niet diegenen die Christus belasteren, indien Christus' eer hun lief is.

Hierop hebben de oude christelijke vorsten goed toegezien. De straf op godslastering

24r

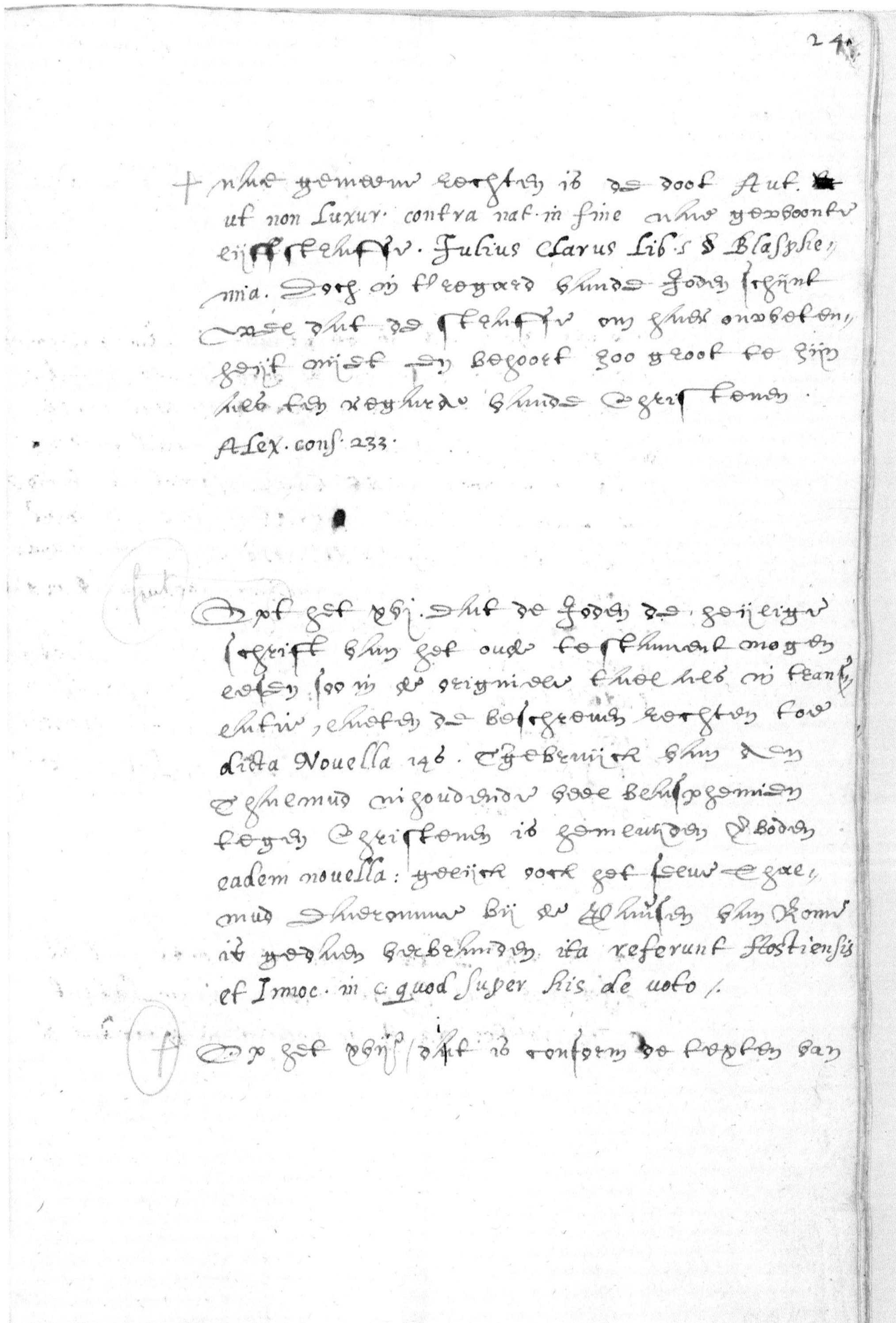

nae gemeene rechten is de doot. *Aut. ut non Luxur. contra nat. in fine* nae gewoonte lijffstraffe. *Julius Clarus Lib. 5 § Blasphe= mia*. Doch in t'regard vande Joden schijnt wel dat de straffe om haer onweten= heijt nijet en behoort zoo groot te zijn als ten regarde vande Christenen. *Alex. cons*. 233.

Opt het xvj. Dat de Joden de heijlige schrift van het oude testament mogen lesen: soo in de originele tael als in trans= latie, laeten de beschreuen rechten toe *dicta Nouella* 146. T'gebruijck van den Thalmud inhoudende veel blasphemien tegen Christenen is hemluijden *ver*boden *eadem nouella*: gelijck oock het selue Thal= mud Daeromme bij de Pausen van Rome is gedaen verbranden *ita referunt Hostiensis et Innoc. in c. quod super his de uoto* /.

Op het xvij[e] da[i]t is conform de texten van

is volgens de algemene rechtspraak de dood, en naar gewoonte de lijfstraf; maar wat betreft de joden schijnt het dat de straf vanwege hun onwetendheid niet zo zwaar behoort te zijn als wat betreft de christenen.[19]

Ad Artikel 16.
Dat de joden de Heilige Schrift van het Oude Testament mogen lezen, zowel in de originele taal als in vertaling, laat de jurisprudentie toe. Het gebruik van de Talmoed, waarin veel godslasteringen tegen de christenen voorkomen, is hun verboden, zoals ook de Talmoed door de Pausen van Rome werd verbrand.[20]

Ad Artikel 17.
Dit conform de teksten in

19 Cod. 1.9.11; Nov. 77; in dit artikel worden twee interessante wetten uit het Corpus Iuris aangehaald, waarvan de eerste, Cod. 1.9.11 expliciet naar Purim verwijst. Volgens deze wet hadden joden de gewoonte kruisafbeeldingen te verbranden met Purim als verwijzing naar de doodstraf die Haman voor de joden had bedacht en die hij uiteindelijk zelf onderging. De keizers zagen hierin, al dan niet terecht, een bespotting van het christelijke kruissymbool. De tweede wet, Novella 77, spreekt over blasfemie in het algemeen, een paraplubegrip waar veel onder geschaard kon worden. Elke vorm van lichtzinnig gebruik van Gods naam wordt zwaar veroordeeld, onder meer uit angst voor aardbevingen en epidemieën! Overigens valt onder blasfemie ook het uitvoeren van 'onnatuurlijke handelingen.' *Iulii Clari Alexandrini Opera omnia, sive practica civilis atque criminalis*, blasphemia; *Consiliorum seu Responsorum Alexandri Tartagni … Liber sextus …*, 153.

20 Nov. 146; De Groot verwijst verder voor de talmoedverbranding naar een decreet van Innocentius IV en het commentaar van Hostiensis hierop. Dit artikel wordt uitgebreid toegelicht in Kedar, "Canon Law and the Burning of the Talmud.".

24v

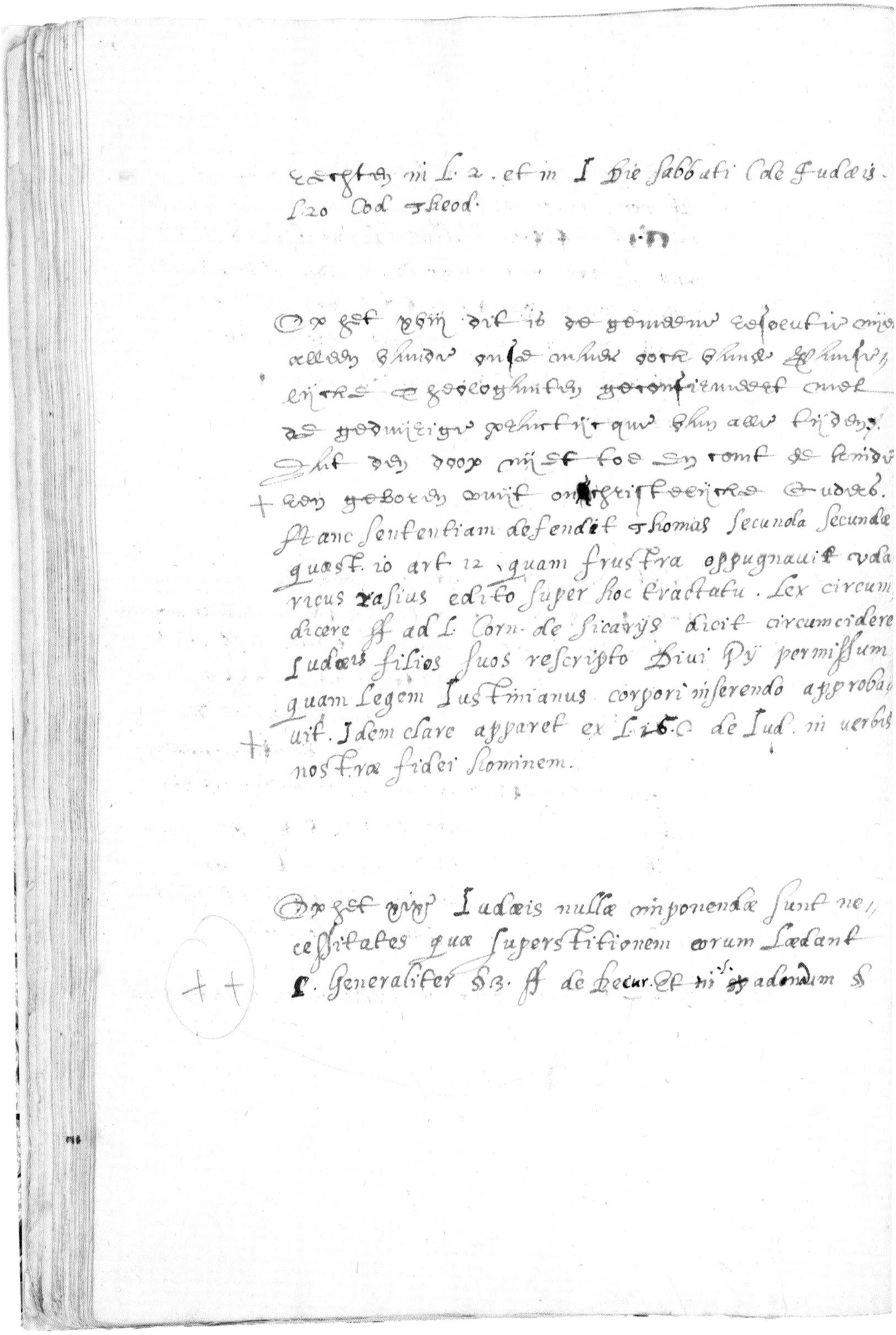

[illegible] in L. 2. et in L die sabbati C. de Iudaeis. l. 20 Cod. Theod.

[illegible] Hanc sententiam defendit Thomas secunda secundae quaest. 10 art. 12, quam frustra oppugnavit Udalricus Zasius edito super hoc tractatu. Lex circumcidere ff ad L. Corn. de sicariis dicit circumcidere Iudaeis filios suos rescripto Divi Pii permissum quam legem Iustinianus corpori inserendo approbavit. Idem clare apparet ex L. 26 C. de Iud. in verbis nostrae fidei hominem.

[illegible] Iudaeis nullae imponendae sunt necessitates quae superstitionem eorum laedant L. Generaliter §3. ff de decur. et in [illegible] ad [illegible] §

rechten in *L. 2 et in L Die sabbati C de Judæis L. 20 Cod. Theod*

Op het xviij dit is de gemeene resolutie nijet alleen vande onse maer oock vande Pause= lijcke Theologanten geconfirmeert met de geduijrige practijcque van alle tijden /. Dat den doop nijet toe en comt de kinde= ren geboren vuijt onchristelijcke Ouders. *Hanc sententiam defendit Thomas secunda secundæ quæst. 10 art 12, quam frustra oppugnauit volab= ricus*[21] *zasius edito super hoc tractatu. Lex circum= dicere ff ad L. Corn. de sicarijs dicit circumcidere. Iudæis filios suos rescripto Diui Pii permissum quam legem Iustinianus corpori inserendo approba= uit. Idem clare apparet ex L. 16. C. de Iud. in uerbis nostræ fidei hominem.*

Op het xix^{e} *Iudæis nullæ imponendæ sunt ne= cessitates quæ superstitionem eorum Lædant L. Generaliter § 3. de Decur. Et in* ·L· *adendum §*

jurisprudentie van de Romeinse keizers.[22]

Ad Artikel 18.
Dit was al een algemeen besluit, niet alleen van ons, maar ook van de rooms-katholieke theologen, overeenkomend met de praktijk van alle tijden, dat de doop niet toekomt aan kinderen geboren uit onchristelijke ouders.[23]

Ad Artikel 19.
Er zullen de Joden geen verordeningen opgelegd worden die hen hinderen bij de uitoefening van hun religie.[24]

21 volab-ricus *lees* Vdalricus.

22 Cod. 1.9.2, Cod. 1.9.13 en Cod. Theod. 16.8.20.

23 De Groot verwijst hier naar Thomas van Aquino, die in zijn *Summa Theologia* 2–2, q. 10 art. 12 betoogt dat er welliswaar vele geleerden zijn die gevonden hebben dat kinderen van Joodse ouders tegen hun wil in gedoopt mochten worden, maar dat dat niet strookt met de algemene gewoonte van de kerk en dat die te allen tijde gevolgd moet worden. Overigens is dit precies één van de passages die Van Ittersum aanhaalt als bronnen van Grotius die hij intensief gebruikte, in navolging van Vitoria: 'Vitoria's *Relectiones XII* served as Grotius' reader's guide to the *Secunda Secundae.* [...] Grotius was paraphrasing Vitoria's *Relection on the American Indians* par. 39, where Grotius mentioned as his sources "St. Thomas in his ST. II-II.10.8", "Gratian's canon *De Iudaeis*" (Decretum D.45.5), "Consilium IV Toletanum par.56" [...] Can it be coincidence that when we turn to Grotius' copy of the *Secunda Secundae* we find underlining in nearly every article of Question 10 [...]? Vitoria's *Relection on the American Indians*, which Grotius read from cover to cover, evidently spurred him on to make careful study of Question 10 of the *Secunda Secundae* [...].' Ittersum, "The Working Methods of Hugo Grotius," 185.

De humanist en jurist Ulrich Zasius heeft dit thema behandeld in zijn *De Iudaeis Quaestionibus tres* (1550), waarbij hij de conclusie trok dat dat wel mocht, maar De Groot vindt hem hier dus duidelijk niet overtuigend. Over Zasius, zie: Rowan, "Ulrich Zasius and the Baptism of Jewish Children." Daarnaast lijkt De Groot een congruentie-regel toe te passen: Aangezien Joden ernstig gestraft dienen te worden als zij een niet-Jood besnijden, mogen Christenen ook geen Joden dopen. Hij verwijst daarvoor naar Dig. 48.8.11 en Cod. 1.9.16.

24 Dig. 50.2.3.3 en Dig. 27.1.15.6.

25r

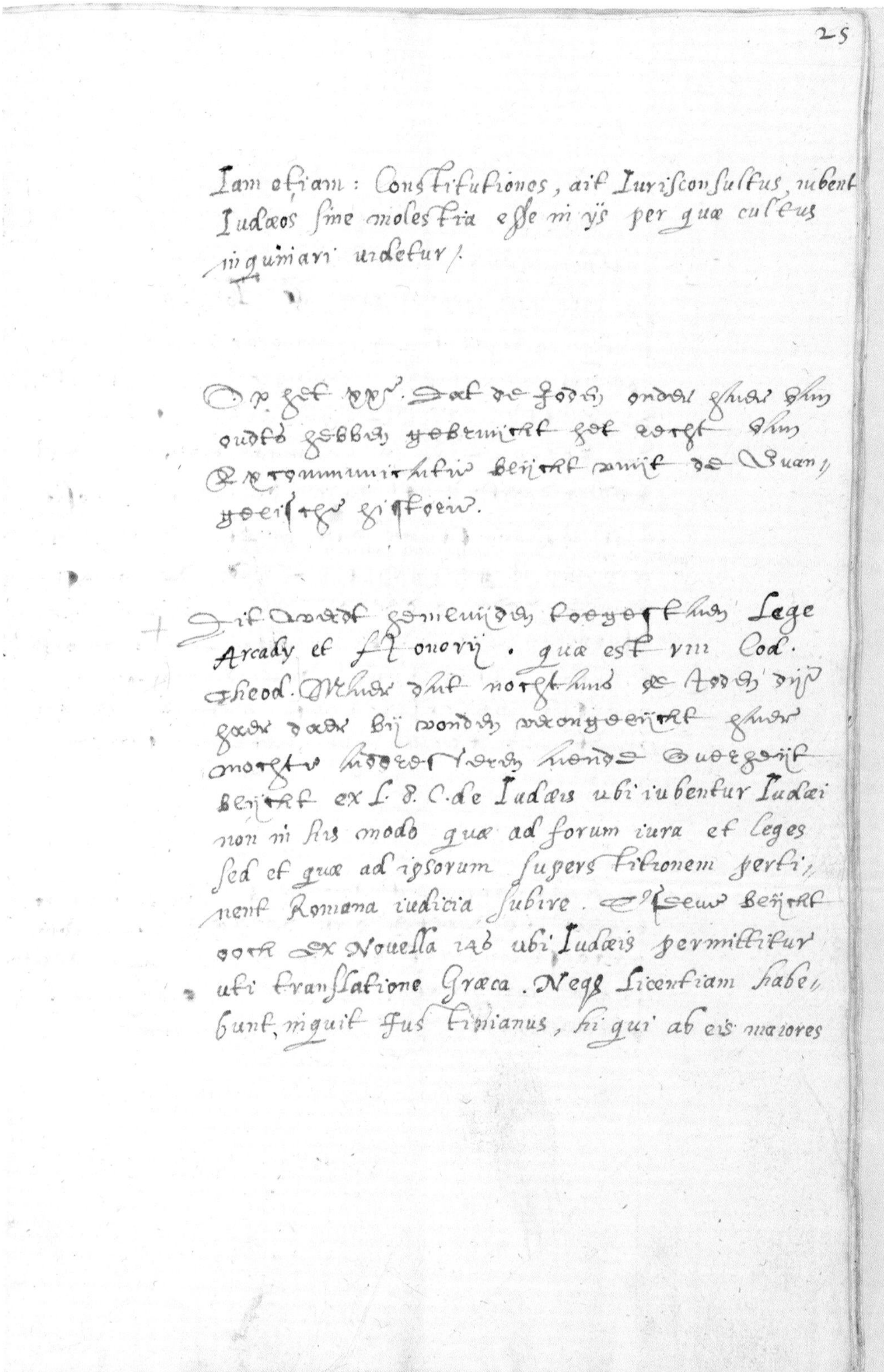

25

Iam etiam: Constitutiones, ait Iurisconsultus, iubent Iudæos sine molestia esse in ijs per quæ cultus inquinari videtur.

[illegible]

Dit wordt gemeenlijck voorgestelt ... Lege Arcadij et Honorij. quæ est VIII Cod. Theod. [illegible] ex L. 8. C. de Iudæis ubi iubentur Iudæi non in his modo quæ ad forum iura et leges sed et quæ ad ipsorum superstitionem perti-nent Romana iudicia subire. [illegible] ex Novella 146 ubi Iudæis permittitur uti translatione Græca. Neque licentiam habe-bunt, inquit Iustinianus, hi qui ab eis maiores

Iam etiam: Constitutiones, ait Iurisconultus, iubent Iudæos sine molestia esse in ijs per quæ cultus inquiriari uidetur /.

Op het xxe. Dat de Joden onder haer van oudts hebben gebruijckt het recht van Excommunicatie blijckt vuijt de Euan= gelische historie.

Dit werdt hemluijden toegestaen *Lege Arcady et Honorij. quæ est* VIII *Cod. Theod.* Maer dat nochtans de Joden dije haer daer bij vonden verongelijckt haer mochte addresseren aende Ouerheijt blijckt *ex L. 8. C. de Iudæis ubi iubentur Iudæi non in his modo quæ ad forum iura et leges sed et quæ ad ipsorum superstitionem perti= nent Romana iudicia subire.* T' selue blijckt oock *ex Novella 146 ubi Iudæis permittitur ubi translatione Graeca. Neq*ue *licentiam hebe= bunt, inquit Justinianus, hi qui ab eis maiores*

Ad Artikel 20.
Dat de joden sinds oude tijden onderling gebruik hebben gemaakt van het recht van excommunicatie, blijkt uit de evangelische geschiedenis.

Dit werd hen toegestaan volgens de Romeinse wetgeving.[25] Maar dat de joden die zich daardoor tekort gedaan voelden, zich niettemin mochten wenden tot de overheid.[26]

25 Cod. Theod. 16.8.8.

26 Cod. 1.9.8. De Groot haalt ook Nov. 146 aan waarin sprake is van Joden die tegen hun religieuze leiders in 'bescherming' worden genomen, dat zij de Griekse bijbelvertaling mogen gebruiken. In dit geval kunnen zij dus een beroep doen op de seculiere autoriteiten t.o.v. de religieuze autoriteiten.

25v

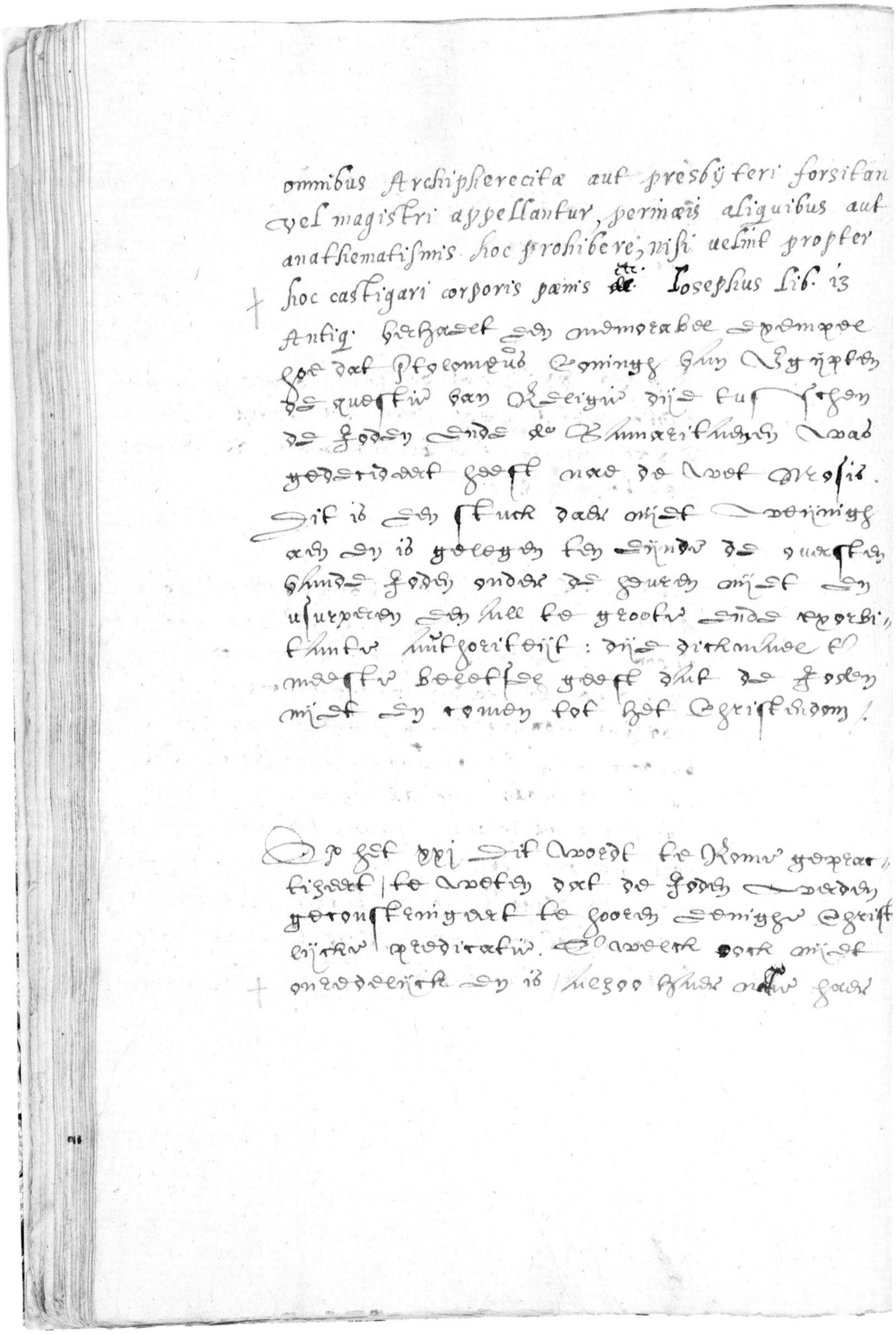

omnibus Archipherecitæ aut presbyteri forsitan vel magistri appellantur, per nais aliquibus aut anathematismis hoc prohibere, nisi velint propter hoc castigari corporis pœnis etc. Iosephus lib. 13 Antiq.

omnibus Archipherecitæ aut presbijteri forsitan vel magistri appellantur, perinœis aliquibus aut anathematismis hoc prohibere, nisi uelint propter hoc castigari corporis pœnis [etc]. *Iosephus Lib 13 Antiq*. verhaelt een memorabel exempel hoe dat Ptolomeus Coningh van Egijpten de questie van Religie dije tusschen de Joden ende de Samaritaenen was gedecideert heeft nae de wet Mosis. Dit is een stuck daer nijet weijnigh aen en is gelegen ten eijnde de ouersten vande Joden onder de heuren nijet en usurperen een all te groote ende exorbi= tante authoritheijt: dije dickmael t' meeste beletsel geeft dat de Joden nijet en comen tot het Christendom /.

Op het xxj Dit wordt te Rome geprac= tiseert / te weten dat de Joden werden geconstringeert te hooren eenighe Christe= lijcke predicatie. T' welck oock nijet onredelijck en is / alzoo Haer nae haer

Flavius Josephus geeft een gedenkwaardig voorbeeld, hoe Ptolemaeus, koning van Egypte, de godsdienstkwestie, die tussen de joden en de Samaritanen heerste, beslist heeft volgens de wet van Mozes. Dit is een zaak van groot belang, omdat de leiders van de joden zich onder de hunnen een al te grote en exorbitante autoriteit aanmatigen, wat vaak het grootste beletsel oplevert waarom de joden zich niet tot het christendom bekeren.

Ad Artikel 21.
Dit wordt te Rome toegepast, namelijk dat de joden gedwongen worden enige christelijke preken aan te horen. Dit is ook niet onredelijk, omdat het hun volgens hun

[26]r

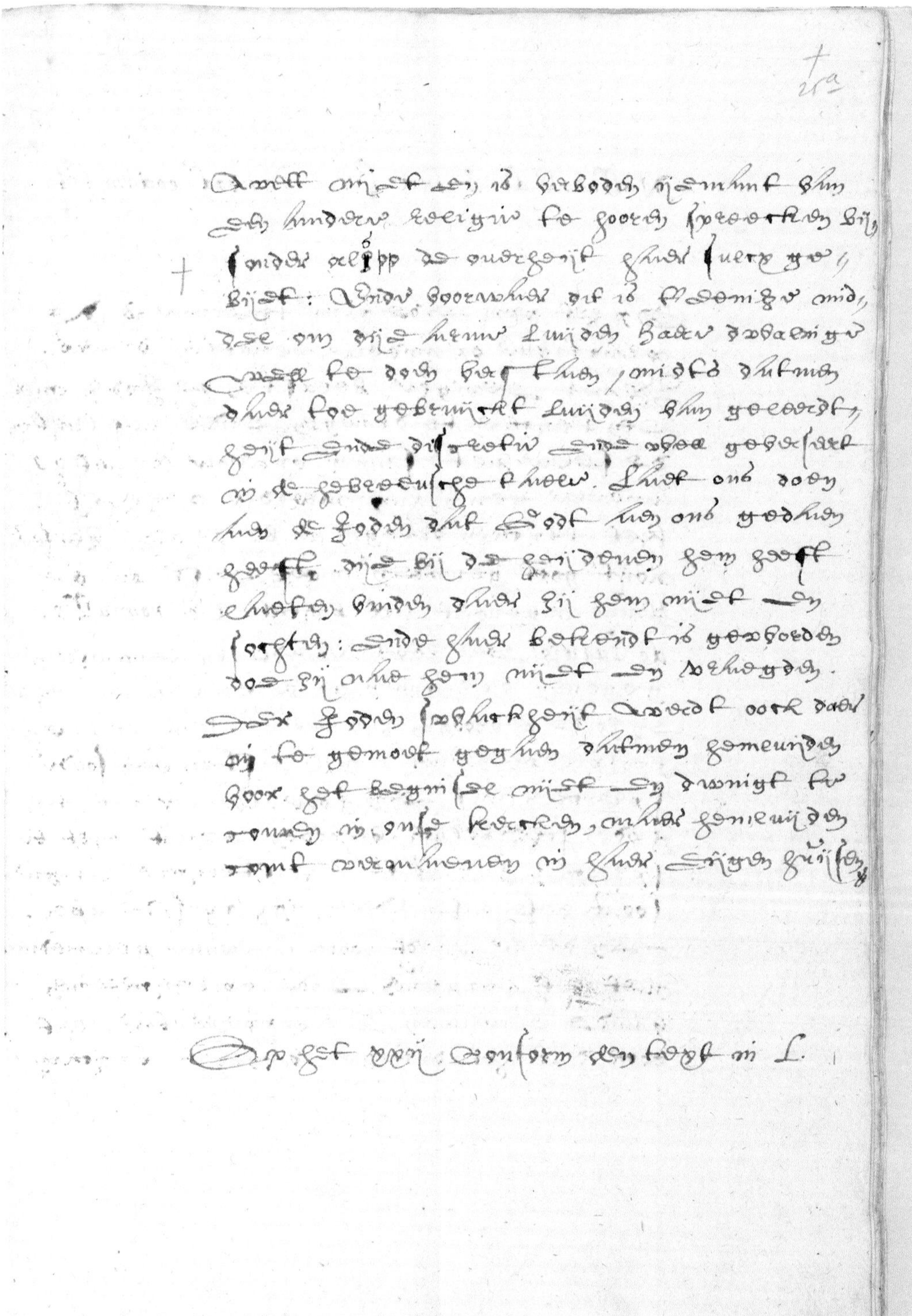

wet nijet en is verboden ijemant van een andere religie te hooren spreecken bij= sonder al^{s}zoo de ouerheijt haer sulcx ge= bijet: Ende voorwaer dit is het eenige mid= del om dije arme Luijden Haere dwalinge well te doen verstaen / midts datmen daer toe gebruijckt Luijden van geleerdt= heijt ende discretie ende well geverseert in de hebreeusche taele. Laet ons doen aen de Joden dat Godt aen ons gedaen heeft dije bij de heijdenen hem heeft laeten vinden daer zij hem nijet en sochten: ende haer bekendt is geworden doe zij nae hem nijet en vraegden. Der Joden swackheijt werdt oock daer in te gemoet gegaen datmen hemluijden voor het beginsel nijet en dwingt te comen in onse kercken, maer hemluijden comt vermaenen in haer eijgen huijsen.

Op het xxij Conform den text in *L.*

wet niet verboden is iemand van een andere godsdienst te horen spreken, in het bijzonder als de overheid het hun gebiedt. En het is stellig het enige middel om deze arme mensen hun dwaling goed te doen inzien, mits men daartoe geleerde en oordeelkundige mensen inzet die goed bedreven zijn in de Hebreeuwse taal. Laten wij voor de joden datgene doen wat God voor ons heeft gedaan, die zich bij de heidenen heeft laten vinden, waar zij hem niet zochten en zich bij hen bekend heeft gemaakt toen zij niet naar hem vroegen. Aan de zwakheid van de joden wordt ook tegemoet gekomen, doordat men hen uit principe niet dwingt in onze kerken te komen, maar hen komt vermanen in hun eigen huizen.

Ad Artikel 22.
Conform de tekst in het Corpus Iuris.[27]

27 Cod. 1.9.14; Cod.Th. 16.8.21 (*niet* 12).

[26]v

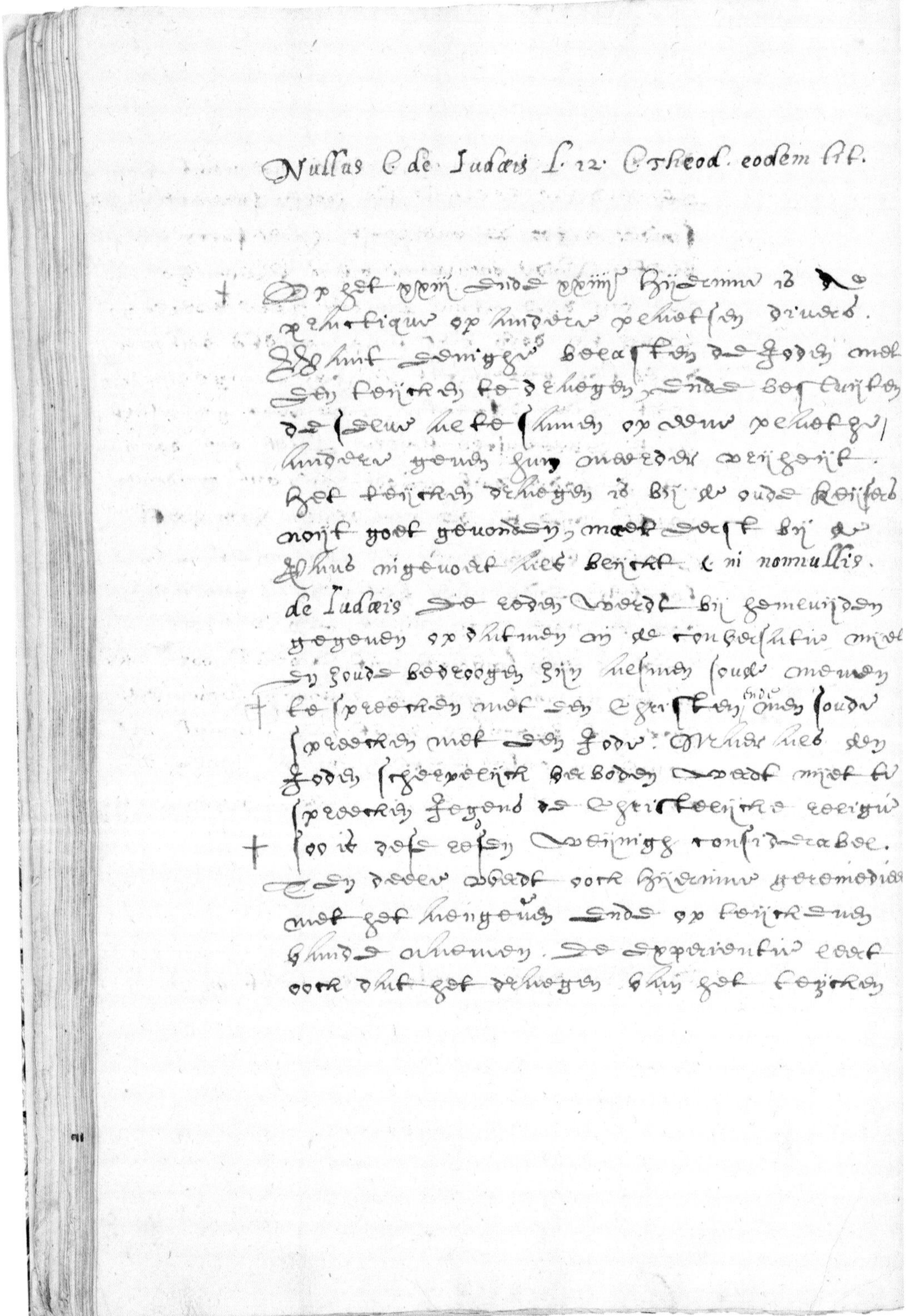

Nullus C. de Iudaeis l. 12 C. Theod. eodem tit.

[illegible]
[illegible]
[illegible]
[illegible]
[illegible]
[illegible]
het [illegible] is bij de oude keijsers
noijt goet gevonden, maer [illegible] bij de
[illegible] c. ni nonnullis.
de Iudaeis [illegible]
[illegible]
[illegible] souden moeten
te spreken met den Christenen [illegible] souden
spreken met den Joden. [illegible]
Joden [illegible] verboden [illegible]
spreken tegens de Christelijcke religie
so is dat [illegible] considerabel.
[illegible]
[illegible]
[illegible] De experientie leert
[illegible]

Nullus C. de Iudœis L. 12. C. Theod. eodem tit

Op het xxiij ende xxiiij^{e} Hijerinne is de practique op andere plaetsen diuers. Want eenighe belasten de Joden met een teijcken te draegen, ende besluijten de selue al te samen op eene plaetze / andere geuen hun meerder vrijheijt. Het teijcken draegen is bij de oude Keijsers noijt goet geuonden, maer eerst bij de Paus ingeuoert als blijckt *C. in nonullis de Iudœis* De reden werdt bij hemluijden gegeuen op datmen in de conversatie nijet en zoude bedroogen zijn als men soude menen te spreecken met een Christen / ^{ende} men soude spreecken met een Jode. Maer als den Joden scherpelijck verboden werdt nijet te spreecken Jegens de Christelijcke religie soo is dese res^{d}en weijnigh considerabel. Ten deele werdt oock Hijerinne geremedieert met het aengeuen ende op teijckenen vande naemen. De experientie leert oock dat het draegen van het teijcken

Ad Artikel 23 en 24.
Hierin is de praktijk overal verschillend. Want sommigen gelasten de joden een teken te dragen en wel iedereen op eenzelfde manier. Anderen geven hen meer vrijheid. Het dragen van een teken is door de oude keizers nooit juist gevonden, maar pas door de Paus ingevoerd.[28] De reden die door hen gegeven werd, was dat men in de omgang niet misleid zou worden, als men zou menen te spreken met een christen terwijl men zou spreken met een jood. Maar als het de joden streng zou worden verboden zich tegen de christelijke godsdienst uit te spreken, dan is deze reden van weinig belang. Deels werd hierin ook tegemoet gekomen door het aangeven en opschrijven van de namen. De ervaring leert ook dat het dragen van een teken

28 CIC X 5.6.15.

26[=27]r

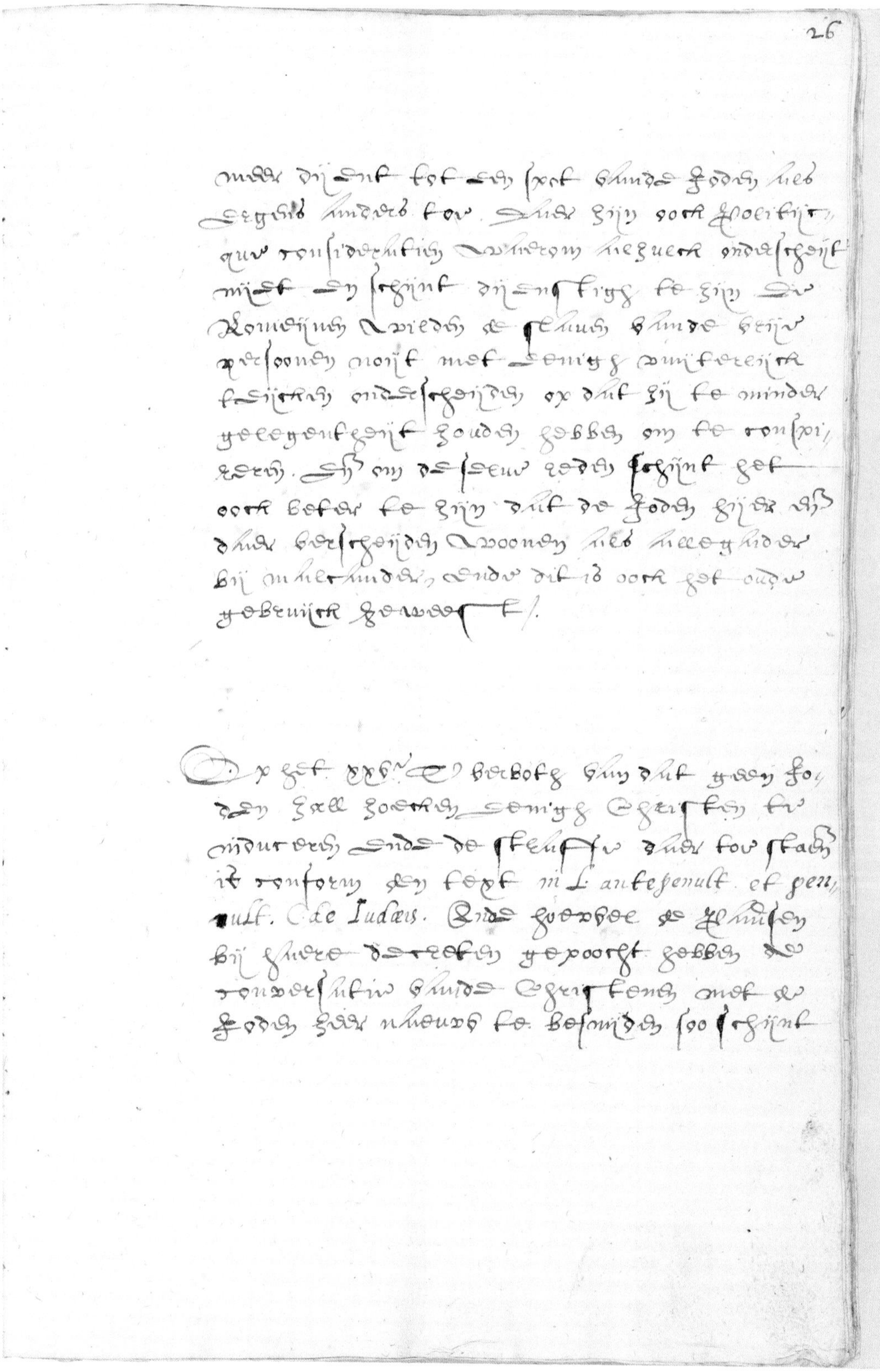

meer dijent tot een spot vande Joden als ergens anders toe. Daer zijn oock Politijc=que consideratien waarom alzulck onderscheijt nijet en schijnt dijenstigh te zijn. De Romeijnen wilden de slauen vande vrije persoonen noijt met eenigh vuijterlijck teijcken onderscheijden op dat zij te minder gelegentheijt zouden hebben om te conspi=reren. En*de* om deselue reden schijnt het oock beter te zijn dat de Joden hijer en*de* daer verscheijden woonen als allegader bij malcander, ende dit is oock het oude gebruijck geweest /.

Op het xxv^{e}. T' verboth van dat geen Jo=den zall zoecken eenigh Christen te induceren ende de straffe daer toe staen*de* is conform den text *in L. antepenult et pen=ult. C. de Iudæis*. Ende hoewel de Pausen bij haere decreten gepoocht hebben de conversatie vande Christenen met de Joden zeer naeuw te besnijden soo schijnt

meer dient tot bespotting van de joden dan tot iets anders. Er zijn ook politieke overwegingen waarom een dergelijk onderscheid niet nuttig lijkt te zijn. De Romeinen wilden de slaven nooit met een uiterlijk teken onderscheiden van de vrije mensen zodat zij minder gelegenheid zouden hebben om samen te zweren. En om dezelfde reden lijkt het ook beter dat de joden hier en daar verspreid wonen dan allemaal bij elkaar, en dat is ook de oude gewoonte geweest.

Ad Artikel 25.
Het verbod dat geen jood enig christen zal proberen te overreden, en de straf die daarop staat, is conform de tekst van het Corpus Iuris.[29] En hoewel de Pausen met hun decreten gepoogd hebben de omgang van christenen met joden zeer sterk te beperken, zo schijnt

29 Waarschijnlijk verwijst De Groot hier naar Cod. 1.9.16 en Cod. 1.9.18.

26[=27]v

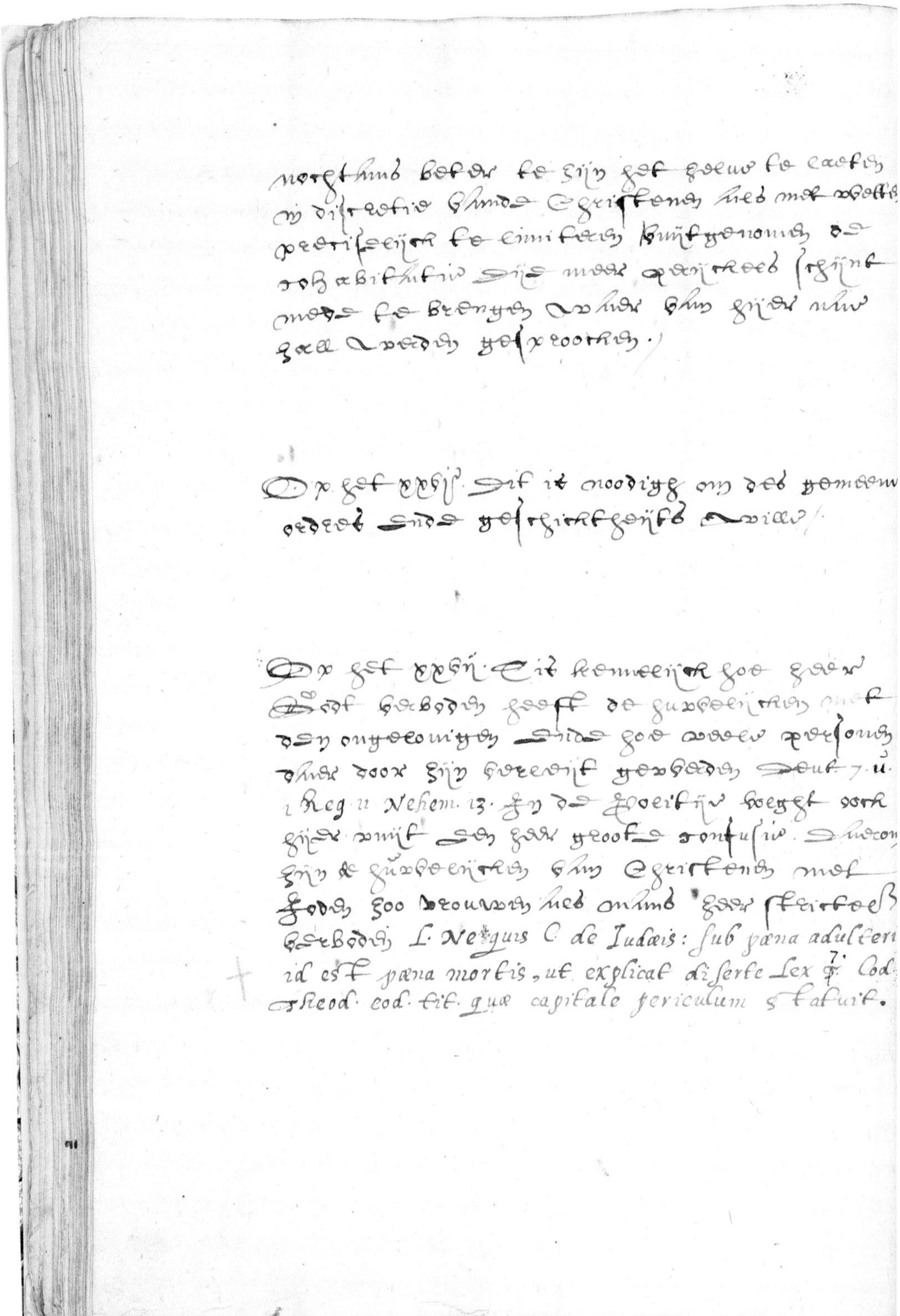

nochtans beter te zijn het zelue te laeten in discretie vande Christenen als met wetten preciselijck te limiteren / vuijtgenomen de cohabitatie dije meer perijckels schijnt mede te brengen waer van hijer nae zall werden gesproocken. /

Op het xxvj^{e}. Dit is noodigh om des gemeene ordres ende geschicktheijts wille /.

Op het xxvij. T'is kennelick hoe zeer Godt verboden heeft de huwelijcken met den ongelouigen ende hoe veele personen daer door zijn verleijt gewerden Deut. 7. u. 7 *1 Reg 11. Nehem. 13.* In de Politije volght oock hijer vuijt een zeer groote confusie. Daerom zijn de huwelijcken van Christenen met Joden zoo vrouwen als mans zeer strickt*elijck* verboden *L. Ne quis C. de Judæis: sub pœna adulterij id est pœna mortis, ut explicat diserte Lex 5 7. Cod. Theod. eod. tit. quæ capitale periculum statuit.*

het toch beter te zijn, dit over te laten aan het onderscheidingsvermogen van de christenen dan deze met wetten nauwkeurig te beperken, behalve het samenwonen dat meer problemen met zich mee schijnt te brengen, waarover hierna zal worden gesproken.

Ad Artikel 26.
Dit is nodig vanwege de algemene regels en gewenste doelmatigheid.

Ad Artikel 27.
Het is onmiskenbaar, hoewel God huwen met een ongelovige heeft verboden, hoeveel mensen hiertoe werden verleid. *Deut. 7:7, 1 Kon. 11, Neh. 13.*[30] Hieruit volgt in de wetgeving ook zeer grote verwarring. Daarom zijn huwelijken van christenen met joden, zowel vrouwen als mannen, strikt verboden.[31]

30 Waarschijnlijk Deut. 7:3; 1 Kon. 11; waarschijnlijk Neh. 13:25–26.

31 De Groot voert hier bewijzen aan uit het Romeinse recht. Hij onderbouwt zijn stelling met de woorden van een 15^{e} eeuwse commentator, die op de geciteerde plaats de vraag bespreekt of dood door het zwaard ook letterlijk uitgevoerd werd en diende te worden, of ook overdrachtelijk genomen kon worden. In ernstige gevallen was daadwerkelijke uitvoering gewenst. Over Joden wordt niet gesproken in de betreffende passage. Cod. 1.9.6, Cod.Th. 3.7 en Cod. 9.9.29. Bartholomaeus a Salyceto, *In VII. VIII. et IX. Codicis Libros Commentaria*, 222.

27[=28]r

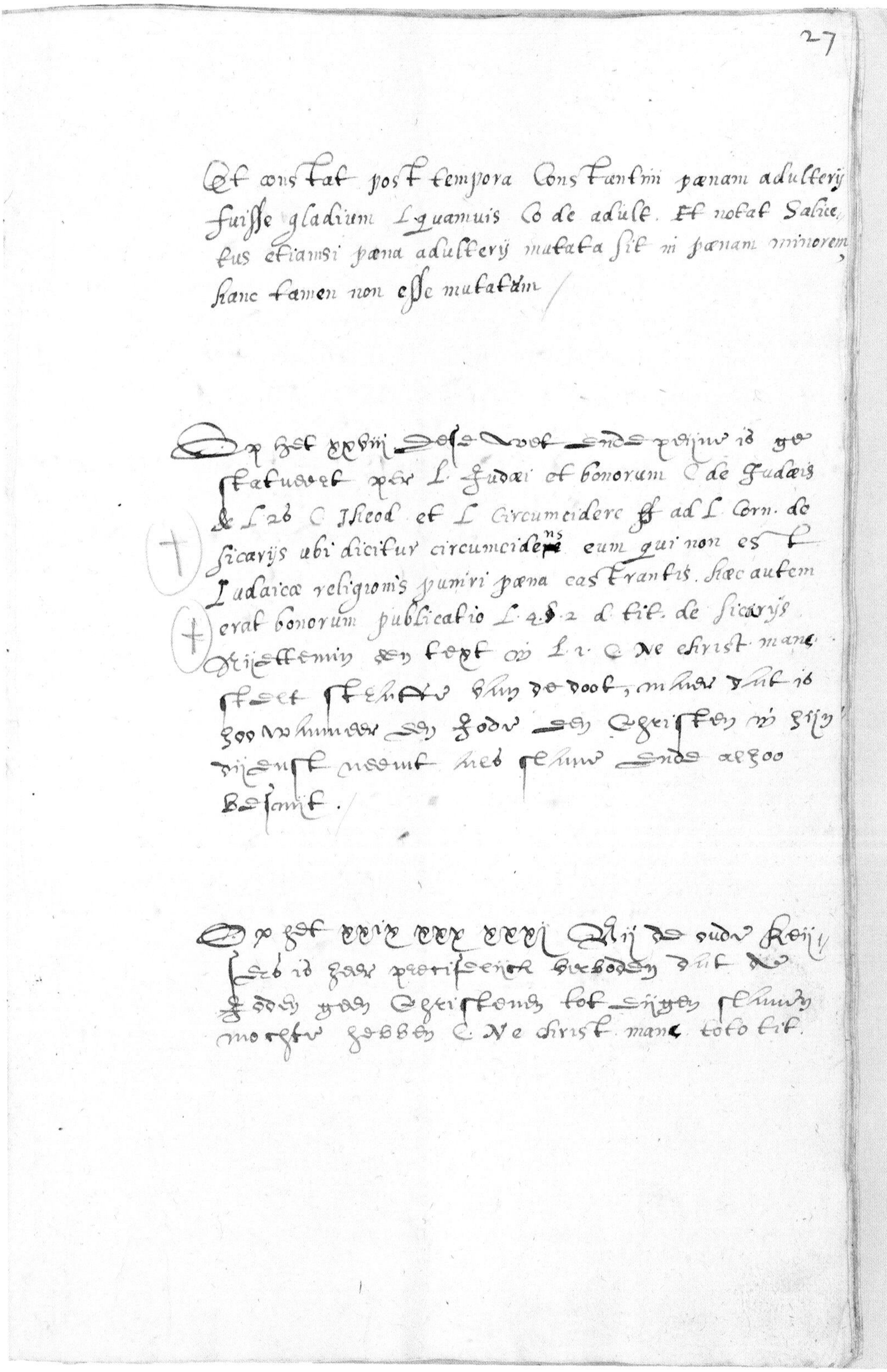
Et constat post tempora Constantini pœnam adulterij fuisse gladium L quamuis Co de adult. Et notat Salicetus etiamsi pœna adulterij mutata sit in pœnam minorem hanc tamen non esse mutatam

[illegible] statuerat per L. Iudaei et bonorum C de Iudaeis & L 26 C Theod et L Circumcidere ff ad L Corn. de sicarijs ubi dicitur circumcidens eum qui non est Iudaicae religionis puniri pœna castrantis. haec autem erat bonorum publicatio L 4 [illegible] 2 d tit. de sicarijs [illegible] L 1 C Ne christ. manc. [illegible]

[illegible] C Ne christ. manc. toto tit.

Et constat post tempora Constantini pœnam adulterij fuisse gladium L. quamvuis C. de adult. Et notat Salcei= tus etiamsi pœna adulterij mutata sit in pœnam minorem, hanc tamen non esse mutatam /

Op het xxviij Dese wet ende peijne is ge statueert per *L. Judæi et bonorum C de Judæis & L 26 C Theod et L Circumcidere ff ad L Corn. de sicarijs ubi dicitur circumcide~~re~~ns eum qui non est Iudaicæ religionis puniri pœna castrantis. Hæc autem erat bonorum publicatio L. 4. §. 2. d. tit. de sicarijs* Nijettemin een text in *L. 1. C. Ne christ. manc.* stelt straffe van de doot, maer dat is zoo wanneer een Jode een Christen in zijn dijenst neemt als slaue ende alzoo besnijt. /

Op het xxix xxx xxxj Bij de oude Keij= sers is zeer preciselijck verboden dat de Joden geen Christenen tot eijgen slauen mochten hebben *C. Ne christ. manc. toto tit.*

Ad Artikel 28.
Deze wet en straf is vastgesteld door de Romeinse keizers.[32] Niettemin bepaalt een tekst in Cod. 1.10.1 de doodstraf, maar dit geldt wanneer een jood een christen als slaaf in zijn dienst neemt en hem dan besnijdt.

Ad Artikel 29, 30, 31.
Door de oude keizers is zeer nadrukkelijk verboden, dat joden christenen tot eigen slaven hadden.[33]

32 De strafmaat was verbeurdverklaring van goederen, net als bij castratie. Cod. 1.9.16; Cod.Th. 16.8.26; Dig. 48.8.11 en Dig. 48.8.4.2.

33 Cod. 1.10, en Cod.Th. 16.9.

27[=28]v

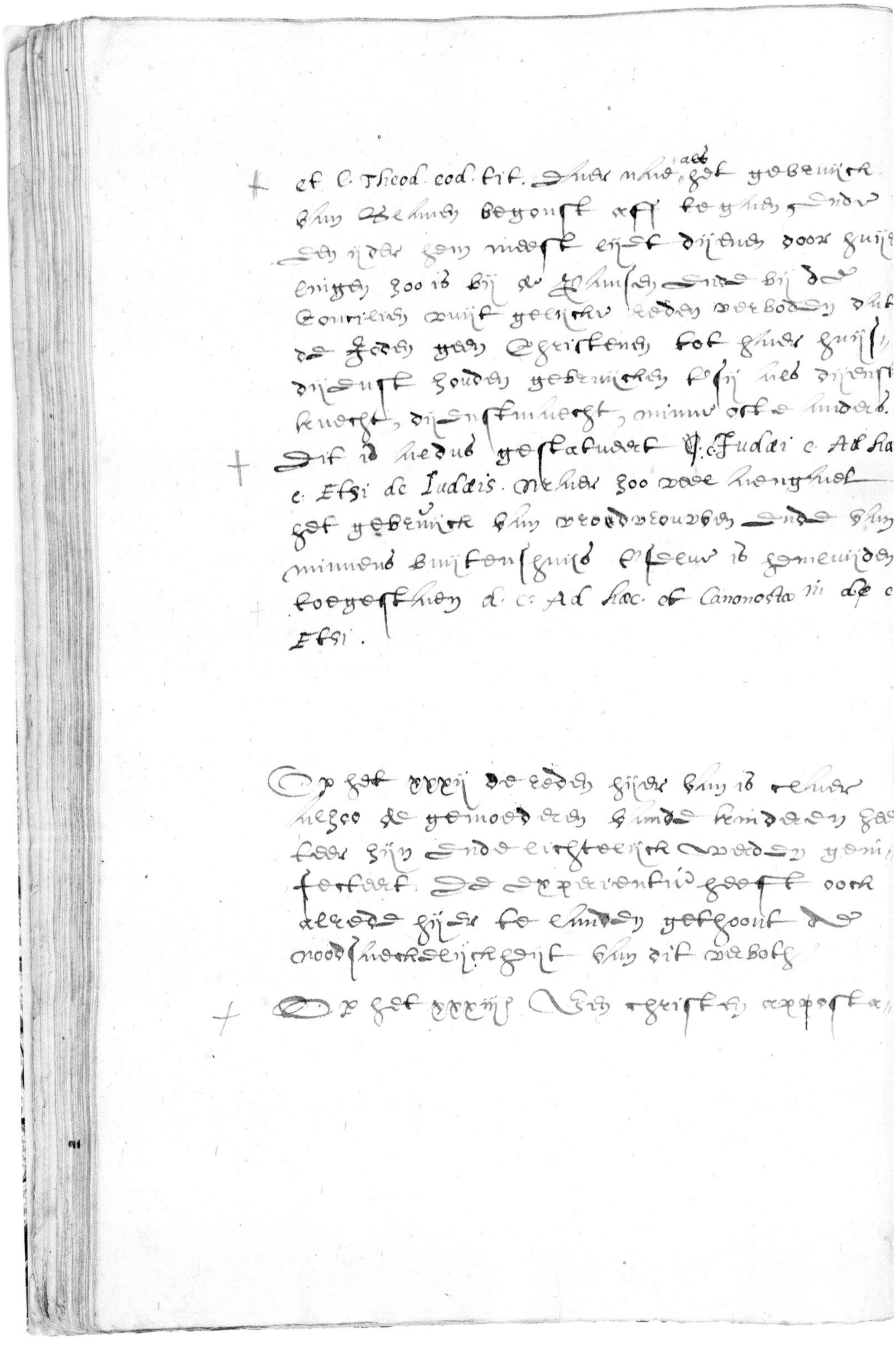

et C. Theod. eod. tit. Daer nae [als] het gebruijck van Slauen begonst aff te gaen, ende een ijder hem meest lijet dijenen door huijr=lingen zoo is zoo is bij de Pausen ende bij de Concilien vuijt gelijcke reden verboden dat de Joden geen Christenen tot haer huijs=dijenst zouden gebruijcken t'sij als dijenst=knecht, dijenstmaecht, minne ofte anders. Dit is aldus gestatueert ~~C.~~ *c. Judæis c. Ad hæc c. Etsi de Judæis*. Maer zoo veel aengaet het gebruijck van vroedvrouwen ende van minnens buijtenshuijs t' selue is hemluijden toegestaen *d. c: Ad haec et Canonosta in d. c c. Etsi.*

Op het xxxij de reden hijer van is claer alzoo de gemoederen vande kinderen zeer teer zijn ende lichtelijck worden gein=fecteert: De experientie heeft oock alrede hijer te landen gethoont de noodsaeckelijckheijt van dit verboth /

Op het xxxiij[e]. Een christen ap~~p~~osta=

Daarna, toen het gebruik van slaven begon af te nemen, en iedereen zich meestal liet bedienen door huispersoneel, is door de Pausen en door de Concilies om dezelfde reden verboden, dat de joden christenen als hun huispersoneel zouden gebruiken, hetzij als dienstknecht, dienstmeid, min of anders. Dit is aldus vastgelegd in het canoniek recht.[34]

Maar voor zover het betreft het gebruikmaken van vroedvrouwen en minnen buitenshuis is het hun toegestaan.[35]

Ad Artikel 32.
De reden hiervoor is duidelijk, omdat de emoties van kinderen zeer gevoelig zijn en gemakkelijk worden beïnvloed. De ervaring heeft ook reeds hier te lande de noodzakelijkheid van dit verbod aangetoond.

Ad Artikel 33.
Een christen, die afvalt

34 CIC X 5.6.8 en 5.6.13.

35 CIC X 5.6.8 en de glos op 5.6.13.

28[=29]r

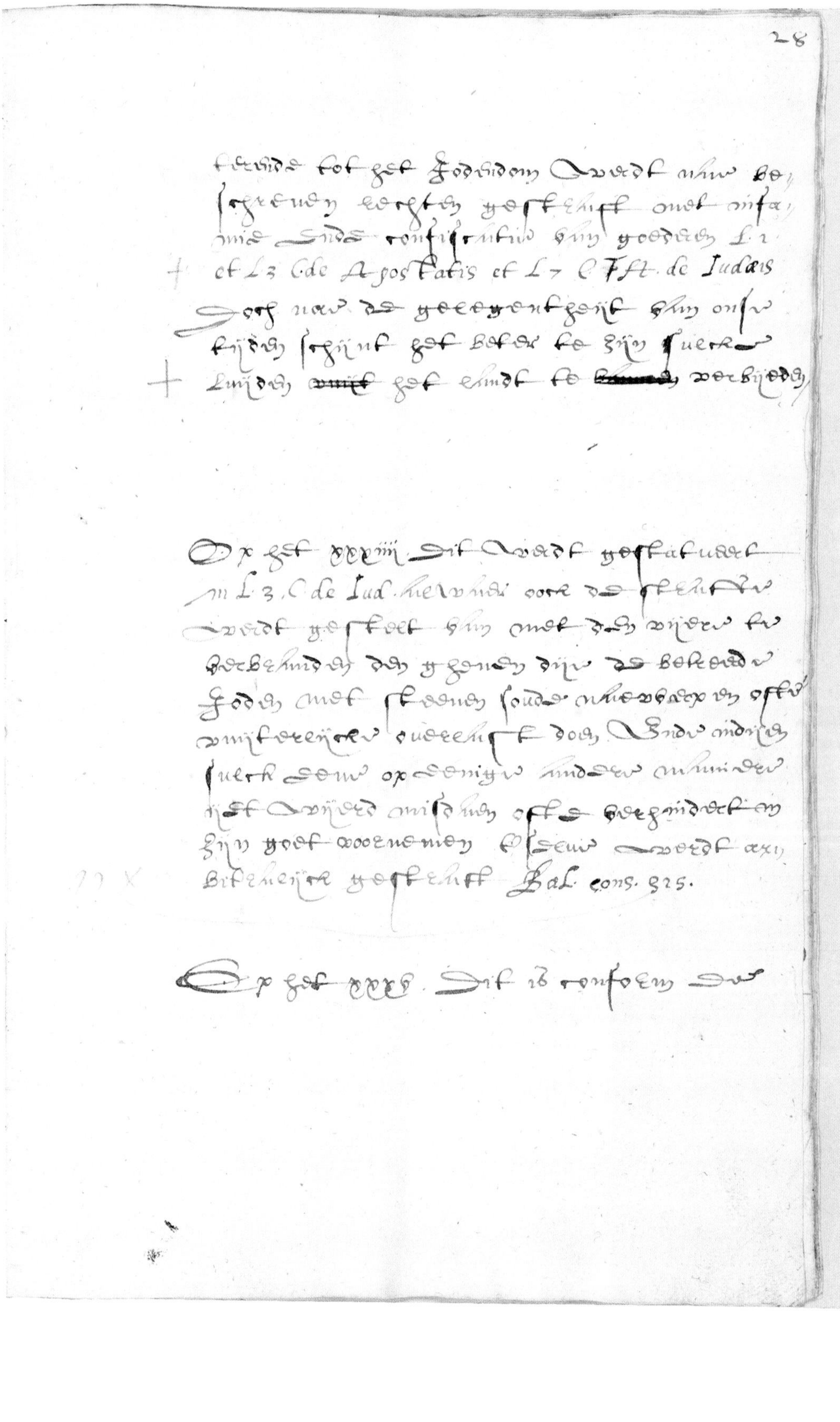

terende tot het Jodendom werdt nae be= schreuen rechten gestraft met infa= mie ende confiscatie van goederen *L. 2 et L 3 C. de Apostatis et L 7 C. TH. de Iudæis* Doch nae de gelegentheijt van onse tijden schijnt het beter te zijn sulcke Luijden ~~vuijt~~ het land te ~~bannen~~ verbijeden /

Op het xxxiiij. Dit werdt gestatueert *in L. 3. C. de Iud.* alwaer oock de straffe werdt gestelt van met den vijere te verbranden den ghenen dije de bekeerde Joden met steenen soude naewerpen ofte vuijterlijcke ouerlast doen. Ende indijen sulck eene op eenige andere maniere ijet wijerd misdaen ofte verhindert in zijn goet voornemen t' selue werdt ar= bitralijck gestraft *Bal cons. 525.*

Op het xxxv. Dit is conform de

tot het jodendom, wordt volgens de bestaande jurisprudentie gestraft met verlies van de burgerlijke eer en confiscatie van bezittingen.[36] Maar gezien de huidige tijd schijnt het beter te zijn, zulke mensen de toegang tot het land te ontzeggen.

Ad Artikel 34.
Dit werd vastgelegd in het Corpus Iuris, waarin de brandstapel als straf werd vastgesteld voor diegenen die naar de bekeerde joden met stenen zouden gooien of hen lichamelijk letsel zouden aandoen. En indien hen op enige andere manier iets werd misdaan of hen zou hinderen in hun goede voornemens, wordt dit op een zelfde manier door de rechter bestraft.[37]

Ad Artikel 35.
Dit is conform de

36 Cod. 1.7.2 en 1.7.3 en Cod. Theod. 16.8.7 (vreemd genoeg niet Cod. Theod. 16.7, dat geheel over afvalligen gaat).

37 Cod. 1.9.3.

28[=29]v

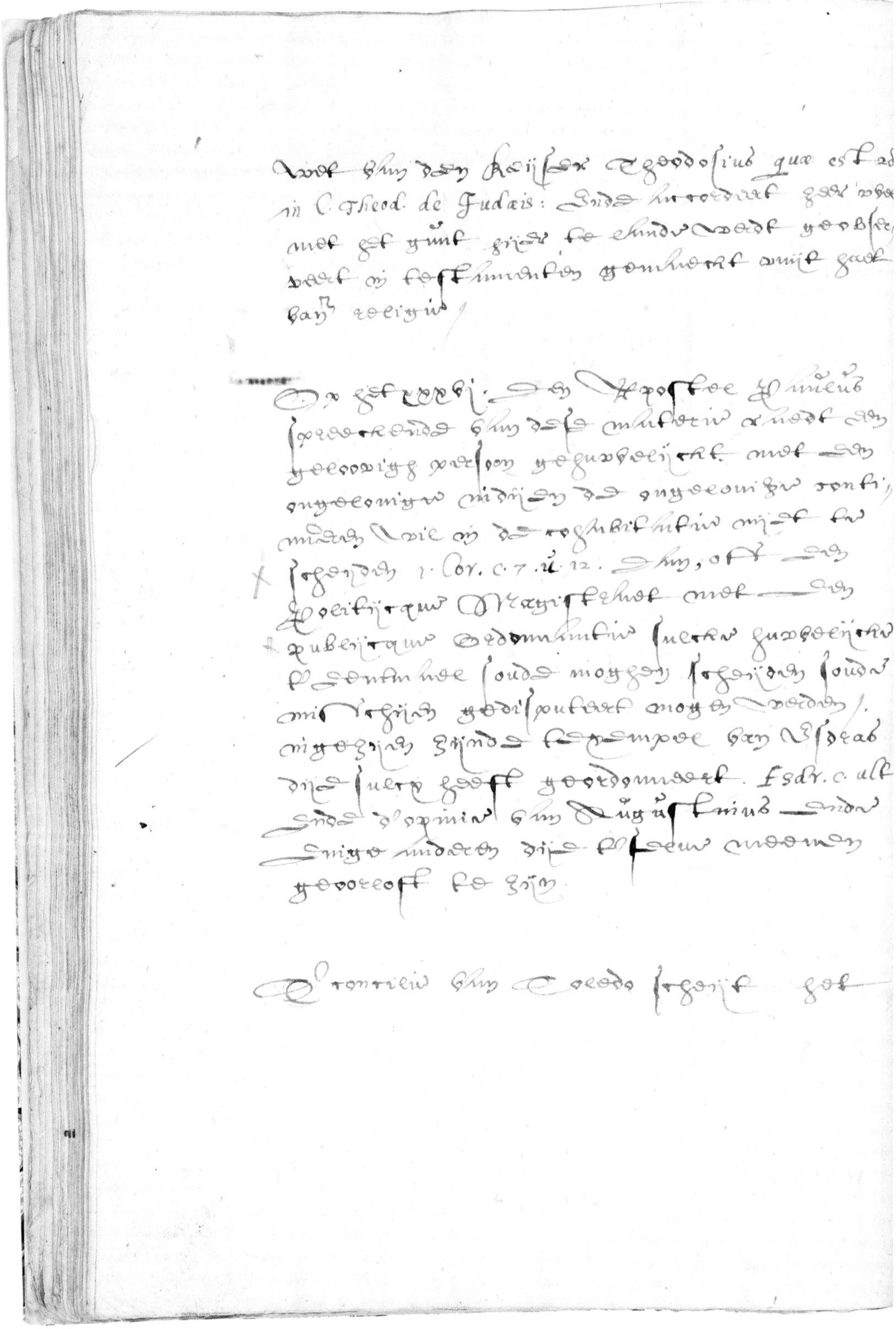

wet van den Keijser Theodosius *quæ est 28 in C. Theod. de Judæis*: Ende accordeert zeer wel met het gunt hijer te lande werdt geobser=veert in testamenten gemaeckt vuijt haet van*de* religie /

Op het xxxvj. Den Apostel Paulus spreeckende van dese materie raedt een geloovigh persoon gehuwelijckt met een ongelouige indijen de ongelouige conti=nueren wil in de cohabitatie nijet te scheijden *1. Cor. c. 7 u. 12*. Dan, oft een

Politijcqe Magistraet met een publijcqe Ordonnantie sulcke huwelijcke t' eentmael soude moghen scheijden soude misschijen gedisputeert moghen werden /. ingezijen zijnde texempel van Esdras dije sulcx heeft geordonneert. *Esdr. c. ult* ende d'opinie van Augustinus ende enige anderen dije t'selue meenen geoorloft te zijn.

T'concilie van Toledo scheijt het

wet van keizer Theodosius, en komt uitstekend overeen met hetgeen hier te lande wordt waargenomen in testamenten, gemaakt uit haat tegen de godsdienst.[38]

Ad Artikel 36.

De apostel Paulus, sprekende over deze materie, raadt een gelovige, gehuwd met een ongelovige, aan niet te scheiden indien de ongelovige de samenwoning wil continueren.[39] Of een stedelijk bestuur door een openbare verordening een dergelijk huwelijk zou mogen beëindigen kan wellicht in twijfel worden betwist, gezien het voorbeeld van Ezra, die dit heeft verordonneerd, en de mening van Augustinus en enkele anderen, die menen dat ditzelfde is geoorloofd.[40]

Het Concilie van Toledo ontbindt het

38 Cod. Theod. 16.8.28.

39 1 Cor. 7:12.

40 Ezra 10:1–44.

29[=30]r

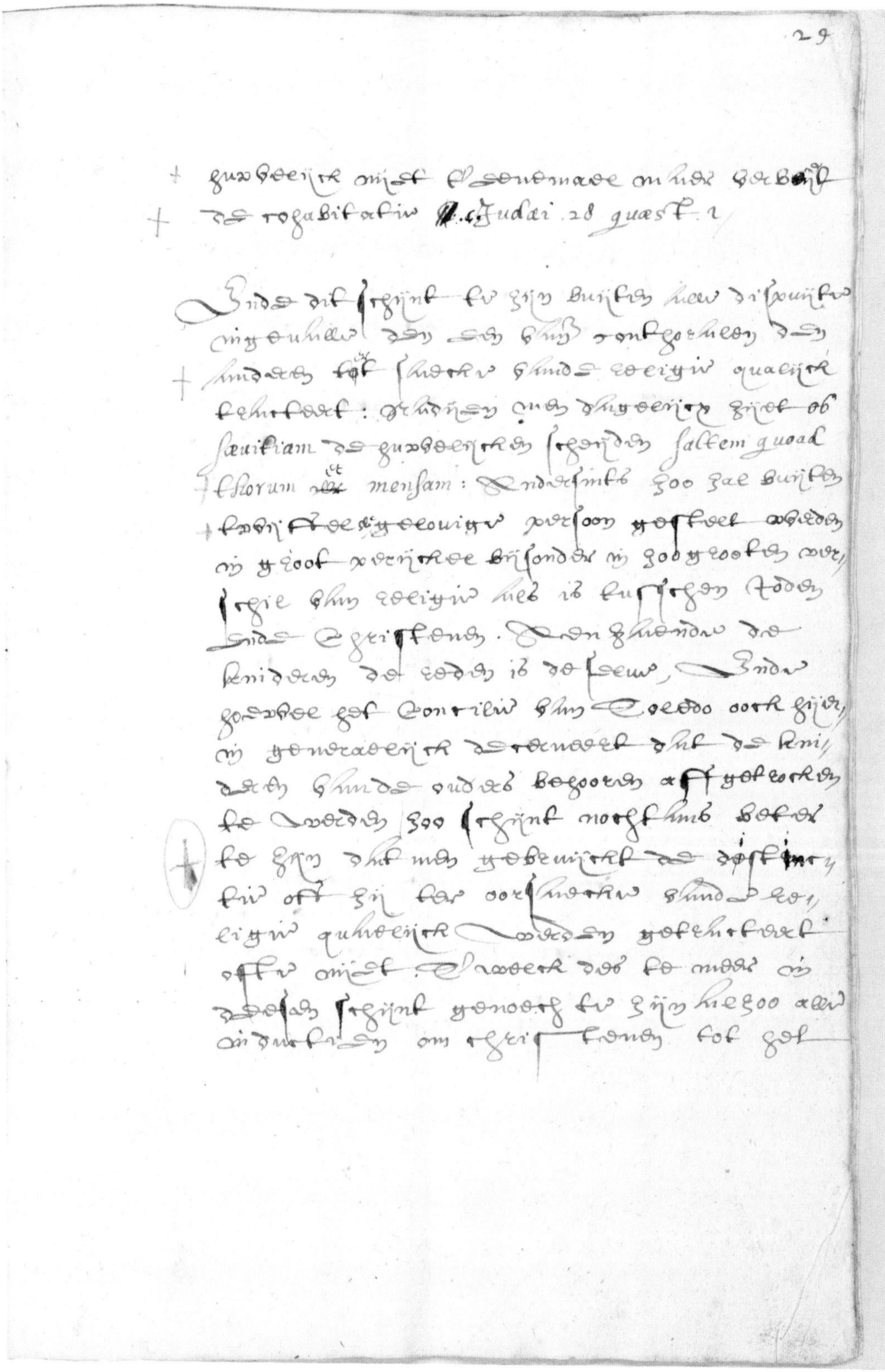

huwelijck nijet t'eenemael maer verbeij^{e}t
de cohabitatie ~~C.~~ *c. Judæi. 28 quæst.* 2 /

Ende dit schijnt te zijn buijten alle dispuijte
ingeualle den een van*de* conthoralen den
anderen ~~tot~~^{er} saecke vande religie qualijck
tracteert: Nadijen men dagelijcx zijet *ob*
sæuitiam de huwelijcken scheijden *saltem*
quoad
thorum ^{et} *mensam:* Andersints zoo zal buijten
twijffel de gelouige persoon gestelt werden
in groot perijckel bijsonder in zoo grooten ver=
schil van religie als is tusschen Joden
ende Christenen. Aengaende de
kinderen de reden is deselue. Ende
hoewel het Concilie van Toledo oock hijer=
in generaelijck decerneert dat de kin=
deren van de ouders behooren affgetrocken
te werden / zoo schijnt nochtans beter
te zijn dat men gebruijckt de ~~de~~^{i}~~ste~~^{i}nc=
tie off zij ter oorsaecke vande re=
ligie quaelijck werden getrackteert
ofte nijet. T'welck des te meer in
deesen schijnt genoech te zijn alzoo alle
inductien om christenen tot het

huwelijk niet eenzijdig, maar verbiedt het onwettig samenwonen.[41]

En dit schijnt buiten alle meningsverschil te vallen, ingeval een van de echtgenoten de andere, betreffende de godsdienst, slecht behandelt; zoals men dagelijks ziet dat wegens wreedheid huwelijken tenminste tussen tafel en bed ontbonden worden.

Anderszins zal zonder twijfel de gelovige in grote moeilijkheden geraken, in het bijzonder bij een zo groot verschil in geloof als tussen joden en christenen. Wat betreft de kinderen, is de redenering dezelfde. En hoewel het Concilie van Toledo ook hier in het algemeen besluit, dat de kinderen de ouders ontnomen behoren te worden, zo schijnt het toch beter te zijn, dat men het onderscheid maakt of zij wat betreft het geloof slecht behandeld worden of niet.[42] Hetgeen in deze des te meer in deze voldoende schijnt te zijn, omdat alle pogingen, om christenen tot het

41 CIC C. 28. q. 1. Hier komen ook de verwijzingen naar Paulus, Ezra en Augustinus vandaan.

42 CIC C.28. q.1. c.11; zie: Brundage, "Intermarriage between Christians and Jews in Medieval Canon Law."

29[=30]v

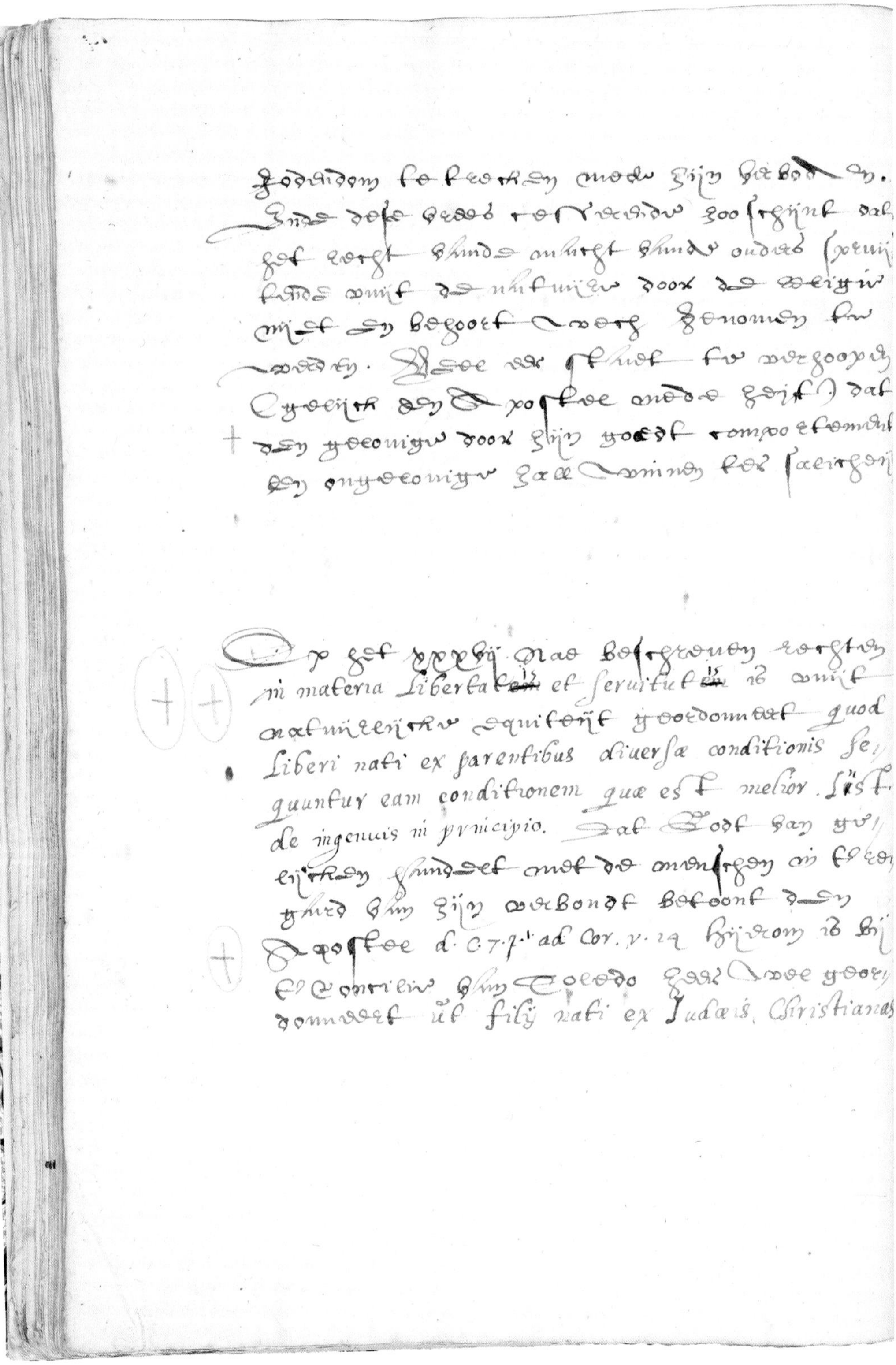

in materia Libertatis et servitutis

Liberi nati ex parentibus diversae conditionis se-
quuntur eam conditionem quae est melior. Inst.
de ingenuis in principio.

d. c. 7. 1. ad Cor. v. 14

ut filii nati ex Judaeis, Christianas

Jodendom te trecken mede zijn verboden. Ende dese vrees cesserende zoo schijnt dat het recht vande macht vande ouders spruijtende vuijt de natuijre door de religie nijet en behoort wech genomen te werden. Veel eer staet te verhoopen (gelijck den Apostel mede zeijt.) dat den gelouige door zijn goedt comportement een ongelouige zall winnen ter salicheijt.

Op het xxxvij. Nae beschreuen rechten *in materia libertatis~~em~~ et servitutis~~em~~* is vuijt natuijrlijcke equiteijt geordoneert *quod liberi nati ex parentibus diuersæ conditionis sequuntur eam conditionem quæ est melior. I~~n~~ust. de ingenuis in principio.* Dat Godt van gelijcken handelt met de menschen in t' regard van zijn verbondt betoont den Apostel *d. C. 7. ad Cor. v. 24* hijerom is bij t' Concilie van Toledo zeer wel geordoneert *ut filij nati ex Iudæis Christianas*

jodendom te bekeren, ook zijn verboden. En door de afnemende angst hiervoor, zo schijnt het, dient het natuurlijk recht van de ouders niet door het geloof afgenomen te worden. Veeleer mag men hopen (zoals ook de Apostel zegt) dat de gelovige door zijn goede gedrag de ongelovige tot diens heil zal overhalen.

Ad Artikel 37.
Na beschreven jurisprudentie aangaande vrijheid en slavernij is uit natuurlijke gelijkheid verordonneerd, dat kinderen, die geboren zijn uit ouders van verschillende status (nl. vrij of slaaf), die status verkrijgen die voor hen het gunstigst is.[43] Dat God de mensen gelijk behandelt ten opzichte van zijn Verbond, zo toont de apostel in 1 Cor. 7:24. Hierom is door het Concilie van Toledo zeer juist verordonneerd, dat kinderen van joden die met christelijke

43 I. 1.4.

30[=31]r

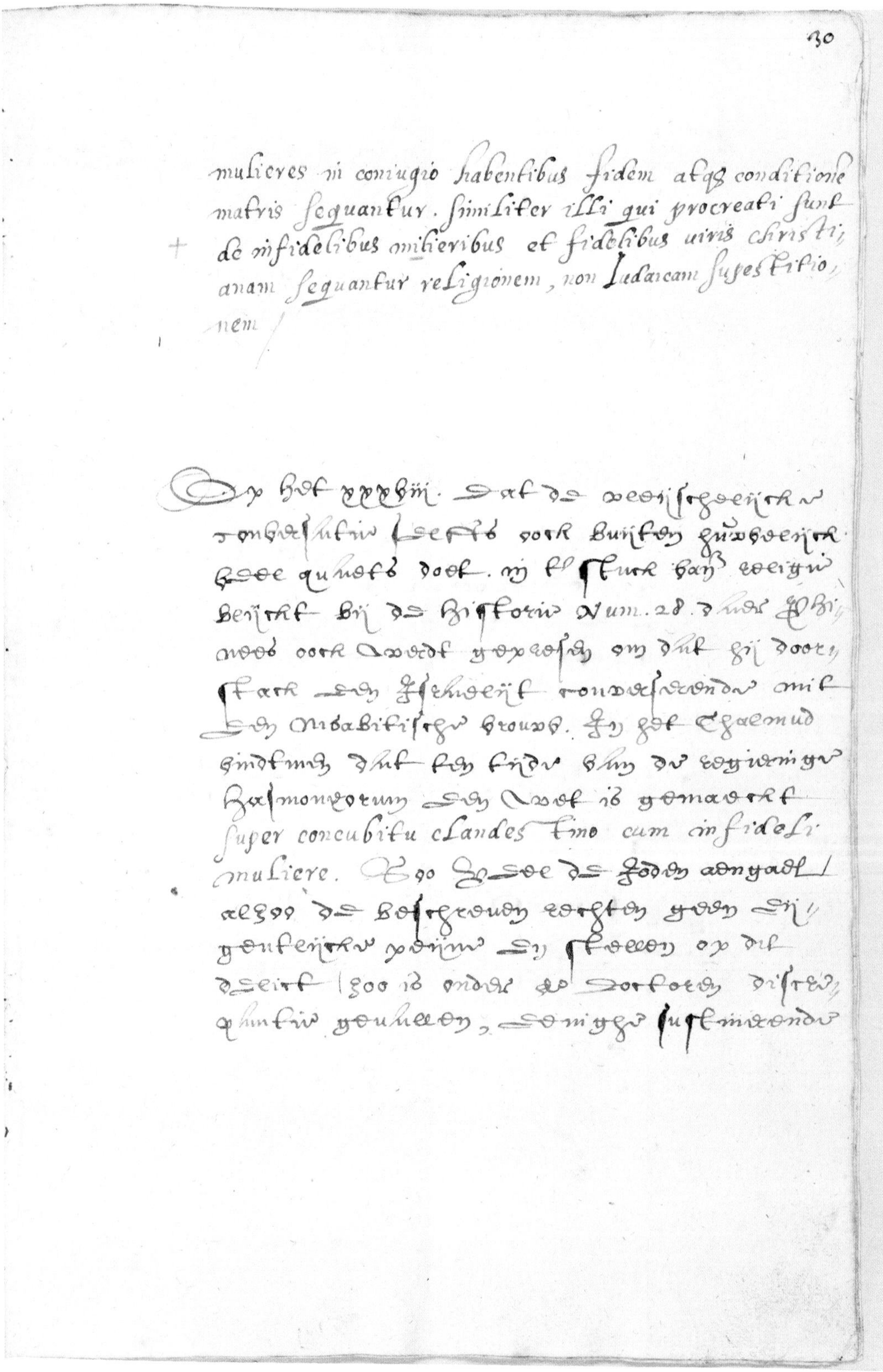
30

mulieres in coniugio habentibus fidem atque conditionem matris sequantur. Similiter illi qui procreati sunt de infidelibus mulieribus et fidelibus viris christianam sequantur religionem, non Iudaicam superstitionem /

super concubitu clandestino cum infideli muliere.

*mulieres in coniugio habentibus fidem atq*ue *condition*em *matris sequantur. similiter illi qui procreati sunt de infidelibus mulieribus et fidelibus uiris christi= anam sequantur religionem, non Iudaicam supestitio= nem /*

Op het xxxviij. Dat de vleijschelijcke conversatie selffe oock buijten huwelijck veel quaets doet in 't stuck van*de* religie blijckt bij de Historie *Num. 28* daer Phi= nees oock werdt gepresen om dat hij door= stack den Israelijt converserende mit een Moabitische vrouw. In het Thalmud vindt men dat ten tijde van de regieringe Hasmonæorum een wet is gemaeckt *super concubitu clandestino cum infideli muliere*. Soo veel de Joden aengaet / alzoo de beschreuen rechten geen eij= gentlijcke peijne en stellen op dit delict / zoo is onder de doctoren discre= pantie geuallen, eenighe sustinerende

vrouwen getrouwd zijn, de godsdienst en de status van de moeder verkrijgen. Op dezelfde wijze dienen zij, die voorgekomen zijn uit joodse vrouwen en gelovige mannen, de christelijke religie te volgen, niet het joodse bijgeloof.[44]

Ad Artikel 38.
Dat de lichamelijke omgang, ook buiten het huwelijk, veel kwaad doet op het gebied van het geloof blijkt ook uit Num. 25:7–8, waar Phineas ook werd geprezen omdat hij een Israëliet doorstak die gemeenschap had met een Moabitische vrouw. In de Talmoed vindt men dat ten tijde van de regering van de Hasmoneeën een wet is opgesteld aangaande de ongeoorloofde bijslaap met een heidense vrouw.

Voor zover het de joden aangaat is er, omdat de beschreven wetten geen werkelijke straf stellen op dit delict, onder de geleerden onenigheid ontstaan: enkelen beweren

44 CIC C.28 q.1 c.10.

30[=31]v

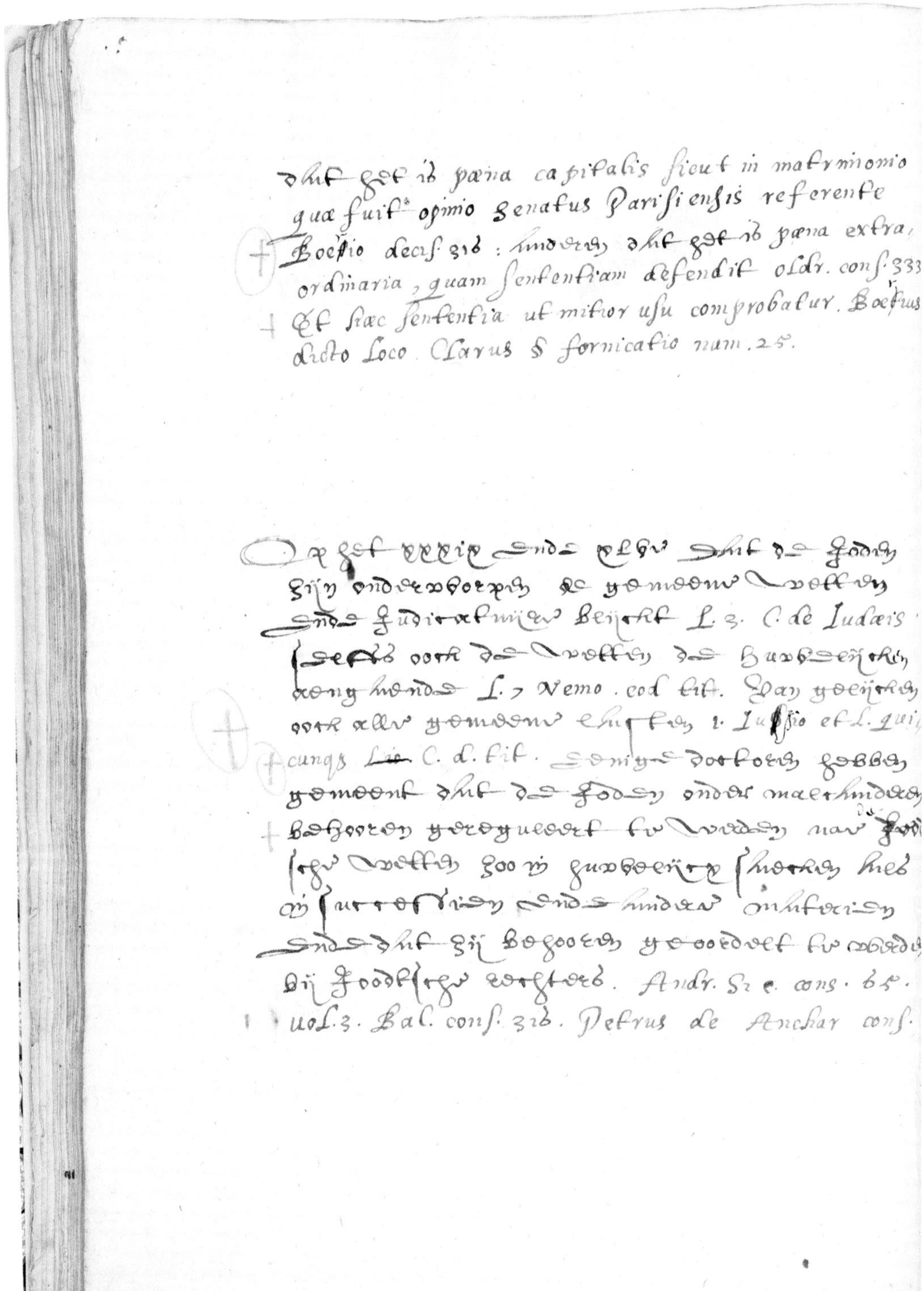

dat het is pæna capitalis sicut in matrimonio
quæ fuit opinio Senatus Parisiensis referente
Boerio decis. 316: andere dat het is pæna extra
ordinaria, quam sententiam defendit Oldr. cons. 333
Et hæc sententia ut mitior usu comprobatur. Boerius
dicto loco. Clarus § fornicatio num. 25.

Oock heeft recht ende reden dat de Joden
hun onderworpen de gemeene rechten
ende Judicatuÿren [illegible] L. 8. C. de Judaeis
[illegible] oock de rechten der Christenen
[illegible] L. 7 Nemo. eod. tit. Van gelijcken
oock alle gemeene edicten l. Jussio et L. qui-
cunque [illegible] C. d. tit. Sommige doctoren hebben
gemeent dat de Joden onder malcanderen
behooren geregueleert te worden naer de Jood-
sche rechten soo in huwelijcken, sterften, met
successien ende andere contracten
ende dat sij behooren geoordeelt te worden
bij Joodtsche rechters. Andr. Sic. cons. 65.
vol. 3. Bal. cons. 316. Petrus de Anchar cons.

dat het is *pœna capitalis sicut in matrimonio*
quæ fuit opinio senatus Parisiensis referente
Boet^{r}io decis 316 : anderen dat het is *pœna extra=*
ordinaria, quam sententiam defendit oldr. cons. 333
Et hæc sententia ut mitior usu comprobatur. Boet^{r}ius
dicto loco. Clarus § fornicatio num. 25.

Op het xxxix ende xLv^{e} dat de Joden
zijn onderworpen de gemeene wetten
ende Judicatuijre blijckt *L. 3. C. de Iudæis.*
selffs oock de wetten de Huwelijcken
aengaende *L. 7 Nemo eod. tit.* Van gelijcken
oock alle gemeene lasten 1. *Iussio et L. qui=*
*cunq*ue *L. 10. C. d. tit.* eenige doctoren hebben

gemeent dat de Joden onder malcanderen
behooren gereguleert te werden nae ^{de} Jood=
sche wetten zoo in huwelijcx saecken als
in successien ende andere materien
ende dat zij behooren geoordelt te werden
bij Joodsche rechters. *Andr. S 2 c. cons. 65.*
uol. 3. Bal. cons. 316. Petrus de Anchar cons.

dat het de doodstraf verdient, net als bij een huwelijk zoals de mening was van het Parijse stadsbestuur, volgens Boerius; anderen dat het een buitengewone straf verdient, welke mening verdedigd wordt door Oldradus. En deze mening om een zachtere behandeling te gebruiken, vindt weerklank.[45]

Ad Artikel 39 en 45.
Uit de Romeinse wetgeving blijkt dat de joden zijn onderworpen aan de algemene wetten en rechtspraak, alsook wat betreft de wetten aangaande het huwelijk; hetzelfde geldt ook voor de algemene belastingen.[46] Enkele geleerden hebben gemeend, dat ten aanzien van de joden onder elkaar de joodse wetten, behoren te gelden, zowel in huwelijkse zaken, in erfenissen, als in andere zaken, en dat zij door joodse rechters berecht dienen te worden;

45 Bohier, *Decisiones*, para. 316; Oldradus de Ponte, *Consilia seu responsa et quaestiones aureae*, para. 333; Clarus, *Opera omnia*, para. fornicatio, no. 25.

46 Cod. 1.9.3, Cod. 1.9.7, Cod. 1.9.5 en Cod. 1.9.10.

31[=32]r

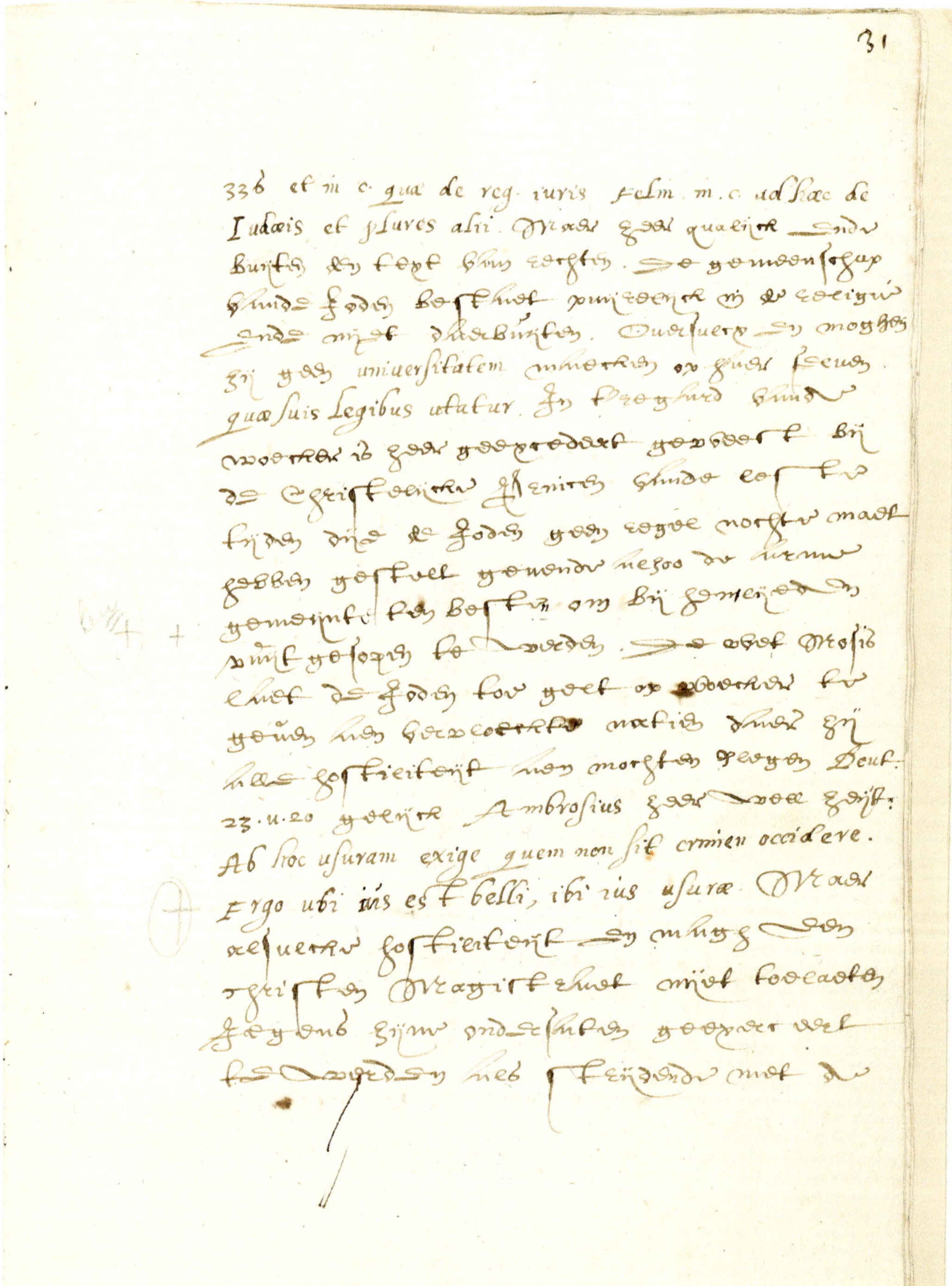

336 et in c. quæ de reg. iuris. Felin. in. c. ad hæc de Iudæis et plures alii. Maer zeer qualijck ende buijten den text van rechten. De gemeenschap vande Joden bestaet puijrelijck in de religie ende nijet daerbuijten. Ouersulcx en moghen zij geen *uniuersitatem* maecken op haer seluen *quæ suis legibus utatur*. In t' regard vande woecker is zeer geexcedeert geweest bij de Christelijcke Princen vande leste tijden dije de Joden geen regel nochte maet hebben gestelt geuende alzoo de arme gemeijnte ten besten om bij he~~m~~nlijeden vuijtgesopen te werden. De wet Mosis laet de Joden toe gelt op woecker te geuen aen vervloeckte natien daer zij alle hostiliteijt aen mochten plegen *Deut. 23. u. 20* gelijck *Ambrosius* zeer well zeijt: *Ab hoc usuram exige quem non sit crimen occidere. Ergo ubi ius est belli, ibi ius usuræ*. Maer alsulcke hostiliteijt en magh een christen Magistraet nijet toelaeten Jegens zijne ondersaeten geexerceert te werden als strijdende met de

maar dit is zeer kwalijk en valt buiten de tekst van de jurisprudentie.

De joodse gemeenschap bestaat zuiver in de godsdienst en niet daarbuiten. Als zodanig mogen zij uit zichzelf geen instellingen oprichten, die zich bedienen van haar eigen wetten.

Met betrekking tot de woeker, deze is zeer vermeerderd doordat de christelijke vorsten de laatste tijd de joden geen paal en perk hebben gesteld, zodat hen aldus als voordeel werd gegeven dat de arme gemeente door hen uitgezogen kon worden. De wet van Mozes staat de joden toe, geld verdiend met woeker te geven aan vervloekte volken, aan wie zij alle vijandelijkheid mogen betuigen. Zie Deut. 23:20. Zoals Ambrosius zeer juist opmerkt: Vraag woeker van wie het geen misdaad is om hem te doden. Dus waar het oorlogsrecht geldt, daar geldt het recht op woeker.[47]

Maar een dergelijke vijandigheid, die wordt uitgeoefend jegens zijn inwoners, mag een christelijk stadsbestuur niet toelaten, want dit is in strijd met het

47 CIC C.14. q.4. c.12.

31[=32]v

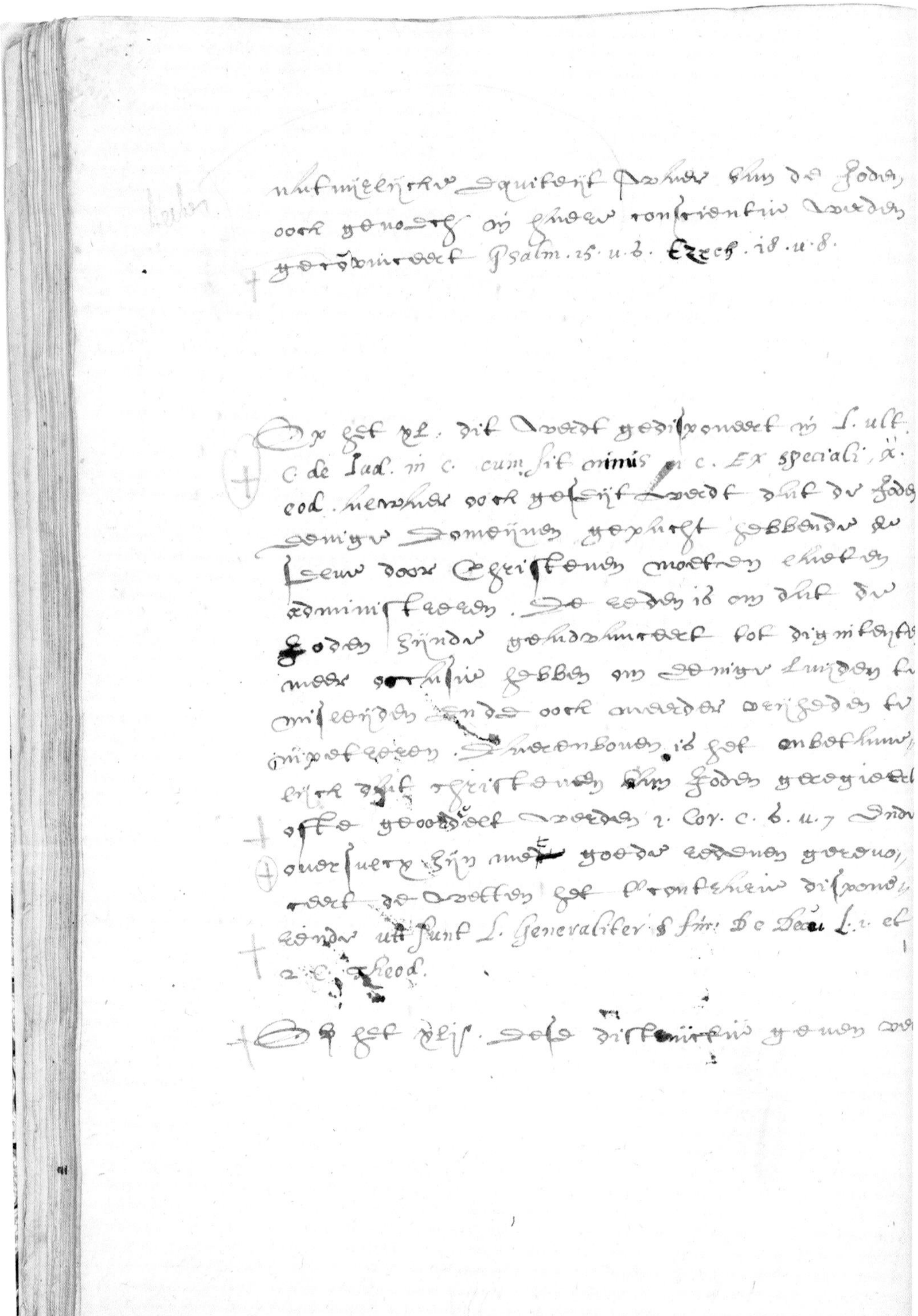
[illegible] equiteyt schuldich sijn de Joden
oock gehouden op haere conscientie worden
gerestitueert Psalm. 15. u. 6. Ezech. 18. u. 8.

Op het xl. dit woordt gedisponeert in L. ult.
C. de Iud. in c. cum sit nimis in c. Ex speciali, x.
eod. [illegible] oock [illegible] woordt dat de Joden
[illegible] [illegible] [illegible] hebbende [illegible]
[illegible] over Christenen moeten [illegible]
administreeren. De reden is om dat de
Joden sijnde [illegible] tot [illegible]
meer servitute hebben om [illegible] [illegible]
[illegible] ende oock [illegible] [illegible]
[illegible]. Insgeliicx is het onbehoorlijck
dat Christenen van Joden [illegible]
ofte [illegible] worden 1. Cor. c. 6. u. 7 ende
oversulcx sijn met goede redenen [illegible]
[illegible] [illegible] [illegible] het [illegible] [illegible]
[illegible] ut sunt L. Generaliter § fin. De Decu. L. 1. et
2. C. Theod.

Op het xlj. dese distinctie [illegible] [illegible]

natuijrlijcke equiteijt waer van de Joden oock genoech in haere conscientie werden geco*n*vinceert *Psalm. 25. u. 6. Ezech. 18. u. 8.*

Op het xL. dit werdt gedisponeert in *L. ult. C. de Iud. in c. cum sit nimis in c. Ex speciali, x. eod.* alwaer oock geseijt werdt dat de Joden eenige Domeijnen gepacht hebbende de selue door Christenen moeten laeten administreren. De reden is om dat de Joden zijnde geadvanceert tot digniteijten meer occasie hebben om eenige Luijden te misleijden ende oock meerder vrijheden te impetereren. Daerenbouen is het onbetame= lijck dat christenen van Joden geregiert ofte geoord^{e}elt werden 2. Cor. c. 6. u. 7 Ende oversulcx zijn me~~d~~t goede redenen gereuo= ceert de wetten het t' contrarie dispone= rende *uti sunt L. Generaliter § fin. De Decu L. 1 et 2. C. Theod.*

Op het xLj^{e}. Dese distinctie geuen ver=

natuurlijk gelijkheidsbeginsel waarvan de joden zelf ook voldoende overtuigd zijn in hun geweten. Zie Ps. 15:6. en Ez 18:8.

Ad Artikel 40.
Dit werd vastgelegd in die Romeinse wet, waar ook in werd gesteld dat de joden die domeinen in pacht hebben, deze door christenen moeten laten administreren.[48] De reden hiervoor is, dat de joden, die bevorderd zijn met ereambten, meer gelegenheid hebben om anderen te misleiden en zich ook meer vrijheden verwerven. Bovendien is het onbetamelijk, dat christenen door joden worden bestuurd of berecht. 2 Cor. 6:7. En zodoende zijn met goede reden de wetten ingetrokken die het tegenovergestelde bepalen.[49]

Ad Artikel 41.
Dit onderscheid maken

48 Cod. 1.9.18.

49 Cod. 1.8 en Dig. 50.2.3.2.

32[=33]r

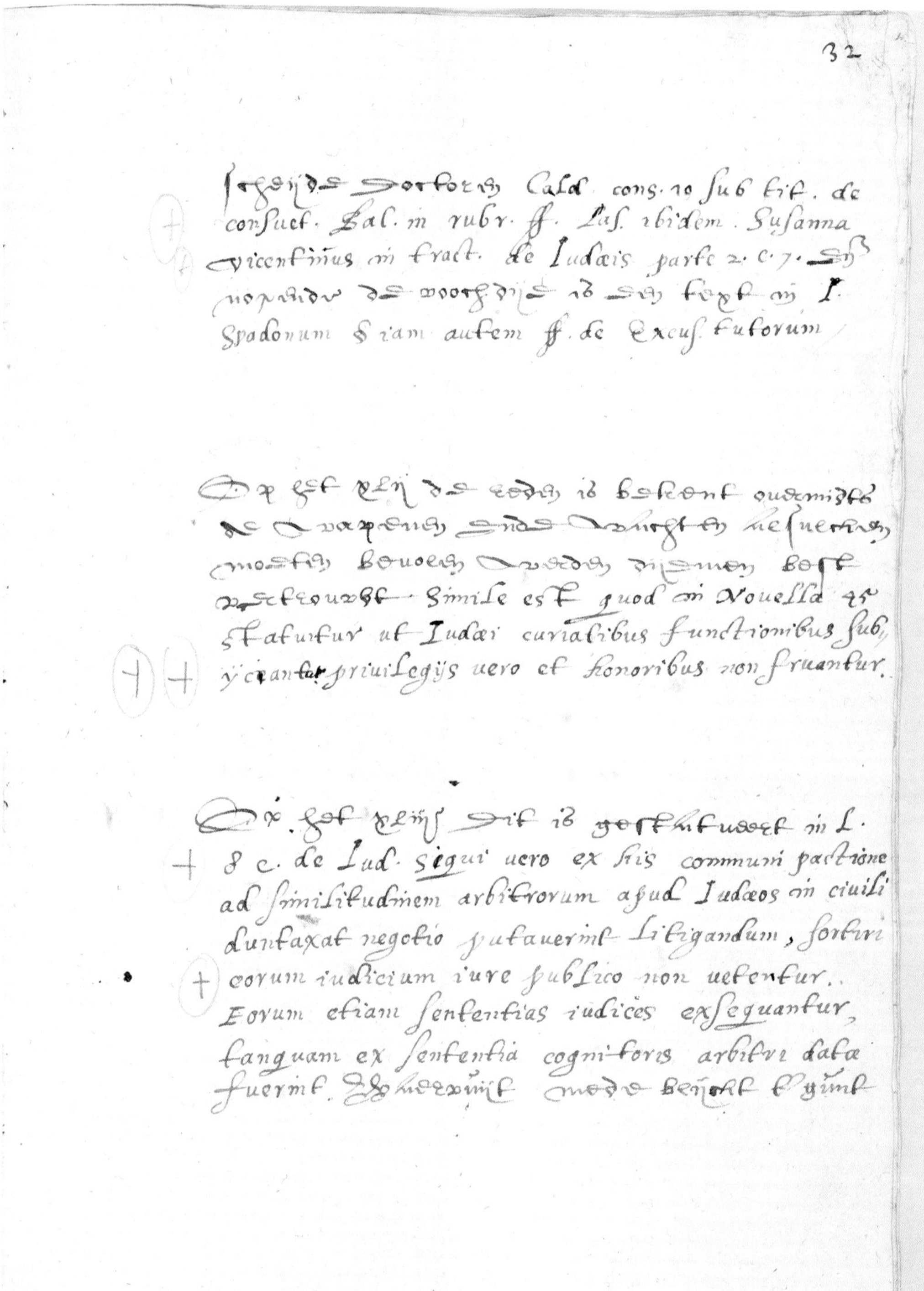
32

Seggen de doctoren Cald. cons. 10 sub tit. de consuet. Bal. in rubr. ff. Jas. ibidem. Susanna Vicentinus in tract. de Iudaeis parte 2. c. 7. [illegible] noppende de voorsz. dinghe is den text in l. Spadonum § iam autem ff. de excus. tutorum

[illegible] het [illegible] de [illegible] is bekent ouermits de [illegible] [illegible] [illegible] [illegible] [illegible] [illegible] [illegible] [illegible] Simile est quod in Nouella 45 statuitur ut Iudaei curialibus functionibus subijciantur privilegijs uero et honoribus non fruantur.

[illegible] het [illegible] dit is gestatueert in l. 8 c. de Iud. siqui uero ex his communi pactione ad similitudinem arbitrorum apud Iudaeos in ciuili duntaxat negotio putauerint litigandum, sortiri eorum iudicium iure publico non uetentur. Eorum etiam sententias iudices exsequantur, tanquam ex sententia cognitoris arbitri datae fuerint. [illegible] [illegible] [illegible] [illegible]

scheijde Doctoren *Cald. cons. 10 sub tit. de consuet. Bal. in rubr. ff. Pas. ibidem. Susanna Vincentinus in tract. de Iudæis parte 2. c. 7*. Ende nopende de voochdije is een text in *1. Spadonum § iam autem ff. de Excus. tutorum* /

Op het xLij^{e} De reden is bekent ouermidts de wapenen ende wachten alsulcken moeten beuolen werden dijemen best vertrouwt *Simile est quod in Nouella 45 statuitur ut Iudæi curialibus functionibus sub= ij ciantat priuilegiis uero et honoribus non fruantur*.

Op het xLiij^{e} Dit is gesttueert in *L. 8 c. de Iud. si qui uero ex his communi pactione ad similitudinem arbitrorum apud Iudæos in ciuili duntaxat negotio putauerint litigandum, sortiri eorum iudicium iure publico non uetentur. Eorum etiam sententias iudices exsequantur, tanquam ex sententia cognitoris arbitri datæ fuerint*. Waervuijt mede blijckt t' gunt

verschillende geleerden. En voor wat betreft de voogdij is er een tekst in de Digesten van Justinianus.[50]

Ad Artikel 42.
De reden is bekend, aangezien wapens en wachtlopen aan diegenen moeten worden opgedragen, die men het meest vertrouwt. Dit komt overeen met wat gesteld wordt in Nov. 45, nl. dat Joden openbare functies dienen te vervullen, maar niet in aanmerking komen voor de bijbehorende privileges en eerbewijzen.

Ad Artikel 43.
Dit is vastgesteld in Cod. 1.9.8:

Maar indien sommigen van hen gemeend hebben, althans in een burgerlijke rechtszaak op basis van een gemeenschappelijke afspraak, hun proces ten overstaan van Joden te moeten voeren, dit naar analogie met scheidslieden, wordt het hun krachtens het recht van publieke herkomst niet verboden een vonnis van hen te verkrijgen.[51]

Waaruit ook blijkt hetgeen

50 Dig. 27.1.15.6.

51 Spruit, Chorus, and Forrez, *Corpus juris civilis*, VII. Codex Justinianus 1–3:224.

32[=33]v

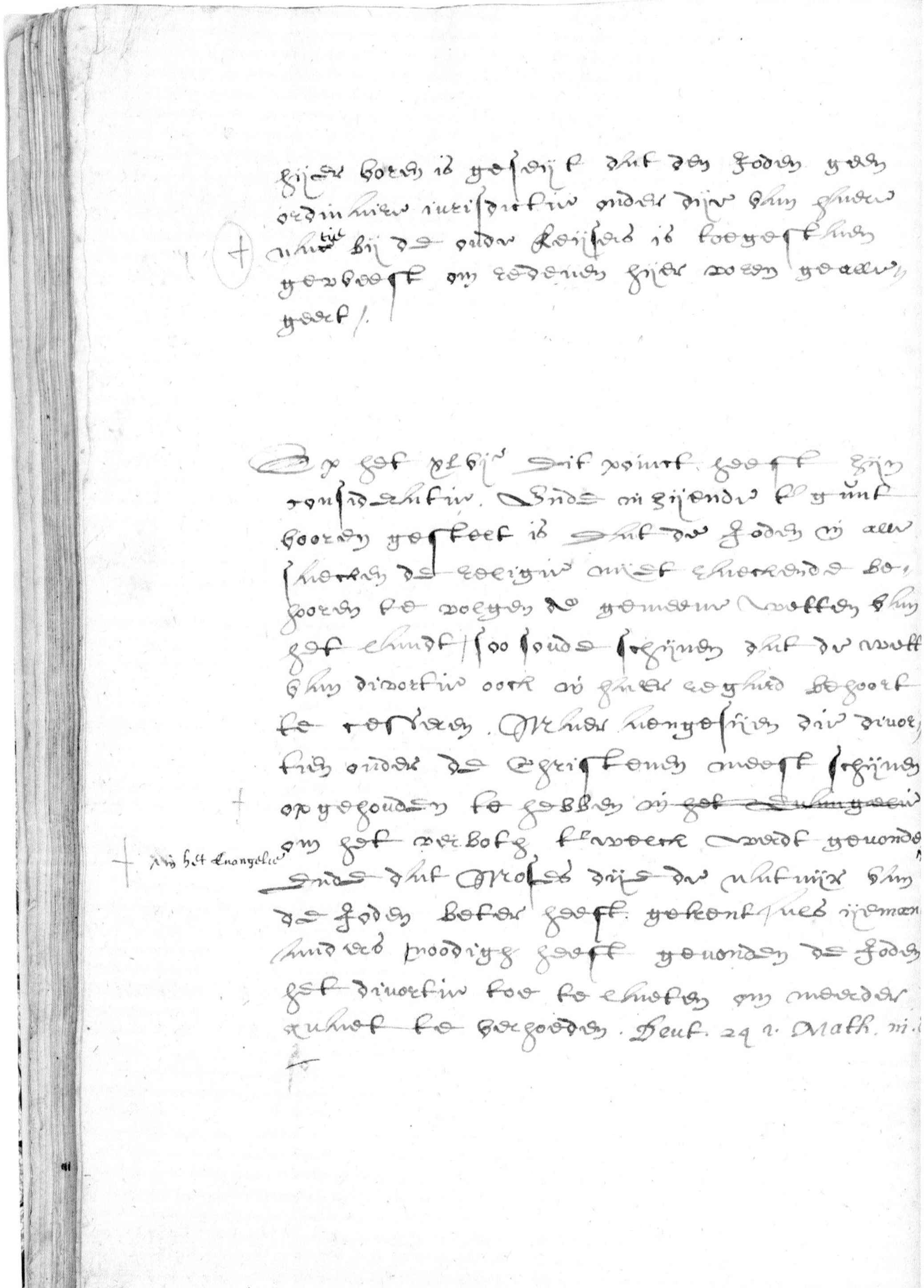

hijer voren is geseijt dat den Joden geen ordinaire iurisdictie onder dije van haere na^{tie} bij de oude Keijsers is toegestaen geweest om redenen hijer voren gealle=geert /.

Op het xLvj^{e} Dit poinct heeft zijn consideratie. Ende inzijende t' gunt vooren gestelt is Dat de Joden in alle saecken de religie nijet raeckende be=hooren te volgen de gemeene wetten van het landt / soo soude schijnen dat de wett van divortie oock in haer regard behoort te cesseren. Maer aengesijen die diuor=tien onder de Christenen meest schijnen opgehouden te hebben ~~in het Euangelie~~ om het verboth t' welck wordt geuonden ↑[in het Evangelie] ende dat Moses dije de natuijr van de Joden beter heeft gekent als ijemant anders noodigh heeft geuonden de Joden het divortie toe te laeten om meerder quaet te verhoeden. *Deut. 24 1. Math. iii. 8*

hiervoor is gezegd, dat de joden door de oude keizers geen normale rechtspraak over hun eigen volk is toegestaan, om redenen zoals hiervoor zijn aangehaald.

Ad Artikel 46.
Dit is een punt van overweging. En inziend hetgeen hiervoor is gesteld, dat de joden in alle zaken die niet religieus van aard zijn, de algemene wetten van het land behoren te volgen, zou het lijken dat de wet betreffende echtscheiding zou moeten vervallen. Maar aangezien echtscheidingen onder de christenen meestal tegengegaan werden door het verbod dat in het Evangelie wordt gevonden, en dat Mozes, die de aard van de joden beter heeft gekend dan iemand anders, het nodig heeft gevonden de joden echtscheiding toe te staan om groter kwaad te voorkomen.

Uit Deut. 24:1 en Mt. 3:8.

33[=34]r

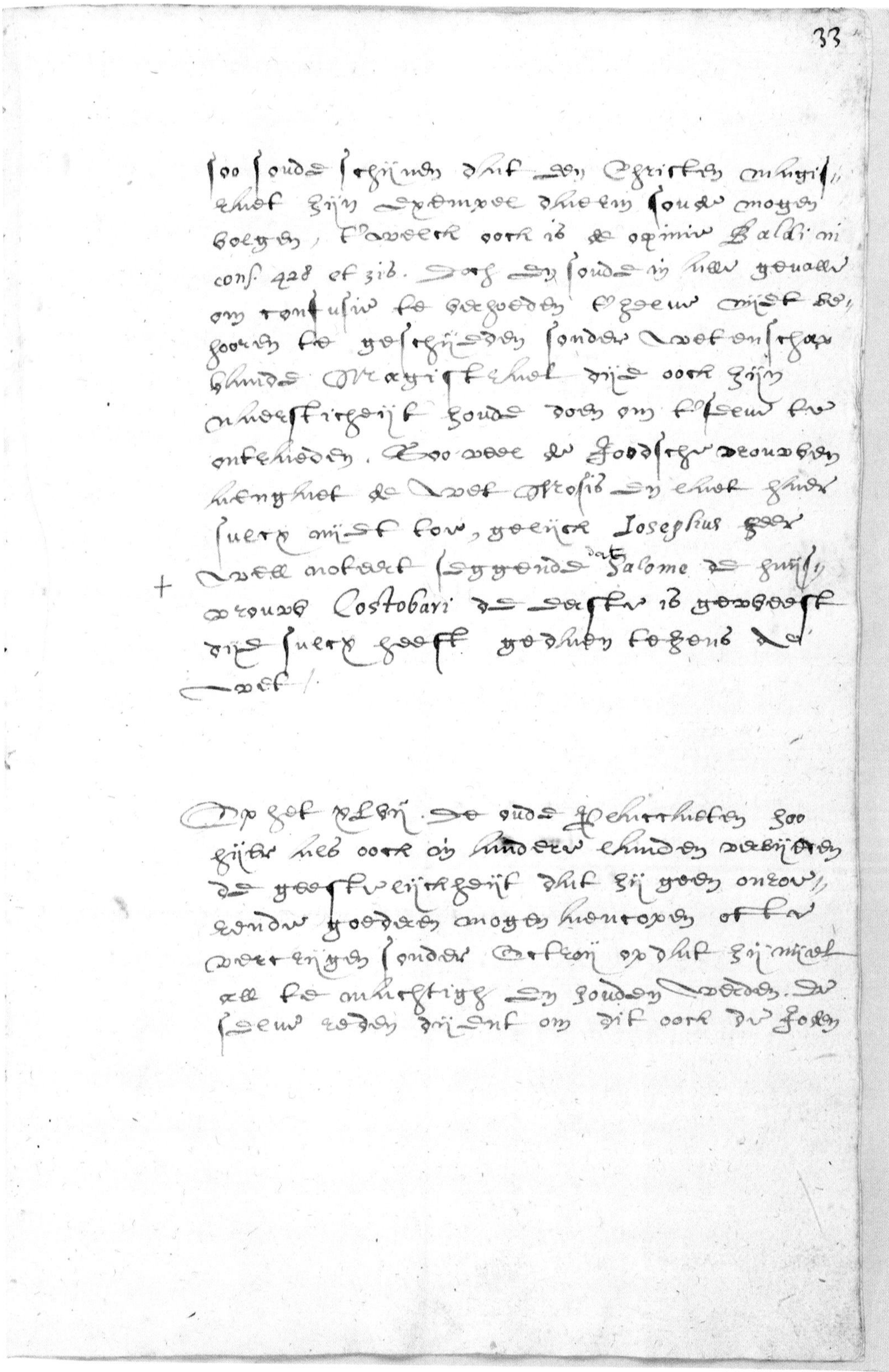
soo soude schijnen dat een christen magis-
traet [illegible] exempel [illegible] soude mogen
volgen, twelck oock is de opinie Baldi in
cons. 428 et 316. Doch [illegible] soude in [illegible] gevalle
om confusie te [illegible] [illegible] niet [illegible]
[illegible] te [illegible] sonder wet [illegible]
[illegible] Magistraet [illegible] oock [illegible]
[illegible] soude [illegible] om [illegible] te
onthouden. [illegible] de [illegible] [illegible]
[illegible] de wet Mosis en [illegible] [illegible]
[illegible] niet toe, [illegible] Josephus [illegible]
seer notabel [illegible] dat Salome de [illegible]
[illegible] Costobari de [illegible] is [illegible]
die [illegible] [illegible] [illegible] tegens de
wet/.

Op het [illegible]. [illegible] oude [illegible] soo
[illegible] heb oock in [illegible] [illegible] [illegible]
de [illegible] dat hij [illegible] [illegible]
[illegible] [illegible] mogen [illegible] of te
[illegible] sonder [illegible] [illegible] dat hij [illegible]
al te [illegible] en souden [illegible]. [illegible]
[illegible] [illegible] [illegible] om dit oock [illegible] [illegible]

soo soude schijnen dat een Christen magis=raet zijn exempel daerin soude mogen volgen, t' welck oock is de opinie *Baldi in cons. 428 et 316*. Doch en soude in alle geualle om confusie te verhoeden t' zelue nijet be=hooren te geschijeden sonder wetenschap vande Magistraet dije oock zijn naersticheijt zoude doen om t' selue te ontraeden. Soo veel de Joodsche vrouwen aengaet de wet Mosis en laet haer sulcx nijet toe, gelijck *Josephus* zeer well noteert seggende dat *Salome* de huijs=vrouw *Costobari* de eerste is geweest dije sulcx heeft gedaen tegens de wet /.

Op het xLvij. De oude Placcaeten zoo hijer als oock in andere landen verbijeden de geestelijckheijt dat zij geen onroe=rende goederen mogen aencopen ofte vercrijgen sonder Octroij opdat zij nijet all te machtigh en zouden werden. De selue reden dijent om dit oock de Joden

zou blijken, dat een christelijk stadsbestuur zijn voorbeeld zou mogen volgen, hetgeen ook de mening is van Baldus de Ubaldis. Maar dit zou in alle gevallen, om verwarring te voorkomen, niet behoren voor te komen zonder dat het stadsbestuur op de hoogte is, en dat dit ook moeite zou moeten doen dit te ontraden. Voor wat betreft de joodse vrouwen, staat de wet van Mozes het hun niet toe, zoals Josephus zeer juist opmerkt, zeggend dat Salome, de vrouw van Costobari, de eerste is geweest die dit tegen de wet in heeft gedaan.

Ad Artikel 47.

De oude verordeningen, zowel hier als in andere landen, verbieden de geestelijkheid, om zonder toestemming van de overheid onroerende goederen aan te kopen of te verkrijgen, zodat zij niet te machtig zouden worden. Dezelfde reden dient om dit ook de joden

33[=34]v

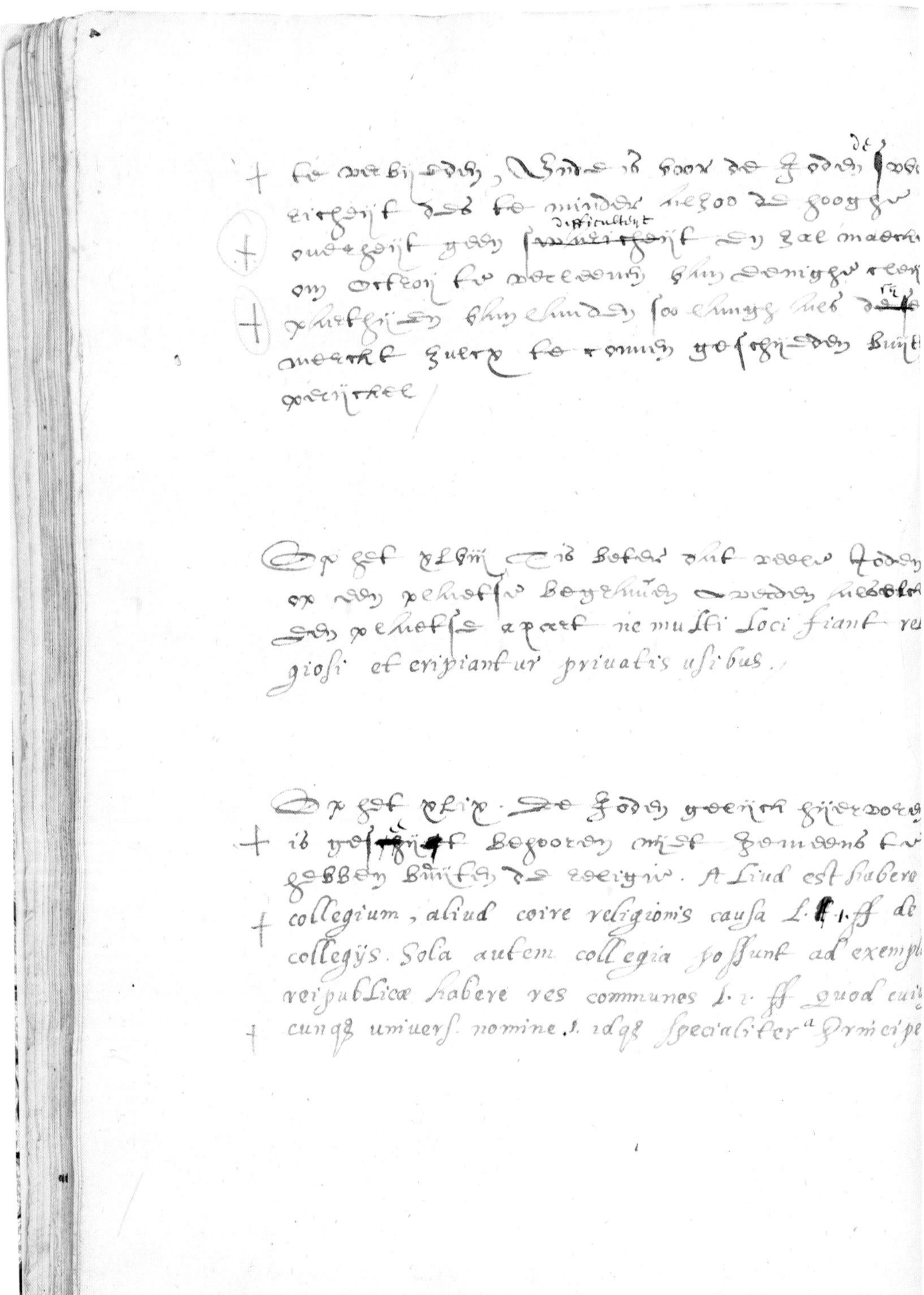
ne multi loci fiant re
gioSi et eripiantur priuatis usibus.
Aliud est habere
collegium, aliud coire religionis causa L. 1. ff de
collegijs. Sola autem collegia possunt ad exempl
reipublicae habere res communes L. 1. ff quod cuiu
cunqz uniuers. nomine. 1. idqz specialiter a Principe

te verbijeden, Ende is voor de Joden de swa= richeijt des te minder alzoo de hooghe ouerheijt geen ~~swaricheijt~~ difficulteijt en zal maecken om Octroij te verleenen van eenighe cleijne partheijen van landen soo langh als ~~dese~~ sij merckt zulcx te connen geschijeden buijten perijckel /

Op het xLviij T is beter dat veele Joden op een plaetse begrauen werden als elck een plaetse apart *ne multi loci fiant reli= giosi et cripiantur priuatibus usibus.* /

Op het xLix. De Joden gelijck hijervoren is ges^e^ijt behooren nijet gemeens te hebben buijten de religie. *Aliud est habere collegium, aliud coire religionis causa L 1.ff de collegijs. Sola autem collegia possunt ad exempl[um] reipublicæ habere res communes L. 2. ff quod cuius= cunq*ue *uniuers. nomine. 1. idq*ue *specialter* ^a^ *Principe*

te verbieden. En deze moeilijkheid is voor de joden minder erg, omdat het hoogste gezag geen bezwaren zal hebben toestemming te verlenen tot enkele kleine stukken land, zo lang zij zelf ervaart dat dit zonder gevaar kan gebeuren.

Ad Artikel 48.
Het is beter dat veel joden op een plaats worden begraven, dan iedereen ergens anders. Opdat niet teveel plekken een religieuze bestemming krijgen en onttrokken worden aan privaat gebruik.

Ad Artikel 49.
De joden behoren, zoals hiervoor is gezegd, niets gemeenschappelijks te hebben behalve de godsdienst. Het is iets anders om een collegium te hebben dan om omwille van de godsdienst bij elkaar te komen. Maar alleen collegia kunnen naar het voorbeeld van de staat gemeenschappelijke bezittingen hebben.[52]

52 Dig. 47.22.1; Livius, *Ab urbe condita*, bk. XXXIX.18.

34[=35]r

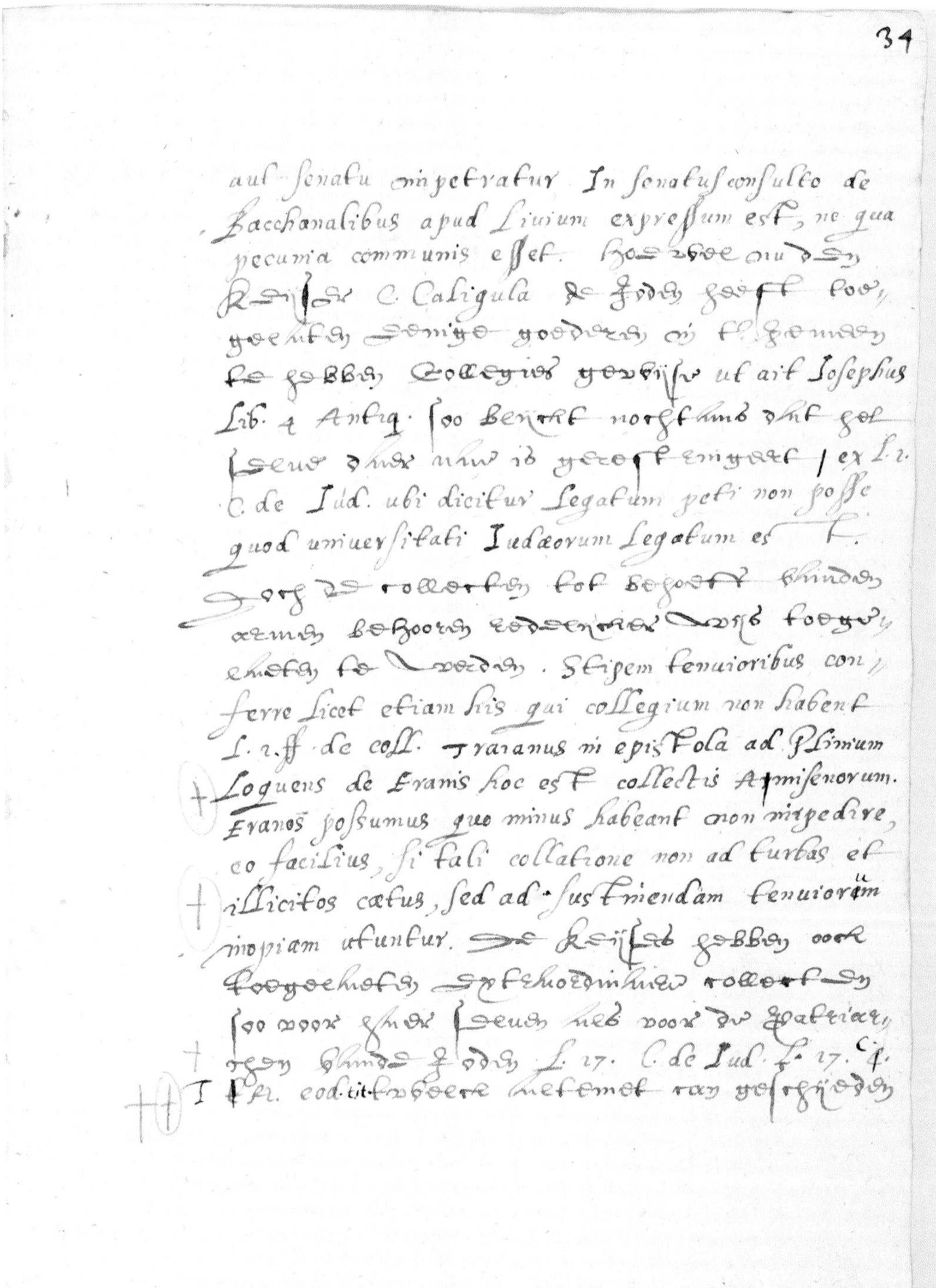
34

aut senatu impetratur In senatusconsulto de
Bacchanalibus apud Livium expressum est, ne qua
pecunia communis esset. [illegible]
[illegible] C. Caligula [illegible]
[illegible]
[illegible] ut ait Josephus
Lib. 4 Antiq. [illegible]
[illegible] / ex l. 2.
C. de Iud. ubi dicitur legatum peti non posse
quod universitati Iudaeorum legatum est [illegible]
[illegible]
[illegible]
[illegible]. Stipem tenuioribus con-
ferre licet etiam his qui collegium non habent
l. 1. ff. de coll. Traianus in epistola ad Plinium
loquens de Eranis hoc est collectis Amisenorum.
Eranos possumus quo minus habeant non impedire,
eo facilius, si tali collatione non ad turbas et
illicitos coetus, sed ad sustinendam tenuiorum
inopiam utuntur. [illegible]
[illegible]
[illegible]
[illegible] l. 17. C. de Iud. l. 17. [illegible]
I [illegible] eod. tit. [illegible]

aut senatu impetratur. In senatus consulto de Bacchanalibus apud Liuium expressum est, ne qua pecunia communis esset. Hoewel nu den Keijser *C. Caligula* de Joden heeft toe= gelaten eenige goederen in t' Gemeen te hebben Collegies gewijse *ut ait Josephus Lib. 4 Antiq.* soo blijckt nochtans dat het selue daer nae is gerestringeert / *ex L. 1. C. de Iud. ubi dicitur legatum peti non posse quod uniuersitati Iudæorum legatum est.* Doch de collecten tot behoeff vanden armen behooren redelijcker wijs toege= laeten te werden. *Stipem tenuioribus con= ferre licet etiam his qui collegium non habent L. 1. ff. de coll. Traianus in epistola ad Plinium loquens de Eranis hoc est collectis Armisenorum Eranos possumus quo minus habeant non impedire, eo facilius, si tali collatione non ad turbas et illicitos cœtus, sed ad sustiniendam tenuiore^{u}m inopiam utuntur.* De Keijsers hebben oock toegelaeten extraordinaire collecten soo voor haet seluen als voor de Patriar= chen van de Joden *L. 17. C. de Iud. L. 17. C. 4. Tth. eod. tit* t' welck altemet can geschijeden

In het senaatsbesluit over de Bacchanaliën is expliciet uitgedrukt dat er geen gemeenschappelijke kas mag zijn. Hoewel keizer C. Caligula volgens Flavius Josephus de joden wel heeft toegestaan enkele gezamenlijke bezittingen per gemeente te hebben, zo blijkt toch, dat dit daarna is beperkt, *ex L.1, C. de Jud., hetgeen Cornelia Salvia gelegateerd heeft aan de gemeenschap van de Joden die in de stad Antiochië gevestigd zijn, kan niet opgeëist worden.*[53] Maar de geldinzamelingen ten behoeve van de armen behoren redelijkerwijs toegestaan te worden. Zelfs zij die geen collegium hebben, mogen geld voor de minderbedeelden inzamelen.[54] Trajanus in een brief aan Plinius, sprekend over publieke inzamelingen voor charitatieve doeleinden: 'Wij kunnen dergelijke publieke inzamelingen niet weigeren, des te meer, als dergelijke inzamelingen niet voor opstootjes en illegale samenscholingen worden gebruikt, maar voor het verlichten van de armennood.'[55] De keizers hebben ook bijzondere geldinzamelingen toegestaan, zowel voor hetzelfde als voor de voornaamsten onder de joden[56] hetwelk zo nu en dan kan geschieden

53 Cod. 1.9.1. Spruit, Chorus, and Forrez, *Corpus juris civilis*, VII. Codex Justinianus 1–3:222–223.

54 Dig. 47.22.1.

55 Plinius Secundus, *Epistularum libri decem*, X, 93.

56 Waarschijnlijk gaat het om Cod. 1.9.17 en Cod. Theod. 16.8.14, 16.8.17 en 16.8.29.

34[=35]v

met kennisse van saecken. Andersints is het zeer dangereux eenige natie ofte secte geldt ofte goedt in t' gemeen te laeten vergaderen

met kennis van zaken. Anderzijds is het erg gevaarlijk een volk of geloofsgroep gemeenschappelijk geld of goederen bijeen te laten brengen.

CHAPTER 3

English Translation: a Remonstrantie on the Regulations to Be Instituted in Holland and West Friesland regarding the Jews

Cis van Heertum

That which others explore with less motivation and without need or prior cause, forces us to consider how to proceed in our country in the matter of the Jews, both those by descent and those by religion. It is reprehensible that without any public resolution, without previous regulations, and in violation of ancient decrees, the Jews have already entered the country in large numbers, and have been treated by the towns and cities with the utmost courtesy, with promises of great liberties and privileges: whereby each is intent on private profit and commerce, but hardly mindful of God's honour and of what is best for the general interest.

It is high time, therefore, that those who have been appointed to represent not the private but the general interest, are motivated to steer that which has already happened in such a direction as to prevent worse.

To put things right in this respect, the principal issues that need to be addressed are the following three:

First, whether the Jews ought to be admitted to this country.

Second, whether they should be allowed to practise their religion.

Third, which means are best suited to prevent their presence and the practice of their religion from causing problems, both with respect to the Christian religion and the public peace.

The first issue, whether the Jews ought to be admitted, is not without problems. Several wise rulers and states can bear witness to this, especially those of the reformed religion, who have always refused this.

The reasons appear to be as follows:

Seeing that religious unity is the greatest strength of a powerful state, it is not advisable to receive people in the country whose religion differs so much from ours. It is true that the sight of these people alone will instil doubt in the weak-minded regarding the principal points that are necessary for our salvation. This is especially so in a country where many people are inclined to novelties and are all too curious about matters that are beyond human comprehension, of whom—God forbid—there are all too many in this country.

We also need to consider the resentment and hatred of the Jews with regard to the Christians, which alone can be expected to lead to all kinds of trouble, rioting and other problems.

It is certain that for thousands of years the Jews have held the malicious view that they do not owe people of other religions even the smallest acts of kindness, to which our Lord bears witness in the parable of the Samaritan, which taught, contrary to Jewish opinion, that the expression 'our neighbours' must not be restricted to members of the same religion. A Roman poet who described the Jewish customs said they would not want to show the way nor a well to an uncircumcised man.

… [they study, observe, and revere the Judaic code, as handed down by Moses in his mystic scroll, which tells them] not to show the way to anyone except a fellow worshipper and if asked, to take only the circumcised to the fountain.[1]

1 *non monstrare vias eadem nisi sacra colenti, / quaesitum ad fontem solos deducere verpos. Juvenal and Persius*, Satire 14, 103.

In the Talmud, the Jews' second bible, it is expressly stated in the treatise called *Avoda Zarah*, that it is a sin to be good to anyone else but a Jew, and specifically that they are obliged to treat badly all those who belong to the sect of Jesus of Nazareth;

that they may break the heads of Christian women, just like serpents;

that they must suffocate a Christian who is dying;

is he near a well, they must throw him in;

is he in a well, then they must cover it with a lid, so that he cannot get out,

and more of the same.

The tenor of the prayers they say three times a day is primarily that the Christians may be destroyed. This is the reason why it is generally accepted and practised that a Jew is not allowed to testify against a Christian, especially in criminal cases, as it is assumed all Jews are hereditary enemies of all Christians.

The enmity and hatred of the Jews lead to very dangerous consequences, especially when they are strong (as we see there is no people that increases and multiplies so greatly), something which both old and new historiography is full of.

In the days of Trajan, when the Jews had come to greater power in the land of Cyrene, they once slaughtered some 200,000 adherents of another religion, using such cruelty that they ate the flesh, drank the blood and dressed themselves in the skins. At around the same time this also happened in Egypt and in Cyprus, where almost 240,000 people were murdered by Jewish hands. A law was made in eternal remembrance of this, stipulating that any Jew who would ever set foot on Cyprus was to be executed.

Under Justin, Justinian and Phocas the Jews who lived in Arabia, Syria and Palestine cruelly murdered large groups of Christians, cutting off body parts of some and frying others in a pot. What is more, when Khosrow, King of Persia, had seized Jerusalem and its surrounding cities and captured many Christians, the Jews bought them from him for a small sum of money and killed some 90,000 of them.

These are horrible examples, but they happened far away from here and a long time ago. Let us now turn to times and places closer to us.

It will be found that, generally speaking, it was a custom of the Jews to torture a Christian man or child and finally crucify them until they died, not only to satisfy their hatred, but also to mock the Christian religion that way. This is very old practice.

Sozomen, Socrates and Nicephorus all tell of a remarkable episode that occurred in Antioch in the days of Theodosius the Younger. The same, however, is related in the histories of all peoples and all times.

It happened in Norwich in England in the Year of Our Lord 1146, in Blois in France in 1272; again in Norwich in 1234; in a village called Forcheim in Germany, in the land of the Margrave, in 1262; in Munich, also in Germany, in 1285; in Bern in Switzerland in 1288; in the city of Prague in Bohemia in 1289; in the city of Vessenge in Thuringia in 1302; in the city of Überlingen in 1331; in Diessenhofen in 1402, in Trento in 1405;[2] in the city of Tirnau in Hungary in 1404, again in Tirnau in 1523; in Bösing in 1529.

These numerous examples not only lend more credence to the matter at hand because so many witnesses agree, they also underscore the fact that these identical consequences must not be put down to a few isolated causes, but solely to the inveterate hatred of the Jews against the Christians: this is certainly something that should be taken into consideration.

Why else is it that the Jews have been banned from France, from England, from Hungary, from Spain and Portugal, and even from the Low Countries where they had lived for so long and had been of great benefit to the princes, if not for these and similar causes?

2 The date has been corrected in the text. There was a blood libel case in Trento in 1475.

FIGURE 17
A woodcut depicting the blood libel case of Simon of Trent, found in Schedel's *Weltchronik* of 1493, which Grotius references in a list of such anti-Semitic allegations

The nature of the Jews is also made clear to us by Holy Writ, where they are called: stiff-necked, uncircumcised in heart, killers of prophets, a generation of vipers; of whom it is said that their father is the devil, who has been a murderer from the beginning, that they act like their ancestors.

What all Christians may expect from them is most emphatically shown when our Lord says: They have called the master of the house *Beelzebub*. What will the members of the household do? The pupil is no better than his master. Consider the death of Jesus Christ, whose blood they have taken upon them and their children. Also consider whether most of the persecutions endured by the apostles were not caused by the malice of the Jews. As Chrysostom put it so eloquently somewhere: that they do not nowadays do to the Christians what they have done to Christ and his Disciples, is not because they lack the will, but the power.

These, therefore, are not the least reasons, why a country that is empty of Jews might object to admitting and receiving them.

There are, however, also excellent arguments for the other side, and these perhaps ought to take priority over the previous ones: arguments which do not result from any expectation of trade and profit (which in all fairness may also be taken into account), but from God's word and from natural, sincere love. The chief reason is that, although generally speaking, the Jews seem to have been cast out by God because of their unbelief to this day, some have nevertheless converted to the true faith in every age so that, as the prophets once predicted, the others may be saved. The apostle Paul furthermore explicitly says that a full conversion of the Jewish people is to be expected finally, to which end God miraculously appears to preserve the Jewish people, distinct and separate from all other people, as a token of the trustworthiness of his promises in the end of times. For this personal and collective conversion all Christians should do their utmost, which will not come about if the Jews are forbidden to live among Christians: For how can they believe without hearing or hear without a preacher? Nor is it unimportant in what kind of Christian company they find themselves. We know that a large part of Christendom has adulterated religion with idolatry, especially the worship of statues, something expressly forbidden by the inviolable law of God, which the Jews justly adhere to in this respect. What hope or probability is there that the Jews will be brought to Christianity if they keep company with Christians such as these? How can they believe that they will find the truth among such people, who do not keep God's truth themselves?

It is important, therefore, to follow God's will, and allow the Jews to live among those Christians who have turned away from idols and idolatry and are therefore rightly called reformed. Faith, which surpasses nature, does not take away that which is given by nature. *Nature has established a kind of kinship between all people*, according to the lawyers.[3] *I am a man, I consider nothing that is human alien to me.*[4] From this natural kinship, which is common to all people, springs hospitality, which is recommended to us not only by Scripture,[5] but also by the pagan authors, and involves receiving strangers and treating them well. The nations that have turned away strangers are everywhere denounced as barbarians and unnatural people.

What race of men is this? What land is so barbarous as to allow this custom? We are debarred the welcome of the beach;[6]

When the apostle Paul enjoins us to be good to all people, in particular our fellow believers, he does presume a closer bond between believers, but does not exclude the unbelievers from the bond of love. Our Lord himself instructs us in what we ought to do when he chides the Jews by means of the parable of the Samaritan, which teaches us that all people, including those of other creeds, are our neighbours. 'Do', he says, 'like your Father who causes his sun to rise and sends his rain on the good and the evil.'

In the same way we must show to all people the common works of natural love, without excluding anyone. Banishment is contrary to nature, as it cuts the community off from nature and is therefore a punishment that ought not to be imposed unless an offence has been committed. These special considerations apply to the Jews even more than to other unbelievers. They are the children of Abraham, Isaac and Jacob, the Israelites, to whom pertain the adoption, and the glory, and the covenants, and the giving of the law, and the service of God and the promises. They are the patriarchs from whom Christ is descended, they are the kinsmen of the Apostles and the first teachers of our religion. Indeed, it is to them that God's prophecies have been entrusted.

3 *Cognationem quandam inter omnes homines natura constituit.* Marginal note: ⟨*L.3.ff. de Inst. et Iur.*⟩ (= Dig. 1.1.3).

4 *homo sum; humani nil a me alienum puto.* Terentius, "The self-tormentor," l. 77.

5 Marginal note: ⟨*Deut. 10. 19 Nom* [*read: Rom.*]. *12. 13 Hebr. 13. 2*⟩.

6 *quod genus hoc hominum? quæve hunc tam barbara morem / permittit patria? hospitio prohibemur harenæ;* Virgil, *Aeneid* 1, 539–540.

When we look for arguments to decide which books in the Old Testament are canonical, we call upon the Jews. As the Apostle says, they are bound to be our enemies as far as the gospel is concerned, but they are loved on account of the patriarchs, who were specially elected by God. The pagans have false gods. The Mohammedans have a false Prophet. The Jews at any rate have the true God and the true Prophets.

The core of their belief is what we believe, too, and that which we believe in addition to this, we prove on the basis of the writings they believe in. In short, as the Ancient Fathers rightly say of them: *Theirs is the origin of truth*.[7] That is why the early Christian emperors and princes, with a good conscience and diligent fervour and bolstered by the advice of eminent theologians, never once considered expelling the Jews, but admitted them to the Roman Empire and defended them against every injustice, which is borne out by their decrees. It is objected that the Jews hate the Christians. This is true, but it would suit us to show that we are Christians and not Jews. We will be Christians, in imitation of Christ, who prayed that God might forgive them, for they knew not what they were doing. We will also be proclaimers, in imitation of the Apostle, who says that his heart's desire was for Israel, for they had a zeal of God, but not according to knowledge.

May God grant that the Christians are not partly the cause of the hatred which the Jews bear them. We know how they are treated in many places. They are mocked, they are insulted, they are pulled about, beaten, have things thrown at them, not only with the connivance but even with the consent of the authorities.

The scholars themselves are the cause of such ill feeling, because they explicitly state that the Jews are slaves, not in a figurative, but in a literal sense, and that they and their possessions belong to the Christian princes. That their children may be taken away from them against their will. That their possessions may be confiscated, even that they themselves may be sold.[8] Many princes were happy to accept this view and used the Jews as sponges, allowing them to suck the blood of the poor through extortionate usury and squeeze them later, for their own profit; which is truly no way to win people's hearts, only to harden the hearts of those who are already hard-hearted.

It is right to think that the Jews have caused great harm to the Christians in the past. However, as the Christians are in power, such harm can be prevented through good laws and close supervision, without it being necessary to expel all Jews for offences that do not concern the individuals but only the people as a whole. *As the teeth of the sons are blunted, because the fathers ate something unripe*.[9] It is obvious that God wishes them to live somewhere. Why not here, then, as well as anywhere else, seeing that the same argument applies elsewhere which might also be put forward here?

I will not even mention certain facts (which, if necessary, can certainly be adduced), which according to history have been laid at the door of the Jews, but have never been examined from a legal point of view, though it is mentioned in some sources, that due to the avarice of the princes in regard of others, Jews have lost their lives or possessions due to the fanaticism of the populace without any form of justice, and that the princes afterwards found ways of concealing this. Should the weak-minded take offence at the sight of and association with the Jews, this could certainly be prevented, partly through good legislation and partly through the efforts of the clergy.

If this should increase it would be more pertinent for the Jews to be of use to the Christian

7 *Habent primordium veritatis.*

8 Marginal note: *c. etsi. de Iud. Zas. in tract. de Iudaeis ratione sexta pro affirmativa. citans Hostiensem, Archidiaconum, Albericum, Oldradum. tenet Tib. Decianus Lib. v. Criminalium c. 13 n. 2.* Grotius here refers to canonical law and to note 24 on p. 153.

9 *ut dentes filiorum obstupescant, quia patres omphacen comederunt.* (Cf. Ezekiel 18:2). ('omphacen' derives from the Greek word ὄμφακα).

religion. First, the scholars among them might be of use to us on account of their knowledge of the Hebrew language.

The steadfastness of the Jews in their religion serves as an example to us and as an argument for the truth of the Holy Scripture of the Old Testament. Observing their unbelief causes us to give greater thanks to God for setting us in the place of the pagans on whom he formerly bestowed his inexpressible grace.

It is impossible to legislate for only one religion in this country. We have numerous religions here; and the least danger is from the one that differs most:

Most bitter are the hatreds of brothers, and easy is the fall from nearby.[10]

The examples of Poland, Germany, even Italy and Rome itself (where they are otherwise all too precise in the matter of religion) can provide practical lessons for admitting the Jews without undermining the Christian faith, namely by drawing up sound regulations, which will be discussed below.

If it is therefore understood (as most arguments seem to tend in this direction), that the Jews may and also should be admitted to this country, it ought to be examined in the second place whether they should or should not be allowed to practise their religion.

To indicate that they ought not to be allowed such a thing, the argument from God's law might be put forward, that idolatry among God's people was strictly forbidden. The princes who did allow this, were sternly rebuked and those who forbade it and effectively prevented it were praised.

Second, that it will probably cause great outcry should the Jews be allowed what was denied the Roman Catholics in our country. However, the following argument can be used to make a strong plea to allow the Jews who have been admitted to the country to practise their religion. For, if such is not allowed, one of two things must happen: either they are forced to accept our religion, or they should be left without any religious practice at all.

The former must be judged as improper and unlawful by all people with common sense, as religion should not be enforced: it may even be argued with good reason that it is a greater sin in the eyes of God to feign the true religion and adopt it against one's conscience, than to continue to adhere to an erroneous opinion through ignorance.

The latter is surely just as wrong and opens the road to pure godlessness, which is far worse than Judaism. No people has ever been so uncivilized as not to observe that the practice of religion is necessary to uphold piety.

This has been affirmed with respect to the Jews, both on the basis of the arguments relating to the first point, the special affection we owe the Jews on account of the dignity of their descent and the rudiment of truth residing in them, as well as from the examples that have been presented above, of the Christian emperors who expressly allowed the Jews the aforesaid religious practice. The same is obvious from the laws, which not only allowed the Jews to have their synagogues but also forbade anyone to molest them there, and which also in a sense conferred dignity and authority on their teachers and supreme governors. The argument relating to the prohibition of idolatry is not valid here. In the first place, the worship of the Jews is not idolatry but worship to God, though adulterated with superstition, even if their ancient ceremonies are abolished, except circumcision, Sabbath and abstinence from forbidden foods. Furthermore the law which has been given to the people of Israel is not such that it is applicable to all peoples and in all ages.

For this law was given to a people that had descended from the same forefathers and had been raised in a religion that was daily affirmed through visible miracles and prophecies: all of which is no longer the case among the peoples of today, except that Christian kindness seems to

10 *acerrima fratrum odia, et facilis ex proximo lapsus*. A text based on Tacit with a reference to the religious conflicts in the Dutch Republic. See: Kaplan, *Muslims in the Dutch Golden Age*, 11–12.

require a different approach in the matter of religion than the relentlessness of the Jewish law.

The Roman Catholics will have no cause to reproach us for tolerating the Jewish religion, as they do the same: not only do they act in the same way as us, but the papal decrees (which guide their consciences) very clearly indicate that the Jews should be allowed their religious practice, though not the Christians who are of a different persuasion than they themselves. *Accept the law you have made yourself.*[11] The cause is very diverse. The congregations of the Roman Catholics, who acknowledge the Pope as their leader and supreme commander, the same who, as a notorious enemy of this state, is suspected, and not without valid reason, of communicating with certain rulers this country must be wary of, are incomparably more dangerous than the congregations of the Jews, whose religion knows neither a leader nor a prince.

Assuming therefore, that the Jews will be admitted to the country and will be allowed the practice of their religion, it is important to take a close look at the legislation that is to be drafted with respect to them,

regarding which two objectives are important in general, namely:

the welfare of the Christian religion and the welfare of the state. Everything that is not contrary to this ought to be allowed the Jews as well as the Christians, so that they may actually experience Christian love.

So let us now draw up a number of articles and next examine them.

1. That all Jews, by descent and religion, who are now in the country or will arrive later, shall individually register their names with the city government of their place of residence within the first eight days following this announcement or their arrival, the parents, however, only need register the names of underage children younger than 14. All this under penalty of a fine of fifty guilders.

2. That all Jews over the age of 14 shall give the following declaration of their faith before the city government: That they believe there is one God, the creator and ruler of all that is, the origin of all that is good, who must be honoured, served and worshipped. That Moses and the Prophets, through God's inspiration, have written the truth; that after death there will be another life, in which the good will be rewarded and the evil will be punished.

3. That they shall at the same time swear an oath of allegiance to the country.

4. That all Jews shall settle within walled cities.

5. That no more than two hundred families are to reside in each city in Holland and West Friesland, with the exception of Amsterdam, where, because of the size of the city, three hundred families may reside. And that, should this number increase, either through the growth of their population or through arrivals from elsewhere, they are to move to other cities.

6. That Jews are to live freely in their places of residence and engage in trade, retailing or local industry as they see fit, and that they shall enjoy the same liberties, exemptions and privileges enjoyed by other citizens and residents without having a special tax imposed on them, provided they adhere to the following rules.

7. That they shall be allowed the free exercise of their religion in the following manner.

8. Namely, they shall designate to the city authorities one, two or three or more of their own houses or of those they occupy, where they will be permitted to gather in order to perform their religious duties at certain fixed hours.

11 *Patere legem quam tuleris.* According to Roman law; for the origin of this saying see: Wilks, *The Problem of Sovereignty in the Later Middle Ages*, 216, n. 1.

9. Provided that no more than a hundred shall gather in each house, under penalty of a fine of two hundred guilders, to be paid by the occupant of the house where the congregation is taking place.

10. Also, that no congregations shall take place in other houses and at other times than those permitted by the authorities, under penalty of confiscation of the house, when it is owned by a Jew or if this is not the case the sum forfeit shall equal the value of the house.

11. That no one shall attend the congregation carrying arms, under penalty of banishment from the city.

12. That no Christian shall enter the place where Jews gather, except officers and members of the city government or those who have been given permission by the authorities, and that they will behave modestly as long as they are there.

13. That no Jew will be so bold, in public or in secret, as to declare anything in violation of the declaration of faith in the second article, on pain of death or else corporal punishment, depending on the case.

14. That no Jew, during their congregation or outside, shall utter blasphemous remarks or profanities against our Lord Jesus Christ or against the Christian religion, on pain of banishment and confiscation of possessions, or a heavier punishment, depending on the case.

15. If the same should happen during the congregation, the house is to be demolished, and if it does not belong to a Jew, the owner is to be compensated out of the possessions of the occupant of the house.

16. Furthermore, Jews in this country will be permitted to own, use and also cause all books to be printed, with the exception of those containing any blasphemies or profanities, as indicated above. This on pain of banishment from the country with confiscation of possessions of those who would have such books printed; and the punishment for those who own and use these books is confiscation of the books and a fine of fifty guilders at the first offence, a hundred guilders at the second, two hundred guilders at the third, and a penalty to be imposed by the judge thereafter.

17. Jews who are summoned to appear in court on a Sabbath day or any other day celebrated according to the law of Moses, shall not be obliged to appear and shall not be sentenced by default.

18. The children who are born from a Jewish father and mother, by descent and religion, shall not be baptized against the will of the parents before they reach adulthood, but they will be circumcised in accordance with their custom.

19. Jews will be allowed to have their own butcher to slaughter and cut the meat in accordance with their custom.

20. Jews may be excommunicated or banned from their congregations by their teachers or others appointed to this end in case of misconduct or erroneous opinions; provided that anyone wishing to make a complaint for having been wrongfully excommunicated is to turn to the city government, which will take due note and will refer to the laws as mentioned in the Old Testament.

21. Christian clergymen will be allowed to visit the congregation of Jews with the consent of the city government, to teach and preach to them about the Christian religion after the aforementioned service has ended, which instructions they are obliged to attend and remain present, under penalty of a fine of a hundred guilders for anyone who should then leave.

22. Nobody may hinder, hurt or insult Jews in their private lives or during their congregations, in word

or action, or impede the practice of their religion. Those who attempt to do so shall be severely punished.

23. Jews will be free to buy or rent houses throughout their places of residence.

24. Without being obliged to wear any badge to distinguish them from the Christians.

25. Jews shall be at liberty to meet, trade and associate with Christians, provided that they will not attempt to convert Christians to their religion, under penalty of banishment from the country and confiscation.

26. Jews shall be obliged, on Sundays and on all prayer days decreed by the authorities, to close their shops and refrain from any work, as do the Christians, to prevent annoyance and confusion, subject to the same penalty as other residents.

27. No Jewish man shall marry a Christian woman, nor a Christian man a Jewish woman, on pain of being punished by the sword, both the man as well as the woman, both the Christian as well as the Jew.

28. No Jew shall circumcise a Christian adult or a child born from Christian parents, under penalty of banishment from the country and confiscation of possessions.

29. No Jew shall have Christians live in his household in any way, whether men, women or children, young or old, under penalty of banishment from the city and a fine of two hundred guilders for the Jew and on the Christian a penalty to be imposed by the judge.

30. However, Christian midwives may assist Jewish women at their delivery.

31. The children of Jews may also be sent to Christian wet nurses outside the house.

32. The children of Jews may not be taught at Christian schools, but Jews will be allowed to set up a number of schools themselves, so that their children can be taught, after notifying the authorities.

33. A Christian who converts to Judaism shall be banished from the country.

34. If a Jew converts to the Christian faith, he shall not be hindered or harmed, under penalty of banishment from the country and confiscation, or also corporal punishment, as the severity of the case requires.

35. The wills that might be made by Jews out of hatred against their Christian kinsmen shall be declared null and void, and they shall be declared intestate.

36. If a woman, son or daughter of a Jew, who has converted to the Christian religion, should complain to the authorities that they are being abused by their husband or respective parents because of their religion, then the authorities, having been notified, shall give permission to the woman or the children to live on their own or with Christians.

37. A child born from a Jewish father and a mother who has converted to the Christian religion or vice versa can be baptized at the request of the Christian father or mother, and being baptized shall not be circumcised, under penalty of banishment from the city and confiscation of half of the possessions of the person who performs the circumcision.

38. If a Jewish man or woman has sexual intercourse with a Christian man or woman out of wedlock, both shall be punished by being whipped and they shall be banished from the country with confiscation of their possessions.

39. All Jews shall furthermore be subject to the same rights, decrees and customs, taxes, levies, judiciary and jurisdiction to which all other citizens of these lands are also subjected, to equal

FIGURE 18 Etching of a circumcision in the Amsterdam Jewish community

punishments like the others, in particular they shall also be subject to the laws regulating the interest on lent money.

40. Jews by descent or religion may not be appointed to any offices in the judiciary, police force or finance or to any other public offices.

41. As a result they will allowed to represent Jews in court and, after prior consent by the Court, exercise the office of a public notary exclusively among Jews and also act as guardians of Jewish children.

42. Nor shall Jews be admitted to the civic militia or security guards of the cities, but they shall pay a tax in lieu of service, like others who are not called to duty.

43. Jews are allowed to be appointed as arbiters between Jews, provided that appeals are possible in this jurisdiction, as in the jurisdiction by others.

44. The parents and next of kin of newly-born Jewish children or of Jews who died, shall submit the name of the child or the deceased to the author-

FIGURE 19 The Jewish marriage ceremony depicted in a book describing Jewish traditions published in Utrecht in 1682

ities within eight days to be officially registered, under penalty of fifty guilders.

45. Jews who wish to marry, shall have the banns proclaimed and the marriage formally confirmed by the city authorities.

46. Jews shall be permitted to give their wives a divorce letter in accordance with the law of Moses, provided that this letter of divorce is submitted to the city government and registered by the clerk's office in the town hall.[12]

47. Jews shall not be allowed to buy land or manors unless by authorization from the highest authority.[13]

48. Jews are permitted to collectively buy one or two plots of land in every city to set up a burial ground and shall have the purchase registered at the city clerk's office.

49. Furthermore the community, group or nation of the Jews shall not receive donations, have inheritances or bequests left to them, nor be allowed to have communal possessions or organize collections other than those that are directly distributed among their poor, under penalty of forfeiture of the aforementioned possessions to the treasury, either inherited or bequeathed; and the persons who encourage the aforesaid money collections shall be punished with banishment from the country and confiscation of possessions, unless the city authorities permit a collection to a certain sum of money in the interest of a cause.

The principal articles will now be explained below.

12 This refers to the so-called *get*, a rabbinical document that enables a husband to divorce his wife.

13 This refers to the States of Holland.

Sub article 1.
Registering names is very useful to monitor people of a different religion. Here is an example from *Livy, 4th Decade, Book 9, which deals with the cult of Bacchus. If any person considered such worship to be ordained by tradition or to be necessary, and believed that he could not omit it without sin and atonement, he was to make a declaration before the city praetor.*[14]

Sub articles 2 and 13.
Among the Jews, as among other religious faiths, there are often some atheists and godless people to be found, who ought not to be tolerated in a good republic. It is important that they are clearly distinguished from the rest, and those who display any kind of godlessness should be punished ruthlessly.

If, however, any among them try to introduce godless sophisms, denying either the Resurrection or the Last Judgement or that angels are made and created by God, We wish them to be expelled from every place and not speak any blasphemy that is far removed from the knowledge of God itself. In case they try to spread such views, We will subject them to the harshest of punishments and will thus purify the Jewish people of the errors they introduced.[15]

Nor will the Jews themselves have any difficulty accepting this as it is drawn from their own traditional testimonies.

Sub articles 3, 4 and 5.
This is intended to force Jews to greater obedience and also to prevent any conspiracies forged in isolated places or also in cities, should they become too numerous.

14 Livy, *History of Rome, Volume XI*, bk. XXXIX.18.8. This passage from Livy has a somewhat peculiar connotation—the fragment here quoted by Grotius is taken from a lengthier passage in which the toleration of an unauthorized cult was shown to have a disruptive effect on Roman society, so that stern measures were eventually required. It is almost impossible that Grotius did not have this negative connotation in mind when he wrote this.

15 Nov. 146.

Sub article 6.
The custom of making Jews pay a tax for their freedom of religion was introduced by the Popes, which exposes their tyranny and greed. The ancient emperors never imposed such a tax, but treated the Jews like all other citizens. Furthermore the free commerce by Jews is explicitly dealt with in article 1.9.9 of the Corpus Iuris Civilis.

Sub article 8.
The emperors traditionally allowed Jews to establish their synagogues, which was afterwards restricted to the extent that they were permitted to repair their old synagogues, but not build new ones.[16] The reason appears to have been that their religion seemed to be endorsed too much by being allowed to build in public spaces. In this country, too, the understanding has always been that there should only be one public religion, so that it is actually better not to allow the Jews the exercise of their religion in public places but in private houses, which is also less noticeable for the people.

Sub articles 9, 10, 11, 12.
It is important to prescribe the number of congregations, so that public disturbances may be averted. The prohibition to carry arms also serves to this end, which is in general imposed by all rulers who condone a religion. The supervision by the city authorities serves to investigate what goes on in their congregations, what they are about and what is being discussed.

Sub articles 14 and 15.
A Christian city government may tolerate some persons who as yet do not know Christ, though not any who malign Christ, if they value the honour of Christ. This is something that has been strictly supervised by the old Christian rulers. Blasphemy is a capital punishment according to common law and carries a corporal punishment according to custom. However, as far as Jews are concerned it

16 Cod. 1.9.18(19), Cod. Theod. 16.8.22 and 16.8.25.

would appear that due to their ignorance the punishment ought not to be as severe as that for Christians.[17]

Sub article 16.
Jurisprudence allows Jews to read the Holy Writ of the Old Testament, both in the original language and in translation. They are forbidden the use of the Talmud, which contains numerous blasphemies against Christians; similarly the Talmud was also burnt by the Popes of Rome.[18]

Sub article 17.
This in accordance with the jurisprudence of the Roman Emperors.[19]

Sub article 18.
This was already a general decree, made not only by us, but also by Roman-Catholic theologians, in accordance with the traditional custom that children born from non-Christians are not entitled to be baptized.[20]

Sub article 19.
No decrees shall be imposed on Jews that will hinder them in practising their religion.[21]

Sub article 20.
That the Jews have traditionally made use amongst themselves of the right to excommunicate, is evident from evangelical history. They were allowed to do so according to Roman law.[22] However, Jews who felt disadvantaged because of it, could nevertheless appeal to the authorities.[23]

Flavius Josephus offers a memorable example, how Ptolemy, King of Egypt, ruled in accordance with the law of Moses in the religious issue

17 Cod. 1.9.11; Nov. 77; two interesting laws from the Corpus Iuris are cited in this article the first of which, Cod. 1.9.11, explicitly refers to Purim. According to this law it was a Jewish custom to burn effigies of the cross at Purim as an allusion to Haman's plan to impose capital punishment on the Jewish people, though in the end it was he who was sentenced to death. The emperors rightly or wrongly interpreted this as a mockery of the symbol of the Christian cross. The second law, Novella 77, discusses blasphemy in general, a comprehensive term that could include a range of things. Any frivolous use of the name of God is severely punished, for fear of provoking earthquakes and epidemics and such! Blasphemy incidentally also stretches to performing 'unnatural acts'. *Iulii Clari Alexandrini Opera omnia, sive practica civilis atque criminalis*, blasphemia; *Consiliorum seu Responsorum Alexandri Tartagni … Liber sextus …*, 153.

18 Nov. 146; with respect to the burning of the Talmud, Grotius furthermore refers to a decree by Innocent IV and Hostensies' comment on this decree. This article is explained extensively in Kedar, "Canon Law and the Burning of the Talmud."

19 Cod. 1.9.2, Cod. 1.9.13 and Cod. Theod. 16.8.20.

20 Grotius here refers to Thomas Aquinas, who argued in his *Summa Theologia* 2–2, q. 10 art. 12 that although many scholars had been of the opinion that the children of Jewish parents could be baptised against their will, the practice is not compatible with the general custom of the church, which should be followed at all times. This is precisely one of the passages cited by Ittersum as sources which Grotius, following Vitoria, made robust use of: 'Vitoria's *Relectiones XII* served as Grotius' reader's guide to the *Secunda Secundae*. […] Grotius was paraphrasing Vitoria's *Relection on the American Indians* par. 39, where Grotius mentioned as his sources "St. Thomas in his ST. II-II.10.8", "Gratian's canon *De Iudaeis*" (Decretum D.45.5), "Consilium IV Toletanum par.56" […] Can it be coincidence that when we turn to Grotius' copy of the *Secunda Secundae* we find underlining in nearly every article of Question 10 […]? Vitoria's *Relection on the American Indians*, which Grotius read from cover to cover, evidently spurred him on to make careful study of Question 10 of the *Secunda Secundae* […].' Ittersum, "The Working Methods of Hugo Grotius," 185.

The humanist and lawyer Ulrich Zasius discussed this theme in his *De Iudaeis Quaestionibus tres* (1550). He came to the conclusion that it was allowed, though Grotius obviously did not find him convincing here. On Zasius see: Rowan, "Ulrich Zasius and the Baptism of Jewish Children." Grotius moreover appears to apply a rule of correspondence: Since Jews are to be punished severely when they circumcise a non-Jew, Christians are also not allowed to baptise Jews. He refers for this to Dig. 48.8.11 and Cod. 1.9.16.

21 Dig. 50.2.3.3 and Dig. 27.1.15.6.

22 Cod. Theod. 16.8.8.

23 Cod. 1.9.8. Grotius also cites Nov. 146 which deals with Jews who are being 'protected' from their religious leaders, and are allowed to have recourse to the Septuagint. In this case, therefore, they can appeal to the secular authorities in relation to the religious authorities.

between the Jews and the Samaritans. This is a matter of great importance as the leaders of the Jews presume to excessive and exorbitant authority amongst their own, which is often the main obstacle stopping Jews from converting to Christianity.

Sub article 21.
This is put into practice in Rome, namely that Jews are forced to attend a number of Christian sermons. Nor is this unreasonable, since according to their own law they are not forbidden to hear anyone of a different religion speak, especially when they are ordered to do so by the authorities. And surely it is the only means by which these unfortunate people can be made to acknowledge the error of their ways properly, provided that learned and judicious people are engaged, with a sound training in Hebrew. Let us do for the Jews what God did for us, who manifested himself among the heathens where they did not seek him and made himself known to them when they did not ask for him. Allowance is also made for the weakness of the Jews as they are, as a matter of principle, not forced to come to our churches, but are exhorted in their own houses.

Sub article 22.
In conformity with the text of the Corpus Iuris.[24]

Sub articles 23 and 24.
The practice differs everywhere in this respect. For some order Jews to wear a badge, each one of them in a uniform manner. Others allow them greater freedom. The ancient emperors never approved of the wearing of a badge, which was only instituted by the Pope.[25] The reason they gave was that nobody would be misled in contact with others, should anyone believe to be speaking to a Christian while actually speaking to a Jew. However, if Jews are strictly forbidden to speak out against the Christian religion, this reason is of little consequence. This is also partly regulated by submitting and registering their names. Experience also teaches that wearing a badge serves to mock the Jews rather than anything else. There are also political considerations at stake why such a distinction does not seem useful. The Romans never wanted to distinguish their slaves from free people by means of an outward token, so that they would have less opportunity to conspire together. For the same reason it would seem more advisable that the Jews live spread across the country rather than all together, which has also been traditional practice.

Sub article 25.
The prohibition that no Jew shall try and convert any Christian, and the punishment imposed, is in accordance with the text of the Corpus Iuris.[26]

And although the Popes attempted through their decrees to impose strict limitations on the relations between Christians and Jews, it seems more advisable to leave this to the discretion of the Christians rather than proscribe them, with the exception of cohabitation, which seems to incur greater problems, as is discussed below.

Sub article 26.
General rules and the desired effectiveness make this necessary.

Sub article 27.
It is unquestionable that God has expressly forbidden marriage with unbelievers, also that many people have given in to temptation. *Deut. 7:7, 1 Kings 11, Neh. 13.*[27]

This has also given rise to a great deal of confusion in the legislation. For this reason marriages between Christians and Jews, both women and men, are strictly forbidden.[28]

24 Cod. 1.9.14; Cod.Th. 16.8.21 (*not* 12).

25 CIC X 5.6.15.

26 Grotius here probably refers to Cod. 1.9.16 and Cod. 1.9.18.

27 Probably Deut. 7:3; 1 Kings 11; probably Neh. 13:25–26.

28 Grotius' evidence is based on Roman law. He substantiates his arguments with the words of a 15th-century commentator, who in the locus citandi discusses the question whether death by the sword was and should

Sub article 28.
This law and punishment have been codified by the Roman Emperors.[29] Nevertheless capital punishment is prescribed by Cod. 1.10.1, but this law applies when a Jew employs a Christian as his slave and proceeds to circumcise him.

Sub articles 29, 30, 31.
It was expressly forbidden by the ancient emperors that Jews kept Christians as their slaves.[30]

Afterwards, when the use of slaves began to decline, and it became customary to employ domestic servants, the Popes and the Councils for the same reason forbade Jews to hire Christians as their domestics, either as servants, housemaids, or wet nurses, or in any other domestic role. This is codified accordingly in canonical law.[31]

They are allowed, however, to employ midwives and wet nurses outside their homes.[32]

Sub article 32.
The reason for this is obvious as the feelings of children are very susceptible and easily influenced. Experience has already shown in this country, too, that this a necessary prohibition.

Sub article 33.
A Christian who apostatizes to Judaism is punished with dishonour and the seizure of his possessions in accordance with existing jurisprudence.[33]

In view of the present times, however, it seems more advisable to deny such people entry to the country.

Sub article 34.
This was codified in the Corpus Iuris, which prescribed death by burning for anyone throwing stones at converted Jews or cause them bodily harm. And if any wrong were to befall them in any other way or if they were hindered in their good intentions, it would be punished by the judge in the same way.[34]

Sub article 35.
This is in agreement with the law of Emperor Theodosius and fully agrees with what is observed in this country with respect to wills made out of hatred against our religion.[35]

Sub article 36.
The apostle Paul, speaking of this matter, advises a believer who is married to an unbeliever, not to divorce if the unbeliever wants to continue to live together.[36] Whether a city government might be allowed to end such a marriage by public order might be contested, in light of the example of Ezra, who commanded it, and the opinion of Augustine and some others, who believe that such a thing is allowed.[37]

The Council of Toledo does not dissolve marriage unilaterally, but prohibits unlawful cohabitation.[38]

And this would appear to be indisputable, in case one of the spouses should abuse the other in regard of religion; in the same way as we daily witness divorces at least from board and bed on the grounds of cruelty.

On the other hand the believer will undoubtedly encounter great difficulties, especially when

actually be practised, or could be taken in a figurative sense. In serious cases the actual practice was to be preferred. There is no mention of Jews in this passage. Cod. 1.9.6, Cod.Th. 3.7 and Cod. 9.9.29. Bartholomaeus a Salyceto, *In VII. VIII. et IX. Codicis Libros Commentaria*, 222.

29 The penalty imposed was confiscation of goods, as was the case with castration. Cod. 1.9.16; Cod.Th. 16.8.26; Dig. 48.8.11 and Dig. 48.8.4.2.

30 Cod. 1.10, and Cod.Th. 16.9.

31 CIC X 5.6.8 and 5.6.13.

32 CIC X 5.6.8 and the gloss on 5.6.13.

33 Cod. 1.7.2 and 1.7.3 and Cod. Theod. 16.8.7 (oddly enough not Cod. Theod. 16.7, which deals exclusively with apostates).

34 Cod. 1.9.3.

35 Cod. Theod. 16.8.28.

36 1Cor. 7:12.

37 Ezra 10:1–44.

38 CIC C. 28. q. 1. This is also the source of the references to Paul, Ezra and Augustine.

confronted with so wide a religious divide as that between Jews and Christians. The same argument applies in the case of children. And even though the Council of Toledo in this respect also generally ruled that the children should be taken away from their parents, it would seem to be more advisable that a distinction is made as to whether or not they are treated badly in the matter of religion. Which would appear to be all the more sufficient in this respect, as all attempts to convert Christians to Judaism are likewise forbidden.[39] And due to diminishing fears in this respect, it would seem that parents must not be deprived of their natural right on the grounds of religion. It is rather to be hoped (as the Apostle also says) that the believer may turn the unbeliever to the road of salvation through their good example.

Sub article 37.
Following written jurisprudence pertaining to liberty and slavery it has been commanded on the grounds of natural equality that children who are born of parents with a different status (i.e. free or slave), will obtain the status that is most favourable to them.[40] That God treats people equally with respect to his Covenant is shown by the Apostle in 1 Cor. 7:24. That is why the Council of Toledo correctly decreed that children of Jews who are married to Christian women, shall acquire the religion and status of the mother. In the same way are those who were born from pagan women and Christian men to follow the Christian religion rather than the Jewish superstition.[41]

Sub article 38.
That sexual relations, whether or not illicit, cause great harm in the matter of religion is also evident from Num. 25:7–8, where Phineas was also praised for thrusting a spear through an Israelite who had intercourse with a Moabite woman. It is found in the Talmud that a law was established during the rule of the Hasmoneans pertaining to unlawful sexual intercourse with a pagan woman.

The scholars are in disagreement where the Jews are concerned, because the written laws do not impose any real punishment for this crime: some claiming the death penalty is to be imposed, as with a marriage, as was the opinion of the Paris city government according to Boerius; others say it calls for an exceptional punishment, a view defended by Oldradus. This view, to apply a more lenient treatment, finds acceptance.[42]

Sub articles 39 and 45.
It is evident from Roman law the Jews are subject to the general laws with respect to matrimonial laws; the same also applies to general taxes.[43]

Some scholars were of the opinion that the Jewish laws should prevail for Jews among themselves, both in matrimonial affairs, in inheritances, as well as in other matters, and that they should be tried by Jewish judges, but this is reprehensible and is not covered by the legal code.

The Jewish community solely exists in its religion and not in any other sense. As such they cannot on their own initiative establish institutions that are based on their own laws.

With respect to usury, this has greatly increased because recently, Christian rulers did not impose any restrictions on the Jews so that they could reap the benefits from the Jews bleeding the poor dry. The law of Moses allows the Jews to lend money at exorbitant interest rates to accursed peoples, towards whom they are allowed to express every hostility.

See Deut. 23:20. As Ambrose very rightly observed: Exact usury from those whom it would not be a crime to kill. Where the rule of war prevails,

39 CIC C.28. q.1. c.11; see: Brundage, "Intermarriage between Christians and Jews in Medieval Canon Law."
40 I. 1.4.
41 CIC C.28 q.1 c. 10.
42 Bohier, *Decisiones*, para. 316; Oldradus de Ponte, *Consilia seu responsa et quaestiones aureae*, para. 333; Clarus, *Opera omnia*, para. fornicatio, no. 25.
43 Cod. 1.9.3, Cod. 1.9.7, Cod. 1.9.5 and Cod. 1.9.10.

there is a right to usury.[44] A Christian city government, however, cannot allow such hostility to be exercised against its citizens, as it is contrary to the principle of natural equality, of which the Jews themselves are also sufficiently convinced in their conscience. See Ps. 15:6. and Ez 18:8.

Sub article 40.
This was set down in the same law which also affirms that Jews who have estates on lease, must have them administered by Christians.[45] The reason for this is that Jews who have been awarded honorary offices have greater opportunity to mislead others and also obtain more liberties for themselves. It is furthermore improper that Christians should be ruled or tried by Jews. 2 Cor. 6:7. And so the laws that prescribed the opposite were revoked with good reason.[46]

Sub article 41.
This distinction is made by a number of scholars. With respect to guardianship, we find a text in the Digests of Justinian.[47]

Sub article 42.
The reason is known, as weapons and watch-keeping should be assigned to those who are to be trusted most. This is consistent with what is stated in Nov. 45, i.e. that Jews are not to be exempt from public office, but are not allowed to enjoy the corresponding privileges and honours.

Sub article 43.
This has been prescribed in Cod. 1.9.8:

If any of them decides to litigate before Jews, after the fashion of arbiters in civil cases only, they are not forbidden to obtain a decision from them by public law.[48]

from which it also appears what has been stated above, that the ancient emperors did not allow Jews general jurisdiction over their own people, for reasons cited above.

Sub article 46.
This is a matter of consideration. And in view of what has been stated above, that Jews should abide by the general laws of the land in all matters not pertaining to religion, it would seem that the law relating to divorce ought to be annulled. However, in view of the fact that divorce among Christians is usually discouraged with a reference to the prohibition found in the Gospel, and that Moses, who knew the disposition of the Jews better than anyone else, considered it necessary to grant Jews divorce to prevent greater evil.

It would appear from Deut. 24:1 and t. 3:8, that a Christian city government would do well to follow his example, which is also the opinion of Baldus de Ubaldis.

However, to avoid confusion, this should in every case not be allowed to occur without prior knowledge of the magistrate, who should also make efforts to dissuade it. As far as Jewish women are concerned, the law of Moses does not allow them a divorce, as Josephus rightly observed, stating that Salome, the wife of Costobarus, was the first to go through with this in violation of the law.

Sub article 47.
The old decrees, both here and in other countries, forbid the clergy to purchase or acquire immovable goods without the consent of the authorities, to prevent them from becoming too powerful. The same reason also serves to forbid Jews the same. And this obstacle is less awkward for the Jews as the highest authority will have no objections to allowing them a few small plots of land, as long as it finds there is no danger to be expected from it.

Sub article 48.
It is better to have many Jews buried in one place, than each in a separate place. So that not too many places will have a religious function and be withdrawn from private use.

44 CIC C.14. q.4. c.12.
45 Cod. 1.9.18.
46 Cod. 1.8 and Dig. 50.2.3.2.
47 Dig. 27.1.15.6.
48 Krueger et al., *The Codex of Justinian*, 231.

Sub article 49.
As has been stated above, Jews ought not to have anything else in common except their religion. There is a difference between having a sodality and having a gathering because of a religion. However, only societies are entitled to communal possessions after the example of the state. In the senate's ruling on the Bacchanalia it was expressly stated that a communal fund was not allowed.[49] Although emperor C. Caligula according to Flavius Josephus did allow each Jewish community to own a few common possessions, it appears that it was restricted afterwards: 'no suit can be brought to recover what Cornelia Salvia bequeathed to all Jews situated in the city of Antioch'[50]

Yet in fairness collecting money for the poor ought to be allowed. Even those without a sodality are allowed to collect money for the poor.[51] Trajan in a letter to Pliny, writing about public collections for charitable ends: 'We will not oppose such public collections, especially when such collections are not meant for riots and illegal assemblies, but for poor relief.'[52]

The emperors also allowed special collections, both for the poor and for the most prominent among the Jews.[53]

which may take place now and then with prior knowledge. On the other hand it is a very dangerous thing to allow a people or a religious group to collect money or goods.

49 Dig. 47.22.1; Livius, *Ab urbe condita*, bk. XXXIX.18.
50 Cod. 1.9.1. Krueger et al., *The Codex of Justinian*, 229.
51 Dig. 47.22.1.
52 Plinius Secundus, *Epistularum libri decem*, X, 93.
53 The reference is probably to Cod. 1.9.17. and Cod. Theod. 16.8.14, 16.8.17 and 16.8.29.

Bibliography

Ambrosius Mediolanensis. *Sancti Ambrosii, Mediolanensis Episcopi, opera omnia … editio prae aliis omnibus completa*. Edited by Jacques Paul Migne. Patrologiae cursus completus: Series Latina 14–17. Parisiis: Migne, 1845.

Bangs, Carl. *Arminius: A Study in the Dutch Reformation*. Nashville: Abingdon Press, 1971.

Barrios, Daniel Levi de. *Triumpho del Govierno Popular, Y de la Antiguedad Holandesa. Dedicalo en el Año de 5443. Daniel Levi de Barrios. A los muy Ilustres Señores Parnasim, y Gabay del Kahal Kados Amstelodamo,* […]. Amsterdam: s.n., 1683.

Bartholomaeus a Salyceto. *Bartholomaei a Salyceto … In VII. VIII. et IX. Codicis Libros Commentaria. Doctissimis quamplurium i. c. adnotationibus illustrata …* Venetiis, 1586.

Blom, J.C.H., David J. Wertheim, Hetty Berg, and Bart Wallet, eds. *Geschiedenis van de Joden in Nederland*. Grondig vernieuwde en uitgebreide tweede editie. Amsterdam: Uitgeverij Balans, 2017.

Bodian, Miriam. *Hebrews of the Portuguese Nation: Conversos and Community in Early Modern Amsterdam*. The Modern Jewish Experience. Bloomington: Indiana University Press, 1997.

Bohier, Nicolas. *Decisiones Burdegalenses: Per excellentiss. ic. dn. Nicolaum Boerium, (…)*. Francofurti: Ex Officina Typographica Nicolai Bassaei, Impensis Sigismundi Feyrabent, 1574.

Briscoe, John. *A Commentary on Livy: Books 38–40*. Oxford: Oxford University Press, 2008.

Brundage, James. “Intermarriage between Christians and Jews in Medieval Canon Law.” *Jewish History* 3, no. 1 (1988): 25–40.

Capella, Martianus. *Martiani Minei Felicis Capellæ Carthaginiensis viri proconsularis Satyricon, in quo de nuptiis Philologiæ & Mercurij libri duo, & De septem artibus liberalibus libri singulares. Omnes, & emendati, & notis sive februis Hug. Grotii illustrati*. Leiden: Ex officina Plantiniana, apud Christophorum Raphelengium, Academiae Lugduno Bat. typographum, 1599.

Catalogue de manuscrits autographes du célèbre Hugo Grotius et de documents importants qui ont servi à la composition de ses ouvrages dont la vente aura lieu le 15 nov. 1864 sous la dir. de Martinus Nijhoff. Den Haag: Martinus Nijhoff, 1864.

Catalogue de vente de la succession de feu D. Henriques de Castro Mz., sous la direction de J. Vita Israel et Jacq. Lamed, courtiers, par le ministère de Mm. Van Leijden, Ritman et Hoorn, notaires. Amsterdam: sn, 1899.

Clarus, Julius. *Opera omnia, sive Practica civilis atque criminalis*. Ed. nova. Francofurti: Schonwetterus, 1636.

Clarus, Julius. *Opera omnia, sive practica civilis atque criminalis*. Lugduni: Sumpt. Horatii Boissat, & Georgii Remeus, 1661.

Cohen, Julie-Marthe. *Onder de hamer: de veelzijdige verzameling van David Henriques de Castro (1826–1898). / Up for Auction. The variegated collection of David Henriques de Castro (1826–1898)*. Amsterdam: Joods Historisch Museum, 1999.

Cohen, Robert. “Memoria Para Os Siglos Futuros: Myth and Memory on the Beginnings of the Amsterdam Sephardi Community.” *Jewish History* 2, no. 1 (1987): 67–72.

Coolhaas, Caspar. *Remonstrantie aen zijne prinslijcke excellentie, ende de edele … zeer vermogende Heeren Staten ende Steden der vereenighde ende gereformeerde neder-Landen, in dewelcke (onder verbeteringe) aenghewezen wordt ’t ghene, dat nootlijck naer eysch der Heyligher Godlijcker Schriftuer … met kleyne moyte verbetert zal konnen werden*. Ter Govde: By Jacobus Migoen, woonende op de Vis-mert inde ladder Iacobsz, 1608. http://proxy.uba.uva.nl:2048/login ?url=http://books.google.com/books?vid= KBNL:UBA000058066.

Deursen, A.Th. van. *Honni soit qui mal y pense? De Republiek tussen de mogendheden (1610–1612)*. Mededelingen der Koninklijke Nederlandse Akademie van Wetenschappen. Afd. Letterkunde, N.R., dl. 28, no. 1. Amsterdam: Noord-Hollandsche Uitgevers Maatschappij, 1965.

Deursen, A.Th. van. *De last van veel geluk: de geschiede-*

nis van Nederland, 1555–1702. De geschiedenis van Nederland, dl. 4. Amsterdam: Bakker, 2004.

"Discours, by forme van remonstrantie; vervatende de nootsakelijckheyt vande Oost-Indische navigatie", n.d. http://primarysources.brillonline.com/browse/dutch-pamphlets-online/discours-by-forme-van-remonstrantie-vervatende-de-nootsakelckheyt-vande-oostindische-navigatie;dutchpamphletskb0kb01829.

Dorsten, J.A. van. *Poets, Patrons and Professors: Sir Philip Sidney, Daniel Rogers and the Leiden Humanists*. Publications of the Sir Thomas Browne Institute, Leiden: General Series, no. 2. Leiden: Leiden University Press, 1962.

"Dutch Pamphlets Online—BrillOnline Primary Sources." Accessed June 2, 2017. http://primarysources.brillonline.com/browse/dutch-pamphlets-online.

Eyffinger, Arthur. "'How Wondrously Moses Goes Along with The House of Orange!': Hugo Grotius' 'De Republica Emendanda' in the Context of the Dutch Revolt." In *Political Hebraism: Judaic Sources in Early Modern Political Thought*, edited by Gordon Schochet, Fania Oz-Salzberger, and Meirav Jones, 107–147. Jerusalem and New York: Shalem Press, 2008.

Eysinga, Willem Jan Mari Van. *De Groots Jodenreglement*. Mededeelingen Der Koninklijke Nederlandsche Akademie Van Wetenschappen Afdeeling Letterkunde Nieuwe Reeks, Dl. 13, No. 1 (1950). Amsterdam: Noord-Hollandsche Uitgevers Maatschappij, 1950.

Eysinga, Willem Jan Mari Van and L.J. Noordhoff. *Catalogue de manuscrits autographes de Hugo Grotius, dont la vente a eu lieu à La Haye le 15 novembre 1864 sous la direction et au domicile de Martinus Nijhoff*. 2me éd. / avec annotations de W.J.M. van Eysinga et L.J. Noordhoff. Den Haag: Nijhoff, 1952.

Frijhoff, Willem. "Religious Toleration in the United Provinces: From 'Case' to 'Model.'" In *Calvinism and Religious Toleration in the Dutch Golden Age*, edited by Ronnie Po-Chia Hsia and Henk van Nierop, 27–52. Cambridge: Cambridge University Press, 2002.

Gelder, H.A. Enno van. *Revolutionnaire reformatie: de vestiging van de Gereformeerde Kerk in de Nederlandse gewesten, gedurende de eerste jaren van de opstand tegen Filips II, 1575–1585*. Patria 31. Amsterdam: Van Kampen, 1943.

Gelder, H.A. Enno van. *Vrijheid en onvrijheid in de Republiek: geschiedenis der vrijheid van drukpers en godsdienst van 1572 tot 1798*. Haarlem: Tjeenk Willink, 1947.

Grafton, Anthony. *Joseph Scaliger: A Study in the History of Classical Scholarship; II Historical Chronology*. Oxford: Clarendon Press, 1993.

Greenblatt, Stephen. *Renaissance Self-Fashioning: From More to Shakespeare*. Chicago & London: The University of Chicago Press, 2005.

Groot, Hugo de. Letter to Georg Michael Lingelsheim, January 25, 1604. http://grotius.huygens.knaw.nl/letters/0049.

Groot, Hugo de. *Meletius, sive, De iis quae inter Christianos conveniunt epistola*. Edited by G.H.M. Posthumus Meyjes. Studies in the history of Christian thought, vol. 40. Leiden: Brill, 1988.

Groot, Hugo de. *Ordinum Hollandiae ac Westfrisiae pietas (1613)*. Edited by Edwin Rabbie. Studies in the History of Christian Thought 66. Leiden: Brill, 1995.

Groot, Hugo de. *Remonstrantie nopende de ordre dije in de landen van Hollandt ende Westvrieslandt dijent gestelt op de Joden*. Edited by Jaap Meijer. Amsterdam: Meijer, 1949.

Haven, Alexander van der. "Conversion on Trial: Toleration of Apostasy and the Trial of Three Converts to Judaism in the Dutch Republic, 1614–1615." In *Contesting Inter-Religious Conversion in the Medieval World*, edited by Yaniv Foḳs and Yosi Yisraeli, 41–60. London and New York: Routledge, Taylor and Francis, 2017.

Haven, Alexander van der. "Predestination and Toleration: The Dutch Republic's Single Judicial Persecution of Jews in Theological Context." *Renaissance Quarterly* 71, no. 1 (2018): 165–205.

Heesakkers, Chris L. *Praecidanea Dousana: Materials for a Biography of Janus Dousa Pater (1545–1604). His Youth*. Amsterdam: Holland University Press, 1976.

Heesakkers, Chris L. and Wilma M.S. Reinders. *Genoeglijk bovenal zijn de muzen: de Leidse Neolatijnse dichter Janus Dousa (1545–1604)*. Leidse opstellen, 18. Leiden: Stichting Dimensie, 1993.

Hellinga, W.Gs. *Van den vos Reynaerde. Diplomatisch uitgegeven naar de bronnen vóór het jaar 1500. I Teksten*. Zwolle: Tjeenk Willink, 1952.

Huijbrecht, R. "Hugo de Groot als advocaat-fiscaal van het Hof van Holland, Zeeland en West-Friesland 1607–1614." In *De Hollandse jaren van Hugo de Groot (1583–1621): lezingen van het colloquium ter gelegenheid van de 350-ste sterfdag van Hugo de Groot ('s-Gravenhage, 31 augustus–1 september 1995)*, edited by H.J.M. Nellen and J. Trapman, 45–56. Hilversum: Verloren, 1996.

Huussen jr., Arend H. "De toelating van Sefardische joden in Haarlem in 1605." Edited by Historische Vereniging "Haerlem." *Haerlem Jaarboek 1991*, 1992, 48–62.

Innocentius IV. *Sanctissimi in Christo Patris Do. Innocentii Papae IIII. Apparatus toto orbe celebrandus, super V Libris Decretalium, & super Decretalibus per eum editis, cum summarijs Do. Pauli Rhoselli, & vita ipsius Innocentii Do. Thoma Diplouatatio autore fidelissimè, quoad fieri potuit, edita: Sub quo Margaritam Baldi nouissimè additam inuenies*, 1540. http://archive.org/details/bub_gb_jlZQIhV8GaIC.

Israel, Jonathan I. *European Jewry in the Age of Mercantilism, 1550–1750*. Oxford: Clarendon Press, 1985.

Israel, Jonathan I. "Manuel López Pereira of Amsterdam, Antwerp and Madrid: Jew, New Christian, and Advisor to the Conde-Duque De Olivares." *Studia Rosenthaliana* 19, no. 2 (1985): 109–126.

Israel, Jonathan I. *The Dutch Republic: Its Rise, Greatness, and Fall, 1477–1806*. Paperback with corr. Oxford: Clarendon Press, 1998.

Israel, Jonathan I. "The Intellectual Debate about Toleration in the Dutch Republic." In *The Emergence of Tolerance in the Dutch Republic*, edited by Christiane Berkvens-Stevelinck, Jonathan I. Israel, and G.H.M. Posthumus Meyjes, 3–36. Studies in the History of Christian Thought 76. Leiden: Brill, 1997.

Ittersum, Martine J. van. *Profit and Principle: Hugo Grotius, National Rights Theories and the Rise of Dutch Power in the East Indies 1595–1615*. Brill's Studies in Intellectual History 139. Leiden and Boston: Brill, 2006.

Ittersum, Martine J. van. "The Working Methods of Hugo Grotius: Which Sources Did He Use and How Did He Use Them in His Early Writings on Natural Law Theory." In *Reassessing Legal Humanism and Its Claims: Petere Fontes?*, edited by Paul J. du Plessis and John W. Cairns, 154–193. Edinburgh Studies in Law 15. Edinburgh: Edinburgh University Press, 2016.

Juvenalis, D. Junius. *De Satiren*. Translated by M. d'Hane-Scheltema. Baskerville serie. Baarn: Ambo, 1984.

Juvenalis, D. Junius, and Aulus Persius Flaccus. *Juvenal and Persius*. Translated by Susanna Morton Braund. Loeb classical library 91. Cambridge, MA: Harvard University Press, 2004.

Kamen, Henry. *Inquisition and Society in Spain in the Sixteenth and Seventeenth Centuries*. London: Weidenfeld & Nicolson, 1985.

Kaplan, Benjamin J. *Muslims in the Dutch Golden Age: Representations and Realities of Religious Toleration*. Golden Age Lecture 4. Amsterdam: Amsterdams Centrum voor de studie van de Gouden Eeuw, Universiteit van Amsterdam, 2007.

Kaplan, Benjamin J. "'Dutch' Religious Tolerance: Celebration and Revision." In *Calvinism and Religious Toleration in the Dutch Golden Age*, edited by R. Po-chia Hsia and H.F.K. van Nierop, 8–26. Cambridge: Cambridge University Press, 2002.

Kedar, Benjamin Z. "Canon Law and the Burning of the Talmud." *Bulletin of Medieval Canon Law* 9 (1979): 79–82.

Kleffens, E.N. van. "Over zes brieven uit het bezit van Hugo de Groot." *Mededelingen der Koninklijke Nederlandse Akademie van Wetenschappen, afd. Leterkunde* Nieuwe Reeks, dl. 23, no. 16 (1960): 7–9.

Koen, E.M., and W.Chr. Pieterse. "Notarial Records in Amsterdam Relating to the Portuguese Jews in That Town up to 1639." *Studia Rosenthaliana* 1, no. 1 (1967): 109–115.

Kromhout, David. "Clashes of Discourses: Humanists and Calvinists in Seventeenth-Century Academic Leiden." Amsterdam University, 2016.

Krueger, Paul, Bruce W. Frier, Serena Connolly, Simon Corcoran, Michael H. Crawford, John Noël Dillon, Dennis P. Kehoe, et al., eds. *The Codex of Justinian: a new annotated translation, with parallel Latin and Greek text based on a translation by Justice Fred H. Blume*. Translated by Fred H. Blume. Cambridge: Cambridge University Press, 2016.

Lefèvre, E., and E. Schäfer, eds. *Ianus Dousa: neulateinischer Dichter und klassischer Philologe*. NeoLatina 17. Tübingen: Gunter Narr Verlag, 2009.

Livius, T. *History of Rome, Volume XI: Books 38–39*. Translated by Evan T. Sage. Loeb Classical Library LCL313. Cambridge, MA: Harvard University Press, 1936.

Livius, T. *Titi Livi ab urbe condita: Tomus VI Libri XXXVI–XL*. Edited by Patrick Gerard Walsh. Scriptorum classicorum bibliotheca Oxoniensis. Oxonii: E Typographeo Clarendoniano, 1999.

Lubbertus, Sibrandus. *Sibrandi Lubberti commentarii ad nonaginta novem errores Conradi Vorstii*. Franekeræ Frisiorum: ex officina Ulrici Dominici Balck, 1613.

Michman, Jozeph. "Historiography of the Jews in The Netherlands." In *Dutch Jewish History: Proceedings of the Symposium on the History of the Jews in the Netherlands: November 28–December 3, 1982, Tel Aviv-Jerusalem*, edited by Jozeph Michman and Tirtsah Levie, 7–31. Jerusalem: Tel Aviv University; Hebrew University of Jerusalem, The Institute for Research on Dutch Jewry, 1984.

Mout, M.E.H.N. "A Comparative View of Dutch Toleration." In *The Emergence of Tolerance in the Dutch Republic*, edited by Christiane Berkvens-Stevelinck, Jonathan I. Israel, and G.H.M. Posthumus Meyjes, 37–47. Studies in the History of Christian Thought 76. Leiden: Brill, 1997.

Nellen, Henk. J.M. "Een tweespan voor de arminiaanse wagen: Grotius en Wtenbogaert." In *De Hollandse jaren van Hugo de Groot (1583–1621): lezingen van het colloquium ter gelegenheid van de 350-ste sterfdag van Hugo de Groot ('s-Gravenhage, 31 augustus–1 september 1995)*, edited by H.J.M. Nellen and J. Trapman. Hilversum: Verloren, 1996.

Nellen, Henk. J.M. *Hugo de Groot: Een leven in strijd om de vrede 1583–1645*. Amsterdam: Balans, 2007.

Nellen, Henk. J.M. *Hugo Grotius: A Lifelong Struggle for Peace in Church and State, 1583–1645*. Translated by J.C. Grayson. Leiden; Boston: Brill, 2014.

Nicholas, D.M. *The Transformation of Europe, 1300–1600*. The Arnold History of Europe. London: Arnold; New York: Oxford University Press, 1999.

Noordkerk, Hermanus. *Handvesten; ofte Privilegien ende octroyen; mitsgaders willekeuren, costuimen, ordonnantien en handelingen der stad Amstelredam ...* Vol. 2. Te Amstelredam: by Hendrik van Waesberge, Salomon en Petrus Schouten, boekverkoopers, 1748.

Oldradus de Ponte. *Oldradi de Ponte ... Consilia seu responsa et quaestiones aureae: in quibus ea quae ad quotidianum usum in forensibus negotiis ... spectant ... perstringuntur ...* ex officina Damiani Zenari, 1585.

Otterspeer, Willem. *Groepsportret met dame I: Het bolwerk van de vrijheid: de Leidse universiteit, 1575–1672*. Amsterdam: Bakker, 2000.

Pantelia, Maria C. ed. "Ἡ Προαίρεσις, -εως." *Thesaurus Linguae Graecae® Digital Library*. Irvine: University of California. Accessed May 12, 2017. http://www.tlg.uci.edu.

Peterse, Hans. "Hugo Grotius und sein Gutachten über die rechtliche Stellung der in Holland (1615)." In *Bundeseinheit und Gottesvolk: reformierter Protestantismus und Judentum im Europa des 16. und 17. Jahrhunderts*, edited by Achim Detmers and Jan Marius J. Lange van Ravenswaay, 211–232. Emder Beiträge zum reformierten Protestantismus 9. Wuppertal: Foedus, 2005.

Pieterse, W.Chr. "Daniel Levi de Barrios als geschiedschrijver van de Portugees-Israelietische gemeente te Amsterdam in zijn 'Triumpho del govierno popular.'" Scheltema & Holkema, 1968.

Plinius Secundus, Caecilius. *Epistularum libri decem*. Edited by R.A.B. Mynors. Scriptorum classicorum bibliotheca Oxoniensis. Oxford: e Typographeo Clarendoniano, 1963.

Rabbie, Edwin. "Grotius' denken over kerk en staat." In *De Hollandse jaren van Hugo de Groot (1583–1621): Lezingen van het colloquium ter gelegenheid van de 350-ste sterfdag van Hugo de Groot ('s-Gravenhage, 31 augustus–1 september 1995)*, edited by H.J.M. Nellen and J. Trapman, 193–206. Hilversum: Verloren, 1996.

Rabbie, Edwin. "Hugo Grotius and Judaism." In *Hugo Grotius, Theologian: Essays in Honour of G.H.M. Posthumus Meyjes*, edited by H.J.M. Nellen, G.H.M. Posthumus Meyjes, and Edwin Rabbie, 99–120. Studies in the History of Christian Thought, vol. 55. Leiden: Brill, 1994.

Ravid, Benjamin C. "The Third Charter of the Jewish Merchants of Venice, 1611: A Case Study in Complex Multifaceted Negotiations." *Jewish Political Studies Review* 6, no. 1/2 (1994): 83–134.

Ravid, Benjamin C. "The Venetian Government and the

Jews." In *The Jews of Early Modern Venice*, edited by Robert C. Davis and Benjamin Ravid, 3–30. JHU Press, 2001.

Resolutien van de Heeren Ridderschap, Edelen, ende Gedeputeerden van de Steden van Hollandt ende West-Vrieslandt, Staets-ghewyse genomen in haer Edele Mog. Vergaderinghe gehouden alhier in den Hage, zedert den vierden Maert des Jaers sesthien hondert en vijfthien, ende eyndigende den seventhienden dito daer aen volgende, Pub. L. No. Nationaal Archief, Den Haag, Staten van Holland, nummer toegang 3.01.04.01, inventarisnummer 49 (1615).

Resolutien van de Heeren Staten van Hollande ende West-Vrieslandt, genomen in haer Edele Mog. Vergaderinge gehouden in 's Graven-Hage zedert den negenthienden January des Jaers sesthien hondert negenthien, Pub. L. No. Nationaal Archief, Den Haag, Staten van Holland, nummer toegang 3.01.04.01, inventarisnummer 52 (1619).

Rohls, Jan. "Calvinism, Arminianism and Socinianism in the Netherlands until the Synod of Dort." In *Socinianism and Arminianism: Antitrinitarians, Calvinists and Cultural Exchange in Seventeenth-Century Europe*, edited by Martin Mulsow and Jan Rohls, 134:3–48. Brill's Studies in Intellectual History. Leiden; Boston: Brill, 2005.

Rosenne, Shabtai. "Hugo Grotius: An Israeli Appreciation." *Grotiana* 4, no. 1 (1983): 67–75.

Rowan, Steven W. "Ulrich Zasius and the Baptism of Jewish Children." *The Sixteenth Century Journal* 6, no. 2 (1975): 3–25.

Salomon, H.P. "Myth or Anti-Myth? The Oldest Account Concerning the Origin of Portuguese Judaism at Amsterdam." *Lias* 16, no. 2 (1989): 275–316.

Scaliger, Josephus Justus. *Scaligeriana sive Excerpta ex ore Josephi Scaligeri*. Apud Petrum Columesium, 1666.

Scott, S.P. "The Civil Law." The Roman Law Library, 1932. https://droitromain.univ-grenoble-alpes.fr/Anglica/Jews_Scott.htm.

Silva Rosa, J.S. da. "David Montezinos, de stichter van de 'Livria D. Montezinos.'" *Centraal Blad voor Israëlieten in Nederland* 29, no. 46 and 47 (1914).

Smit, J.G. "De Rotterdamse jaren van Hugo de Groot." In *De Hollandse jaren van Hugo de Groot (1583–1621): lezingen van het colloquium ter gelegenheid van de 350-ste sterfdag van Hugo de Groot ('s-Gravenhage, 31 augustus–1 september 1995)*, edited by H.J.M. Nellen and J. Trapman, 125–143. Hilversum: Verloren, 1996.

Somos, Mark. *Secularisation and the Leiden Circle*. Leiden; Boston: Brill, 2011.

Stein, Siegfried. "Moneylending." In *Encyclopaedia Judaica*, edited by Michael Berenbaum and Fred Skolnik, 2nd ed., 14:436–443. Detroit: Macmillan Reference USA, 2007.

Swetschinski, Daniel M. *Reluctant Cosmopolitans: The Portuguese Jews of Seventeenth-Century Amsterdam*. London: The Littman Library of Jewish Civilisation, 2000.

Swetschinski, Daniel M. "Tussen middeleeuwen en Gouden Eeuw, 1516–1621." In *Geschiedenis van de joden in Nederland*, edited by J.C.H. Blom, R.G. Fuks-Mansfeld, and I. Schöffer, 53–94. Amsterdam: Balans, 1995.

Swift, Louis J. "St. Ambrose on Violence and War." *Transactions and Proceedings of the American Philological Association* 101 (1970): 533–543.

Tartagni, Alessandro. *Consiliorum seu Responsorum Alexandri Tartagni ... Liber sextus ...* apud haeredes Alexandri Paganini, 1610.

Terentius, P. *P. Terenti Afri Comoediae*. Edited by Robert Kauer and Wallace Martin Lindsay. 2nd ed. Scriptorum classicorum bibliotheca Oxoniensis. Oxonii: E typographeo Clarendoniano, 1926.

Terentius, P. *Komedies*. Edited by J.M. Hemelrijk. Translated by J. Hemelrijk. Ambo-Klassiek. Baarn: Ambo, 1993.

Terentius, P. "The self-tormentor." In *Terence I*, translated by John Anthony Barsby, 171–303. The Loeb classical library 22. Cambridge, MA: Harvard University Press, 2001.

Tex, Jan den. *Oldenbarnevelt: II. Oorlog 1588–1609*. Haarlem: H.D. Tjeenk Willink & Zoon, 1962.

Tracy, James D. "Erasmus, Coornhert and the Acceptance of Religious Disunity in the Body Politic: A Low Countries Tradition?" In *The Emergence of Tolerance in the Dutch Republic*, edited by Christiane Berkvens-Stevelinck, Jonathan I. Israel, and G.H.M. Posthumus Meyjes. Studies in the History of Christian Thought 76. Leiden: Brill, 1997.

Vergilius Maro, P. *Eclogues. Georgics. Aeneid: Books 1–6*. Translated by H. Rushton Fairclough. Vol. LCL 63. The Loeb Classical Library. Cambridge, MA: Harvard University Press, 1999.

Vergilius Maro, P. *Aeneas*. Translated by P.H. Schrijvers. Groningen: Historische Uitgeverij, 2011.

Vlessing, Odette. "על ראשית יהודי פורטוגאל באמסטרדאם: עובדות ומעשיות." *Pe'amim: Studies in Oriental Jewry / פעמים: רבעון לחקר קהילות ישראל במזרח*, no. 51 (1992): 81–98.

White, Peter. *Predestination, Policy and Polemic: Conflict and Concensus in the English Church from the Reformation to the Civil War*. Cambridge: Cambridge University Press, 1992.

Wilde, Marc de. "Offering Hospitality to Strangers: Hugo Grotius's Draft Regulations for the Jews." *Tijdschrift Voor Rechtsgeschiedenis* 85, no. 3/4.

Wilks, Michael. *The Problem of Sovereignty in the Later Middle Ages: The Papal Monarchy with Augustinus Triumphus and the Publicists*. Cambridge: Cambridge University Press, 2008.

Wolff, Moses. *De geschiedenis der joden te Haarlem. Deel 1: 1600–1815*. Haarlem: Erven F. Bohn, 1917.

Wtenbogaert, Johannes. *Remonstrantie by de zes colloquenten vander remonstranten weghen in de Haeghsche conferentie bekent … Waer in sy hare bedenckinghen openen over het houden der synoden*. Den tweeden druc. Tot Rotterdam: by Matthijs Bastiaenszboec verkooper op't Steygher in Iosephus, 1618.

Yeivin, Ze'ev, and Haim Hillel Ben-Sasson. "Crafts." In *Encyclopaedia Judaica*, edited by Michael Berenbaum and Fred Skolnik, 2nd ed., 5:263–272. Detroit: Macmillan Reference USA, 2007.

Zwarts, Jac. *De eerste rabbijnen en synagogen van Amsterdam, naar archivalische bronnen*. Amsterdam: Menno Hertzberger, 1929.